Sunset
MIDWESTERN
LANDSCAPING
BOOK

Edited by Craig Bergmann, ASLA

SUNSET BOOKS INC. · MENLO PARK, CALIFORNIA

Sunset Books

VP, General Manager: Richard A. Smeby
VP, Editorial Director: Bob Doyle
Production Director: Lory Day
Director of Operations: Rosann Sutherland
Art Director: Vasken Guiragossian

**Sunset's *Midwestern Landscaping Book*
was produced by:**

Editor: Craig Bergmann
Senior Editor, Sunset Books: Bridget Biscotti Bradley
Managing Editors: Larry Olsen, Pamela Cornelison
Art Director, Production Manager: Alice Rogers
Photography Editor: Jane A. Martin
Computer Production Manager: Linda Bouchard
Senior Editor: Tom Wilhite
Writers: Steve Cory, Natalia K. Hamill, Maryalice Koehne,
    Marty Ross, Sally Roth, Denny Schrock,
    Ronald C. Smith, Kim W. Todd, Anne Marie Van Nest
Landscaping with Plants Writer: Jan Riggenbach
Consulting Editors: James Grigsby, Roger Holmes, Hazel White
Contributors: Roy L. Taylor, Bonnie Blodgett, Romalda Lopat
Illustrators: Deborah Cowder, Lois Lovejoy, Rik Olson, Mimi Osborne,
    Erin O'Toole, Mark Pechenik, Reineck & Reineck, Wendy Smith,
    Jenny Speckels, Elisa Tanaka
Copy Editors: Pamela Evans, Julie Harris, Rebecca LaBrum, Lura Dymond
Proofreader: Christine Miklas
Production Coordinator: Danielle Javier
Editorial Coordinator: Audrey Mak
Indexer: Nanette Cardon

Cover: Photography by Ian Adams.
Garden by Craig Bergmann Landscape Design, Inc.

10 9 8 7 6 5 4 3
First printing October 2001

For additional copies of the *Midwestern Landscaping Book,* or any other
Sunset book, call 1-800-526-5111 or visit us at www.sunsetbooks.com

FOREWORD

The cultivation of a garden is surely one of life's most satisfying endeavors. I feel a sense of accomplishment when I have planted and cared for healthy, eye-catching plants. In particular, an ornamental crabapple that has grown to maturity and is covered with beautiful red-pink buds. A peegee hydrangea that seems to have more flower heads than leaves, even in the heat of July. And delphiniums rocketing higher than the tallest bamboo stakes I own.

As a professional gardener, it is rewarding to hear from clients that their new garden has literally changed their lives. They've made more time to enjoy the out-of-doors. They feel at one with nature as they witness butterflies collecting nectar from the flowers of a butterfly bush. They notice the morning dew on the bluest new growth of a spruce tree in spring. Or they take in the grandeur of the stately bur oak that nature sited so beautifully some 200 years ago.

My personal gardening education started early, when my father gave me a 20-by-20-foot plot in the garden for my fifth birthday. It was my very own to plant and tend, and I did so throughout grammar school and high school. Here, the gardening seed was sown. There were successes and there were also failures. Questions had to be answered. Plants had to be positioned. My gardening library needed to grow.

For more than half a century, gardeners from novices to pros—myself included—have relied on Sunset to help them solve gardening and landscaping problems. With the *Western Landscaping Book* in 1997, Sunset established a unique regional approach to garden design and construction that now extends across the entire U.S..

We Midwesterners now have a comprehensive resource with outstanding examples of local garden design, landscaping plans, recommended plant lists, and tips for creating garden structures, as well as fine examples of garden art and other finishing touches.

This book—written by expert Midwestern garden writers, landscape architects, and horticulturalists—celebrates the regional gardening styles of our part of the world. It also reflects the ways in which gardens are being redefined as extensions of our homes. Gardens are now designed as outdoor rooms that can be used and enjoyed in all four seasons. Native and pioneer plants are valued and preserved. Boundaries between cultivation and nature are beginning to blur. The result is an expansion of our horizons to include the best of our gardening heritage as well as the benefits of modern technologies. When natural conditions are severe, careful planning and gardening practices are now able to adapt and preserve plants to bring us continual joy and beauty.

Whether you want to landscape a rooftop in downtown Chicago, create a bog garden in the North Woods, repopulate a country-style garden with wildflowers in Iowa, or find hardy grasses to thrive in a cold, dry patch of Nebraska, this book can help turn your vision into reality.

Craig Bergmann, ASLA
Editor

THE MIDWESTERN DIFFERENCE

Narth, South, East, and West meet in the Midwest, the crossroads of the continent. The region extends from the cotton and rice fields of southern Missouri to the birch and tamarack forests of northern Minnesota and beyond into the Saskatchewan, Manitoba, and Ontario plains, and from urban manufacturing centers in Ohio to the wide-open prairies in the west. Significant changes in temperature from south to north and differences in soil type and rainfall from west to east make the Midwest not a single common region but rather a series of transition zones in the middle of North America.

TOPOGRAPHY. The glaciers that carved out the Great Lakes also shaped most of the Midwest into gently rolling plains. As the last of the glaciers retreated, a vast inland lake formed, its waters blocked from flowing north into Hudson's Bay by the wall of ice. The old lakebed now forms part of the Red River valley of North Dakota and Minnesota. Lakes and bogs formed in low spots throughout Minnesota, Wisconsin, and Michigan. The melting glaciers also carved out the nation's largest river systems, the Mississippi, Missouri, and Ohio. As these rivers sliced through the plains, they formed bluffs and hills that rival mountain slopes.

The same great water systems that defined the landscape opened the Midwest to European exploration. The Mississippi, Missouri, and Ohio Rivers as well as the Great Lakes served as the first avenues of access to the region. The influence of French explorers who followed these natural waterways is still evident in the names of many river towns, such as St. Louis and Ste. Genevieve, Missouri, and Prairie du Chien and La Crosse, Wisconsin. Later, settlers from the East Coast and many European nations followed the same waterways to establish new communities. With the advent of a moldboard plow capable of cutting through tough sod, and railroads to carry human and agricultural cargo, thousands of immigrant farmers sought a better life in the Northwest Territories.

The mountains of the Midwest don't reach soaring heights. The Ozarks of Missouri are very old and are now worn down to rolling hills of clay and limestone. The tallest peak, Taum Sauk Mountain, rises only 1,772 feet above sea level. Even the highest mountains are referred to as the Black Hills. Not far from the famous Mount Rushmore presidential display, Harney Peak climbs to more than 7,242 feet at the western edge of the region in the South Dakota mountains.

CLIMATE. Annual precipitation ranges from a scant 15 inches in western reaches of the Midwest to over 40 inches in the east. Storm systems from the Pacific Ocean drop most of their moisture on the western slopes of the Rocky Mountains, leaving the western plains high and dry. Storms sweeping up the Mississippi River valley from the Gulf of Mexico gain energy, resulting in greater precipitation the farther south and east one goes in the region. During the growing season, thunderstorms and local downpours alternate with extended dry periods. Only tough plants adapted to dry cycles can thrive in this climate without periodic watering.

The winds that sweep across the flat plains of the Midwest have shaped its character. Windborne soil deposits, called loess, are responsible for much of the deep, fertile prairie lands that became corn, wheat, and soybean fields in the prairie states. The lack of natural mountain barriers means that most of the region is exposed to drying winds that challenge plant life.

The Midwest is famous for cold winters. Temperatures below zero are standard throughout the region; temperatures of −20 to −40 degrees are common in the northern Midwest. Near the Great Lakes, snow arrives in November or December and remains until late spring. On the High Plains, in the Ozarks, and in the Ohio River valley, however, warm spells occur throughout the winter, creating widely fluctuating temperatures. Plants in these areas must be adapted to extreme cold, temperature changes, and fierce winter winds.

In summer, temperatures in the 90s and 100s are common toward the south and west. The moderating influence of the Great Lakes keeps the northeast cooler, but an occasional heat wave can affect plants and humans there as well.

PLANTS. In the northern woodlands, spring brings a dazzling wildflower display, with ephemerals such as spring beauty *(Claytonia virginica)*, Dutchman's breeches *(Dicentra cucullaria)*, wake robin, bloodroot, and wild cranesbill *(Geranium maculatum)*. Prairies burst into bloom in late summer with asters, goldenrod, Joe Pye weed *(Eupatorium purpureum)*, and grasses. In fall, the trees come to the fore in blazing shades of red, orange, and yellow. In winter, after the foliage has dropped to expose the skeletal structure of trees and shrubs, sunlight reveals a tracery of shadows on the snow, brightly colored berries on the branches, the rich texture of tree bark, and the warmth of ornamental grasses.

Native plants give the Midwestern gardener a wealth of material for landscaping. Some of the most beautiful plants, such as paper birch *(Betula papyrifera)* and balsam fir *(Abies balsamea)*, thrive only in the cooler zones and languish in the warm southern areas of the region. Imports from East Asia, Japan, and Europe have enriched the diversity of ornamentals. Protection from the cold in sheltered locations and from temperature fluctuations under mulches helps the marginally hardy exotics survive. There is no shortage of plants that can be successfully grown in the Midwest.

CONTENTS

FINISHING TOUCHES 268

REGIONAL PROBLEMS AND SOLUTIONS 304

LANDSCAPE PLANS 336

MATERIALS AND TECHNIQUES 360

GARDENS OF THE MIDWEST

In a region where moisture from the Great Lakes, frigid northern winds, and warm, wet southern air create an unpredictable mix of climates, Midwestern gardeners face a wealth of challenges.

Time-tested plant choices, including native and hardy varieties, is one key to success. In urban and suburban patios, container gardening provides flexibility and versatility. In rural areas, wildflower gardens attract wildlife, and vegetable and herb gardens can flourish by sheltering plants from the hot summer sun.

Outstanding examples of Midwestern garden design abound in the following pages. From spare woodland styles near the Great Lakes to sturdy shortgrass styles of the arid High Plains, and from dense northern forests to lush ornamental displays in the south, there is something here to spark every imagination.

The North Woods

The rugged North Woods, covered with birch, poplar, pine, and maple forests, extends east of Lake Winnipeg in Manitoba into Minnesota, Wisconsin, and to the shores of the Great Lakes. These forested areas gradually thin to mixed woods and grasslands to the south and then meet the prairie. Snow and ice have carved out low sites for thousands of lakes and bogs here, and in the process have broken up the granite bedrock into the stones and gravel that pass for soil.

Because the growing season is cool and short, color is intense and bloom times are condensed here. Flowers that fade in the peak heat of summer in the rest of the Midwest— delphiniums, lupines, and fuchsias—grow with gusto through the region's brief summers. Ornamental trees such as red-berried mountain ashes and white-barked birches, which languish in the heat of the Lower Midwest, exhibit their full glory in the north.

Relaxed informality is typical of North Woods garden landscapes. Many homeowners blend their yards into the surrounding natural beauty. Why struggle to maintain a mowed lawn on a shady, gravelly site when native ground covers of wild ginger, violets, and ferns clothe the ground naturally? American columbines, Dutchman's breeches, and New England asters add color, while boggy sites feature cattails, arrowhead, and tamarack.

The popular cottage garden style works here, combining mounded, spiked, and trailing perennials in a tapestry of colors, forms, and textures. Early spring bulbs such as snowdrops and crocus start off the season while snow still blankets the ground. Annual flowers, iris, lilies, daylilies, and roses provide color through early summer, and chrysanthemums, goldenrods, asters, and ornamental grasses shine in the late summer and autumn.

In urban gardens, woodland retreats reminiscent of lake country are recreated on a smaller scale. Overhead canopies of vines on trellises soften urban architecture and further the illusion of a country setting in the city. Fountains and ponds contribute soothing sounds and small wildlife habitats.

With space and sunlight restricted, container gardening is a key feature of urban gardens. Colorful combinations of annuals and perennials can be tucked into sunny pockets in the yard; cooler pastels, whites, and variegated foliage plants in pots can enliven dark corners. Container gardening in shade is easier, as the pots don't dry out so quickly, the soil is easily amended, and the containers can be moved indoors for winter.

Because winter is the longest season here, woody plants that provide structure and color in those bleak months are important. Bright red stems of redtwig dogwood are spectacular against a backdrop of newly fallen snow. The red fruits of winterberry and cranberry highbush not only add color but also provide food for wildlife. The evergreen foliage of eastern white pine, red pine, and white cedar is a welcome contrast to the otherwise gray and white winter landscapes. Soon enough, the snow melts, bringing forth bloodroots and spring beauties to start nature's cycle once again.

ATTRACTING WILDLIFE
With native plantings

During the past decade, Thom and Linda Gode have transformed their 60-acre property 20 miles west of Minneapolis from a barren cornfield into a domestic garden and wildlife haven.

Thom says of their garden and surrounding property, "The process of building is as important as the completion." In keeping with that philosophy, the Godes informally studied the garden designs at Monticello and Williamsburg, then made many of their design decisions and plant selections based on what they learned at those historic sites.

Their plan resulted in a series of fenced gardens on the north and south sides of their mid-18th-century-reproduction home. These gardens produce abundant vegetables, herbs, flowers, and fruit.

Beyond the acre occupied by the house and gardens, the Godes emphasize native species that are both beautiful and attractive to wildlife. "This land is very different than it was 10 years ago," says Thom. "When we first moved here, the only animals we saw were three crows and a misguided beaver. Now we have thirty or forty species of birds, deer, turkeys, pheasants, coyotes, woodchucks, rabbits, and foxes."

The Godes have planted 20 acres of prairie grasses and wildflowers and have restored two wetland areas. They plant 2,000 trees every spring and are currently working on a maze the size of a football field, using native redtwig dogwood. The dense foliage of the dogwood provides cover for wildlife, the coral red stems add a brilliant shot of color to the winter landscape, and birds relish the milky white fruit.

FACING PAGE This restored prairie garden grows right up to the herb garden boundary. It contains big bluestem *(Andropogon gerardii)*, little bluestem *(Schizachyrium scoparium)*, purple coneflower, Indian grass *(Sorghastrum nutans)*, rudbeckia, and Queen Anne's lace.

RIGHT A small apple orchard grows in prairie grass outside the herb garden. The 'Haralson' apples shown here withstand low winter temperatures and produce well.

BELOW A combination of design elements shape this garden. A staggered picket fence, stone walls, geometric raised beds, and mulched pathways provide structural definition. Sheared evergreen arborvitae are strong forms year-round. The Godes don't cut back the garden in the fall. Instead, dried seed heads remain to provide food for birds and visual appeal through the winter months.

WEAVING A GARDEN PATHWAY
Up a Minnesota hillside

When clients ask Steve Ruce for advice about landscape design, the owner of Heliotrope Garden Design in Orono, Minnesota, tells them to begin with a well-thought-out plan. But that's not how he created the garden he shares with Irene Silber. Rather, it evolved over a 2-year period when Steve and an employee, Duane Peterson, worked on it during their spare time.

"We live on a hill that is actually a big mound of clay," Steve explained. "It's hard as brick when it's dry and like grease when it's wet. We began by installing a herringbone pathway that goes from one level to another via a series of steps. The different rectangular and square garden beds just evolved to fit the paths."

Unlike the herringbone central path, the side paths were made with colored cement pavers in basketweave designs. Seven distinct levels have developed from the paths' installation. The lowest level begins near a marsh; there Steve rotates vegetables each year and includes flowers as ornamentation.

On the second level, Steve installed a heated bed with a thermostat so he could actually pick a salad on a subzero day. "It was lots of fun to go out in the snow to harvest lettuce and spinach, but the cost of electricity was prohibitive," he said with a laugh.

The elevation rises as the garden approaches the house. Because the garden faces east and south, it catches all possible sun so that annuals and perennials as well as vegetables can flourish. Russian sage and coneflowers enhance one bed, while a collection of oriental poppies followed by long-blooming perennials fills another. A series of eight circles of allium fill another bed, surrounding annuals that vary from one year to the next.

A compelling water feature that is actually built into the deck of the upper level provides the soothing sounds of a fountain near the seating area. On all levels, rectangular and square beds are planted with perennials, old roses, and lilies.

FACING PAGE The garden overlooks a marsh and wooded area in the background that is protected by a combination of conservancy efforts. In the foreground, dwarf conifers provide a transition from other parts of the property to the deck.

ABOVE In the background is a vine-covered arbor over a path that leads to the house. Pots surrounding the water feature contain lavenders and rosemaries. Elephant's ear *(Colocasia esculenta)* graces the rectangular, 18-inch-deep pool.

TOP RIGHT A close-up shows one of a collection of birdhouses handmade from recycled barn wood by local craftspeople. The *Agave americana* in a pot is the variety from which tequila is made.

RIGHT On the second level of the garden, ornamental allium borders a bed filled with 'Anteres' and 'Brunia' lettuces. Shell peas begin their climb up the string latticework on the background structure.

PIONEER PARADISE
Near St. Paul

After restoring her 1898 farmhouse, Lynn Steiner turned her horticultural talents to the 18 acres surrounding her home. She focused first on the front-entry area, taking her inspiration from walled gardens in Savannah and Charleston to create an intimate and welcoming space.

Lynn fashioned an enclosed entry garden by borrowing the exterior walls from her house and garage and building a picket fence on the two remaining sides. "I needed some way to contain the garden and create definition," said Lynn.

The gardens have a different feeling elsewhere on the property. Bricks salvaged from stockyards in nearby St. Paul are laid out to form rigid linear paths, while a variety of plants mix happily to soften the formal layout of the planting spaces. Curved lines and natural stone combine with large drifts of ornamental grasses and coneflowers.

The boulder garden is a series of three tiers holding a hillside that backs up to a swimming pool. The boulders were previously blasted from the earth when the property was used as a gravel quarry. Stones salvaged from an old patio around the farmhouse are laid as stepping-stones throughout the garden.

ABOVE The delicate petals and brilliant shades of herbaceous peonies belie their north-country adaptability.

RIGHT Annual bright red poppies mix easily with perennials such as hot yellow coreopsis (*Coreopsis grandiflora* 'Early Sunrise') and purple anise hyssop (*Agastache foeniculum*). Self-seeding annuals require care when weeding in spring, but they are the backbone of the casual cottage-garden style.

LEFT A picket fence encloses this welcoming entry garden, where colorful annuals and perennials mix with culinary herbs and vegetables. The tall purple spikes of *Liatris spicata* 'Kobold' in the foreground attract many kinds of butterflies, and the sturdy stems make 'Kobold' an excellent cut flower. In the background are red poppies, coreopsis, and purple anise hyssop.

BELOW Large swaths of perennials are featured in the terraced boulder garden at the back of the house. Russian sage, purple coneflower, black-eyed Susan, Joe Pye weed, sedum 'Autumn Joy', and ornamental grasses put on a colorful late-summer display.

A GARDEN FOR STROLLING
Above the St. Croix

Perched near the top of a bluff above the scenic St. Croix River in a suburb of St. Paul, the Lappi garden is a remarkable design and engineering feat. Six terraces span the width of the 1-acre property, connected by wide grass walkways that encourage visitors to experience the garden from different angles.

"It really is a strolling garden," explains Paulette Lappi. "You can stroll at the top of a bed and look down on the plantings, or you can look up at the beds from the bottom." To encourage multiple views, the tallest plants are placed in the center of the wide borders, with shorter plants next to the walls and the down-hill sides of the beds.

Walls ranging in height from 3 to 5 feet retain the terraces on the steep slope. Besides holding the soil in place, the walls serve as a handsome backdrop for plantings and provide structural interest.

"When you've got lemons, you make lemonade," jokes Paulette, as she explains that the property was a fill site for two quarries in the 1800s. Paulette and her husband Larry have used the stone to create retaining walls, a streambed, a waterfall, and a small pool.

LEFT A boulder-lined stream integrates two sides of the property with different grades. It ends in a waterfall and empties into a pool that attracts wildlife. Daylilies, hosta, coreopsis, and creeping thyme flank this part of the stream.

ABOVE Terraced plantings connected by grass walkways lead visitors gently around the steep grade. Trumpet vine rambles over the railing near the deck, providing nectar for hummingbirds.

LEFT To maximize visual impact, each bed contains large masses of just a few different species. This bed contains oriental lilies, coral bells, bearded iris, and sedum. Ground covers such as lamb's ears edge the upper and lower sides of the beds, to hold in soil.

FLOWERS FOREVER
In an everlasting harvest

Mary Lomax was a confirmed vegetable gardener until she planted a seed packet of everlastings—flowers that retain their color and form even after they are harvested and dried. "One year I planted a package of mixed seeds, the next year I planted more, and the next thing you know, the vegetables were out of my gardens," Mary said.

Now she grows thousands of everlasting flowers on 3 acres in Galena, in northern Illinois, every summer. Her business, Cedardale Farm, specializes in annual and perennial flowers that can be used in long-lasting bouquets. She starts her annuals from seed beginning in March and continues planting until May, when the first wildflowers are harvested to dry.

Thousands of flowers in her growing fields stretch in spectacular waves of color down to the surrounding farmland. Daisylike, everlasting *Helipterum roseum* flowers are among the most popular for drying. (Many gardeners use the term *everlasting* to refer to all flowers that hold their color and form when dried, but *H. roseum* is the true everlasting flower.) Lomax especially likes the bright tropical colors and flame-shaped plumes of cockscombs, which are both flashy in the garden and among the best annuals for drying.

When the flowers are at their most brilliant, she cuts them on long stems, bundles them together with rubber bands, and hangs them upside down on wires strung across her drying house. Success depends on low humidity and limited exposure to light. Properly dried flowers should last for months, all the way through a long, cold winter.

ABOVE In the production field in high summer, a great wave of mealycup sage *(Salvia farinacea)* is planted in front of showy red-crested cockscomb *(Celosia* 'Red Velvet'). Also in view are globe amaranth *(Gomphrena globosa),* zinnias, Joe Pye weed *(Eupatorium purpureum),* and ornamental grasses grown for their dramatic plumes. A hayfield lies beyond.

FACING PAGE TOP Fall is the season for making wreaths and other arrangements. This wreath has a twiggy birch base purchased from a hobby shop. At the center are three freeze-dried peony flowers. Flower spikes of pink larkspur *(Consolida ajacis)* and old-fashioned bridal wreath spirea *(Spiraea × vanhouttei)* radiate around the center. A few panicles of hydrangea are tucked in at the bottom.

RIGHT Raised beds outside the shop are reserved for favorite annual and perennial flowers. Dahlias, in the foreground at left, and bright pink anemones *(Anemone × hybrida)* are not typical dried flowers—it takes special care to preserve them successfully. Mary Lomax grows them here just because she likes them.

A MIRROR IMAGE
Reflecting nature's patterns

Sixty miles north of Toronto on the top of a rolling hill, sits a garden that is foreground to magnificent panoramic views of the countryside beyond. The gardener gathered her inspiration for it from natural pastures in adjacent fields. Masses of native plants, grasses, and perennials have been planted in a prairie style to mimic the surrounding countryside.

The natural topography of the garden accentuates the weathered boulders that rise from the soil in strategic locations. Inside a rustic split rail fence is an ornamental potager, or kitchen garden, situated between the house and barn. In traditional fashion, four segments of vegetables, fruits, herbs, and flowering annuals and perennials are grown here. A rustic obelisk in the center of the potager is made from willow branches, continuing the theme of recycling the countryside.

In a concession to the natural environment, some plants—such as hardy shrub roses—have been selected that will tolerate the hardships of −30 degree winter temperatures, periodic summer drought, and constant wind.

The owner has a keen sense of design, color, and scale. She has created many striking plant combinations that reflect nature's designs just outside the garden. The beds that line the walk to the front door contain drought-tolerant thyme and lavender, which create an effect similar to that of nearby stands of low-growing crown vetch with upright chicory accents. Large masses of black-eyed Susan, purple coneflower, and false sunflower billow with blooms in a garden near the house, copying a nearby wildflower meadow but in a "refined country" style.

ABOVE Tough, hardy perennials and ornamental grasses have been planted in masses to create the feeling of a refined country garden. Liatris, miscanthus, tufted hair grass *(Deschampsia cespitosa),* 'Goldsturm' rudbeckia, purple coneflower *(Echinacea purpurea),* and orange- and yellow-blooming sneezeweed *(Helenium autumnale)* complete this picture.

FACING PAGE TOP Ox eye, or false sunflower *(Heliopsis helianthoides),* planted just outside the split rail fence, creates an informal screen of bright yellow daisies. The gently rolling farmland can be seen beyond.

FACING PAGE BOTTOM The ornamental potager is both decorative and functional. Herbs, vegetables, onions, sunflowers, and zinnias add texture and form to this garden. The twig obelisk marks the center of the quadrants.

CREATING PRIVACY AND SHADE
In urban Winnipeg

You would never know it, but the Corby house and garden sit squarely on the corner of a busy intersection in a very urban area of Winnipeg, Manitoba. "Over the years, we've created an oasis in a busy city environment," says Allan Corby.

The Corby's extensively landscaped property is designed as a continuous series of gardens. The front yard garden consists of several large free-form beds planted with a mix of evergreen trees and shrubs and flowering perennials. The beds are strategically placed to screen the view of a service station across the street, while a 6-foot fence shields the property and provides privacy from a busy street on the

other side. The result gives the feeling of a shaded and secluded park that is both beautiful and functional.

Movement through the gardens and the transition zones between gardens was an important consideration for the Corbys. Therefore, a gated pergola along the side of their home was added to lead visitors from the front to the back of the property.

The 50-by-50-foot sunny backyard is landscaped with a large deck, a brick patio, and lots of colorful containers. The Corbys consider the deck an outdoor living area, and they entertain there frequently. At the back of the property, a low fence keeps their two dogs out of the raised beds in the vegetable garden.

FACING PAGE TOP Large beds with dense plantings screen the house from a busy street, while an inviting grass path leads visitors through the front garden.

FACING PAGE INSET A planter of coleus, begonia, and vinca vine adorn the gate leading to the pergola.

LEFT Purple lupine, bearded iris, and painted daisies bloom in the front garden in late spring. To get lush plant growth like this, the Corbys dug out the heavy clay soil and amended with a mix of organic materials to improve drainage.

BELOW The back of the 1920s house is surrounded by a brick patio and deck. Colorful annuals and two dogs happily coexist because all the plantings are confined to aboveground containers.

THE
GREAT
LAKES

Climate and soil differences define two distinct growing regions around the Great Lakes. The warmer southern borderlands consist of sand dunes and rocky shorelines. A short distance inland are marshlands, and just a few miles farther inland are forests and pastures with rich soils. To the north and west of the lakes, the climate is colder and the soil thinner. Conifers dominate this tough North Woods environment.

The "lake effect" is the product of water and wind combining to make temperatures closer to the lakes warmer in winter and cooler in summer. Along the southern shores, spring plants bloom a little later, but average temperatures are 10 degrees warmer. In fall, plants on the southern side may avoid killing frosts for weeks longer than in the north and west. The lake effect significantly expands the range of plants available for the garden.

In winter, bluffs and hills along the southeastern coastlines lift the cold, moist air traveling across the lakes, producing heavy "lake-effect snow." This extra snow cover protects perennials and low conifers from desiccating winter winds, but it may also harm deciduous trees or large conifers.

Instead of fighting against nature to create formal lawns with clipped hedges, Great Lakes gardeners have embraced a style that works with nature. Well-defined garden structures are softened by shrubs, trees, perennials, vines, and ornamental grasses that combine in an informal style. Both shady woodland and sunny meadow gardens reflect this natural style.

Woodland gardens are found at the base of towering deciduous and conifer trees. The soil below these trees has a dark, spongy, humus layer at the surface. These woodland conditions are often excellent for creating shady wildflower or perennial gardens. The larger trees give protection and cool summer air, while shrubs and small trees form a transition zone between planted beds and the forests beyond.

Sunny areas south of the lakes are ideal for gardens bursting with colors and textures. This meadow style of gardening combines the informality of an English cottage garden with the rusticity of a country garden. Rolling hills, pastures, and wild and domestic animals add to this casual style. Perennials and ornamental grasses are featured, particularly durable ones that offer a long blooming season. Drought-tolerant perennials that form one dense mass of blooms are preferred.

Garden ornaments are often featured as accents in these meadow gardens, whereas in woodland gardens a mossy granite stone might be the accent piece. Rustic cedar is often used to build an arbor or a split rail fence that divides pastures from perennial beds closer to the house. Twigs from local willow and cedar can be made into benches, chairs, or tables. Rusty iron sculptures may be added to give these gardens an aged look.

The Great Lakes themselves are a natural focal point. For houses situated high above the coastline, the main axis of the garden is often designed to end in a panoramic view of freighters and sailboats on the lake by day and the fiery orange sun setting on the lakes in the evening.

An Elegant Update
With views in mind

When landscape architect Craig Bergmann was asked to update a fine old garden and integrate it with the property's 1920s house in Lake Forest, Illinois, he looked forward to the challenge. "The owner loves brilliantly colored flowers and realized the potential of this site," said Bergmann. "We worked to enhance a great existing planting plan and added modern ideas and up-to-date technology while considering the client's wishes."

Creating incredible vistas of the garden from the front door and other areas of the house was one priority. By organizing and renovating the gardens, Bergmann refined and maximized many views from the interior of the home.

One of the biggest obstacles his firm overcame was finding a sufficient number of proportionately large plant materials to match those original to the site. "We are always looking for mature plants for our projects," Bergmann commented.

Because of this insistence on maintaining the same scale as the existing plants, the landscaping looks as though it has been in place for 5 years or more. "It's wonderful to inherit and incorporate high-quality old plants," Bergmann said. "Since the original drainage was good and the original design was well planned, there was immediate gratification with the new installations because of the mature background."

FACING PAGE By renovating existing boxwood hedges and yew globes and adding a seasonal planting border, the designer provided a charming new vignette for the viewer.

LEFT Combining vividly colored flowers such as *Lilium lancifolium flaviflorum* 'Yellow Tiger', *Crocosmia* 'Lucifer', and *Monarda didyma* 'Jacob Cline' adds pizzazz to the garden.

BELOW Integrating the house and garden, this full-sun parterre features annuals canna 'Pretoria' and yellow rocket snapdragons surrounded by roses. It is a favorite place to relax and enjoy views of the main lawn and surrounding herbaceous borders.

RIGHT The roof deck is a popular place to catch the rays, for people and plants as well. Lightweight fiberglass containers with the look of terra-cotta are used because they weigh far less than other types. Here, impatiens, herbs, and a variety of annuals provide green accents.

FACING PAGE A popular area on the lowest level features a large table and concrete stools designed by Maya Lin, creator of the Vietnam Veterans Memorial in Washington, D.C. Pots filled with fuchsias and other flowering annuals complement the permanent plantings in the beds.

BELOW On another side of the building, a fish pond is a permanent feature on the lowest level. Inside, a bedroom overlooks window boxes above the pond.

SHARING ROOFTOP GARDENS
And urban history

Ever since 1925, when this grand old building was built in the Old Town section on the north side of downtown Chicago, its residents have embellished and enjoyed the roof decks on eight different levels. Rooftop gardening may seem to be a new trend, but this building is proof of the long-term viability of such spaces once they are established.

"It's a living, breathing thing, with artists still working on it," said Tannys Langdon, whose architectural firm Carl Street Studios shares the building with another business and several condominiums. "It was very forward-thinking for the original architect to incorporate these outdoor living spaces into the design."

Because each of the suites has four levels, the owners share all the gardens. "This is the first year we've had any thematic plantings, but now we have a butterfly garden, and it's really something to see butterflies so high up in a city garden," Langdon said.

Living in the city loses its edge for a while when residents have access to serene decks. Clients are also attracted to this area, where business is regularly conducted. "Everyone sees the roof decks as a communal living space, and it enriches all our lives," Langdon commented.

Besides the plantings and a fish pond, the brick and tile work on the lower decks also commands the attention of all who visit. Some of the tiles, which are stamped with names like Grubey and Batchelder, are now also found in antique shops. "At the time they found their way to the decks, the tiles were probably end runs or leftovers from other jobs. They add to the art moderne, art deco, eclectic feeling of it all."

BOTH CASUAL AND FORMAL
A friendly blend of styles

By planting their own garden in a casual style highlighted by occasional formal plantings, Craig Bergmann and James Grigsby overcame a number of challenges faced by Midwestern gardeners. Because the garden in Wilmette, Illinois, lacks a great deal of sun, they rely on perennials and woody plants that flourish in partial sun. "We have very unusual plants, but a collection of plants doesn't make a garden," said Grigsby. "Rather, we orchestrate colors and textures to blend into a unified whole."

Since the space is too small for separate gardens, the designers established a series of distinct areas beginning at the entry arbor, which is flanked by a collection of unusual potted dwarf conifers that overwinter in the nursery. When they bought the property in 1986, only a 70-year-old saucer magnolia tree thrived in a protected location. Because of judicious pruning, it is now one of the oldest cultivated specimens in the Chicago area.

Under its boughs flourishes a woodland garden of spring ephemerals, including European ginger, variegated Solomon's seal, and a collection of hellebores. These are followed by the deciduous rhododendron 'Parade', which blooms with coral-orange flowers around July 4. Waiting in the wings to provide August color is a mature colony of oakleaf hydrangeas.

As guests follow the path through the garden, they pass the long border with a natural espaliered fringe tree (*Chionanthus virginicus*) underplanted with perennials and tender plants that provide continual interest. The designers complement whatever is in bloom at the time with their collection of stone ornaments.

FACING PAGE At the entry arbor, visitors pass a collection of potted dwarf conifers before viewing the plants inside the gate, which demonstrate a restrained color palette and variegated foliage.

LEFT This detail shows potted 'New Design' tulips, fuchsias, and *Hebe buxifolia* 'Purpurea'. The designers prefer to plant tulips in pots rather than directly in the soil, so that the root zones of established plants aren't disturbed. Pots also have the advantage of being easily moved wherever color is desired.

BELOW A potted fuchsia collection flanks the entrance to a Lord & Burnham greenhouse (circa 1900) first used by a local high school. It was moved to this site in 1960. Also on the property is a renovated farm-implement store that serves as a design studio.

RIGHT A collection of pots along the garden edge hold bulbs and tender plants in May.

BELOW A softly curving path invites a stroll through "sun-thrifty" perennials to the venerable *Magnolia × soulangeana,* while a 'Wintergreen' boxwood hedge frames *Cornus mas* 'Golden Glory' at left. Foreground plantings include a potted chartreuse euphorbia, *Myosotis* 'Victoria Blue', lamiums, a dwarf conifer, and 'White Triumphator' tulips.

ABOVE Throughout the gardens, unusual combinations of carefully selected plants inspire visitors. Here, *Thalictrum rochebrunianum* consorts with *Heliotropium arborescens* 'Alba', *Lavandula multifida*, *Lobelia* 'Summer Meadow', and *Origanum rotundifolium* 'Kent Beauty'.

LEFT In this view, a combination of perennials and shrubs provides textural interest, with phormium as an accent.

A ROMANTIC GARDEN
For a suburban cottage

When Jim Shartle began his front yard garden, he didn't realize that it would change the style of his house or that guests and neighbors would thank him for providing such a visual treat. "Our house evolved as the garden grew. We added a sunroom to enjoy the view, and we even painted the brown trim of the house white to blend with garden structures," said Jim, who, with Dave King, bought this "typical two-story colonial" in Schaumberg, Illinois, 26 years ago. "I worked from front to back and finally added a path around the house to connect the two. I began by adding a little here and there, but I never expected to be surrounded by gardens."

Continual blooming annual daisies, like Shasta daisies, and *Verbena bonariensis* are just two of Jim's favorites that tie the garden beds together. If they reseed in places he doesn't expect, he simply transplants them or weeds them out.

Jim credits his garden success to double-digging all the beds, removing big clumps of clay, and then adding peat moss and humus from the compost pile. He brought in bags of topsoil and refilled them with the clay he removed from the garden.

A collection of urns throughout the garden and different Adirondack chairs complete the decoration.

ABOVE A concrete urn overflowing with vivid annuals nestles among equally brilliant perennials such as purple coneflower in the backyard.

LEFT A stepping-stone path connects the front yard to the backyard's "secret garden." Jim purposely placed the large urn planter filled with dracaena, geraniums, and trailing annuals in the center of the path. The detour around the urn draws visitors' attention to the closely planted borders on either side.

RIGHT The homeowners searched local flea markets for garden artifacts such as this Adirondack chair and two-story birdhouse. Phlox, black-eyed Susan, daylilies, and impatiens provide a colorful background border.

A COUNTRY RETREAT
In an urban patio

Creating illusions of space in a small enclosed city garden came naturally to Nancy McIlvaine, an interior designer and owner of the Chicago art gallery Portals Ltd. "It's our haven in downtown Chicago," she said. "We wanted the serenity of water in a very small space, and we use the garden all year round."

When they bought the townhouse 8 years ago, the McIlvaines asked landscape architect Doug Hoerr to help them take their indoor decor outdoors. Hoerr began by replacing concrete pavers with flooring of Wisconsin lannon stone and brick, and then he added a pergola and the wood trellis wrapped on two walls that disguises a wood fence. In one corner, water trickles into a raised pool from an olive jar converted into a fountain. This becomes a focal point as well as a special water feature.

The Beaux Arts formality of the garden's accessories softens the walls of the modern building, but it can't overcome the threats of nature. "The garden looks so peaceful, but the soil was hostile and the wind forms a tunnel," said McIlvaine. "That's why we replaced and fertilized the soil and why we chose plants like miniature daffodils and iris that aren't affected by the wind."

FACING PAGE Trompe l'oeil techniques, such as the mirrored trellis and the broken pediment and arched trellis over the door, give an informal, playful effect while creating the illusion of space in this enclosed urban patio. Repeating white lily-of-the-Nile (*Agapanthus africanus* 'Albus'), 'Pink Swirl' impatiens, and different varieties of astilbes, Asiatic lilies, and caladiums adds to the feeling of unity.

TOP An antique fox statuette sounds a whimsical note as it peers around plantings of impatiens, caladiums, and heuchera in a nook. The owners' collection of pots and antique oil jars contribute individuality to the scene.

RIGHT TOP Water adds still another element to the small L-shaped space. Pots filled with trailing sedums perch on the staggered stone ledges. The pool is filled with pots of water lilies and blue lily-of-the-Nile.

RIGHT BOTTOM An ornamental pear tree backed by climbing rose and hydrangea vines adds dimension to the dining corner. Lighted in the evening, white lilies and astilbe catch the eye and lead it to the smaller caladiums and impatiens.

A GREENHOUSE LEGACY
Uncovering a dream

A buckthorn thicket, one of the many banes of Midwestern gardeners, had smothered the old greenhouse foundations on the former Albert Lasker estate in Lake Forest, Illinois, by 1987. That's when visionaries Gwil and Bruce Newman bought the little house that had been attached to the greenhouse, along with the two-thirds-acre plot of buckthorn-shrouded ruins. Recalls Gwil, "We killed the buckthorn and then the weeds that grew in their place. We replaced the clay soil in the former potting sheds. Then we ran into drain tile and broken glass that we removed from the soil."

Gwil's familiarity with estate gardens and classic European gardens gave her the vision and determination to transform the forlorn thicket into a classic layout of separate themed gardens. The property includes bowers, patios, fountains, and even two pavilions in addition to the greenhouse ruins that begged to be filled with blooms once again. Although dogwood and some varieties of boxwood wouldn't flourish in the Chicago suburb's climate, Gwil found hardy rhododendrons, astilbes, asters, and roses that acclimated well.

The couple's project eventually came to the attention of the director of the Chicago Botanic Garden, who advised them to allow one specimen of buckthorn to flourish. Now they meticulously remove the buckthorn seedlings that sprout every year.

ABOVE Deteriorating walls were capped and at least 12 gardens with separate themes were created in the ruins of the old greenhouse. Purple asters and sweet autumn clematis ramble in the foreground, softening the formality of the walled gardens.

CENTER A metal fountain from Mexico that is surrounded by evergreen shrubs forms a focal point on one patio. In the background, the lone surviving buckthorn tree shades the area.

FACING PAGE BOTTOM Hidden in a leafy bower covered with wisteria and clematis is a replica period bench that invites passersby to tarry awhile.

ABOVE The entire home wraps around the garden and provides inviting views from inside. Chaise longues on the patio are situated to view a pond inspired by Monet's in Giverny. Plantings around the patio include English delphinium *(D. elatum)*, *Nepeta* × 'Six Hills Giant', yarrow, crocosmia, and crown-pink *(Lychnis coronaria)*.

LEFT Since Diane's favorite color is orange, she is particularly fond of the native perennial butterfly weed *(Asclepias tuberosa)*.

A PRIMARY LANDSCAPE
With an international flavor

The more color the better for Diane and John Patience, who delight in entertaining family and friends in their garden. Saturating their surroundings with bright, primary hues reminds the couple of Mediterranean countries and of Mexico, favorite destinations when their garden in Winnetka, Illinois, is covered with snow.

"I love visiting exotic and unusual gardens all over the world and then, in my garden, creating that ambience," says Diane. To that end, she has mixed the deep, bright oranges of trumpet vines and butterfly weed with the intense blues of delphiniums and spectacular pink tones of spider flower.

To convert their garden vision to reality, the couple turned to landscape architect Craig Bergmann. His company designed, installed, and maintains the gardens around the 1920s home, which was previously surrounded by lawn and yew hedges. Now, besides relishing the bright colors of annuals and perennials in her collection of flowerpots, Diane delights in the view of a pond on the property, where herons, black-capped mergansers, wood ducks, and mallards come to call.

ABOVE Inspired by fresh-air cafés in Italy, Spain, and Morocco, the pergola is covered by honey suckle, trumpet vine, and sweet autumn clematis. More flowering plants, such as deep lavender *Agapanthus* and 'Pink Cascade' geraniums, fill Diane's containers from all over the world.

FORMAL ELEGANCE *Revisited*

Lively plantings in classical urns punctuate parterres laid out in a classic Greek design in Audrey and Jim Altounian's garden in a north Chicago suburb. These containers are an important element of the updated garden. Besides herbs and annuals, which are commonly planted in containers, shrubs—including *Hydrangea macrophylla* 'Nikko Blue'—flourish in these urns.

Once part of a large estate, the three-quarter-acre lot containing the former carriage house was landscaped during the 1950s by designer Catherine Cole Church, whose work has withstood the test of time. Says Audrey, "I fell in love with the garden. That's why we bought and then remodeled the house. It's a wonderful, peaceful getaway. We knew it had great bones, and we wanted to improve what was there."

The couple asked landscape architect Douglas Hoerr to connect all the garden areas so that there is a continuous path to follow and experience each part. Hoerr also improved the site by adding color and texture in the landscape. One of his main principles is that a garden should be as delightful when viewed from the house as when people walk through it.

CENTER Formal boxwood hedges surround parterres created within the foundation walls of an abandoned greenhouse. Designer Doug Hoerr updated the original plan and included pots with seasonal plantings in each of the parterres.

FACING PAGE INSET In spring, this classic urn overflows with fuchsia and variegated ivy, while bleeding heart and ferns dominate the parterre plantings. As the seasons change, so do the potted plantings. During any single year, each urn may contain a variety of annuals, perennials, herbs, shrubs, and even vegetables with attractive foliage.

ABOVE An entirely different perspective on the garden is gained from the gazebo, which serves as a screened-in porch for cocktails before dinner or as a reading room.

LEFT An iron fountain from England featuring a child holding a goose provides a focal point on a brick path leading away from the house.

ADAPTING ENGLISH STYLE
To a Chicago home

A sunken garden, burgeoning with bouffant perennials and annuals, continues in display mode from May to early November in one area of this updated formal garden, which borders a rippling canal. The garden complements an English-style home in Hinsdale, Illinois. Since the owners admire and collect English furniture and artifacts, they called on landscape architect Craig Bergmann to create a design reflecting an English aesthetic.

After revitalizing the canal—previously filled with soil and planted with red wax begonias—Bergmann established a true English border with 90 percent perennials and 10 percent annuals. Bergmann's signature juxtaposition of informal plantings with formal structure defines this fascinating garden. Ornamental grasses and unexpected annuals like *Verbena bonariensis* add airy accents.

"It's a Midwestern interpretation of the Edwardian time period," said Bergmann. "One can be inspired by gardens in any part of the world, but the trick is to interpret and not copy what you see. It's important to have a sense of place and integration with the surrounding landscape."

FACING PAGE Water lilies now blossom in the restored canal. Fountain grass and *Boltonia asteroides* 'Snowbank' form a fine backdrop for lamb's ears, purple alum root (*Heuchera micrantha* 'Palace Purple'), and 'Japanese Bishop' dahlias in the foreground.

RIGHT A newly constructed strolling path of old street brick provides access to the canal in the sunken garden. *Pennisetum alopecuroides* 'Hameln' in the foreground and *Miscanthus* 'Silver Shadow' in the background complement the eclectic mix of annuals and perennials.

LEFT Since only the central set of steps is now used to enter the sunken garden, two other unused sets of steps serve as pedestals for a pair of antique terra-cotta oil jars. In the foreground, the foliage of German iris provides a foil for 'Alert' aster and 'Huntington' silver artemisias interplanted with *Verbena bonariensis*. Feather reed grass *(Calamagrostis × acutiflora)* provides accents.

BELOW A hillside bank is filled with rescued native wildflowers. Dappled light from the mature trees creates interesting effects on the ferns and flowers below.

ABOVE Masses of native wildflowers bloom in May. Yellow lady's slipper *(Paphiopedilum calceolus)*, pink lady's slipper *(P. acaule)*, wake robin *(Trillium grandiflorum)*, may apple *(Podophyllum peltatum)*, and foamflower *(Tiarella cordifolia)* carpet the hillside.

PRESERVING WILDFLOWERS
In a hillside garden

This garden near Detroit in Bloomfield Hills, Michigan, features a natural hillside planted with layer upon layer of native wildflowers. In the 1970s, when the property was purchased, it contained traditional landscaping around a 1920s brick home. However, when the owners heard that a subdivision was about to be built nearby, they developed a plan to preserve native wildflowers along a 50-foot bank at the edge of the forest. They removed invasive trees and shrubs, cleared the wooded bank, and transplanted wildflowers from the subdivision property to theirs before the bulldozer could plow them under.

As these rescued plants grew and thrived, some were divided and offered for sale at nearby Cranbrook House and Gardens. The profits support the maintenance and preservation of the 40-acre gardens surrounding Cranbrook House. It is hoped that these wildflowers will flourish in their new homes and contribute to a growing awareness of a naturalistic garden style.

This plant rescue program of 20 years is now a model for other cities and towns that wish to preserve the beauty of native plants for future generations to enjoy.

LEFT Jack-in-the-pulpit *(Arisaema triphyllum)* shows its distinctive purplish green–striped spathe (or "pulpit") and inner spadix (or "Jack").

BORROWING FROM NATURE
A garden of transitions

Nestled between Lake Michigan and a large oak forest, this garden borrows from the beauty of both. Part of a large summer camp on the eastern shores of Lake Michigan, near South Haven, the 10-acre garden is ringed by oak woods, the lake, the house, and a meadow.

Landscape architect Douglas Hoerr pulled together all of these zones as a complete picture. The modernized house, 200 feet from the lake, is Art Deco style, featuring big, bold shapes in curvilinear forms. Between the house and lake is a meadow of tall grasses and native wildflowers, including New England asters *(Aster novae-angliae)*, that are spectacular in the fall. A feeling that nature is on the move pervades this area, as the forest plays tug-of-war with the meadow.

Closer to the house the wilderness recedes, and perennials, annuals, and herbs take over. An informal pattern is borrowed from the wildflower area and repeated with these introduced plants. Most of the garden is sheltered from the wind by a 40-foot bluff at the lake's edge. The garden has a planned vista from the house to the lake that is perfect for watching glorious sunsets at the end of the day.

Because sand and gravel are the predominant soil types, with clay areas in the ravines, Hoerr chose tough, self-sustaining plants that mimic the indigenous species. These include fragrant sumac *(Rhus aromatica* 'Gro-Low'), 'Nearly Wild' roses, ornamental grasses, and spike gayfeather.

FACING PAGE TOP A naturalistic planting of lily turf *(Liriope)* flows like a river toward a grouping of hydrangeas. Fountain grass *(Pennisetum)* is planted in the lily turf as an accent.

FACING PAGE BOTTOM Informal annuals spill out of 1920s-era cement urns. These heirloom pieces were collected by the owner's father and now provide distinctive accents along the 60-foot-long-pergola that leads from the house to the service area and family parking. A gravel walk leads past an old bollard-and-ball light.

ABOVE The challenge of integrating the landscape with the natural environment is met well here, as shown by these informal transition plantings of *Hydrangea paniculata* 'Tardiva' and spreading junipers abutting the lawn.

RIGHT Tough, durable sedums in the perennial beds next to the guest parking provide spectacular fall color. Sedums 'Vera Jameson' and 'Autumn Joy' contrast vividly with the blue oat grass *(Helictotrichon sempervirens)*. The combination of these plants was inspired by the meadow landscape.

A Bog and Pond Garden
Welcomes wildlife to the city

In only 10 years, an amazing transformation has occurred in this garden in Grand Rapids, Michigan. A low, open area that had flooded during heavy rains was reconstructed as a secluded garden containing bogs, ponds, a boardwalk, and a dry streambed. Instead of fighting nature, it has been modified to good advantage as a delightful bog and pond garden.

The serenity of this garden is the result of carefully screening the property from the street, sidewalk, and neighbors. A berm was planted with tall ornamental grasses along the street side; several large spruce and bald cypress trees frame the property on the neighbors' sides. This natural screening has created a microclimate that is as much as 10 degrees warmer than other areas of the city.

Distinctive plants growing in and out of the water include Kuma bamboo grass *(Sasa veitchii)*, yellow groove bamboo *(Phyllostachys aureosulcata)*, Joe Pye weed, swamp milkweed *(Asclepias incarnata)*, marsh marigold *(Caltha palustris)*, self-seeding cardinal flower, and turtlehead. Even the bald cypress are ideally suited to a wet, swampy area.

The garden owners, Milt and Barb Rohwer, have extended their living room and kitchen windows from floor to ceiling to take advantage of the view during all seasons. A small courtyard at the back of the property offers a view of another garden filled with waves of Siberian iris. Attention to the placement and amount of foliage and texture has resulted in a garden with a naturalistic style.

FACING PAGE Large spruce, bald cypress, and tall ornamental grasses create a very private garden in the city. The secluded retreat is a haven for wildlife, including ducks, woodchucks, squirrels, raccoons, and butterflies.

ABOVE LEFT A rustic boardwalk takes visitors on a journey over the ponds and past masses of ornamental grasses. The deck and boardwalk add significantly to the garden's water theme.

ABOVE RIGHT A removable canvas roof and screening are installed on the deck so that the garden can be appreciated in comfort during the summer months. A collection of flowering annuals adorns the deck, catching the late-day sun.

LEFT The shape of the shiny bergenia leaves is echoed across the pond by the larger leaves of coltsfoot *(Petasites japonicus)*. Local native Michigan fieldstone provides an attractive edge to the pond.

A MULTI-USE GARDEN
Making the most of a small backyard

Only a small, kidney bean–shaped patch of lawn remains from what once filled the backyard of Nancy Hayer and Steve Gartman. 'Nearly Wild' roses, astilbes, delphiniums, catmint, and flowering ground covers and annuals now fill almost all of this small garden in Shorewood, Wisconsin, one of Milwaukee's oldest suburbs.

"The owners are well traveled, and both had definite perceptions of what the garden should become," said landscape designer Chris Miracle of La Rosa Landscape Company. Among the challenges they gave Chris were grade changes, providing privacy, and hiding utility poles. The clients wanted a cutting garden, fragrance, ongoing color, bold foliage, vines, and year-round interest. Steve is

also a bird-watcher, so he wanted to attract butterflies and birds to the garden. Chris was able to "shoehorn" many features into a limited area: "Because of the English Tudor style of the home, we chose an understated color palette that also relies on foliage for a refined look that fits nicely into the space."

Now the garden complements and extends the house. "When we moved in, these beautiful French doors led to nothing," gestured Nancy. "As we began work, we found the remnants of a stone patio covered by turf in this area." Steve designed an arbor outside the French doors and added antique chimney tops as focal points in two beds. Now the couple enjoys these mementos of their trips daily when they pause for coffee in the arbor.

FACING PAGE A raised bed edges the rear of the property and provides privacy as well as a backdrop for a small patio. In the foreground, roses, lady's-mantle *(Alchemilla mollis),* catmint, and sedums surround an antique English chimney top used as a planter.

RIGHT An arbor, reached through gracious French doors from the house, provides a perfect spot to relax. A path leads from the arbor through meticulous beds of perennials that include dephiniums and more roses.

LEFT Bordering the walk to the front door of the English Tudor–style home, pachysandra, boxwood, and shrub roses formally welcome visitors.

RIGHT With limestone bedrock about a foot below the surface of the soil, planting holes had to be excavated for many shrubs and trees. Sharp pieces brought to the surface were used to create a series of low walls.

BELOW Bright green arborvitaes (*Thuja occidentalis* 'Emerald') form a transition between the informal meadow and the more formal gardens surrounding the renovated house.

LIMESTONE MEETS GRANITE
At Lake Ontario

At the northeastern end of Lake Ontario is a 5-acre garden built to preserve beautiful views of the nearby lake and surrounding pasturelands. This garden is a rustic blend of limestone and granite, shrub roses, a wildflower meadow, rock gardens, and cottage-style perennial borders.

The garden perches on an escarpment with a sharp drop to the lake, where fierce north winds drive the temperature down to −30 degrees in winter. The garden was originally pasture, with cattle grazing right up to the kitchen windows, so the first challenge was to keep the cattle away from the plants. After many cow-moving exercises, a fence was built to define the pasture and garden areas. Then it was possible to plant wide beds of perennials next to the house.

As they began to plant, the owners discovered that the soil was very shallow and the limestone bedrock very close to the surface. In some places, the soil was only 12 inches deep. Digging out planting holes by excavating stone looked to be a long and laborious job, so raised planting areas were constructed instead. Even a pond had to be raised about 30 inches above ground because of the shallow soil.

Unlike most of the property, a section of the garden south of the house has rich and fertile soil, thanks to the effects of the continental ice sheet that transported soil and rounded granite boulders into a lower valley 12,000 years ago. This sloped area has become a rock garden that is sheltered from the wind, making it a valuable microclimate a good 10 degrees warmer than its environs.

RIGHT TOP Hardy maiden pinks *(Dianthus deltoides)* are tucked into a crevice in the limestone at the home's front door.

LEFT The late-day sun heightens the foliage contrast provided by a red-leaf shrub rose *(Rosa glauca)* planted behind a green-leaf variety. The large groupings of fragrant shrub roses greet visitors traversing the mown paths to investigate the wildflower meadow beyond.

BELOW A square wooden cedar arbor, one of many on the mown paths, is covered in edible grapes and provides a shady spot to rest while looking back through the wildflower meadow to the restored 1830s farmhouse.

ABOVE The limestone rock garden contains low-growing perennials, such as dwarf campanulas and dianthus, and hardy evergreens, such as dwarf junipers and pines. In the background is a rustic wooden arbor that is well suited for supporting Virginia creeper *(Parthenocissus quinquefolia)* and clematis.

RIGHT Nature left an ideal rock garden site here 12,000 years ago, with larger boulders at the base and progressively smaller stones up the slope.

A WOODLAND GARDEN
Of contrasting textures

A few blocks from Lake Ontario, in greater Toronto, is a neighborhood of tall, older trees sheltering 1950s-era brick bungalows. In this suburban woodland setting, a remarkable garden thrives under the protection of silver maples and a large weeping copper beech. These outstanding trees are what first prompted the owners to purchase the 100-by-200-foot corner lot.

The garden site was once under water as part of Lake Iroquois, which was formed at the end of the Wisconsin glaciation when the Laurentide ice sheet retreated. The soil is therefore sandy up to a foot deep, providing ideal drainage for such plants as Japanese tree peonies and daphne. But the owners have struggled through the years to amend this sandy soil with compost, mulch, and leaves so they could include plants that don't like such good drainage. One of their success stories has been their blooming shrub roses, but foliage is the star of the show.

The garden has been designed to emphasize foliage contrasts in blue, purple, chartreuse, and red. Blue hostas, dwarf blue spruce, burgundy-leaved eastern redbud (*Cercis canadensis* 'Forest Pansy'), purple weigela, Japanese maples, and a cedar hedge provide much of the color.

FACING PAGE An invasive thug is effectively used as an accent in this garden. Variegated Japanese knotweed is grown in a large plastic pot sunk into the soil, to effectively contain its roots. New shoots are orange-coral when young and resemble bamboo. Clouds of white flowers appear late in summer.

RIGHT The 1950s bungalow has been skillfully camouflaged with Japanese maples and climbing hydrangea *(H. anomala petiolaris)*. Golden variegated Japanese forest grass *(Hakonechloa macra* 'Aureola') springs from the brick planters at the end of the front walk.

BELOW This bed began life as a perennial border, but as the garden's one sunny spot it has evolved into an informal cottage-style garden that includes woody and annual plants. On view are the pink-blooming 'Lavender Dream' shrub roses, white and pink musk mallow *(Malva moschata)*, and blue love-in-a-mist *(Nigella damascena)*.

AN URBAN SANCTUARY
Leaving the city behind

The pressures of Toronto city life have inspired this garden's owner to create his own version of paradise in a narrow urban lot just 20 by 115 feet. When he bought the property in 1991, he found a boring garden with nondescript lawn and daylilies that needed work. Having never gardened before, he decided to take courses to learn about perennials, woody plants, and landscape design.

The first project involved replacing the lawn by the garage with a patio enclosed by planting beds, creating a cozy garden room. Next he built a 5-foot-high cedar fence around the entire garden and excavated a 1-foot area within the garden to create more planting beds.

The task of removing the heavy Toronto clay was daunting. The beds were raised a foot above grade with an attractive foundation of old bricks. New soil containing triple mix (loam, compost, and manure) and coarse sand was added to the beds. The raised beds and cedar fence have created a warm microclimate, so plants can now be grown that are hardy to −10 degrees.

The raised beds outline a half-moon-shaped interlocking brick patio that is perfect for dancing under the moonlight. Two huge containers on the patio are used to add color during the gardening season. From May to July, they hold indoor tropical plants that have been moved outdoors. From August to October, these are replaced with *Sedum* 'Autumn Joy', red fountain grass (*Pennisetum setaceum* 'Rubrum'), and trailing ivy or vinca for a glorious fall foliage and flower show.

FACING PAGE Large artistic clay planters form an attractive accent on this interlocking-paver patio beside a brick-lined raised bed. A former swing set was transformed by the previous owner into a Japanese-style torii gateway. A wild, natural look is achieved through careful plant selection.

ABOVE A secret entrance to the storage shed lies behind this chair. Silver lace vines (*Fallopia baldschuanica*), also appropriately called mile-a-minute, are allowed to tumble naturally across the top of the shed. An upright juniper and other dense plants hide the building from sight.

THE PRAIRIE

The Prairie was once the pioneers' "sea of grass," an ocean of endless waves of wind-ruffled beauty that in reality could be confounding in its vast emptiness to those accustomed to the settled East. The central prairie states of Illinois, Iowa, and Indiana were home to the classic tallgrass prairie. The drier western part of this region, extending into eastern Nebraska, Kansas, and the Dakotas, was home to shorter grasses. The eastern areas were once fingers of the prairie peninsula, where stretches of grassland mingled with patches of forest.

Vigorous, long-lived, and incredibly deep rooted, the prairie grasses made a sod so firm that it could be cut and stacked like bricks and used to build sod houses. Turned to the plow, the ultra-rich soil of the prairie now waves with corn and wheat instead of wild grasses, which today are relegated to restoration areas and gardens.

The soils in this region are the most fertile on the continent. Thousands of years of grasses living and dying have created a deep, loose loam that is slightly alkaline and quick to drain, yet retains moisture in its lower levels and remains soft on the surface even when dry.

Today very little remains of the original prairie, but the legacy of the sea of grass lives on in restoration prairie gardening, sometimes called the New American Garden style, thanks to the beauty, diversity, and rugged constitution of the plants born in grasslands. Dozens of varieties of grasses flourish in restored gardens alongside native wildflowers. Tall perennials are the rule, along with lower-growing annuals that cram their abbreviated life cycle into the short period between spring thaw and overshadowing grass growth.

Though the bright cones of *Rudbeckia*, *Echinacea*, and *Ratibida* and vertical plumes of gayfeather can evoke the prairie, few gardeners are content to stop there. Cheery golden sunflowers, asters, goldenrods, daffodils, roses, and peonies add color. Old favorites, including irises, phlox, and lilies, will shrug off severe winters and occasional droughts to bloom again another year.

Formal English-style gardens flourish in cities, towns, and suburbs, but in the countryside, where farming predominates, practicality is the rule. Most country yards have a flourishing patch of vegetables with a few ornamental plantings. A venerable clump of lilacs may beckon at a corner of the house, or an old shrub rose will stand as centerpiece in a neatly mown front yard. Small splashes of marigolds, red *Pelargoniums*, and other bedding annuals add color with little care in summer.

Cottage gardeners intoxicated with color have the opportunity to indulge themselves in the longer growing season to the south, where many late bloomers are available and experimenting with delicate plants can be worth the ever-present risk of unseasonable weather. Grasses and flowers stretch tall in the summer heat and then turn orange and gold during a long Indian summer, when the prairie seems to go on forever in all its glory under wide blue skies.

RECLAIMING A FAMILY TREASURE
Timeless elegance in a small Indiana town

When a husband and wife have totally different gardening styles, it can lead to a battle in the backyard—or, in this case, to two separate gardens, 20 miles apart. Rusty Harrison's garden is at the family homestead in Attica, Indiana, a small town on the bank of the Wabash River in the west-central part of the state. Ann Harrison's garden surrounds their cabin retreat in the nearby countryside (see pages 72–73).

Rusty's masterpiece garden has old roots. His grand-father built a sunken formal garden on the property in the 1920s to complement an English-style house. In the 1950s, his parents replaced the original house with their own modern ranch house and simplified the 3-acre gardens.

Several years later, it was finally Rusty's turn. "I always knew I would want to work with the garden," he says. "It seemed to be asking me to bring it back." Today, the formal heritage of the gardens has been restored. With help from design professional Ron Tisdale and from Bob and Rosella Jenkins of Jenkins Country Gardens, Rusty laid out

three levels of 60- by 350-foot tiers, echoing the original sunken garden.

Controlled elegance is the theme, and in this garden, neatness counts. Carefully clipped hedges form the living sculpture of the geometric beds. Rectangles, circles, and classic curlicues are outlined in the four-season green of boxwoods and then filled with a changing show of lilies, peonies, and daylilies—plus fragrant lilies-of-the-valley planted by Rusty's mother years ago.

Winter is one of the biggest challenges. Fickle temperature swings and drying air can damage the boxwood, even when a hardy variety is used. Over the years, Rusty has replaced demanding roses with reliable annuals and switched from vegetables to ornamentals. Specimen conifers and hedges keep the formal personality alive during the cold, often snowy season.

Well-used seating areas beckon throughout the garden. "My husband loves the planning and loves reading," explains Ann Harrison. "You can often find him sitting in his garden."

FACING PAGE Formerly a rose garden, this tier of the garden retains its formal feeling even though the roses are long gone. Young trees anchor hedged plantings of annual begonias in the foreground. To discourage weeds, the paths were lined with plastic, then topped with layers of limestone gravel, powdered limestone, and pea gravel. A brutal cold snap of −20 degrees a few years ago killed 600 boxwood plants, which had to be replaced with a hardier variety.

RIGHT Both an homage and a passion, Rusty Harrison's formal gardens pay tribute to his grandfather's garden, which existed on the same site. 'Enchantment' lilies ignite the early summer view. Evergreen hedges and conifers maintain a palette of green, and the contrasting paving adds color in the winter.

BELOW The understated container filled with silver *Helichrysum*, and a bold ring of hostas at its base provides an elegant juxtaposition to the Lutyens style furniture seen beyond.

ABOVE A small pond in a shady nook provides contrast to the foliage mix of color and texture seen here along a mosaic-patterned bluestone walk.

RIGHT The riotous color of butterfly weed, lilies, golden privet, annual amaranthus, and salvia fill the border.

RIGHT A gracious weeping spruce holds court in this centerpiece of conifers. The blue spruce and creeping juniper beneath contribute horizontal lines for visual balance as well as a feast of texture and subtle color. Hidden from view is a granite basin with a fountain, which brings nature's music to the bench nearby.

LEFT For the transition from the formal gardens to the woods beyond, Rusty Harrison wanted something rustic, "a little bit of a folly." This Arts-and-Crafts-style gazebo is visually separated from the formal garden by a woodland of old shade trees interplanted with young spruce and pines.

A COUNTRY CABIN
Offers a four-season retreat

Ann Harrison rarely sits still when she's in her garden. Outdoors, she would rather weed than read. "I love to putter. Ever since I was a small child, I've had my hands in the soil," she says.

For years, Ann helped with the gardens at the Harrison home in Attica, Indiana (see pages 68–71). But when the couple built a rustic retreat 10 years ago, Ann planned a garden that is country casual and all her own.

About 20 minutes from the Harrison's town home, the log cabin is nestled among deep ravines in the countryside, backed by existing woods and a sandstone cliff that drops off sharply to a creek 250 feet below.

"The country is simply wonderful year-round," says Ann, so her garden is an all-season show-off, with conifers and red- and yellowtwig dogwoods tucked in everywhere to keep things interesting in winter. Existing woodland becomes part of the garden picture, especially when the trees turn in fall or when spring is heralded by that mist of green.

Calling upon the same design professionals that had worked with the town garden, Ann made a centerpiece out of a drainage swale that ran near the cabin. "It was deep, and full of brush," she remembers. "But that heavy clay soil holds water, so we made a pond out of it." The 12-foot-deep pond has a practical side hiding beneath its serenity—it's a handy water source in case of fire.

While Ann's husband, Rusty, prefers to plan before planting, Ann favors the hands-on approach. Moving plants around to try out new combinations is simply part of the pleasure. "Sometimes," she laughs, "I have to move a plant six inches to make me happy."

ABOVE A dwarf blue spruce cools the warm colors of yellow daylilies and fuchsia-colored petunias. The entrance to the pier is a popular spot with friends, family, and even the cat and dog. A feeding frenzy by 2-foot-long koi ensues whenever food is scattered on the water.

ABOVE A swale filled with brush has become a tranquil pond, the dense clay soil now doing what it does best—hold water. Although the living room and porch of the cabin offer views of the water, Ann says the best place for pond-watching is the little porch they attached to the garage, shown here.

ABOVE A weathered wood goose greets visitors to this country cabin in the heart of the Midwest. Tough, hardy 'Stella de Oro' daylilies require little care and bloom for months.

RIGHT This flagstone path to the garage meanders through mixed shrubs and perennials. In summer, the variegated redtwig dogwood (center right) lightens the greenery; in winter, its bare, red-barked stems flare against the snow.

CAREFUL PLANNING
Brings blooming fall color

Most people rely on foliage to provide the bright colors that frame every view of the Midwest in fall, but Jim Lukes expects his flowers to contribute some special effects as well. His 2-acre garden on the bluffs of the Iowa River in Decorah bursts into bloom just as the trees begin their spectacular fall show. Asters, chrysanthemums, boltonia, rudbeckia, and fall-blooming clematis make up the gardening season's grand finale until frost knocks the last blooms back in October.

Before the gardens were established, Jim planted trees to create privacy for the house and give the garden an elegant setting. His property is large enough for sweeping perennial gardens and two ponds, one with a 4-foot waterfall. Dark evergreens form a distinguished backdrop for the garden year-round, but they look especially handsome in fall against the bright perennials and the decorative plumes of ornamental grasses.

Jim mulches garden beds with a 3-inch layer of bark chips to help control weeds and maintain moisture in the soil. As his garden expands, he continues to search for plants that tolerate the growing conditions of the Midwest. His goal is to have color year-round. "Summer is not a problem," he says, "but if you don't prepare for fall color, you won't have it."

BELOW Feathery pink plumes of a tamarisk tree (*Tamarix parviflora*) float lightly above a pond. The dark foliage of a purple beech (*Fagus sylvatica* 'Atropunicea') provides a shadowy contrast. In the background are the bluffs of the Iowa River.

FACING PAGE Silvery plumes of feather reed grass (*Calamagrostis × acutiflora* 'Karl Foerster'), bright yellow 'Goldsturm' rudbeckia, and the red-splotched gloriosa daisy (*Rudbeckia hirta* 'Indian Summer') are at their best in late summer.

ABOVE A billowing cloud of *Boltonia asteroides* 'Snowbank' blooms before the twining green leaves and fragrant white flowers of sweet autumn clematis. Behind them is a barn now used as a potting shed.

LEFT Backed by the ornate pergola, the cascade's banks host plants of striking textures. A mound of fuzzy lamb's ears (*Stachys byzantina* 'Big Ears') on one side echoes the blue-green tint of spiky cheddar pinks (*Dianthus gratianopolitanus* 'Bath's Pink') on the other. Crinkly bronze leaves of carpet bugleweed (*Ajuga reptans* 'Catlin's Giant') emerge from a thick mat of *Mazus reptans*.

FRENCH FORMALITY
With a difference

The formality of the French garden style and the lush abundance of the English garden style mix nicely under tall midwestern oaks in this Canton, Ohio, garden. Clearly expressing owner Jacqueline Gill's roots in southern France, elegant structures linked by formal paths connect the garden to the French-style house. Hundreds of perennial flowers, a cascading stream, and a large pond contribute English informality. The result is an elegant, inviting garden that appears to be hidden in an enchanted woodland.

Six years ago, Jacqueline and Robert Gill engaged garden designers Sabrena Schweyer and Samuel Salsbury to help them revise a landscape plan that had gone awry. They reorganized the spaces, redesigned an existing pond, and added the cascade. They moved hundreds of perennials and shrubs and opened up a view of the lawn. The new design was tied together by repeating silver and pastel colors throughout.

Close to the house, the garden style is formal and the palette restrained. Pink polyantha roses and soft purple catmint bloom all summer long in beds beneath the stone balustrade of the patio. Deeper in the garden, however, the plantings become more diverse and the structures less formal. A brick path connects with stone stairs leading down to a tree-sheltered pergola at the edge of the large pond.

ABOVE A stone wall wraps around a grassy nook by the large pond. The wall and stairs were constructed with stone salvaged from the foundations of old barns. In this part of the garden, the colors and textures are bold. Purple-and-white bear's breech *(Acanthus mollis)* stretches up before the oversize leaves of Japanese coltsfoot *(Petasites japonicus giganteus)*.

ABOVE The garden is formal but inviting near the house. A cascading stream starts near the gazebo, seen at far right, so the soothing sound of the water can be heard from the patio.

LEFT Chartreuse and magenta brighten a mixed border near the house. Magenta bush clover (*Lespedeza thunbergii* 'Gibraltar') is surrounded by the chartreuse foliage of *Spiraea thunbergii* 'Ogon'—sometimes called mellow yellow spirea—and of a variegated false cypress (*Chamaecyparis obtusa* 'Crippsii'). In the background, *Hydrangea paniculata* 'Tardiva' lifts its panicles like great torches.

FACING PAGE A brick walkway on one side of the property winds under an arbor on the way to the backyard. Oakleaf hydrangea, hostas, lady's-mantle *(Alchemilla mollis)*, Japanese painted fern *(Athyrium nipponicum* 'Pictum'), and Japanese anemones flourish in beds along the shady path. Hanging baskets full of annuals are suspended from the arbor.

RIGHT The 100,000-gallon pond at the bottom of the property is a garden of its own, where water lilies, iris, and three dozen koi thrive. The pergola's pyramid-shaped roof was designed to echo the formal roof style of the house.

SHOWY PERENNIALS
From an Iowa cornfield

The country life called Lee Zeike and Lindsay Lee 15 years ago when they moved to rural Decorah, in the rolling hills of northeastern Iowa. There they built a small house and a large nursery, where they sell bone-hardy perennials that flourish with little care.

Willowglen Nursery's display gardens sit on a natural terrace on old farmland. The heavy clay soil is rich with minerals, but Zieke and Lee amended it with lots of compost to lighten it and improve drainage. Great drifts of black-eyed Susans, asters, hollyhocks, and ornamental grasses grow to enormous proportions in this sunny garden. The show of color begins in June and lasts until October.

When the garden was first designed, the owners arranged plants with hot red, yellow, and orange flowers in beds farthest from the house. Cool pinks and blues were planted closer to the entrance to the garden. Now their planting style is bolder—brilliant colors splash all through the borders. Bright pink phlox flash at the feet of snow-white asters and pop up again in the midst of black-eyed Susans.

INSET ABOVE A great wave of white New England aster (*Aster novae-angliae* 'Wedding Lace') tumbles out of raised beds near the nursery's workshop. Behind it, the tall flowering plumes of feather reed grass (*Calamagrostis* × *acutiflora* 'Karl Foerster') form a dramatic natural curtain.

ABOVE A sea of thousands of 'Goldsturm' rudbeckias blooms for weeks in midsummer. Silver feather miscanthus (*Miscanthus sinensis* 'Silberfeder') and Siberian graybeard (*Spodiopogon sibiricus* 'West Lake') begin blooming at the same time. These ornamental grasses' showy flowering panicles last until frost.

FACING PAGE TOP RIGHT An old-fashioned combination of hollyhocks (*Alcea rosea*) and Siberian catnip (*Nepeta sibirica*) blooms near an old barn on the property. The catnip is cut back after it blooms in June so that it will produce another round of flowers.

FACING PAGE BOTTOM RIGHT Midwestern gardeners love hydrangeas, but not many varieties can survive truly cold winters. *Hydrangea paniculata* 'Tardiva' puts on a spectacular show late in summer and thrives despite winter temperatures that drop well below zero.

ABOVE The variegated foliage of two dappled willows (*Salix integra* 'Hakuro Nishiki') shines from a bog garden in the midst of the woodland. Bright yellow marsh marigolds *(Caltha palustris)* light up the bog in spring.

RIGHT Canadian-bred hardy climbing rose 'William Baffin' and clematis 'Mme le Coultre' thrive on an arbor at the entrance to the rose garden. Hendley protects the crowns of the roses with a mound of mulch every winter.

A WOODLAND EDEN
In urban Ohio

Burt Hendley started this 3-acre garden from scratch in 1987 when he and his wife Susan bought their property in Zanesville, Ohio. The woodland garden is planted on hard clay soil, but Hendley built up free-form beds to support a collection of about 200 rhododendrons and other woody plants. Pine bark, garden loam, and peat were mixed to provide a lighter soil for the shallow-rooted plants.

Inspired by the collection of deciduous and evergreen magnolias at Dawes Arboretum in Newark, 25 miles northwest, Hendley has planted a number of magnolias in his garden. He especially favors *Magnolia grandiflora* 'Bracken's Brown Beauty', a Southern magnolia that stands up to midwestern winters.

Hendley does most of his planting in fall, when he makes the rounds of local nurseries looking for end-of-season bargains. Through the years he has planted hybrid rhododendrons, native and evergreen azaleas, witch hazels, willows, hollies, dwarf conifers, and seven varieties of oakleaf hydrangea around the property.

Although this is a city garden, deer can be a problem. The Hendleys have solved it by sharing their home with two standard Schnausers, Leo and Josie, who patrol the garden and keep the deer at bay.

ABOVE The gently rolling Appalachian foothills provide a tranquil setting for dogwoods (*Cornus* × *rutgersensis* 'Constellation') blooming under a canopy of oak trees in May. A grove of summer-flowering sourwood trees *(Oxydendrum arboreum)* provides a backdrop for a bed of rhododendrons and azaleas.

TOP LEFT A stonemason built these handsome "natural" stairs leading down through the trees. Under the deciduous canopy are collected 50 different varieties of hostas.

DRAWING INSPIRATION
From a garden laboratory

Tracy DiSabato-Aust writes garden books. Between the intricate mixed beds of flowers and shrubs in the front yard of her garden and the tumble of perennials at the back, she finds plenty of material for inspiration.

She calls her garden, located northeast of Columbus, Ohio, Hidden Haven. "This garden is a living laboratory, but it is also for pleasure, and it reflects my style," she says of the dense collection of plants around her log house. She tests plants for winter hardiness and drought tolerance, evaluates their performance in different conditions, and works on plant combinations. For 10 years she has worked with perennials, but she recently started incorporating more woody shrubs in her plantings.

Healthy soil is the foundation for Tracy's exuberant garden. Compost, cottonseed meal, and alfalfa meal are worked generously into the planting beds when they are first dug and are used again as a topdressing on established beds. A good organic base doesn't require a supplement of commercial fertilizer—she doesn't use any chemical fertilizers or pesticides at all.

Tracy chooses her plant combinations carefully, considering shape, texture, and color. Mellow blues and purples are her favorite colors, but in summer the garden tends toward brighter oranges and reds.

Everything in this garden has to survive without a lot of pampering. "I believe in selecting the proper plant from the start," she says. "It's survival of the fittest around here."

FACING PAGE Drifts of perennials overflow mixed borders along the front walk. Black-eyed Susan, phlox, and coneflower provide bright summer color. A yellow honeysuckle (*Lonicera periclymenum* 'Graham Thomas') blooms on a trellis against the house.

LEFT From the deck behind the house, the view of the backyard is spectacular in summer. Brown-eyed Susan *(Rudbeckia triloba)* blooms toward the back of the garden. Behind it tower tall plumes of Joe Pye weed (*Eupatorium purpureum maculatum* 'Gateway').

BELOW Rustic chairs made by an Ohio artist congregate under a large maple in the shade garden. The pale yellow flowers of fennel (*Foeniculum vulgare*) peer over a hellebore's evergreen foliage in the background. The blue pot contains an ornamental rhubarb *(Rheum palmatum tanguticum)*.

OLD-TIME ABUNDANCE
Gardening with a free hand

A profusion of colorful annual and perennial flowers thrive in this casual garden near Cleveland in Hudson, Ohio. During the 20 years she has lived in her house, landscape designer Valerie Strong has eliminated almost all the turf, saying, "a traditional green lawn seemed like a waste of good garden space to me."

Valerie's house sits on a terrace 3 feet above the street, and the garden starts at the front retaining wall. There are no formal flower beds, just drifts of plants along a series of gravel paths. She didn't start with a master plan—all she wanted was a garden with color and fragrance throughout the growing season.

Annual flowers are allowed to find their own places in the garden. Dame's rocket, spider flower, love-in-a-mist, and cosmos reseed in different places every year. If the plants look good, Valerie lets them grow where they will.

She also grows old roses, scented geraniums, lavender, thyme, and two species of flowering tobacco (*Nicotiana alata* and *N. sylvestris*) for their fragrance and their old-fashioned charm.

A sweet-scented wild honeysuckle climbs an arbor near the back door, where it draws lots of hummingbirds. A small pond in the front yard and two more in the back attract frogs and dragonflies to her fragrant, free-form garden.

FACING PAGE INSET In late spring, bright purple
alliums pop up all around the cottage garden.

ABOVE Trailing pink petunias and silvery artemisia
tumble together at the bottom of an ivy-covered
retaining wall at the front of the property. Pansies
bloom in a stone trough on top of the wall.

CENTER A red-roofed garden house is the centerpiece of the backyard. Many of the old-fashioned
plants in the garden were given to Valerie as cuttings
or divisions, including the climbing pink rose. Just in
front of the garden house, the tall foliage and bright
yellow flowers of *Iris pseudacorus* shoot up at the
edge of the pond.

THE
PLAINS

From Saskatchewan south through the western Dakotas, Nebraska, and Kansas, the historical advance and retreat of massive glaciers has crushed the land into flat tables and shallow bowls, thinned the sugar-fine sand of Nebraska's sandhills, deposited rich loess soil in the east, and carved out streams and canyons. Unique land formations like the Pine Ridge escarpment and the Bad-lands rise like sentinels from these rolling expanses of land.

Were the Plains undisturbed by agriculture, the entire region would be cloaked in short- and midgrass prairie plants. Stretching their roots to depths exceeding 10 feet, the grasses continue to blanket large areas of the Plains where shallow soils and limited rainfall will not support woody plants. Occasional groves of cottonwood and willow and stands of mountain mahogany, ponderosa pine, and limber pine, controlled by lightning-triggered wildfires, stand in stark contrast to the flat grasslands.

Winds charge unchallenged across these open spaces, wringing the last drops of moisture from the soil. Yet many ornamental native wildflowers and hardy trees and shrubs introduced from the eastern deciduous forests have been able to adapt to these dry and windy growing conditions.

Gardeners in the Plains must provide what nature lacks, selecting plants adapted to the region, modifying hot and windy conditions with shelterbelts and windbreaks, and amending the soils to help increase fertility and retain moisture.

Owners of large properties create gardens here with managed spaces closer to the house and transition plantings that blend with the more distant landscape. These naturalized gardens require little maintenance and allow native plants such as yucca, gramas, and bluestems to find their own places. Local limestone becomes the background for rock gardens or is used to construct borders and walls tumbling with vines like purple poppy mallow. Kitchen gardens enhanced by ornamental grasses and shrubs provide edibles and cutting flowers such as penstemons, pinwheel coneflowers, and sunflowers.

But not all Plains gardens are rustic and natural. Many formal and contemporary styles flourish here, using plants as architectural features to enhance garden structures. Traditional gardens tie lakefront or riverfront properties to their houses, marsh gardens include colonies of reeds and cattails, and suburban water gardens use stone to move water and create focal points. Backyard ponds provide a social setting and garden habitat for birds and other wildlife to interact, while butterflies and bees are attracted to goldenrod, gayfeather, and wild roses.

Blooming prickly pear cactus, aromatic bee balm, and velvety spiderwort add fragrance and texture to these garden landscapes. Creeping mahonia, one of few broadleaf evergreens to flourish here, forms thick mats of foliage. Sumac colonizes the grasses and dons a red cloak in autumn to replace the color of the wildflowers.

But the true glory of the Plains remains the sea of moving grasses standing against a backdrop of limestone under an endless, restless sky.

DETERMINATION IS THE KEY
To success in Saskatchewan

BELOW A stone bench at the edge of the pond provides a focal point as well as a place to view the fish. In the foreground, primroses and miniature hostas combine with iris and coral bells.

Most farmers diligently clear their fields of rocks, but Connie Reavie hauls them into her 4-acre garden set among the fields of the family farm in the rural Carrot River area of eastern Saskatchewan. Now, rocks pave paths through her shade garden, border the large pond, and provide accent notes throughout. "My husband couldn't believe I'd have rocks hauled here from northern Saskatchewan," she said.

Reavie began collecting plants 20 years ago and created her garden on land that was originally flat and bare. When her children were young, she raised vegetables, but then she discovered "the wonderful world of flowers."

Not one to be stymied by annual temperature dips to −20 degrees and summer highs in the 90s, Connie always finds room for a new arrival. "I'm not always particular about what fits together," she said. "I like having an element of surprise and am delighted to find a little jewel that has overwintered even though it shouldn't have."

By covering new plants with mulch in fall or putting them in sheltered spots, she is able to overwinter perennials that don't usually grow this far north. Because the garden is so large, she mulches only a few plants every winter, but has had particular luck with the Explorer and Morden series of roses, clematis, and a 'Carol Mackie' daphne that is planted in a sheltered spot. "I'll throw a little straw on them for a few years, and then they're on their own," she said.

Ever practical and resourceful, Connie hand-dug a pond that holds 5,000 gallons of water. Now, besides the welcome sounds and reflections that water provides, the aquatic and bog plants provide this plant collector with a whole new area to explore. "We get such hot, dry summers, seeing the water lilies and fish in the pond and the cattails, astilbes, and other bog plants in bloom is a real treat."

ABOVE Besides gardening, Connie finds time for making pottery that she sells at retail outlets. She includes original pieces in her garden, such as this pitcher and bowl that she fashioned into a fountain.

RIGHT Because the surrounding countryside is so flat, the Reavies turned this natural depression in the earth into a dry streambed and built a bridge across it. Here sedums, lamiums, and daylilies combine with dianthus and campanula.

LEFT This arbor, made of willow twigs found on the property, welcomes guests to the shade garden. In the foreground, a "Welcome" plaque made by Connie is surrounded by lamiums.

A SHOWPLACE OF UNUSUAL PLANTS
Where only the fittest survive

Feeling like a North Dakota pioneer, this gardener had to conquer thistles and brome grass before his property in Minot could be turned into a garden. After applying herbicides, he disked the land under and left it fallow for 2 years to make sure the undesirable weeds were truly gone. Then he seeded small sections of lawn, only to lose it all to drought in the third year. One bright solution to the problems of low annual rainfall and a salty well on the property was to create a surface water hole to store snowmelt water.

During the past 25 years, flower beds have been added one by one, for a total of 15 islands scattered around the perimeter of the lawn. The garden is a showplace of many different ornamental grasses, annuals for a summertime display of color, and drought-resistant perennials to extend the season. Many plants have come from other rock-garden enthusiasts belonging to an international seed exchange program. Two small bog gardens, made from inexpensive children's pools filled with peat moss and sand, contain a collection of native orchids.

Because the property is near a gravel township road, groups of people often stop and visit. Granite stones have been used as accents for the largest bed, a rock garden. Flat granite pieces make excellent stepping-stones through this garden, allowing visitors a closer look at the plants, many of which sport identification labels.

The biggest vertical accents in the garden are the encircling windbreaks of blue spruce. They break up the endless horizon of the plains and send the eye skyward. The perennials and grasses also contribute to the feeling of a garden reaching for the sky.

Key challenges faced by this gardener are water conservation and finding unique, drought-tolerant plants. The garden receives only 16 inches of rain per year. The numerous annuals are given supplemental irrigation immediately after planting and into the early summer, and thereafter get water only during a summer drought. The remaining plants must tolerate the dry environment. New plants get only two chances for survival—if they don't thrive after being planted twice, they are not replaced.

LEFT Strong vertical accents of feather reed grass (*Calamagrostis × acutiflora* 'Karl Foerster') swaying in the wind create a nice contrast against the horizontal branches of a blue spruce. A lavender-blue fleabane (*Erigeron* 'Azure Fairy') has been appropriately placed to hide the base of the ornamental grass.

FACING PAGE A piece of western cedar from the Badlands has nicely weathered the elements and has become the focal point for this wild bed. Yarrows, bluebells, wild columbine, and poppies have been chosen because they will self-seed and create an informal display that requires just a little periodic weeding.

ABOVE Only the fish in this pond won't survive the severe winters in North Dakota. All the plants in this 10-year-old lily pond are hardy. Native water lilies thrive because they are planted 2½ feet below the surface of the water.

LEFT A mounded rock garden containing native granite boulders also includes drought-hardy 'Stella de Oro' daylily and several types of hen and chicks (*Sempervivum tectorum*). In the center, a pink *Sempervivum* is in flower with exotic upright flower structures.

IMAGINATIVE RECYCLING
Holds back a hill

Transforming the side of a hill in Rapid City, South Dakota, was a challenge that Gale and Janice Holbrook lived with for several years before setting to work to create an area that now is a joy to behold.

"We built the house 15 years ago and couldn't stand looking at the view," said Janice. Then Gale decided to recycle on a grand scale. He brought home pieces of sidewalk, breaking them up with a sledgehammer and trundling them down the hill in a wheelbarrow to create retaining walls that never fail to impress visitors.

"They really think it's natural rock," said Gale. "The secret is to have the broken side to the outside so that the smooth side of the concrete never shows. The rough side looks more like natural limestone." As he scoured the town for broken driveways and sidewalks, Gale became friendly with many contractors, who were always happy to see him come to their construction sites to haul away concrete debris.

As the retaining wall was being constructed, Gale created pockets behind the rock where Janice planted blue spruce, juniper, perennials galore, clematis, and three kinds of sedums that bloom at different times during spring and summer.

"They take turns performing," said Janice. "At different times they provide a mass of white flowers followed by red, pale pink, and two different shades of yellow. It's a truly spectacular display."

FACING PAGE Although it's not part of their hilltop property, the Holbrooks cleaned up this slope, planted wild roses and yucca, and now enjoy the borrowed view of canyons and trees in the distance.

TOP LEFT This potted cactus, brought from Arizona, didn't bloom for 6 years even though it overwintered in the house. Then it finally put on a display for the patient Holbrooks.

ABOVE Delphinium and clematis in the foreground nearly obscure the cracked-concrete wall. Sedums provide continuous color during three seasons, and evergreens enhance the winter view.

A PHOTOGRAPHER'S EYE
Using annual color to compose garden portraits

Cheryl Richter's vision and love of dramatic color combinations have inspired this appealing urban garden in Lincoln, Nebraska. Colorful annuals have been used in the same way that a florist would arrange a cut-flower design for a table centerpiece. Given the extensive use of containers, the garden can be changed on a whim to create a new image.

Large London plane trees shade the front of Cheryl's garden, which surrounds a prairie box house built in 1908 in the Hillsdale Historic District. Flowering crabtrees and thornless honey locusts, which are able to thrive in the heavy clay soil, also line the neighborhood streets.

No matter what the design of the moment, a riot of summerlong color greets visitors around the perimeter of this garden. Long-blooming perennials are grouped to bloom simultaneously. Most of the annuals—geraniums, petunias, zinnias, salvia, and cleome—are tough and reliable. Coleus and sweet potato vine are used to create a dark or light foliage contrast to the flowering plants.

ABOVE Ready for all visitors, these 1950s-style metal chairs in turquoise, orange, and chartreuse provide a welcome in front of the garage. Anything goes in this celebration of color.

An eccentric mix of containers creates many different moods and themes in this garden—including a southwestern bed, with pots from Mexico. But containers make dealing with the inconsistent Nebraska weather even more challenging. One way Cheryl has successfully countered summer heat is to mix water-holding crystals with the soil to reduce the need for frequent watering. Careful observation of soil color and of the plants for signs of thirst has also helped her cope with maintaining so many annuals. Sometimes large containers are chosen so that plants won't dry out quite so fast.

Another weather challenge is the forceful winds. Each summer, some of the less sturdy plants must be staked or cut back. Doing so has the added benefit of increasing plant density.

ABOVE A visit to the Sonoran desert was the inspiration for this annuals garden surrounding a small pond. Random swirls of color create naturalistic drifts that flow in a pattern reminiscent of that of desert wildflowers. Large-leaved castor beans provide a contrast to the fine-textured flowering annuals below them.

LEFT A local Nebraska artisan has created a whimsical bench that is perfect for this quiet spot in the garden. Barn boards create a resting spot for guests; a basket of annuals is a great accent at the base of the bench.

RIGHT A mosaic-covered container purchased at a Mexican market in the Texas hill country contributes to the southwestern feel of this annual display. Frilly 'Kiwi Fern' coleus, 'Terra Cotta' million bells *(Calibrachoa)*, and the daisylike flowers of 'Lemon Symphony' *Osteospermum* and white 'Super-cascade' petunias add color among the bright green sweet potato vines (*Ipomoea batatas* 'Terrace Lime').

A NESTLED COTTAGE
In Nebraska Pines

The country garden of Sue and Walt Gardner in Lincoln, Nebraska, developed as many good gardens do—one area at a time, working toward a goal of blending spaces, structures, and plants into a harmonious whole.

The Gardners first built a deck to connect the house with the 3-acre garden. Tennis courts and a swimming pool followed. Construction of the striking glass atrium allowed a nearly seamless connection between inside and outside spaces near the house. A casual mix of woody and herbaceous plants flow around the edges of paths and patios to unify this lush retreat. Walt's love of water inspired him to build two ponds, connected by the twists and turns of a bubbling stream down the hill to the garden's latest addition, a guest cottage.

Modeled after a French cottage as well as Nebraska's historic sod houses, the house is tucked among perennials and shrubs that soften its corners, frame its windows like wide-open eyes, and flow up its wedgewood blue walls to the wildflower-covered roof.

Building the straw-bale cottage tested the Gardners' commitment and endurance, from obtaining a construction permit to organizing a family bucket brigade to carry soil to the roof. Straw-bale construction consists of tightly bound bales of straw, stacked and pinned and then finished with a mortar or stucco surface that waterproofs and binds the straw together. It is extremely long lasting and energy efficient, as the nearly 3-foot-thick walls provide excellent insulation.

A rubber liner and large beams support 12 inches of heavy soil and a soft carpet of hand-planted grasses and perennials on the roof. An automatic irrigation system provides regular watering, and a hidden system of drain tiles and gutters carries away any extra water under ground. The result is a charming cottage that looks as if it has been nestled here forever among the pines.

FACING PAGE A dwarf Alberta spruce accents the path as it winds through perennials and shrubs to the cottage. Blue and white annual bachelor's buttons *(Centaurea cyanis)* mirror the lavender on the roof; in spring, *Iris sibirica* 'Caesar's Brother' adds dark purple to the color scheme.

ABOVE Grasses and perennials on the cottage roof were chosen for their cool colors: among them are several lavenders, moss roses, snow-in-summer *(Cerastium tomentosum),* and wild prairie petunias *(Ruellia humilis).* The cottage peeks from behind layered shrubs of red-leaf Japanese barberry *(Berberis thunbergii* 'Atropurpurea') and spreading juniper.

ABOVE Soft masses of cranesbill, silver artemisia, and bright blue larkspur and spiderwort fill stone walls that line a brick path between the deck and cottage. Blue sky is reflected in the bowl of a simple copper birdbath.

LEFT An airy bridge over a meandering stream leads to the hot tub garden, screened from direct view by a globe arborvitae and redleaf barberry. The vertical accent of horsetail *(Equisetum hyemale)* stands as a formal contrast to the rounded shrubs and stones.

PLANNING PAYS OFF
On a busy city lot

Matt and Judy Veatch's Victorian home was built in Lawrence, Kansas, in 1891. Back then it was in the country, but today it sits on a busy corner surrounded by traffic. Though they didn't mind sharing their garden, the Veatches didn't want their yard to be a public park, so Matt enclosed it with a 4-foot "hospitality fence" that passersby can see over to enjoy the garden.

Matt, a historical archivist, and Judy, a mechanical engineer, are both research oriented and methodical. They spent many hours studying gardening materials before breaking ground. They finally agreed on an informal garden style inspired by English designers Rosemary Verey and Adrian Bloom.

Matt worked out the overall layout for the garden beds and developed a custom database with all the plants he and Judy were thinking of putting in the garden. Then Matt used a commercial landscape design software package to arrange the plants within each bed.

The shady backyard features three large planting areas that contain plants of a particular color. "Blue garden" has a host of plants with blue foliage or blue flowers, "chartreuse garden" contains plants with yellow-green foliage and flowers, and "green garden" is made up of plants in varying shades of green.

The couple continues to experiment with a variety of plants, and they don't hesitate to eliminate those that don't perform in the challenging Kansas heat and wind. Monkshood *(Aconitum)*, lupine hybrids, and foxglove have all gone to the compost heap.

Plantings of great summer performers include hosta, daylily, black-eyed Susan, purple coneflower *(Echinacea purpurea)*, catmint, tall sedum *(Sedum spectabile)*, bluemist spirea *(Caryopteris × clandonensis)*, 'Sea Foam' rose, dwarf fountain grass *(Pennisetum alopecuroides* 'Hameln'*)*, and many different varieties of Japanese silver grass *(Miscanthus sinensis)*.

ABOVE The foundation planting beds around the front porch of this Victorian home are much deeper than is typical. Bold curves sweep out into the lawn, creating ample space for layered plantings. River birch *(Betula nigra)* and porcupine grass *(Miscanthus sinensis* 'Strictus') anchor this bed, while drifts of layered perennials create depth.

RIGHT The shady backyard garden consists of several large, free-form beds around a brick patio and wood deck (shown on facing page). That area is blocked from public view by a taller fence with tightly spaced slats.

FACING PAGE From a second-story roof, the bird's-eye view shows how the "blue garden," "green garden," and "chartreuse garden" wrap around the main walkway in the backyard. Adirondack chairs and a small table are placed in a quiet nook where the couple enjoys sitting.

A JAPANESE-STYLE GARDEN
That stands up to heat

This backyard in suburban Overland Park, Kansas, has been transformed from a sloping site with a concrete slab patio, a fence, and lots of turf into an inviting outdoor room filled with color and texture, thanks to the hard work and ongoing attention of garden owners J. D. Perkins and Joe Hudec.

Because the home is situated on a sloping site, the builder graded the property to raise the house and patio from the surrounding ground. This provided a dry basement, but it left an awkward area in which to garden. To deal with the lack of a level planting area around the patio, J. D. and Joe hauled in loads of soil to create large berms anchored by rock. They built one fish pond nestled against the patio and added a smaller fish pond a few years later. The whole area is covered by a handsome wood arbor spanning almost 55 feet. The arbor is a strong structural element that unifies the area adjacent to the house.

The garden is now divided into two areas. The space nearest the house is dedicated to entertaining. Spring blooming bulbs, flowering trees and shrubs, and evergreen conifers provide seasonal interest and privacy on the rest of the property. The garden is loosely based on the Japanese style, with bermed planting areas, rock, fish ponds, carefully pruned Japanese maples, and conifers.

According to J. D., his biggest challenge is finding plants that look great in the heat and humidity of July and August. "We garden on the edge in this part of the Midwest," he laughs. The spring garden is filled with reliable bulbs and azaleas, but the summer garden depends on tropicals and annuals that can hold their own through weeks of temperatures over 90 degrees. Color and texture are combined in such summer standbys as coleus, wax begonias, other begonias with large colorful leaves, ivy geraniums, and sweet potato vine.

FACING PAGE Berms and stone were used to elevate the area near the patio. Red-tinged caladiums, impatiens, and geraniums are coordinated with a red-leaf Japanese maple in this example of color echoing color.

ABOVE The front steps are built of concrete pavers in a mix of subtle colors and shapes chosen to suggest cobblestones. *Spiraea japonica* 'Limemound' and hosta 'August Moon' line one side of the walk, while an evergreen yew and Colorado blue spruce provide year-round interest.

ABOVE Wisteria grows up and over the wood arbor covering a fish pond and the patio. Fragrant clusters of purple blooms drip down through the openings in the arbor when the vine blooms in April.

LEFT This passageway between the front and side yards was poorly drained, so the owners paved it with limestone flagstones and fast-draining ¾-inch river rock.

The Lower Midwest

Magnificent rivers and rolling hills define the landscape of the Lower Midwest. The Ohio River forms the southeastern boundary of the region, while the Missouri skirts its northern reaches and the Mississippi meanders through its heart.

West of the Mississippi, the Ozark mountains rise up from the surrounding plains. Wind, water, and time have softened these mountains from craggy peaks to gently undulating mounds of clay, limestone, and granite cloaked with oaks and pines. Farther east, the topography appears similar, but the oak- and hickory-covered hills were formed by rivers and streams carving through an upland plateau, seeking an escape to the sea.

Early migrants from Virginia and Kentucky gave much of the Lower Midwest a decidedly southern flavor. Wealthy landowners recreated the plantations of the South complete with expansive vistas, allées of stately trees, and large homes. That early southern influence remains today. Nowhere else in the Midwest can one find Southern magnolias, crepe myrtles, and mimosas as standard landscape plants.

The Shady Retreat and Savanna Spotlight are two garden styles that derive from this southern heritage. To escape the heat and humidity of summer, gardeners construct a Shady Retreat, a private conversation corner tucked under the shade of a tulip poplar or sour gum. Subtle shades of greens, golds, and whites from hostas, vinca, and euonymus contribute to the soothing effect.

For a bolder statement in the landscape, the Savanna Spotlight mimics the scattered woodlands, where oaks and hickories are interspersed with open grasslands. The resulting mix of sun and shade enables gardeners to grow many flowering perennials, annuals, and spring bulbs such as crocus and daffodils. The flowering plants appreciate the afternoon shade as much as the gardeners do.

Southern plants survive in the Lower Midwest because winter temperatures remain warmer here than in the rest of the Midwest. This region also receives more moisture than areas farther north and west, so water gardens have a natural appeal. The cooling effect of water in the landscape is appreciated through the warm summer months and underscores the importance of water to the region's history.

An unpredictable rainfall pattern has made waterwise gardens a popular recent garden style. Plants are grouped by moisture needs for easy irrigation. Soils are amended with organic matter to hold more water. Use of thirsty plants is minimized; instead, drought-tolerant plants such as ornamental grasses and sedums are featured.

The New American Garden style is also popular here, in which native purple coneflowers, prairie dropseed, little bluestem, and goldenrods combine to imitate nearby prairies.

Unlike the rest of the Midwest, where summer quickly shifts to winter, spring and fall linger here, deliciously displaying the pastel blossoms of springtime flowering dogwoods and redbuds and the rich fall colors of sugar maples and sweet gums. To fully appreciate gardening in the Lower Midwest, take a cue from nature and plan for a four-season display in the landscape.

ANTIQUE URNS AND VICTORIAN PLANTERS
Define a shady space

Twenty years ago, Jim Fitterling began the process of converting an 80-by-40-foot space behind a condominium in Kansas City's historic Westport district into a beautiful garden.

ABOVE Visitors are immersed in the fragrance of a reblooming honeysuckle as they enter this urban oasis through a gate between the parking area and the garden. In the foreground, the pale foliage of *Spiraea japonica* 'Goldmound' contrasts with a bright Asiatic lily and warm yellow sundrops *(Oenothera fruticosa glauca)*.

A retired art teacher and artist, Jim used his summers to learn to garden. Today his garden is a little bit English and a little bit French, with lots of American ingenuity. "I love the abundant plantings of the English garden style tucked into the structure of the French parterres," he says.

In his plan, Jim relied on classic elements of design, such as a central axis to connect the main perennial garden to its surrounding spaces. Rather than using many plants, he repeated a few plant combinations to create rhythm.

Jim and his partner, Leonard Raynor, built a knee-high dry-laid native stone wall along the rear property line, then placed large antique urns and Victorian planters as focal points within the defining lines of clipped 'Green Gem' boxwood and burning bush hedges.

Walnut trees adjacent to the property's boundaries on three sides presented a particular challenge. Besides casting deep shade, they were poisoning other plants. By excavating to a depth of 18 inches and using new soil amended with compost, Jim and Leonard were able to reduce the toxic effect that the walnuts were having on other plants.

Their efforts have been rewarded by a beautiful garden than survives midwestern summers with only 5 hours of sunlight a day.

ABOVE The trunk of a redbud tree and a Victorian planter emphasize the transition between the shade garden and the central beds. Evergreens, including spruce, yews, and boxwood, provide year-round structure. The foxgloves, lilies, coreopsis, and cosmos fill in for a colorful midsummer show.

BELOW Seen from beneath the delicate canopy of a redbud *(Cercis canadensis),* an antique Sarasota urn filled with annuals invites further exploration of the central perennial beds. The slight offset and differing heights of the clipped boxwood hedges form a virtual gate through which the turf path winds.

ABOVE Displayed against a clipped hedge of Washington hawthorn that screens meter boxes, another antique urn filled with annuals is circled by clipped boxwood and English ivy. *Penstemon digitalis* 'Husker Red' sends its spires of pale pink flowers skyward above dusky red foliage in the adjacent perennial border.

RIGHT A small pond is tucked into the curved elbow of a native stone path leading from the central beds to the shade garden. A narrow band of several varieties of hosta, lady's-mantle *(Alchemilla mollis),* and carpet bugleweed softens the edges and blends with the shady green backdrop under a river birch.

FIREWORKS
In a country garden

Flamboyant colors are not accents in this country garden in Columbia, Missouri—they are the heart of the garden. "I have a tendency to plant things that are gaudy, loud, vibrant, and rich," Gay Bumgarner says. "There's nothing subtle about it."

Gay plants in great brushstrokes of color in her series of gardens hidden in a valley near Grindstone Creek. A garden dominated by orange blooms is accented with chartreuse, yellow, and purple flowers. The colors in her red garden are fiery and completely unabashed. "It's somber, there's so much of it," she says. Even in her shade garden, red coleus and caladiums flash among cool ferns and tropical elephant's ears.

Gay also likes to plant pockets of annuals in front of established perennials. She tries new plants and new combinations to change the palette every year.

Most of her 11-acre property is wild. A creek provides the rugged native limestone and gravel she uses to define flower beds and construct paths and patios.

Three arbors made of native red cedar from the property link the different garden spaces. One is the gateway into the sunny main garden; another leads into the shade garden. The third arbor opens onto grassy paths leading into fields and woods. "Each arbor prepares the visitor for the garden beyond," says Gay. "You forget one garden when you go into the next one."

CENTER The tiny foliage of *Mazus reptans* spreads naturally to meet a gravel path through the shade garden closest to the creek. Ferns from the nearby woods have been transplanted into this garden. Tropical elephant's ears *(Colocasia esculenta)* and caladiums thrive here in Missouri's hot summers.

RIGHT Rich red Asiatic lilies flourish at the edge of the red garden. This arbor, with its lush canopy of bittersweet *(Celastrus scandens),* leads to grassy paths and the fields and woods beyond.

TOP RIGHT Tall cannas and the enormous leaves of castor bean (*Ricinus communis*) dominate the red garden in high summer. Japanese blood grass (*Imperata cylindrica* 'Rubra') and red star clusters (*Pentas lanceolata*) mixed with dahlias are planted just in front of a twiggy Japanese barberry (*Berberis thunbergii* 'Atropurpurea') showing deep claret foliage.

RIGHT A grapevine bench on its own platform of limestone rocks faces back toward the house from deep in the sunny garden.

SENSORY DELIGHTS
In the heart of St. Louis

Asplashing fountain is always within earshot in Douglas MacCarthy's 2-acre garden in St. Louis. The moving water of his 13 fountains doesn't just cool the air and mask the noises of the city. For Douglas, who is blind, the bubbling, splashing, and dripping of the fountains also help him identify the various spaces in his expansive garden.

From mid-March through October, Douglas lives in a garden house on his property, passing through the garden every morning and afternoon on his way to and from work.

When he bought the property in 1980, the garden did not exist. Over the past 20 years, working with landscape designer Charles Freeman, he has developed ten different garden spaces on the property. All of them were designed to provide a sense of enclosure.

"Gardens don't just get put there; they should evolve," Douglas says. "Nature changes them. New plants and ideas come along." He can't see the flower colors in the garden's sunny areas, but he enjoys their fragrances and textures and relishes the sense of intimacy and enclosure in each of the distinct spaces.

This garden's style was influenced by European gardens and by the designer's southern roots. Visiting other gardens has helped Douglas appreciate the possibilities of his own, which he has furnished with wonderful antiques—gates, statues, and fountains—bought on trips around the United States and in Europe.

LEFT Lush variegated hostas line a brick path leading toward the house. On a column near the gate, a lead monkey contemplates the scene.

ABOVE The spectacular foliage of *Fallopia japonica* 'Variegatum' seems to float on either side of the gate between two garden spaces.

RIGHT TOP Exquisite wrought-iron gates from Harrogate, England, open into the Italian garden from the perennial garden. A hornbeam *(Carpinus)* hedge, trimmed to 9 feet high, encloses the Italian garden. Variegated hostas gleam on either side of the gate.

RIGHT BOTTOM The fountain at the center of the North Carolina garden actually came from New Orleans. The blue paint was inspired by garden ornaments at Hidcote Manor Garden in Gloucestershire, England. Around the fountain, hardy 'Green Velvet' boxwoods are trimmed into tight balls.

EASY DOES IT
An old-fashioned summer garden

When the owners of this country garden in Columbia, Missouri bought their 65-acre property 15 years ago, they first installed a big pond. Then they dug a series of garden beds around their property and filled them with all the flowers they love. From a shaded deck at the back of the house, they have a 180-degree view of their flower garden, a cutting garden, and their three-fourths-acre pond.

This strictly informal garden did not start with a master plan, and the color palette was not difficult to work out— all colors go together in nature, the owners say. From spring's first jonquils through the daylilies and phlox that bloom in the heat of high summer, old-fashioned flowers prevail. Cottage pinks (*Dianthus plumarius*) bloom alongside pale and dark blue delphiniums (*D. × belladonna* 'Belladonna' and 'Bellamosum'), sturdy hybrids that come back year after year. Blue pincushion flower (*Scabiosa columbaria*) and pink and white phlox extend the season.

Late summer in Missouri can be hard on plants, with temperatures well over 90 degrees for weeks. Old-fashioned flowers stand up to the heat best, say these gardeners.

The clay soil is built up with topsoil and manure to lighten it and improve drainage. Instead of commercial fertilizer, compost is used to top-dress the beds. "It's all trial and error," the owners say. "The errors just don't show."

FACING PAGE Colorful lantanas at one edge of the pond give way to native plants on the far side. The golden flowers of annual *Bidens ferulifolia* shimmer in the bright summer sun.

RIGHT Pink petunias tumble out of flower boxes around the shady deck. The boxes are planted with different annual flowers every year.

BELOW A flower bed stretches along the fence around the vegetable garden. Established clusters of bright yellow Asiatic lilies, at right, almost obscure the fence. Cheerful annual pansies crowd together at the front of the bed.

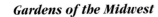

THROUGH AN APPLE TUNNEL
To a delightful herb garden

This thoughtfully planned herb garden in the center of Kansas City is part of a larger garden occupying half an acre on three adjacent lots. Other areas of the property include a formal vegetable garden, a perennial border, and a woodland garden.

Americans are beginning to realize that English gardens are about balancing structure and hardscaping with plants," says the owner and designer. One enters the herb garden through an opening in a low stone wall. Brick paving defines the symmetrical space, while a large fountain serves as the focal point. In contrast to the red brick, the pebble paving looks like a rug spread under the fountain. An arbor of apple separates the herb garden from the adjacent vegetable garden.

"The less you have a vista," says this accomplished gardener, "the more important it is to enclose the spaces and make garden rooms." Within the planting areas, small deciduous trees and shrubs and evergreen boxwoods and conifers provide additional structure and texture. They serve as backdrops for the herbs, perennials, and annuals that fill the garden.

After the last of the herbal bounty is harvested and winter settles in, this garden continues to provide pleasure. Paving and architectural ornaments throughout the garden provide form and interest. The apple branches make interesting tracery against the arbor. A heated fountain runs all winter, enticing birds to drink and bathe.

ABOVE The apple tunnel separating the herb garden from the vegetable garden leads to perennial and woodland gardens. An early 20th-century column serves as a focal point as visitors pass through the tunnel. 'Liberty' and 'Jonafree' apples are espaliered against its metal framework, while scarlet runner bean flowers and purple clematis add color.

LEFT An aerial view of the apple tunnel and herb garden shows how garden rooms can be constructed using a formal layout softened by informal plantings. Hardy sheared boxwood (*Buxus microphylla japonica* 'Winter Gem') provides evergreen structure in some planting areas.

BELOW The marble urn in the center of the fountain is a mid-19th-century piece. The unusual fountain "finial" is a potted aloe. The collection of container plants includes scented geraniums, dianthus, and rosemary.

FACING PAGE BOTTOM The Colonial Revival home demanded that the garden design be formal. But within planting beds, plants grow lush and loose. Here we see 'Winter Gem' boxwood, the reblooming David Austin rose 'Abraham Darby', 'Bright Lights' Swiss chard, garlic, and the reblooming tall bearded iris 'Immortality'.

PLANNING YOUR GARDEN

When you want to create a beautiful and functional place for outdoor relaxation, the reality of your bare or overgrown yard may seem utterly daunting. So before you turn your first shovelful of soil, close your eyes and picture your dream garden. Does it have a spacious deck or patio for parties? Is it serene and secluded? Or is it lively with a profusion of flowering plants blooming in random exuberance? Whatever your fancy, make a wish list of your favorite garden styles and plants. Then use the information on the following pages to help you plan space for your activities, choose a garden style, and work with your soils and microclimates. The result will be a garden that reflects the nature of your site and your dreams.

PLANNING WITH A PURPOSE

How you design your property can greatly enhance the pleasure of living in your home. When it is thoughtfully planned, landscaping does far more than merely beautify. It can provide recreation areas and places to entertain. Well-placed trees, shrubs, and arbors temper the weather and cut down on heating and cooling costs. A good design can also add much-needed living space to your home in the warm seasons and provide a window on the natural world throughout the year.

Explore your garden's potential

Think of the spaces between the exterior of your house and the edges of your property as potential outdoor rooms. For example, a house that lacks a foyer gains a welcoming entry with the addition of a well-designed front garden. An entrance garden also improves the appearance of your house and symbolizes the return to a comforting haven for you and your family.

Space behind the house or along its sides can become an outdoor room, spacious enough to host large gatherings. Paving or decking defines the room's dimensions. Planting or fencing around it ensures privacy and lends a comforting sense of enclosure. Furniture—for dining or lounging—further defines its identity.

A garden room of your own

You can also make room in your garden for sports and hobbies. A swimming pool is great for family entertainment. A large deck or patio can double as a dance floor or an exercise room, while a sunny bit of ground can be transformed into an herb garden for an enthusiastic chef. For the artist in the family, a shady grove may serve as a sylvan studio.

Even narrow areas on the sides of a house can be put to good use. On the shady side, consider a garden for strolling, bright with bulbs in spring and lush with ferns and shade-loving wildflowers in summer. A sunny strip is perfect for vegetables such as tomatoes and beans, which can be trained to grow vertically, and columnar or espaliered fruit trees against a wall. Or turn the sunny area into a nursery or a cutting garden. Where privacy is an issue, the side yard may be the place to plant a privacy screen.

For those times when it is too cold or too hot to spend time outside, viewing the garden through windows visually extends the house outward. A living tableau of plants that monitor the seasons can be enjoyed from inside as well as out, and planting for wildlife will enliven your vistas with birds and butterflies.

Reflect your lifestyle

The potential uses of spaces around houses are as individual as the people who live in them. When you begin designing your garden, don't be bound by convention. Think of what you and your family want and need and proceed from there. Particularly in backyards, you should feel free to indulge your own unique interests and pastimes.

LANDSCAPING GOALS

A. Create privacy. The walled patio is really an extension of the living room. It creates an enclosed space and conceals the front yard from passersby.

B. Invite entertaining. A broad deck wraps around the family and dining rooms to offer space for dining parties or relaxation in view of, but removed from, the swimming pool.

C. Provide recreation. The swimming pool is a great way to cool off on hot summer days. A trellis—creating a transition between house and garden—provides privacy and a sense of enclosure while it shelters the spa.

D. Modify the climate. Draped in deciduous vines, this arbor shades southern exposures from the summer sun. In winter, when the vines are dormant, it allows the low winter sun to shine through and warm the home's interior. Around the pool, plantings along the fence filter strong winds.

E. Beautify the property. Lush plantings between the sidewalk and the patio wall create an attractive view from the street, soften the lines of the house and wall, and add color.

F. Grow a kitchen garden. Raised beds along the south edge of the side yard offer an ideal spot for raising herbs and vegetables, and are convenient to both the kitchen and the garden work area next to the garage.

G. Attract wildlife. Wildlife plantings and a birdbath, sited to be visible from inside the house and from the deck, lure birds and butterflies to the garden.

H. Reduce water use. A small lawn saves more water than a large one would; other features that lower water use are an automated irrigation system, the grouping of plants with similar water needs, and a liberal application of mulch throughout the garden.

*A WELL-DESIGNED
LANDSCAPE*

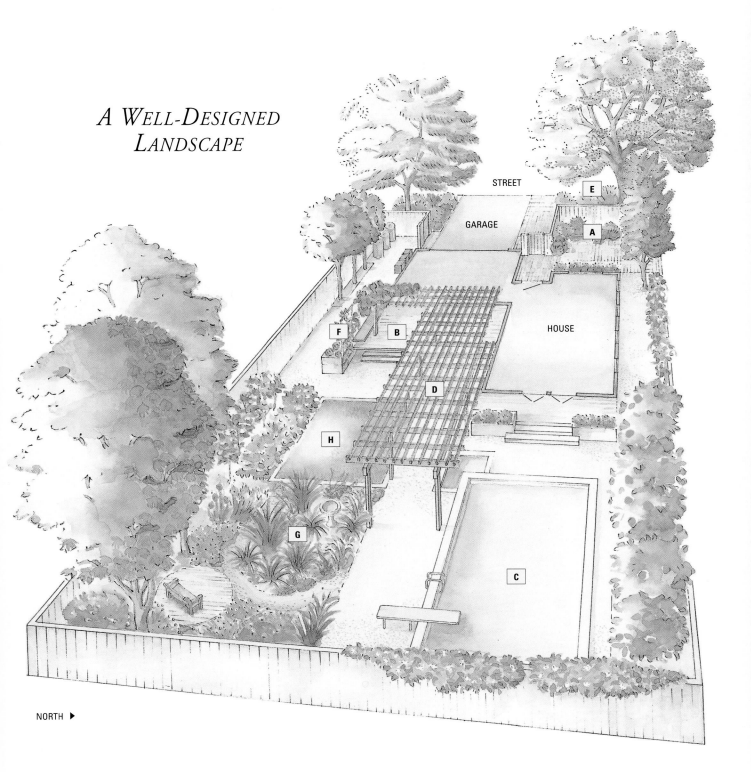

STREET

GARAGE

HOUSE

E

A

F

B

D

H

G

C

NORTH ▶

A WELL-PLANNED GARDEN

A. Edible and ornamental plants share a bed in this garden. Straplike leaves of leeks, rough-textured Italian kale as well as beans and white-flowered garlic chives mingle with nasturtiums, orange Gem marigolds, red zinnias, and tall spider flowers *(Cleome hasslerana)* to create a garden that is as beautiful as it is utilitarian.

B. A stone wall encloses one side of this low-maintenance garden. Boulders and rock shards serve as ground cover, while rock slabs make up the paving, pond edging, and bridge. Most of the plants, including the dwarf conifers, need little maintenance.

MEETS A VARIETY OF NEEDS

C. Beautiful and easy to care for, the bulbs and flowering trees in this Kansas City garden light up a large slope every spring. By summer, it's a cool, leafy place, with dappled sunlight flickering over the periwinkle *(Vinca minor)* ground cover. The redbud tree casts welcome patches of shade on the lawn.

D. Recreation takes place in naturalistic splendor in this swimming pool set into a wooded hillside. Rustic sandstone coping around the pool and rocks flanking a waterfall enhance the natural look. Plantings include a Japanese maple, juniper, cotoneaster, rhododendron, and a weeping white pine, which contrast with the forest setting.

E. Relaxation is the main use of this courtyard garden. High walls keep out street noise, creating a secluded hideaway in an urban area.

THE EFFECT OF MICROCLIMATES

In planning a landscape, it's important to consider the weather and climate in both your region and your garden. The path and angle of the sun, the seasons of the year, and the wind patterns around your property all affect your opportunities for outdoor living, your choice and placement of plants, and the overall design of your landscape.

Have you ever wondered why, in a warm, south-facing garden, the flowers of a star magnolia are ruined by a late frost, while just down the street the fuzzy buds of another star magnolia—this one facing east—have yet to open? Microclimates are responsible. Most gardens have several microclimates—areas that are a little warmer or cooler, wetter or drier, more or less windy than others. Microclimates are created by a combination of factors, including sun angle, wind direction, and the exposure and topography of your site.

Air temperature and movement

Because warm air rises and cold air sinks, cool air tends to "pool" in low places and to back up behind obstacles such as hedges and houses, creating frost pockets. Slopes are the last features in a landscape to freeze, because cold air constantly drains off them, mixing with nearby warmer air as it flows. Flat areas, by contrast, cool off quickly as heat radiates upward, especially during nights when the air is still and skies are clear. Any overhead protection reduces this loss of heat.

In most gardens, the house influences the garden's microclimates. A house blocks the wind, creating warmer, protected pockets on its leeward side. In these warm microclimates, plants not generally hardy in the area may survive the winter. Conversely, beds in the teeth of the northwest wind won't support marginally hardy plants: their colder microclimate may slow plant maturation,

and the appearance of flowers may be as much as a week behind gardens in milder situations.

Soil moisture

Soil moisture has a profound effect on the local climate and growing conditions. Moist soil in winter helps insulate tender plants, because as water freezes it gives off heat. Also, cold doesn't penetrate moist soil as deeply as it does in dry soil. In summer, moist soil cools its surroundings as water evaporates from it; that's why summer heat records frequently occur during extended droughts. The lesson here is that sufficient soil moisture reduces temperature extremes.

Garden structures and paving

As gardeners with courtyards can tell you, what grows inside a garden wall is usually a lot different from what grows outside it. This is because, in addition to blocking cold winds, walls store heat during the day (especially if they're made from dark-colored material) and release it at night, keeping the enclosed garden warmer. Dark-colored paving stores heat, too. As a result, plants growing near walls or paving tend to survive the winter better than those in exposed spots.

Sun and shade

In summer, the morning sun rises in the northeast, arcs high across the southern sky, and sets to the northwest. This long passage means extra hours of daylight, which benefits many vegetables, annuals, perennials, and flowering trees and shrubs. By contrast, the winter sun rises in the southeast, passes low across the southern sky, and sets to the southwest. Days are much shorter, which triggers the blooming of short-day plants such as hellebores and witch hazels.

That shifting sun angle means longer shadows in winter and shorter ones in summer. Thus, plants hidden in shade in winter are often in the sun in summer. The pattern of sun and shade also varies according to the time of day. At noon, when the sun is highest, shade is hard to find. So you need to plan for these changes, lest one day you find a prized shade-loving plant just stewing in the sun.

Exposure

Slopes that drop toward the south or southwest get more heat and light during the day than those that drop toward the north or northeast. Similarly, walls that run east and west reflect extra heat and sunlight onto plants growing on their south side and less on plants growing on the north side. Heat lovers such as prairie grasses and many herbs flourish in full sun. But the soil dries much faster there, so be attentive to the water needs of these plants.

COLD-AIR POCKETS

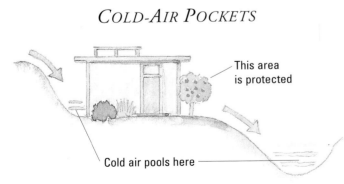

This area is protected

Cold air pools here

Cold air flows downhill like water and gathers in basins. It can be dammed by a barrier such as a house, wall, or fence. So if you build a sunken patio or planting area, you may find yourself shivering even when higher or more protected surroundings are balmy.

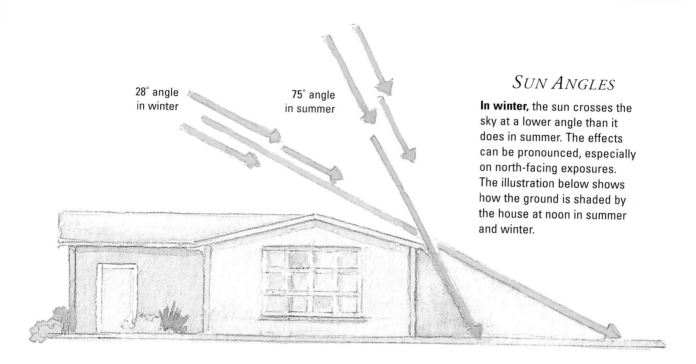

SUN ANGLES

In winter, the sun crosses the sky at a lower angle than it does in summer. The effects can be pronounced, especially on north-facing exposures. The illustration below shows how the ground is shaded by the house at noon in summer and winter.

28° angle in winter

75° angle in summer

SUMMER AND WINTER SHADOWS

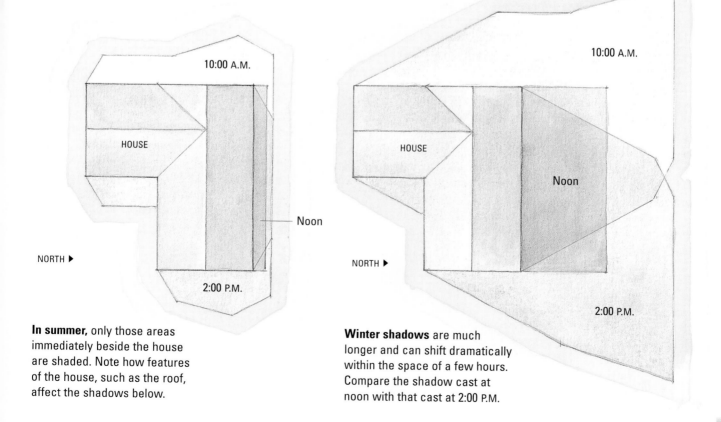

In summer, only those areas immediately beside the house are shaded. Note how features of the house, such as the roof, affect the shadows below.

Winter shadows are much longer and can shift dramatically within the space of a few hours. Compare the shadow cast at noon with that cast at 2:00 P.M.

SOILS OF THE MIDWEST

More than any other factor, your soil will determine which plants will thrive in your garden. Although you can modify your soil to expand the range of plants you will be able to grow, you can never completely change it.

The map on the facing page, prepared by the Soil Survey Staff at the USDA's Natural Resources Conservation Service in Lincoln, Nebraska, shows the various soil types distributed across the Midwest. The western half of the area mostly enjoys *prairie soils,* which have a deep, dark layer at the surface, usually highly fertile and needing no additional amendments. This is the soil type found through large sections of the Great Plains in the central states and into the southern prairie, where wheat and other grains are grown. The eastern half of the Midwest also has mostly good soil, called *alkaline, high-nutrient soils.* Among the more challenging soils dotted about the Midwest are *new soils,* which may be deep sand or river-deposited clay, but which are generally inert and need organic matter and nutrients to grow plants successfully. Also likely to be difficult are *sandy soils,* found mostly around the upper Great Lakes in Michigan and Wisconsin. These soils have been created by ancient glaciers and often contain gravel and stones; they are usually also acidic. The areas of *organic soils* have high water retention and may need drainage systems. (The new soils may also be overly wet.) *Alkaline, clay-based soils* have a high clay content and are difficult to cultivate; a band of these soils is located along the North Dakota and Minnesota state borders and in many areas of western South Dakota. The *low-nutrient soils,* mostly found in southern Missouri, have an acid pH.

The reason experts speak of modifying soil rather than changing it is that the provenance of soils is ancient. It has taken eons for the soil in any one place to take on its distinctive characteristics. Glaciers have moved across the land, skimming off the surface in some places and depositing rocks and minerals in others. Rivers have deposited silt, vegetation has grown up and decomposed, and wind and rain have weathered rock. Human civilization has also had an impact on the development of soil character. Rather than try to change a soil that has developed over thousands of years to suit your plant choice, choose plants compatible with the existing soil type—chances are you will be more successful.

Soil texture

One of the ways garden soils are characterized is by their texture, described as sandy, silt, or clay. Sandy soil has relatively large particles, drains quickly, and usually doesn't hold nutrients well. Silt has intermediate-size particles that fit together more tightly and hold more water and nutrients. Clay has tiny particles that hold

nutrients and water well but allow little air to reach plant roots. When clay dries, it becomes as hard as brick. The perfect garden soil is loam—a light, crumbly mixture of approximately equal parts of sand, silt, and clay, with at least 4 percent organic matter by weight (which can translate to 25 percent by volume). Organic matter does a good job of holding what plants need—water, nutrients, and air—and it is loose enough for roots to penetrate easily. Most gardens don't start out with loam, but you can develop it by adding organic amendments such as compost.

Soil tests

Two tests can be done right in the garden to reveal the characteristics of your soil. A quick test to determine the ratio of sand, clay, and silt is the settling method. Take a cup of soil and place it in a quart glass jar. Add a cup of water. Different types of particles settle out in layers after 2 minutes, 20 minutes, and 24 hours. After 2 minutes, the sand and organic layers should be visible. After 20 minutes, the silt layer is visible, and after 24 hours the clay layer can finally be seen. To quickly determine the water-holding ability of garden soil, take the following test 3 days after a plentiful rain or major irrigation. Dig a hole in the garden 6 inches across and 1 foot deep. If the soil is dry at the bottom of the hole, the soil is not holding enough moisture. Fill the hole with water and let it drain. As soon as it is completely drained, fill the hole with water again. Record how long it takes for the water to drain completely from the hole the second time. If it takes more than 8 hours, water is not draining fast enough for most plants to thrive.

If your soil has a high sand content, annual applications of compost, loam, or manure will increase its water-retention abilities and raise the nutrient levels. If your soil retains too much water, the drainage can be improved in many ways: Adding more sand to the soil layer below the plant roots will provide slightly more drainage. Building a raised bed and modifying the soil is often effective for vegetables, annuals, and perennials. Bigger drainage problems can be solved by creating a French drain, which employs a sloped trench and gravel to remove the water. Perforated drainage pipes work even faster than gravel to remove excess water.

Soil pH

Soil pH, or the degree of alkalinity or acidity of a soil, is another trait that can influence what can or cannot be grown in your garden. Every plant has a preferred pH, which is measured on an acid-to-alkaline scale of 0 to 14. The preferred pH will be the same as that in the plant's native region, which is why choosing plants native to your area almost always results in successful growth. The optimum range for most plants is between 6.0 and 7.5 pH. If soil is acidic, it has a pH lower than 6.5 and will make nitrogen, phosphorus, and potassium less available. If soil has a pH that is above 7.5, it is alkaline, and manganese, phosphorus, and iron micronutrients become increasingly unavailable for plants. However, many plants are adaptable enough to grow in soils ranging from pH 5.5 to 7.5.

While you can amend soils to alter their pH—for example, make them more alkaline by adding lime or more acid by adding peat, sulphur, or acid fertilizer—it will only be for the short term. If you live in an area with naturally acid or alkaline soil, you will have to repeat the amendment periodically. For an accurate soil test and recommendations for the correct amount of soil amendments needed each year to change pH, contact your county's Cooperative Extension Service. Consider that it may be easier to go with the flow and choose plants suited to the pH you already have.

No matter what the general soil type in your area is, you may be surprised to find pockets of a quite different type in your backyard. For example, the lime from concrete walks or foundations may leach into adjacent garden beds, raising their pH. Experiment with different plants in problem areas. Ultimately, the plants' health will tell you whether they are in the right soil.

SOILS OF THE MIDWESTERN UNITED STATES

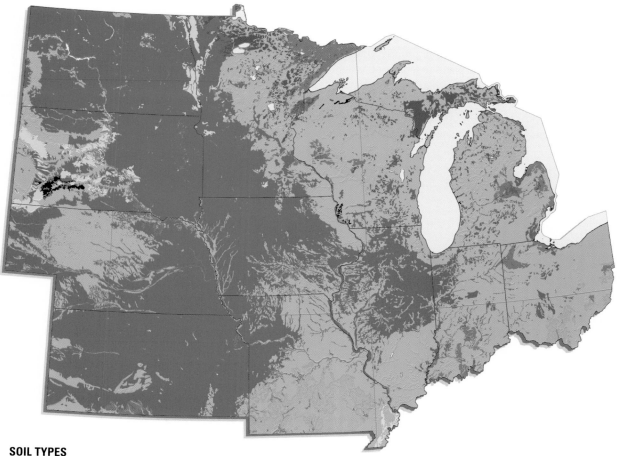

SOIL TYPES

- Alkaline, High-Nutrient Soils (Alfisols)
- New Soils (Entisols)
- Organic Soils (Histosols)
- Young Soils (Inceptisols)
- Prairie Soils (Mollisols)
- Sandy Soils (Spodosols)
- Alkaline, Clay-Based Soils (Vertisols)
- Low-Nutrient Soils (Ultisoils)
- Rock Outcrop
- Water

UNDERSTANDING YOUR SITE

Before tackling the design of your garden, you need to understand the opportunities and problems presented by your property, then find a way to balance those features with your goals for the garden. The preceding pages on microclimates and soil will help you identify many of the natural conditions on your site. You will also need to evaluate any man-made features in your garden and any plantings that have been introduced, especially trees and shrubs. Sketching out these features on paper gives you a base plan, a working document for the design stage.

You'll save yourself hours of measuring if you can find a plot of survey that gives actual dimensions and the orientation of your property, a topographical plan with contour lines showing high and low points and the exact shape of your site, or architectural plans that depict the site plan with the location of all buildings. If none of these are available, you will need to measure your property yourself and transfer the dimensions to a base plan, preferably on graph paper. Use a scale of ¼ inch for 1 foot if possible; larger properties may require ⅛ inch per foot.

If you slip this base plan under a sheet of tracing paper, you can sketch garden designs to your heart's content. This gives you a chance to try out a variety of ideas before laying out everything on site—or worse, installing a structure or plantings only to find they don't suit the space, the property's microclimates, or your needs.

Starting to plan

Next, identify those aspects of the garden that you wish to keep as well as those you want to change. If you have just moved into your home, don't pick up your shovel and start digging yet. Try to live with a new property for a full year; you will get to know your garden through the seasons and can experiment with various plans. A design you make with a thorough knowledge of your garden will fit the land better. Don't be afraid to be ruthless; there is no need to design your garden around an existing feature, living or nonliving, just because it is there.

If you are landscaping just one area of your garden, consider the impact the upgrade will have on the rest of the site. Suppose you wish to plant a row of trees to add privacy to your front yard. Would this create too much shade? Keep the big picture and the garden as a whole in mind, both for the present and for the future.

A Base Plan

SHOW THE FOLLOWING ON YOUR BASE PLAN:

Compass directions, which will help you identify exposures and patterns of sun and shade.

Boundaries and dimensions of the lot and the outlines of the house and other structures.

Location of all windows and doors on your house; note the height of their sills above the exterior grade.

Eaves, overhangs, downspouts, and drains.

Existing paved areas; their condition and usefulness.

Existing steps or ramps; their condition and usefulness.

Location of easements and setback boundaries.

Existing plants: sizes, shapes, and general health of all plants, especially trees.

Topography: high and low points, slope gradients.

Soil conditions: areas that have been raised or filled; soil texture, fertility, and pH.

Direction of prevailing winds throughout the year.

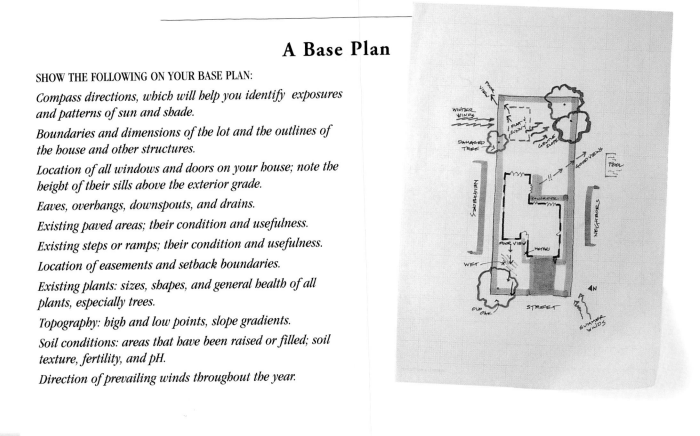

ANALYZING YOUR GARDEN

Here are some of the problems and opportunities presented by this site. The final design on page 121 shows how the landscaper deals with each of these fixtures and issues.

A. **The front view** from the living room is of noisy street traffic, passersby, and parked cars.

B. **Damp pockets of soil** provide a place for moisture-loving plants.

C–D. **Warm air blows** in summer from the southwest **(C)**; winter winds blow from the north **(D)**.

E. **Concrete terraces** reflect excessive heat into the home, and they are too small for entertaining.

F. **Neighbors' homes** are very close to the property line, thus limiting privacy.

G. **Gently sloping land** and existing trees give the garden a natural atmosphere.

H. **Open, sunny areas** in the rear and in the south side yard offer space for a swimming pool or for sun-loving plants.

I–J. **Rear views** from the patio are pleasant in one direction **(I)** but unpleasant in another **(J)**.

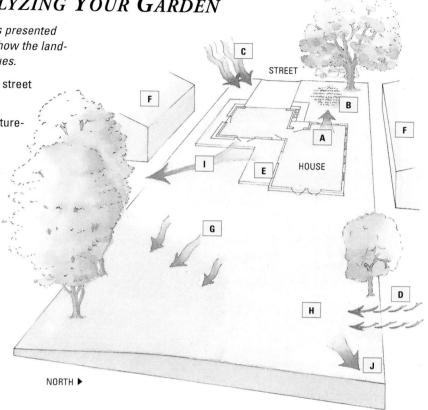

NORTH ▶

Other Considerations

Local zoning or other laws may restrict or prohibit your planned construction. Consult the following documents, agencies, or individuals before proceeding with your design, and note any relevant restrictions on your base plan.

YOUR PLOT OF SURVEY:

Exact location of property lines

Easements or rights-of-way

Building restrictions

Tree removal restrictions

Covenants governing fences, decks, pools, ponds, sheds, dog runs, satellite dishes, and outbuildings

YOUR LOCAL BUILDING OR PLANNING DEPARTMENT:

Setback requirements

Height limitations for fences, buildings, or other structures

Depth and fencing requirements for pools and ponds

Lot coverage guidelines

Safety codes for pools and spas

Requirements for firewalls between adjacent buildings

Open burning restrictions for firepits

Building codes for all construction

Tree or historic preservation ordinances

Building permits for fences, retaining walls above 30 inches in height, other garden structures, and electrical or plumbing work

YOUR WATER COMPANY:

Restrictions on water use for irrigation, pools, and water features

Limitations on the size of lawns

YOUR LOCAL UTILITY COMPANY:

Location and depth of underground utility lines

Building or planting limitations under power lines

Setbacks from transformers and utility corridors

YOUR NEIGHBORS:

Their views into your property (and your view into theirs) and your mutual need for privacy and quiet, sunlight and air flow

Their concerns about existing trees and other plants, structures, and shared walks or driveways

Homeowners' association restrictions

MIDWESTERN GARDEN STYLES

Gardens in the Midwest are as varied as the region itself, adapted to the different growing conditions that can be found within short distances and based on styles from many parts of the U. S. and around the world. The combination of Midwestern soils and climate creates growing conditions that range from moist shade to blazing sun.

The unpredictable and often limited rainfall in the Midwest has influenced the development of gardens that can be sustained with low maintenance and little use of scarce resources. Instead of tending an expansive lawn, Midwestern gardeners are increasingly opting for swaths of meadow under mature trees, giving way to naturalized planting areas to better complement the culture of their large oaks, maples, and beeches, and to conserve water.

A combination of native and adapted plants is often chosen for the plants' ability to survive and thrive in these regional conditions. By using plants that have already proven themselves, gardeners ensure their success. Even the historical or traditionally styled gardens of colonial times take on a distinctly Midwestern flair when populated with grasses and coneflowers, and surrounded by prairie—and they are far less likely to succumb to a Midwest winter.

Local materials not only blend well with the surrounding landscape, giving it a sense of individuality, but they are also practical, affordable, and durable. Garden structures or pavements constructed of regional-type stone, or of brick, add to the sense of place.

The successful choice of a particular garden style is based on lifestyle and architecture, site, and willingness to provide the level of maintenance that is required by some of the more formal designs. The right garden style is the one that matches your individual requirements and lets you showcase your creativity. In Midwestern gardens, the sky is literally the limit.

A. Naturalized gardens are perfect examples of the creative approach Midwesterners use in managing their environment. Shady, mysterious woodlands and bright, sunlit prairie gardens where plants are used in drifts and allowed to reach their natural shape and size provide gardeners with great enjoyment for not much work. This lush prairie garden in Missouri is filled with year-round color, texture, and movement, requiring little from the owner beyond a spring mowing and an occasional enjoyable stroll. Beard tongue *(Penstemon),* pale coneflower *(Echinacea pallida),* bright yellow plains coreopsis, and yarrow float above grasses that will soon form the autumn and winter show.

B. Country gardens in the Midwest combine practical needs like windbreaks and vegetable gardens with ornamental native and introduced plantings around outdoor living spaces. In this garden, bright purple coneflowers *(Echinacea purpurea)* mingle with native grasses along the curved entrance walk and form an inviting, low-maintenance transition to the mowed lawn and distant pasture.

C. Rock gardens provide a unique growing environment for plants that require good drainage and lean soil. They serve a practical purpose as well, stabilizing slopes and carrying excess rain in a defined path through the garden. The rocks themselves become an artistic feature; their craggy or smooth surfaces, home to lichens and mosses, are constantly changing with the movement of the sun. Native plants join introduced species in this rock garden, combining to create a beautiful and low-maintenance display. Soapwort *(Saponaria)* joins prickly pear cactus *(Opuntia humifusa),* and bright yellow primrose to provide four-season waves of color near river birch and creeping junipers.

D. Shade gardens offer welcome relief from the sun and wind, using layers of trees, shrubs, and perennials to form rich textures and distinct spaces. Elements of traditional Eastern gardens find their way into many Midwestern shade gardens, in the details seen in pavements, benches, and garden structures. The shaded seating area in this Illinois garden is brightened by lavender petunias against a casual shrub border. The sense of a calm, cool place to sit is heightened by the contrast between the shady patio and the sunlit lawn in the background.

E. Water gardens in the Midwest take many forms, from classic swimming pool settings and formal reflecting pools to elaborate cascades and ponds. The many lakes, marshes, and creeks offer their own natural inspiration to gardeners who want to introduce the soothing or exciting sound of water—and the wildlife it attracts—to their homes. An intriguing collection of ornamental plants frames the cascading rivulet that spills into this pond in Ohio. A deeply colored Japanese maple and steel blue globe spruce focus attention on the figurine. Water lilies and papyrus carry the lush greenery of the surrounding landscape into the water itself.

F. Kitchen gardens have been part of Midwestern tradition ever since the pioneers relied on their gardens for food. Contemporary versions combine vegetables, herbs, and fruit trees—often arranged in traditional patterns based on colonial gardens—with tried-and-true perennials and annuals. Often located just outside the kitchen door, these gardens are a pleasant jumble of color and texture, with cutting flowers and culinary snippets within easy reach of the cook. The entrance to this one is through a weathered arbor that supports birdhouses and grapevines and blends with the enclosing fence. Colorful salad greens and cutting flowers in raised beds are easily reached from the mulched paths.

G. Classic gardens, with their clean lines and symmetric patterns, suggest serenity and grace. These gardens often have a strong and immediately apparent relationship to the architecture of the house or the enclosing wall, with an axis connecting one element to another. The choice of plants is based on constructing good "bones" for the garden that endure all seasons. Garden ornamentation or furniture is usually placed at one of the focal points in a classic garden. Midwestern gardens designed in the classic style may rely on deciduous shrubs or even grasses for some of the formal structure. The intricate iron gates with brick columns in this classic garden swing wide as the perfect frame for a simple stone fountain.

H. Courtyard gardens are characterized by the small amount of space available for all of the activities and materials usually present in gardens. They may be designed as the entrance to a town-house or as the entire garden for a small urban property. The busy schedules of working couples may require that gardening be done on a smaller scale. Courtyard gardens can combine interesting paving with raised planters, containers, walls, fences, sculpture, and furniture. The result is a small space with great variety, offering places to sit or stroll in sun or shade and plantings that change with the seasons. The multiple levels in this enclosed courtyard provide space for a rich mix of annuals and perennials, including purple coneflower, delphinium, salvia, yarrow, and daisies. Vines growing up the cool gray fence add to the layered feeling.

I. Asian-style gardens evoke a sense of serenity and simplicity that appeals to many Midwestern gardeners who find themselves pulled in too many directions. Characterized by a palette of materials that is rich in texture yet soothing to the eye, Oriental gardens also use contrasting shapes to emphasize different areas. Here, a proud stand of Siberian iris shares space with the complementary textures and colors of a lacy fern, coarse-leafed hostas, and the deep red of a Japanese maple. The lantern, as focal point at the end of a meandering stepping-stone path, is framed by similar plants, which provides a strong connection between separate parts of the garden.

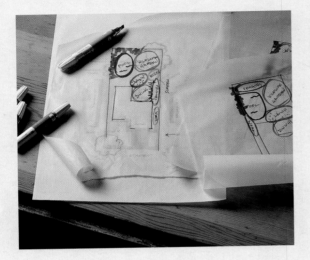

Bubble Diagrams

To experiment with various arrangements of space in your garden, try the designer's trick of using simple "bubble diagrams." These quick studies can be drawn on tracing paper over the base plan you have made of your property. Each bubble (which can be a rough circle, square, or oval) should represent a particular activity or garden space that you hope to incorporate into the design, and each should be approximately the size and shape needed. Make the bubbles different colors to distinguish them from one another (use green for planting areas, blue for a pool, and brown for decks and terraces, for instance).

Let the bubbles overlap where activity spaces will merge with each other. Where spaces need to be separated, draw a line to suggest a screen or barrier. Simple cross-hatching can designate areas that need overhead protection from the sun. Show steps as sets of parallel lines, and roughly indicate entrances to the house or front yard.

Sketch several versions. With each one, consider the microclimates, potential views, and existing features identified on your base plan. Note how well the placement of activities in each diagram takes advantage of the warm spots and shady areas in your garden. Look for smooth transitions from one space to the next, and address practical issues by including spaces for work, storage, and service areas.

After you have drawn several diagrams, lay them out and compare the different arrangement of spaces, then settle on the one that will form the basis for your final design.

DESIGNING YOUR GARDEN

Now that you understand your site, have identified its basic features, and found a garden style you like, you are ready to put your creativity to work. The first step is site planning—creating and arranging the activity spaces in your garden. Study carefully how all these spaces relate to the rooms inside your home, and try to locate the outdoor activity spaces near their indoor counterparts. For example, if young children are a part of the family, place their outdoor play space near a room in the house where you spend a lot of time, so that you can easily keep an eye on them. Organize vegetable and herb gardens near the kitchen, if possible, to make it easy to bring the harvest to the table. Decide whether some areas of the garden should serve multiple functions—whether a sheltered walkway could also screen a driveway or your neighbor's garage.

Look at the entire garden, and lay out spaces that will flow logically and easily from one to the other. Plan a circulation path that won't require walking through a work area or past the trash cans to get to outdoor seating. Settle on an arrangement of planted areas that will permit grouping plants according to their watering needs. As you sketch, you'll begin to make general decisions about the plants and structures you'll need and where they should go. You'll need to refer frequently to your base plan to remind yourself of site features and conditions. Bubble planning (left) can help you explore options and designs.

Odd-shaped lots

Don't worry if your lot isn't a simple rectangle. Most homes don't have rectangular lots. In fact, topography and street patterns mean that most lots have somewhat irregular shapes. For example, a subdivision's cul-de-sac results in pie-shaped lots with little street frontage and plenty of privacy toward the rear. Whatever the size and shape of your lot, the tips and techniques described here will help you make the most of it.

But before you get carried away with the excitement of creating a whole new garden, carefully consider how much time, effort, and money you're willing to put into it. If the commitment looks daunting, don't despair. Just break the project into stages—most important ones first, less important ones later—and complete them as time and money allow.

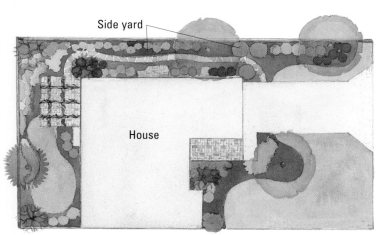

A. Garden home lot

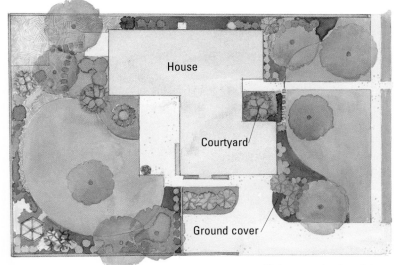

B. Large suburban lot

C. Cul-de-sac lot

THREE LOTS, THREE SOLUTIONS

A. Garden home lots typically lack privacy, and, because of their length and narrowness, they can look like bowling alleys. Here, a side-yard planting anchored by evergreens adds privacy. Broadleafed evergreens flanking the path at the front corner of the house also block views of the side yard from the front, giving the front yard its own space. Segmenting the lot like this makes the narrow property seem wider.

B. Large suburban lots often feature huge, shapeless lawns that merge into those of the neighbors. Here, curving beds of evergreen ground cover border lawns in both front and back, transforming mundane grass areas into dynamic design elements. Ground cover beds in front also guide visitors to an iron gate that marks the entry to a secluded courtyard. Down-sizing the lawn in back simplifies maintenance while still leaving plenty of room for family recreation.

C. Cul-de-sac lots are often shaped like slices of pizza, with narrow street frontage and wide backyards. Dividing such lots into a series of garden rooms, each one hidden from the other, diverts attention from the odd shape. Here, densely planted shrub beds in the front yard border a gracefully curving lawn, drawing your eye. In back, an undulating lawn disguises the property's angular lines. The backyard affords ample room for a variety of needs, including a terrace, a children's play area, perennial beds, a small fruit orchard, and a work area.

THE LANGUAGE OF LANDSCAPE DESIGN

Whatever landscape style you choose, your plan will be more successful if you copy some of the simple techniques that landscape professionals use to make beautiful gardens. First, it helps to familiarize yourself with some of the basic design terms used by landscape architects, garden designers, and garden writers. Some terms are used throughout the broad field of design. "Focal point" and "symmetry," for example, are often used by architects, interior designers, and graphic artists alike. Other terms, such as "borrowed scenery," are specific to landscape architecture. As you read through this book, you'll see these terms used to describe the features of various gardens. And, if at any point in the process of making your garden you decide to hire the services of landscape professionals, you'll have an easier time communicating with them if you understand their lingo.

The texture of plants and other garden elements such as boulders, paving, fences, and even ornaments may be fine or coarse, delicate or bold. Above, emerging hostas and fine-textured snowflakes (Leucojum) *stand out against the ruggedness of a log.*

A. A focal point is an object, such as this jar at the end of a path, which draws the eye due to its placement in the garden. In formal gardens, a focal point is usually placed in the center or at the end of an axis. In less formal gardens, a focal point may appear anywhere, but its distinctiveness attracts attention and draws you closer.

B. Borrowed scenery is a concept adapted from Japanese gardens in which views beyond the borders of a garden are incorporated into the design to make the garden seem larger. Here, the open fields make the garden feel more spacious because they are a part of the view.

C. An accent draws attention to itself by contrasting boldly with its surroundings. The bright yellow of this potted chrysanthemum set in front of the dark conifers and pale grass plumes grabs your attention.

D. An axis is the centerline of a view or walk. An axis can be curved, but it does not fork or branch. Here, it runs along the brick path, up the steps, and across the deck into the trees at the edge of the garden. In formal gardens, elements often align on either side of an axis.

E. Symmetry exists when matching elements are balanced on either side of a central axis; it is most commonly seen in formal gardens. Asymmetry occurs when those elements are different, an effect that may be found in both formal and informal gardens.

DESIGN BASICS

Every good garden owes its effectiveness to certain basic design principles. These rules have proven themselves again and again, and they apply to all areas and levels of garden design, from the most elaborately detailed arbor to the simplest of borders.

You can learn a lot by studying gardens that you visit or see in magazines, as well as those illustrated on these pages and throughout this book. Try to relate the elements that make these gardens work to the design principles illustrated here. Then keep them in mind as you plan your own garden.

In a well-designed garden, no one plant, structure, or feature is completely dominant. Rather, all the parts work together to establish a sense of *unity*. Make sure that all of the elements—structures, beds, borders, and water features—are in *proportion* to the rest of the garden and in *scale* with the size of the house and property. By *repeating* certain plants, colors, and materials, you can bring *rhythm* and *emphasis* to the design. And you can create a feeling of *harmony* in the garden by balancing simple lines and forms with a *variety* of different plants and structural materials.

A. Repetition of narrow, upright conifers in this garden introduces a pleasurable sense of order to the exuberant mix of plantings. The evergreens provide a place for your gaze to linger and then move on in a subtle rhythm, from conifer to conifer, through different parts of the garden.

B. Simplicity is the result of restraint. It keeps an elegant, understated scene from becoming cluttered and unfocused. Here, a simple curved retaining wall beckons visitors into the garden beyond.

C. Unity of design ensures that the garden reads as one beautiful whole rather than as a hodgepodge of disparate elements. Here, the repeated serpentine shapes, brick edgings of the beds, and massed hydrangeas tie the parts of the garden together. Repeating a single type of paving stone in different areas, for example, can also unify a design.

D–E. Scale refers to the balance between sizes of various site elements, including the house, walk, fence, containers, and plantings. No one feature should overpower the others. In this garden (D), the modest-size house calls for low plantings, a small lawn, and a single, medium-size shade tree out front. A large house calls for a bolder approach, such as tall shrubs or a grove of trees (E) to balance the visual weight of the architecture.

DESIGN TRICKS

In addition to basic design principles, professionals have an array of tricks at their disposal— techniques that help overcome typical challenges or simply make the garden more attractive and livable for occupants and visitors alike.

Some of these ideas are very basic, such as considering the dimensions of the human body when designing the height and size of structures in the garden. For example, the best ratio for stair risers and treads is based on the dimensions that are most comfortable for people to climb (see page 392). Similarly, pathways are most comfortable to walk abreast on when they are more than 4 feet wide, and built-in seating for decks or benches should be 16 or 17 inches deep.

Other techniques involve altering the perception of space by manipulating materials, colors, and textures, or by placing elements in such a way as to mask the size and shape of a space.

Bring your garden design to life by incorporating some of these tricks. They can be particularly helpful if you are renovating or upgrading an existing landscape or if there is a particular area of your garden with which you have never been especially pleased.

As you develop your ideas, refer to your bubble plan and the basic design principles to make sure you haven't forgotten your original intentions amid the flurry of other considerations. There will be plenty of opportunity to add whimsy and interest to the garden as you choose plants, structures, and accessories to complete your garden's design.

A. Create a perspective. A large element in the foreground enhances depth. Framed by the cherry tree branches and blossoms, the background appears deeper than it is. The strong forms and colors of the conifers in the midground help the perspective.

B. Use elements to suggest space. The walls of raised perennial beds, the steps leading up to the arch, and the arch itself all suggest that this area is an entry-way to a larger area. However, the arch only implies additional space beyond: the garden ends at the hemlock hedge.

C. Conceal part of the garden. Creating a number of different spaces—some open, some hidden—makes a garden seem much larger than it is. This imaginative platform up in the trees keeps children's playthings out of general view but is attractive to people of all ages.

D. Use contrast to create interest. Contrast makes a garden lively to the eye. It is often achieved by playing with color, but it can be created in many ways—for example, by alternating a sequence of shady and light-filled spaces, by placing dark materials with pale ones, or, as shown here, by mixing vertical and horizontal tropical plants in a pond.

E. Soften hard lines. Geometry and classic lines can be delightful in a garden, giving it order and strength. To lessen the formality, soften the edges of paving with billowing plants such as the lavender catnip *(Nepeta)* growing in this garden. The young hedge rising around the fountain, if left untrimmed or trimmed only lightly, will soften the outside edge of the stone circle.

A

DESIGNING FOR PRIVACY

For most people today, privacy is a valuable commodity and essential to the success of a garden. Noisy streets and bright lights shining through your bedroom window at night—these are just some of the intrusions brought about by houses that are built close together on small lots or located near roadways.

Fortunately, most privacy problems can be solved at the planning stage with creative landscaping. Well-positioned hedges, fences, or walls can shield your house from the street or from neighbors. A tree or an arbor can block the view of your property from a hillside above. A combination of walls or berms, plants, and maybe a fountain or other water feature can even soften the noise of a busy street nearby.

In addition to shielding you from the outside world, creating privacy has some extra benefits. Walls and berms, carefully placed, can create outdoor "rooms" and add interest to the garden.

B

Identify the intrusions

Before you can create privacy, you must determine exactly what you want to block out or be shielded from—and when. Walk around your property, identifying areas that require covers or screens. Also try to evaluate how plantings and additional structures will affect your neighbors, the patterns of sun and shade in your garden, and any views you want to preserve.

A particularly annoying privacy problem might seem to call for a stand of fast-growing, closely spaced trees or shrubs. But don't overdo it. You may end up replacing or removing such plants, because fast growers are often not long-lived. You can, however, plan ahead for selective removal, such as taking out every other shrub in a closely spaced hedge. Or combine both fast- and slow-growing plants, knowing that you'll remove the less desirable ones as the better species mature.

A. Rapid and dense in its growth, privet *(Ligustrum)* is the ideal deciduous hedge plant. Sheared into a formal hedge, as shown here, it screens views, mitigates noise, and withstands difficult conditions such as dry soil and city pollution.

B. 'Skyracer' tall moor grass *(Molinia caerulea arundinacea)* provides an unusually soft, vertical summer screen for this front yard in St. Paul, Minnesota.

C. A berm of shrub roses shields the house from the glances of passersby and buffers noise from the traffic while maintaining an attractive, welcoming approach to the house.

D. A solid barrier, such as this brick wall around a Missouri courtyard garden, provides the most effective buffer to sound. The setback in the wall allows space for the elegant black trellis, supporting espaliered pear trees, and planters that are a comfortable height for sitting or setting things on.

E. A beautifully symmetrical hedge of arborvitae *(Thuja)* alternating with 'New Dawn' and 'William Baffin' roses clothes the fence separating two properties. The dense evergreens screen sights, sounds, and wind, as well as providing winter interest.

SCREENING SOUND

What can you do to foster quiet in the garden? Plants alone won't deflect noise generated by street traffic or neighbors. It takes a solid barrier—a fence, earth, or even a thick wall. But keep security concerns in mind. If barriers create shadows near entrances, for example, install outdoor lights for night visibility.

Berm. A mound of soil planted with shrubs and trees buffers sound from a neighbor's yard or a busy street. It also provides a leafy privacy screen. Dense evergreen plants are best for this use.

Wall fountain. The soothing burble of falling water is effective in masking nearby noise. The water doesn't so much drown out annoying sounds as create a pleasant distraction. (A wind chime, strategically placed, can be a less costly alternative.)

Berm

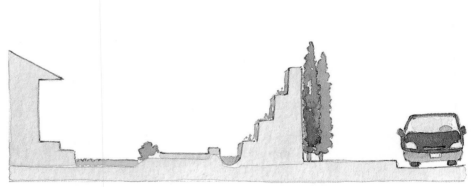

Wall fountain

SCREENING VIEWS

What can you do to hide an unsightly view or create a secluded area when planting alone can't do the job? Fence structures combined with plantings to soften their surfaces offer excellent options.

Fence. A fence will shield an undesirable view when it is at least slightly higher than eye level, or approximately 6 feet. To add privacy without extending a fence, mount a trellis or a planter box on top. Another option, for a long side yard, for example, is to stagger a fence with sections of clipped hedge.

Fence

Good-neighbor gardening

Always think about your neighbors before you begin any building, planting, or pruning along shared property lines.

First, find out exactly where the boundaries of your property are, so you don't end up building or planting on your neighbors' property. Also check local ordinances, restrictions, and easements that could affect your plans (see page 129). Many communities have guidelines or laws that protect beautiful views.

Any fences, hedges, or plantings on the property line belong to both you and your neighbor as tenants-in-common. So before you begin, talk to your neighbor about what you'd like to do and how it will look or be maintained. If you can't come to an agreement, you may need to install your fence or screen just inside the boundary of your property.

Under certain circumstances, you can prune branches and roots that extend over your property from a neighbor's tree, but only up to the boundary line. You may not trespass on your neighbor's property to prune a tree. Further, if the construction or pruning you do on your property affects the health of plants on your neighbor's property or alters the integrity of the plants' shapes, you may be liable for damages.

Use common sense when planting near property lines. Don't plant trees or shrubs that will eventually outgrow their space or extend too far into neighbors' yards, robbing them of sunlight. If you have a tree with limbs that reach into another's yard, work with your neighbor to remove or to prune the branches. Avoid planting species that drop a lot of debris (such as pine, catalpa, and horsechestnut) and those that have weak branches (poplar and silver maple) or aggressive roots (willow and most maples). Also take into account the root zone of large existing trees that may overlap with your planned planting area. If you don't consider these trees' well-being, who will?

CREATING PRIVACY

A. Screen of clipped hedge blocks wind and neighbor's view; prune up trunks to add height yet allow room for beds below.

B. Arbor covered with vines provides overhead protection and enclosure.

C. Single tree placed at front corner of driveway blocks view of entrance.

D. Fence with gate offers security.

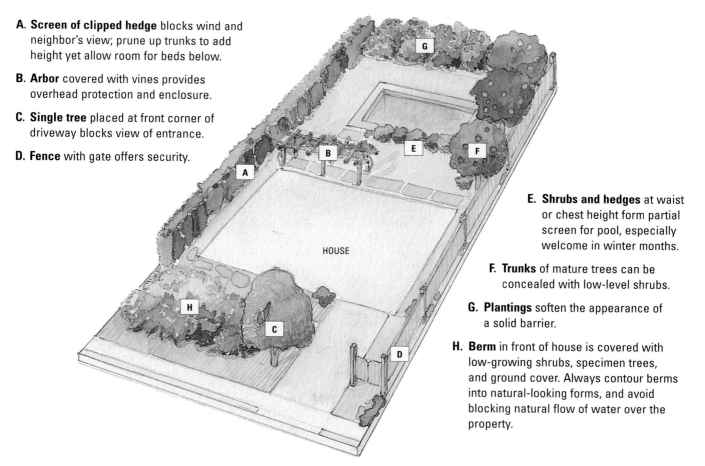

E. Shrubs and hedges at waist or chest height form partial screen for pool, especially welcome in winter months.

F. Trunks of mature trees can be concealed with low-level shrubs.

G. Plantings soften the appearance of a solid barrier.

H. Berm in front of house is covered with low-growing shrubs, specimen trees, and ground cover. Always contour berms into natural-looking forms, and avoid blocking natural flow of water over the property.

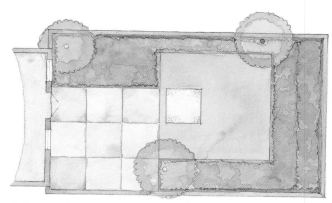

A. Square plan

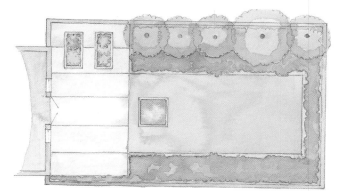

B. Rectangular plan

ONE GARDEN, THREE WAYS

A–C. These simple plans were created for the same basic lot using one of three different geometric shapes (square, rectangle, or circle) to guide the design. Each design presents a similar arrangement of paved terrace, small lawn area, and planting beds with a mix of ground covers, shrubs, and trees. The repetition of a different geometric shape gives each design a distinct character, but all share a contemporary feeling.

To follow this approach in your own garden, select a shape that appeals to you and use it for the largest element in your design—perhaps the terrace, lawn area, or swimming pool. Repeat the shape in smaller elements such as the flower beds, vegetable garden, and garden pond.

Shapes that emphasize the diagonal—offset squares or triangles—make a garden appear larger. Long rectangles or circles, especially when symmetrically placed, appear more formal. Whatever shape you use, play with the alignment and position of elements in a symmetrical or asymmetrical arrangement. Eventually you will settle on a balance that pleases you.

TOOLS OF DESIGN

Once your experiments with bubble diagrams result in a preliminary sketch and you have walked through a mock-up of the design, lay a clean sheet of tracing paper on top of it. On this sheet, begin drawing the various elements of your final design—paved areas, walls or fences, arbors, lawns, pools, flower and shrub beds, or dog runs. This schematic drawing will look rough at first but will gradually take shape as you continue.

Working with shapes

At this point, keep in mind two more tricks of the garden designer. First, work with clear, simple shapes. Second, relate those shapes to the lines of your house. A design consisting of such familiar shapes as rectangles, squares, circles, and curves is a lot easier to make sense of than one dominated by trapezoids, hexagons, and abstract shapes. Repeating a familiar shape can bring simplicity and order to your design, unifying beds, borders, paving, and other features. To add interest, you can vary the sizes of shapes you work with or let them overlap. But don't use too many different shapes unless you're looking for a very lively, complex design.

Working with grids

Once you have settled upon an attractive general design, it's time to plan it more exactly. For this, graph paper is essential. While it's easiest to visualize using a 1:1 ratio (one paper square per square foot of yard), you could use a larger module—for example, one square on the paper representing a 5-by-5-foot square of yard. Then, if you design each of the garden's elements to fit into one or more 5-by-5 modules, the overall plan will take on a pleasing unity.

In the plans for a rectangular lot on the facing page, each grid square represents 5 square feet. Notice how each element—lawn, walkway, terrace, deck—is composed of multiples of the 5-by-5 square module. Even the circular and diagonal lines relate to this basic unit of space. The elements are not always single units standing alone, however; you will want to allow some to intersect or overlap to further unify the design.

C. Circular plan

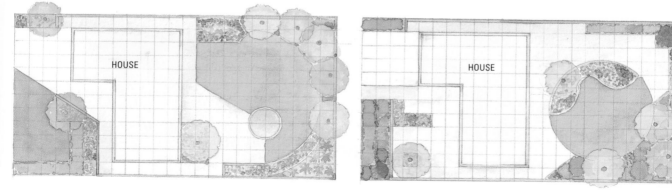

VISUALIZING A GRID

D. Connect the garden to the architecture of your house with imaginary grid lines that run out to the garden from major features of the house. Here, lines marking the doorways, windows, and corners of wings have been drawn on the plan of the garden. Elements such as flower beds, paved terraces, and pools can then be placed within this irregular grid pattern.

THREE PLANS FOR A RECTANGULAR LOT

E–G. The three plans at right and below use the same simple 5-by-5-foot grid to show very different design solutions for a rectangular property. Garden **E** incorporates a large overhead trellis or arbor to shade a portion of the paved terrace, while an L-shaped fence and planting bed screen a vegetable garden, compost area, and work area from view. Garden **F** allows more space for a sweeping lawn, backed up by a curving line of trees to enclose the garden; a round pond echoes the curve of the lawn. Garden **G** places a bold, circular lawn just off center, almost surrounded by a paved surface of varying width.

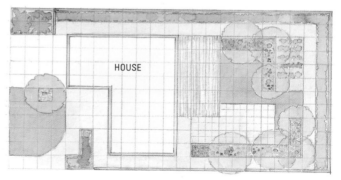

HOUSE

E. Large trellis

HOUSE

F. Spacious lawn

HOUSE

G. Circular lawn

FROM PLAN

B efore drawing up your final plan, you may wish to consult a landscape professional to assist with some element of the design or its implementation. Although many homeowners prefer to tackle the entire design and construction of their garden themselves, others rely on various professionals to help with some of the steps along the way.

The role of the landscape architect

Creating a garden can call for the addition of patios, decks, dining areas, play yards, shade structures, drainage systems, and perhaps a pool or spa. Designing such structures and relating them to a coherent plan for your outdoor environment is where a *landscape architect* comes in.

In addition to determining the most effective use of paving, planting, and lighting, landscape architects are licensed to design exterior structures, solve site problems such as ungainly slopes and poor drainage, and give advice on siting a house and locating service lines, entries, driveways, and parking areas. A landscape architect is familiar with landscape and building materials and services and can suggest cost-saving options.

For individual services or for a simple consultation, landscape architects can work at an hourly rate. More commonly, however, a landscape architect provides a complete package, from conceptual plans to construction drawings and supervision of an installation; fees will depend on the complexity of the project, its length, and the degree of supervision required.

Other professionals

Landscape architects are not the only professionals involved in the creation of fine gardens. The terms *landscape designer* and *garden designer* apply to professionals who may be self-taught or may have the same academic credentials as landscape architects but lack a state license. The focus of their work is more likely to be residential gardens, and if you are not in need of a complex deck construction or high retaining wall, they may well serve your needs.

Their fees will probably be lower than those of a landscape architect. A landscape designer usually works in conjunction with a *landscape contractor,* an important professional, especially when major construction—beyond the limits of do-it-yourself projects—is involved. A licensed contractor is trained in methods of earth-moving and construction as well as planting.

TO REALITY

You may work directly with a contractor, or your landscape architect or designer may select and supervise the contractor. In either scenario, the contractor will submit a bid, either as a lump sum or as a figure based on the estimated time and materials. The latter approach allows more modifications during construction.

Finally, there are professionals who work primarily with plants. *Horticulturists* are trained in the selection and care of garden plants; many have some design training as well. If you are merely looking for plants to complete a design, you can work with a horticulturist. *Arborists* are trained in the care of trees and other woody plants; although not usually able to prepare a design for your garden, they can guide you in identifying healthy trees and those needing pruning, shaping, removal, or protection during construction. Local nurseries may also offer design services and may have talented designers on their staffs; but beware of "free" design services, as the designer may be obligated to work only with plants and other materials offered by the employer.

Finding the right professional

Begin by identifying the professional services you need. Be realistic in assessing the amount of work you want to do yourself. Collect names from friends and neighbors—even if it means knocking on doors when you spot a good design. Then call each of the designers or contractors whose work you like to set up an interview, either at your home (there may be an hourly fee for this) or at their offices (often free). Inquire about the nature of their work, their workload, and their fees. Most important, ask for references—other residential clients whose gardens may give you an idea of the range and quality of the designer's work or the caliber of the contractor's construction. Ask to view these finished projects. Above all, you must feel a rapport with the professional; you will be working closely on the design and installation of your garden, and you will want to find someone with whom you feel comfortable.

When the designer of your choice makes the first visit to your site, use the time wisely. Prepare in advance a list of wishes, needs, and problems that must be dealt with in the design. Make sure everyone in the household has had a chance to participate in this step. Give serious consideration to your budget and your time schedule. When a design is complete, meet with the contractor and the designer to make certain that the contractor understands the design and is comfortable working with the materials proposed.

To protect yourself from surprises, be sure to request a contract from any professionals you hire. This legal agreement should spell out the services to be provided, the schedule to be followed, and the fees to be charged.

Computer-Aided Design

Of the several dozen landscape CD-ROMs and software programs currently on the market, most are for Windows-compatible computers and are similar in format: You must first electronically render your site by means of the program's computer-aided drafting tools, and then you must experiment with the placement of structures, plants, and accessories.

Some programs allow you to work from a scanned image of your property; others require you to position shapes to create an electronic design. Some programs can manipulate elements, such as slopes, or provide a three-dimensional view of the design.

Once the plan is accurate and to scale, you can start to place various elements in the digital landscape. Many programs offer such choices as perennials and annuals, trees and lawns, and even special effects such as lighting, shade patterns, growth rates, or seasonal changes. Some offer extensive databases of plants, and some allow you to print out your final plans to show to a landscape or nursery professional.

These landscape programs can be fun to use, but they can't give you good design advice. The best electronic garden design tool may be a plant encyclopedia that helps you select plants for your garden on the basis of specific search criteria, such as flower color, bloom time, growing conditions, or regional adaptability.

THE DESIGN MOCK-UP

Whether you have completed the design of your garden yourself or have in hand a professionally rendered landscape plan, the next step is to translate the design to your property. If you are having difficulty visualizing the finished garden or can't quite decide on the specifics of certain elements, you may wish to mock up the design on your property. Seeing an approximation of the layout on site in the form of stakes, strings, and markings will help you determine the exact dimensions necessary for some features, such as decks, terraces, and walks. Even if you feel your paper plan is final, be prepared to make some adjustments as you lay out the design on site until the arrangement of spaces and elements feels just right.

There are a variety of methods for staking out your design. Choose the one that works best for your situation; the choice will

A flexible boundary. Where your design is mostly curving lines and free-form shapes, snake a garden hose to lay out the lines to your liking. The hose can be curved at nearly any radius, especially if it is warm. As an alternative, use PVC pipe that you will later use for your irrigation work; the pipe can be softened in the warm sun and gently bent to mark your design.

Colored powder. Limestone or gypsum, common soil amendments, can be used to lay out free-form designs such as the outlines of beds and borders. Powdered chalk of various colors is useful if you have overlapping elements. Measure corner or end points, then dribble a line of powder along the outlines. To make changes, simply brush the powder into the soil and start again.

likely depend on which features predominate—straight lines or curving lines, geometric forms or free forms, specimen plantings or mass plantings. Use materials that you have on hand or that can be found at your local hardware store or garden center, such as bamboo or wooden stakes, kite string, clothesline or garden hose, powdered gypsum, lime, or even flour.

Live with your design layout for a few days before making any final decisions or beginning construction. Walk through or sit in your mock garden several times to be sure that it provides you with the spaces you need, circulation paths that are comfortable, and garden areas that suit your interests and the time you have to spend maintaining them. When you are ready to begin construction, mock-up techniques will also come in handy. Staking is often used to mark an area of concrete to be poured; colored powder can show the true boundaries of planting areas in borders and beds, and a hose snaked along a pathway can help guide the placement of pavers or bricks.

Strings and stakes. For straight or gently curved lines, mark each corner with a short stake and connect them with strings to outline paving areas, deck construction, pathways, hedges, and planting beds; use taller stakes to mark fences and walls. Then test how they affect traffic circulation through the garden and whether they block any important access points or views.

A mock garden. Tall stakes can stand in for trees, fountains, sculpture, or posts for overhead construction. Large pieces of cardboard on the ground can indicate paving or decks; cardboard can also represent fences and walls. Note any shadows cast by your planned vertical barriers. The neighbors might stare, but you will get a much better sense of how your design is shaping up.

LANDSCAPING WITH STRUCTURES

Structures can give your garden shape and dimension. By paying attention to the materials you use to build them, you can enrich your outdoor space with subtle texture and color.

Garden structures also play strong architectural roles. Fences and trellises can create separate "rooms." Low, wide walls can provide seating as well. Gazebos and arbors add shelter, privacy, and support for plants. Spas, decks, and patios can recreate the ambience and convenience of an indoor room for enjoyment outdoors.

Structures can be the costliest part of the garden, so plan them with care, and learn about your local building codes before you start. The design should blend well with the architecture of your house and its setting. Choose the most durable and suitable materials you can afford to ensure that your structures are long lasting as well as pleasing.

ARBORS AND TRELLISES

Arbors and trellises, along with other garden structures such as pergolas, lath houses, and gazebos, can be among the most interesting elements of your garden. They provide a visual change of pace by leading the eye upward. Along with fences and walls, they contribute to the structure of the garden by strengthening its composition.

Two of the simplest vertical structures, arbors and trellises have both decorative and practical functions. They can support climbing plants, tie together garden areas, define zones of use, direct foot traffic, and mask a plain or unsightly feature, such as a garage or dog run.

Though not as large or imposing as pergolas, which traditionally function as covered walkways, arbors tend to be sizable structures that afford a peaceful shelter to relax and reflect.

Generally rendered less imposing by simple design and graceful arches, arbors can be partly attached to a house wall or roof or else built freestanding, colonnade-style. The frame of most arbors is similar in construction to that of many patio overheads and some gazebos, but arbors are generally less enclosed.

Trellises serve primarily as plant supports; they may be freestanding or mounted to a wall, a fence, the side of a house, or a deck to serve as a windbreak or privacy screen. You can make your own trellis from twigs or lattice panels, or buy a commercial model at a garden center or through a mail-order supplier. Some types are made of wooden strips or lattice; others of natural vines, plastic, or wrought iron. Whatever the material, the trellis must be strong enough to support the weight of mature plants and durable enough to stand up to the rigors of your climate.

Tucked into a corner of the garden, this simple arbor provides a quiet place to sit and watch hummingbirds drawn to the feeder, and to enjoy the surrounding plantings in privacy.

A. This weathered trellis serves as a focal point in the garden, breaking the horizontal plane of plantings and sending the eye up to take in the clematis 'General Sikorski' cloaking the frame.

B. A simple, rustic overhead combines sturdy 6-by-6 posts with spare roof framing. Vines snake up the posts and out across plain galvanized pipes. A raised, casual tub fountain provides soothing sounds of water.

C. An arbor with trellised sides and curved rafters offers interesting places for plants to climb. This one is made of plastic, so it is virtually maintenance free. Structures such as this one are often available in kit form.

A BASIC ARBOR

Beams bridge posts; local codes specify sizes and spans

Lattice screen adds privacy and shade; doubles as a trellis

Piers of cast concrete are embedded in poured concrete footings

A. Part of a boundary fence, this graceful, arched trellis shows just its top under a blanket of *Clematis × jackmanii.* The trellis not only provides a beautiful focal point in the garden, but acts as a privacy screen as well.

B. The rustic charm of this cedar-pole arbor is heightened with clematis. The posts are sunk in holes that are then filled with concrete. Fasten the top pieces with 12-inch spikes or lash them together with copper wire.

Designing an arbor

The key to arbor construction is to think of a crisscross or stacking principle, with each new layer placed perpendicular to the one below it. Although you build an overhead from the ground up, you should design it from the top down. First choose the kind of roof you want. That decision will influence the size and spacing of the support members below.

Whether freestanding or attached to a building, the structure is held up by a series of posts or columns. These support horizontal beams, which in turn support rafters. In a house-attached overhead, a ledger (see page 371) takes the place of a beam, and the rafters are laid directly on the ledger. The rafters can be left uncovered or covered with 1 by 2s, lattice, poles, or grape stakes.

Rafters sit atop beams and are spaced for plant support or shade. Orientation determines the extent of shade cast below

Posts are 4-by-4 lumber or larger; post-to-beam connections may need bracing. Metal anchors secure posts to piers or to a concrete slab

Concrete footings extend below the frost line, supporting posts and the weight of arbor and plants

Shopping for a Trellis

An easy and attractive way to support twining and vining plants is with handcrafted trellises, available from garden retailers and mail-order suppliers. Some sources carry an impressive array of trellises, ranging from hand-forged metal to woven willow, that can serve as decorative elements as well as plant supports. Woven wooden or vine trellises bring a casual or rustic touch to the garden, while the architectural wooden and metal ones generally look more formal.

These trellises are simple to use. Most come ready to install. Just push the posts into the soil next to a wall or in a planter box, plant a vine nearby, and wrap the stems around the supports. A few need minor assembly, and some wooden ones with "feet" must be anchored to a wall.

For the creative do-it-yourselfer, hardware stores and home centers also stock lattice panels (both redwood and pressure-treated), copper pipe, chicken wire, and assorted fasteners that can be fashioned into a trellis. Cut a lattice panel with a circular saw, and fasten to fence posts or a wall. Use lag screws or galvanized nails for fastening to wood and expanding anchors for stucco or masonry. Leave some room between trellis and wall.

Both of the trellises shown here are simply con-*structed. At top, four arched, prefabricated trellises were lined up, anchored in concrete, and fastened to the walls with barbed nails. The trellises were joined with overhead 2 by 2s. The trellis at right, cloaked with clematis 'General Sikorski', is constructed of gray-stained cedar strips fastened to the brick wall.*

In most cases arbors are built from standard-dimension lumber. To increase the life of an arbor, use only pressure-treated or naturally decay-resistant materials such as redwood or cedar heartwood. Open arbors don't collect much rain or snow, so they need only support the weight of the materials themselves, plus the weight of any plants growing on them. For added lateral strength, brace the structure where the posts meet the beams.

As you plan, check with your local building department to find out about the regulations affecting the size, design, and construction of your project. In most communities, you'll have to meet building codes and obtain a building permit before you begin work. For do-it-yourself details, see pages 370–371.

DECKS

A deck sets the stage for outdoor activity and extends the total living space of a house. A properly planned deck forms a focal point in the landscape, redefines grade, and provides new views of the garden and its surroundings. Built to accommodate seating, tables, or a hot tub, a deck can function as an outdoor room.

Decks can abut the house or tuck into a remote corner of the garden. The classic attached deck is typically accessed from the house through French or sliding doors from a living room, kitchen, or master bedroom—or all three. So when planning your deck, keep in mind interior traffic patterns as well as outdoor ones.

Why build a deck rather than a patio? Your site or the style of your house can be determining factors. A deck can bridge bumps and slopes or "float" over swampy low spots that might sink a brick patio. Decking lumber is resilient underfoot, and it doesn't store heat the way masonry can, making a deck cooler in hot areas.

A low-level deck can link house and garden at flower height, offering a new perspective on garden beds. Such a deck makes a good replacement for an existing concrete slab—you can often use the slab as a base for the deck. A low-level wraparound deck links interior spaces with a series of boardwalks or landings. You can follow your home's shape or play off it with angular extensions or soft curves.

If you're faced with a hilly site, try cantilevering a deck over the steep slope, or plan on a step-down, multiplatform arrangement like the one shown at right.

Detached decks form quiet retreats, whether tucked behind lush plantings or elevated to catch afternoon sun or shade. The route to such a deck can be direct or circuitous. You can enhance the feeling of a hideaway with the addition of an overhead, a fountain, or a spa or hot tub.

Design options include decking patterns (see page 367) and railing styles. Often the railing is the most visible element. The ultimate feel of a deck is determined by the details, and safety is the only limit.

Pressure-treated lumber (see page 363) is the most affordable material for building a deck. The wood, typically southern pine, has been treated with chemical preservatives that guard against rot, insects, and other sources of decay. Other options include redwood or cedar heartwood, which are more pleasing visually and naturally resistant to decay, but much more expensive.

Coat any deck periodically with a wood preservative or stain (see page 365) to prevent water absorption and reduce the swelling and contracting that lead to cracking, splintering, and warping. Pressure-treated lumber can be stained to look remarkably like redwood.

A. This multilevel deck of pressure-treated lumber runs the full length of the house, linking the interior with the outdoors. Steel railings, built-in benches, and deck-level planters give the structure continuity and an open, contemporary feel.

B. The warm, rich tones of redwood heartwood are elegantly showcased here. Overlapping angles and changes in decking direction signal steps, highlight benches and planters, and turn a potentially plain deck into an architectural statement.

C. Removable sections of parquet decking cover this flat roof. The railing is capped with a continuous planter box. An enormous pot brings a small tree right onto the deck.

Deck-building guidelines

Lumber grades vary greatly in appearance and price. One cost-saving idea is to determine the least expensive lumber for decking and railing that's acceptable to you (see pages 362–363). Whatever the species and grade of the visible wood you choose, use pressure-treated lumber for the substructure. It stands up to weather and in-ground conditions and is less expensive.

A deck can be freestanding or, as shown here, attached to the house with a horizontal ledger. Concrete footings secure precast piers or poured tubular pads, which in turn support vertical wooden posts. One or more horizontal beams span the posts; smaller joists bridge ledger and beams. The decking itself, typically 5/4-by-6 or 2-by-6 lumber, is nailed or screwed to the joists. The design shown, while standard, is but one of many options.

Overheads, railings, and steps are often integral to a deck's framing. Though it may be feasible to add these extras later, it's simplest to design and build the whole structure at once. While you're planning, think about whether you'll need to install plumbing pipes for running water or wiring for electric outlets and outdoor light fixtures. If you need extra storage space or planters, build them into the deck as permanent features.

One advantage of building a deck as a do-it-yourself project is that much of the engineering work has probably been done for you. Standard span tables (listing safe working spans by dimension for each of the common lumber species) are widely available—most lumberyards have them. Remember that these are minimum guidelines; for firmer footing, reduce the spacing between them or choose beefier members.

Posts taller than 3 feet may require bracing, especially in areas prone to high winds. Decks elevated 20 inches or more above existing grade must be surrounded with 3-foot-high railings for safety, with slats no more than 4 to 6 inches apart (again, check local code). A railing must not be climbable by young children. Fascia boards, skirts, and other trim details can dress up the basic structure.

A low-level deck is the simplest kind to build, but a simple raised deck like the one shown at right can also be constructed by a homeowner. Generally, decks that are cantilevered out from an upper story or over water or a promontory must be designed by a qualified structural engineer and installed by a professional. Decks on steep hillsides or unstable soil or those more than a story high should receive the same professional attention.

A BASIC DECK

Decking boards are nailed or screwed perpendicular to joists; they are typically 5/4-by-6 or 2-by-6 lumber

Storage bin can be concealed under built-in bench

Railings (maximum openings specified by local code)

Fascia (trim)

Rim joist secures joist ends

Planters on deck require adequate drainage; deck must support weight of soil and plants

Doors to deck lead from dining or living room, kitchen, or bedrooms. French or sliding doors are best choices

Electric lighting may be 120 volt or 12 volt and may require a permit to install

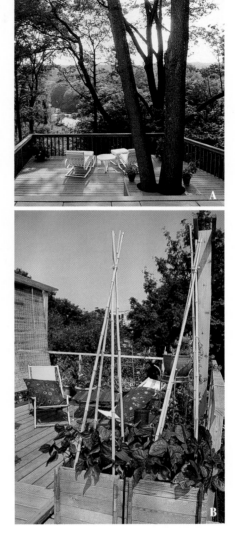

A. **Built out over a steep hillside,** this deck takes on the feel of a tree house. A hole was cut in the decking to accommodate the mature tree that provides shade.

B. **This tiny rooftop deck** functions as resting place and container garden. While in the process of adding the requisite railings, the designer—who specializes in rooftop architecture—hung woven screens to enhance the cozy feeling and privacy of the space.

Ledger secures deck to house framing. Flashing guards against moisture

Beams bridge posts; they may be single timbers or twin 2-by members that "sandwich" posts, as shown

Joists are typically spaced 16 or 24 inches center-to-center and secured to rim joist and ledger with joist hangers

Posts are secured to piers with post anchors. Minimum post sizes and spacings are set by local codes

Piers are made of precast concrete and embedded in poured footings

Poured-concrete footings extend below the frost line

FENCES AND GATES

Fences and outdoor screens can transform a garden into a secure, attractive retreat from the outside world. When well designed, they filter the sun's glare, turn a biting wind into a pleasant breeze, and help to muffle the cacophony of street traffic, noisy neighbors, and barking dogs. As partitions, they divide the yard into separate areas for recreation, relaxation, gardening, and storage. Fences serve many of the same purposes as walls, but fences are generally less formal and imposing in appearance, easier to construct, and, when you calculate labor costs, less expensive.

Most fences are built partly or entirely of wood. The versatility of wood as a fencing material is reflected in the wide variety of its forms—split rails, grape stakes, dimension lumber, poles, and manufactured wood products such as plywood and tempered hardboard. Though the design possibilities are endless, wooden fences fall into one of three basic types: post-and-rail, picket, and solid board. The one you choose may depend on the function the fence is to serve; a board fence may be the best choice for a full privacy screen, for example. Fences can also be designed to edit views with the inclusion of louvers, slats, lattice, or see-through trellises that provide a glimpse of what lies beyond.

Alternative materials beyond boards, slats, and timbers include plastic, galvanized wire, plastic mesh, and ornamental iron. Vinyl fences are readily available, easy to maintain, and simple to install. If you don't like the look of wire or mesh fencing, plant annual vines such as morning glories or climbing nasturtiums for temporary, quick cover, or install evergreen plantings for permanent cover (see pages 222–223).

Whatever your choice of fencing, coordinate the fence with the style and materials of your house. A picket fence that would be too dainty for a contemporary stone-and-glass house might look fine with a colonial brick or clapboard structure. Louvered or board fences, however, can complement a variety of house styles.

Most communities have regulations restricting fence height. In many places, the maximum allowable height is 42 inches for front-yard fences and 6 feet for backyard fences. Tall fences are also more difficult to build and require more materials. An alternative way to gain more height is to train a plant to clothe the top of a fence.

Post-and-rail zigzags mark boundaries. Poppies and roses dress up the fence with scarlet blooms.

Normally, a boundary fence is commonly owned and maintained by both neighbors. Make every effort to come to a friendly agreement with your neighbor on the location, design, and construction of the fence. (One option is a "good-neighbor" fence with crosspieces mounted in alternating directions.) If you can't come to an agreement, you can circumvent the problem by building the fence entirely on your land, within your property boundary.

Choosing a gate

Place a gate for access, to frame a view, or to make a design statement in tandem with the fence. You may want to build the gate in a style and material that match the fence, but you can also choose a contrasting material or design, such as a wooden or wrought-iron gate within flanking brick pilasters. A low picket gate or one made of airy lath invites people in with its open, friendly appearance; a high, solid gate guards the privacy and safety of those within.

The minimum width for a gate is usually 3 feet, but an extra foot creates a more gracious feeling. If you anticipate moving gardening or other equipment through the gate, make the opening wider. For an extra-wide space, consider a two-part gate or even a gate on rollers designed for a driveway.

A. An arbored gate and picket fence made of unfinished, heavily weathered wood provide a pleasing contrast with bright-colored climbing plants and a well-tended garden beyond. The heartwood of redwood or cedar can turn gray like this and last for decades with no maintenance.

B. Its unique herringbone pattern sets this split-rail fence apart from the crowd. Open fences such as this one have the effect of merging the property with the surrounding landscape and serve more as psychological barriers against intrusion than as true privacy fences.

C. This traditional picket fence is a perfect midpoint between the white clapboard house and the rustic stone wall that fronts it. For variation, the space between pickets can be either wide or narrow, and tops can be pointed, rounded, spearheaded, or double or triple saw-toothed.

Building a fence

Most wood fences have three parts: vertical posts, horizontal rails or stringers, and siding. Posts are usually 4-by-4 timbers; rails are usually 2 by 4s. Fence siding can range from rough grape stakes to ready-cut pickets, from finished boards to plywood panels. Posts should be made of pressure-treated lumber or of decay-resistant redwood or cedar heartwood. Redwood can be left to weather naturally, but fir or pine rails or siding should be painted or stained.

If your fence will be on or near the boundary line between your property and your neighbor's, make certain you have the property line clearly established. If there's any doubt, call in a surveyor to review it.

Few lots are perfectly smooth, flat, and obstruction free. If your fence line runs up a hill, build the fence so that it follows the contours of the land, or construct stepped panels that will maintain horizontal lines (see pages 368–369).

Building a gate

A basic gate consists of a rectangular frame of 2 by 4s with a diagonal 2-by-4 brace running from the bottom corner of the hinge side to the top corner of the latch side. Siding fastened to the frame completes the gate.

Choose strong hinges and latches. It's better to select hardware that's too hefty than too flimsy. Plan to attach both hinges and latches with long galvanized screws that won't pull out, and be sure to use galvanized hardware.

A. This classic wooden gate welcomes visitors with its low, widely spaced rails and cheerful yellow paint.

B. A traditional picket gate creates a pleasing contrast with the dense stone wall surrounding this lakeside garden, beckoning visitors to pass through and wander down the pathway.

C. This formal gate, set in a solid brick wall, is nearly a door. Painted a solid white, it nicely sets off the aged patina of the bricks.

D. Bamboo sets the theme in this garden: the gate's frame and rails mirror the living bamboo lining a pathway to it.

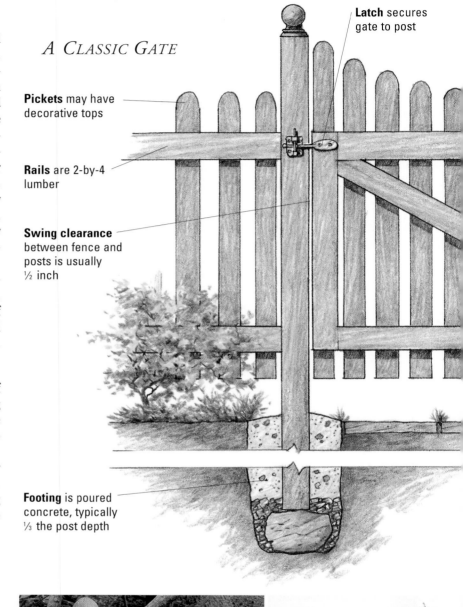

A CLASSIC GATE

Latch secures gate to post

Pickets may have decorative tops

Rails are 2-by-4 lumber

Swing clearance between fence and posts is usually ½ inch

Footing is poured concrete, typically ⅓ the post depth

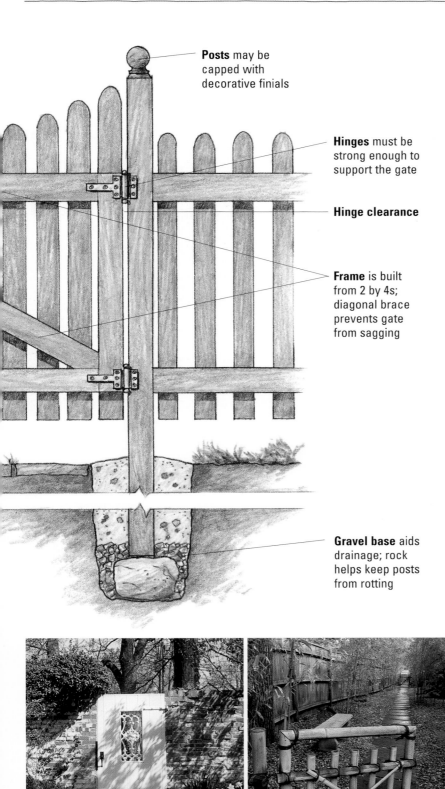

Posts may be capped with decorative finials

Hinges must be strong enough to support the gate

Hinge clearance

Frame is built from 2 by 4s; diagonal brace prevents gate from sagging

Gravel base aids drainage; rock helps keep posts from rotting

E. **Clean pickets** gain appeal from this custom design; the options are endless.

F. **Alternate-width boards**, a kick-board, bamboo horizontals, and detailed posts combine to create a contemporary look for this wood fence.

G–H. **Decorative elements** such as the grapevines of the cast-iron fence and a "fish" gate handle lend personality to the practical.

GREENHOUSES AND LATH HOUSES

In a climate where killing cold is a reality of winter, a greenhouse broadens the scope of gardening, making it possible to overwinter tender perennials—and even tropical plants—and to get a head start in spring with seedlings and cuttings.

If designed to do so, a greenhouse can double as a conservatory. The heated greenhouse shown opposite, top, is furnished with a table and chairs in summer. Most of the plants are taken outside when the weather warms, so there is plenty of room to sit, and the family has a glassed-in space with a broad view of the garden.

There are three kinds of greenhouses: cold, cool, and warm. A cold greenhouse is heated only by the sun. Though unsuitable for tropical plants, it provides protection for plants that are

borderline hardy, and it extends the growing season in spring and autumn. A cool greenhouse is heated, keeping the ambient temperature above 45°F—warm enough to overwinter frost-tender plants. A hothouse, used for growing tropicals, must be kept above 55°F at all times.

A local nursery or landscaping contractor may know of natural ways to keep a greenhouse warm in your area. The unheated greenhouse shown above manages to keep the temperatures inside above freezing throughout the winter. The greenhouse is located on the south side of the property to catch as much sun as possible. A long mirror mounted inside on the north-facing wall catches the sun and reflects it back, and the black gravel floor absorbs the

Constructed with old windows so that it resembles a pretty summerhouse rather than a utilitarian workspace, this greenhouse is an attractive garden feature.

heat. In winter, 11 water-filled barrels covered with black plastic are positioned under the benches. The water heats up during the day and radiates that warmth at night.

Accessories available for greenhouses include heaters, ranging from small electric units to large natural gas heaters; thermostatically controlled fans to circulate the air, keeping the temperature even throughout the space and helping prevent mildew and condensation; vents, including automatic models that open and close on their own as the temperature inside fluctuates; water-misting systems; benches and shelves, also known as staging; and lights.

Depending on your budget, you can have anything from a basic, unheated greenhouse, either freestanding or attached to the house, for relatively little money, or a state-of-the-art marvel outfitted with all the bells and whistles of modern computer technology.

A. Because this greenhouse was built as an extension of the house, heat is shared between the two spaces, saving on energy. The shade cloth cools the greenhouse in summer.

B. Akin to a small greenhouse and easy to build, a cold frame is an inexpensive way of extending the growing season in spring and autumn and of protecting container plants from winter winds.

C. During the hot months, deciduous trees nearby help cool this greenhouse; in winter, the sun shines on the glass for full-strength heat.

Lath houses

A lath house is a multifunction space. With its filtered light, a lath house is an ideal place to start seeds and cuttings in warm weather; it is also an excellent space for potting because it screens the work area from view. You can also use a lath house as a plant hospital and as storage space for out-of-season plants.

Locate a lath house in full sun, with the lath strips running north and south; this way, the shade will shift evenly as the sun moves from east to west. For durability, build it of naturally rot-resistant wood, such as the heartwood of cedar or redwood, or of pressure-treated lumber. The floor under the workbenches can be left as bare soil, but pave the areas where you walk and stand with gravel, stepping-stones, or concrete to keep your feet dry. Adding an automatic mister or drip watering system will save hours of watering.

A. The filtered shade and protected environment provided by a lath house are ideal for seedlings and young plants.

B. A lath house made of trellising is an attractive as well as useful feature in the garden.

GARDEN SHEDS

For anyone who loves to garden—as opposed to simply maintaining a given landscape—a garden shed is a necessary luxury. Where else do you store all the tools and equipment necessary to do the job?

Older properties often have outbuildings that lend themselves admirably to storage. Add a few hooks to the wall for hanging rakes, shovels, and hoes, install some shelves, and you have an excellent place to keep your gardening supplies.

Prefabricated sheds, which come in sections ready to assemble, are relatively inexpensive. Or you can custom-build a storage room that blends with the architectural style of your home. If you are putting up a new structure on your property, even a prefabricated kit, check with your local building authorities. Some communities require permits.

Choose the site for a storage shed carefully. Unless the shed exterior is designed to be a special garden feature, you will probably want to tuck it into an obscure corner of the property. At the same time, it needs to be situated where it is convenient for getting the tools and supplies you need. Choose a level site, and one that is easily accessible by wheelbarrow or cart. It's much easier to wheel supplies about the garden than to make several trips with armloads of tools.

If a plain shed strikes you as an eyesore, dress it up with a false window or cover it with trelliswork painted a pretty, contrasting color. Plant a vine to mask the structure, at the same time adding a pleasing vertical element to your garden design. With little work, a utilitarian shed can be transformed into a charming asset.

A. Resourceful homeowners in Missouri cobbled together this garden shed using salvaged doors, windows, and weathered wood from a 19th-century barn.

B. An old farm structure has been modified to serve double duty as a greenhouse and garden shed. Large south-facing acrylic plastic panels let in the sun. Two large doors can be opened to dissipate heat in the summer.

C. A bed of everblooming dianthus leads the way to an outhouse that has been converted into a tool and potting shed.

GAZEBOS

An enclosed garden structure is a refuge from household bustle—a place to sit quietly or to host a party on a warm evening. It provides shade during the day and shelter during cool evenings, yet is open to breezes, the scent of flowers, and—if near a pool or fountain—the sight or sound of water.

When most of us say we're going to sit outside, we walk out our back door directly onto a patio or deck. But putting a structure away from the house changes how you perceive and use the outdoor space. To find the best site for the structure, walk around your property, glancing back at the house. Look for a vantage point that provides long, diagonal views across the garden; avoid unsightly areas such as the toolshed or garage in favor of a striking bed or a grape arbor. Consider which exposure you want—if your main deck or patio is in full sun, you may prefer to find a shady corner, for example. Then start to think about the

design of the structure itself. The walkway leading to the gazebo may itself add to the view.

Choosing a gazebo

Reminiscent of country bandstands in small-town parks, gazebos can be romantic garden hideaways. The traditional gazebo is a freestanding version of an overhead, with either six or eight sides and sloping rafters joined in a central hub at the roof peak. Often the hexagonal or octagonal sides are partly enclosed with lath, lattice, or even metal grillwork.

Gazebos have come a long way from the old-fashioned Victorian-style version. Construction can either be substantial, with hefty corner columns and stacked beams, or light, with little more than four posts connected by pairs of 2 by 6s. The design may be enhanced by such features as path lighting or downlights, built-in benches or swings, window boxes, fountains, or spas.

Late-afternoon sun warms this traditional gazebo, which was assembled from a kit. Rocking chairs that match the framing offer a comfortable spot for the homeowners to enjoy their garden.

Ready-Made Gazebos

If building an entire gazebo from scratch appears a bit overwhelming, look into building one from a kit. Several companies manufacture traditional gazebos in kit form, complete except for the foundation. You construct the gazebo atop a concrete slab, deck, or foundation of piers or crushed stone. For most types, assembly takes a weekend or two and requires only basic tools and skills and the assistance of a helper.

Even though a kit costs less than a custom gazebo, it's still a major investment, so be sure you know what you're getting. Connections should be made with galvanized or brass hardware, and machining should be carefully done so that assembly is relatively easy. Details, such as railings or bracing, are worthy of close scrutiny. Read the assembly directions beforehand to see if they are clear and easy to follow.

Find out whether the gazebo is made from redwood or cedar heartwood or from less expensive softwood or pressure-treated lumber. Can the wood be finished naturally or must it be painted? If the latter, is it available preprimed?

Also, make sure you know what's included in the price of the kit. Who pays for delivery? Are flooring and floor framing included? What about benches, screens, and steps? Many kits allow you to choose between open railings or lattice panels and other finishing details.

A. This Asian-style open-sided pavilion offers shelter for outdoor dining, rafters for hanging plants, and a prime spot for enjoying both swimming pool and burbling stream.

B. Atop a raised platform, a simple frame becomes an "engawa," or viewing platform, overlooking a large serene pond.

PATHS

Although it's true that the shortest distance between two points is a straight line, garden walkways often work best when this idea is ignored.

In fact, a path is most interesting when it provides a series of experiences along the way. It can alternately reveal and conceal special plantings, a piece of sculpture, a small bench, or a pleasing view. On a small lot, space expands when you obscure the pathway's end or use "forced perspective," gradually diminishing the width of the path to make it appear longer.

Tailor your choice of materials to the task at hand. Major access walks should be made of brick, pavers, concrete, unglazed tile, or uniform stone slabs for easy traffic flow and an even, nonskid surface. Leave space between pavers for low-growing crevice plants such as creeping thyme or sedums.

A rustic path of gravel or bark chips can meander through the garden, its serpentine form leading you around each bend until the path ahead disappears, its uneven texture and natural colors blending into the surroundings.

Fieldstone, rough cobbles, wood rounds, and other casual stepping-stones also make appealing paths, especially when embedded in a less expensive, contrasting filler material such as river rock or wood chips.

Another choice is lumber—redwood or cedar decking atop a pressure-treated base, or pressure-treated timbers or "railroad ties" laid side by side.

Well-defined, broad edgings include brick, landscape timbers, or concrete. Steel ribbon edging is all but invisible.

Unless you've chosen a highly porous material like gravel, plan to pitch the path slightly to one side for drainage, or build it with a slight crown in the center. Runoff needs about ¼ inch of slope per foot.

A

At night, shielded path lights (see page 291) provide plenty of illumination but little glare. Their low-voltage wires can be snaked through garden plantings, adjacent to planting beds, or along edgings.

How wide should your path be? It depends on how you'll use it. If it will wind discreetly through a garden and serve only as a walking surface, 2 feet is adequate. To allow room for lawn mowers and wheelbarrows, make it 3 feet wide. For two people to walk abreast, as on an entry path, it should be 5 feet wide.

Finally, if your terrain is a little too steep for comfortable walking, plan for one or more broadly spaced steps.

A. If a path will not be heavily trodden, grass works fine. Rows of asclepias, nicotiana, and iris on either side define a meandering path to a large flower bed. Grape and berry vines can be seen in the distance.

B. Concrete slabs with exposed aggregate alternate with sections of loose stone in this Missouri garden. Large stones form a border on either side of the path.

C. Large flagstones set directly in well-tamped soil form first a small patio, then a path. Be sure the stones are low enough that you can run the lawn mower over them. Position the pathway stones to accommodate an adult's natural stride.

D. Gray concrete pavers look natural when laid in somewhat haphazard fashion. Here, they complement natural stones near a small pond.

PATIOS

Many people think of a patio as a simple rectangle off the back door. If you have a small, flat lot, perhaps that's your best design option. But with even a little more space, you can expand a patio in almost any direction.

Consider a detached, protected patio in the corner of your lot, or a series of interrelated patios connected by steps. A neglected side yard off a small, dark bedroom may be the spot for a private, screened sitting area. Or an existing driveway could be converted: concrete turf blocks soften a drive's appearance yet allow for traffic; planted areas between flagstones and pavers achieve the same effect. Enclosed by a gate and accented with plantings, the area could become an entry courtyard.

Basic paving options for patio floors include masonry units, poured concrete, and loose materials such as gravel and wood chips. Your choice depends mainly on whether you would prefer a formal or an informal patio. Brick, trimmed stone, and cobblestones look formal if laid in a symmetrical pattern. Irregular flagstones or mossy bricks laid in sand achieve a softer, cottage-garden look, as do spaced concrete pavers.

A smooth poured concrete surface—the first choice for many patios of the past—takes on a friendlier look if it is textured, stamped, or topped by exposed aggregate. You could also leave plant pockets in a freshly poured slab, or shape curved forms and fill them with concrete. The resulting pads—with plant spaces in between—can be smoothed, textured, and finished to resemble natural stone or seeded with another texture (see pages 378–379).

The bricks outlining these bluestone pavers emphasize the geometric shapes of the stones and add visual interest with color and texture. Used as edging, they also provide a frame for the patio.

When combined, masonry and low-level wooden decking complement one another and allow greater flexibility for your patio in shape, texture, and finished height. Although masonry surfaces must rest on solid ground, decks can span sloping, bumpy, or poorly draining areas nearby.

Remember that whether you lay it, hammer it, set it, or pour it in place, a patio almost always requires an edging. Repeat the edging material elsewhere—on paths, for example—to visually link elements in the landscape. Edgings can also connect different areas of a garden. A brick-edged patio, for example, may taper off to a brick path.

A. Little more than a wide spot in the mulch pathway that leads from the house to the garden, this mossy stone patio was carefully designed to blend with its shady surroundings. Even the choice of furnishings evokes a natural harmony.

B. Flowering shrub dogwoods gaze like spectators at this circular patio made of common brick. This material requires regular sealing so the bricks won't crack. Some more durable concrete pavers are tinted to mimic used common brick.

C. Natural brick pavers and bluestone live in harmony with planters and flower beds featuring elephant's ear, fountain grass, and chrysanthemums.

Patio-building pointers

Most patios are constructed either as a poured concrete slab or as a surface atop a bed of clean, packed sand.

A concrete slab suits heavy-use areas and formal designs. The slab should be at least 4 inches thick and underlaid with 2 to 8 inches of gravel. Wooden forms define the slab's shape. A thinner concrete pad, typically 3 inches thick, can serve as a base for masonry units such as ceramic tile or flagstones set in mortar.

For casual brick, paver, and cobblestone patios and walks, use a sand bed (see pages 380–381). A layer of gravel provides drainage and stability; damp sand is then carefully leveled—or "screeded"—on top. Paving units, either spaced or tightly butted, are prevented from shifting by edgings.

In general, patios laid in sand are good do-it-yourself projects. Concrete work is more demanding because there's little room for error; the trick is to pace your formwork and to limit the "pour" to small sections at a time.

If you're thinking of adding an overhead to your patio, you'll find building instructions on pages 370–371. Posts can straddle the paving area atop concrete piers and footings, or they can be affixed directly to the patio surface with post anchors.

A. Here is a cool spot on hot summer days. Crabapple and yew trees allow only dappled sunlight to play on this patio, made of large flagstones set in mortar.

B. These concrete pavers are laid in a basketweave pattern. A limestone retaining wall allows for stand-up flower gardening and gives the area the feel of a room.

C. Reflecting the facade of the house, this brick patio is set in sand for an informal look. Despite the expansiveness of the patio—which means no grass to mow—the herringbone brick pattern lends a sense of containment.

D. White patches in these once-used bricks unify the house and patio. The color, size, and pattern of the brick you choose will create a specific feeling in your patio area.

Renovating Concrete

If you have a deteriorating patio or driveway, you can either demolish it and build anew or, in some cases, install a replacement surface. Asphalt is usually best removed, but an existing concrete slab, unless heavily damaged, can serve admirably as a base for brick, pavers, tile, or stone. Another possibility is to construct a low-level deck over the slab. Or you can break up damaged areas of concrete and let casual plantings grow in the resulting gaps.

Professional solutions include the treatment of concrete with one of three methods: bonding, staining, or topcoating. In bonding, a mix of colored cement and a binder is sprayed over the entire surface. Then cracks are blended into a network of faux grout lines created by stenciled patterns or by a special tape that's later removed. The cost, depending on the complexity of the design, ranges from one-quarter to one-third that of total replacement.

Several companies also offer chemical stains in a variety of colors that can be applied directly to the surface of an existing slab to give it a camouflaging patina. Contractors will often score a cracked concrete slab into shapes and apply different colors of stain to them to draw the eye away from the cracks.

A topcoating that completely covers a cracked concrete surface can make a dramatic change. One innovative covering is made of ground-up bits of colored recycled rubber bonded together with a clear epoxy. Other contractors specialize in adding aggregate topcoats or floating on a new colored mix, which can then be stamped or textured.

PLAY YARDS

Kids love the outdoors and need a place to expend their energy. Yet young children (and some older ones) have little sense of danger, so play areas must be both fun and safe. The first decision to make when planning a play yard is where to place it. Preschoolers feel safer—and can be more easily watched—if the play area is close to the house. You may prefer to corral older, noisier children within view but farther away.

Also take into account sun, wind, and shade. Hot sun increases the risk of sunburn and can make metal slides or bars, as well as concrete walks, burning hot, so install slide surfaces facing north. If your property is in the path of strong winds, locate the play yard inside a windbreak of fencing or dense trees. Dappled shade is ideal. If you have no spreading foliage, position the play yard on the north side of your house, construct a simple canopy of lath or canvas, or plan a play structure that includes a shaded portion.

Many public playgrounds feature metal or plastic play structures rather than timber because wood may eventually rot, break, and splinter. Still, wood is a warmer and friendlier material—and a good-quality wooden structure will last as long as your children will be using it.

Some timbers used in play structures are pressure-treated with a chemical preservative, especially if they'll be buried underground. Though the Environmental Protection Agency considers these chemicals safe in regulated amounts, check the kind of preservative used before purchasing or building a play structure, and consider alternatives such as rot-resistant cedar or redwood.

Perhaps you'll want a play structure scaled beyond your youngster's present abilities. Some structures allow you to add or change components as your child grows. Many mail-order companies offer structures that you can assemble yourself. Before you buy, try to view an assembled structure and talk with the owners to evaluate its safety and design. Look through the instructions beforehand to be sure you can carry out the assembly.

Allow at least 6 feet of space around all sides of swings, slides, and climbing structures for a fall zone, then cushion it well. A 3-inch layer of wood chips is one choice; increase the depth to 6 inches under a swing. Shredded bark holds up well, even in windy areas or on slopes. Use ¼- to 1-inch particles of bark. Sand provides another safe landing for falls. For children, the more sand the better—even a depth of 12 inches is not too much. Building a low wall around a play yard will help to contain loose materials, keeping the cushion thick and reducing the cost of replenishing.

Turf grass also makes a functional play surface. (But avoid mixtures that contain clover, as its flowers attract bees.) Keep grass about 2 inches high for maximum cushioning.

If your little one will be pedaling a riding toy or tricycle, plan a smooth concrete path at least 2 feet wide, preferably as wide as 4 feet. Gravel paths are frustrating for kids on wheels and for very young walkers.

The need for fencing along property boundaries is obvious. Also securely fence the play area from the driveway as well as from any pool, spa, or other body of water. You may need to fence off sharp or heavy tools, garden supplies, and garbage cans, too.

Gangplanks, turrets, and ramparts, all coated in electric colors, ensure plenty of fun.
Forgiving wood chips and ground cover provide a cushioned, safe play surface
and link the structure with the garden.

Buying components for a play center

Home centers typically carry a fairly wide selection of parts for building a play center—slides, swings, rope ladders, and monkey bars. Companies sell these parts separately or in kits. If you find a kit that matches your needs, buy it, even if it costs a bit more than separate components; the instructions will save you plenty of time and work.

Plan to build a play center that your children will still enjoy 5 years from now, when they are much bigger. A slide that seems too high or a rope ladder that is daunting now will be just right in a few years. Check to see that swings can be easily adjusted for height.

Elaborate structures look impressive, but often, simpler is better. A partially enclosed area 5 or more feet above the ground, reachable by ladder, is many children's idea of play heaven. Small children can exercise their imaginations for hours in a sandbox.

A. A cockeyed house in Brookside, Nebraska, seems almost to be melting. Bright colors and a fake chimney make it completely clear that this is a space for children. Plants with outlandishly large flowers and leaves complete this wacky scene.

B. Stained pine presents a quiet facade, but this structure packs playhouse, ladder, observation deck, slide, swing, and storage bins into one dynamic design.

C. The lucky owner of this rustic child-size cabin has a mini-garden out front—a trellis and a friendly nasturtium-covered scarecrow.

D. Playground equipment like this comes in kit form. Here, a single swing is set next to a modest climbing structure. Older children may climb on the horizontal piece above the swing. A bed of sand will cushion falls.

E. This child's house has many features of a grown-up home, with steps, a door, and a window flower box. Cedar shakes top the roof. Blue painted plywood siding is trimmed with white boards at the corners and eaves.

F. How can you build a tree house without damaging a tree? Try setting a playhouse on stilts. Massive 6-by-6 posts, sunk deep in holes that are filled with concrete, provide enough lateral strength to keep this structure from swaying, even when children swing from the railing.

PONDS AND FOUNTAINS

It doesn't take much water to soothe the soul—even the smallest pond can have a cooling effect on a garden. The size of your pond will be restricted by the space available, but its shape and style are limited only by your imagination. If you wish to start small, consider the portable decorative pools available at garden centers and statuary stores, or create your own tub version (see page 299).

Large traditional ponds of brick, concrete, fitted stone, or tile can blend into contemporary gardens as easily as formal ones. They present the opportunity to introduce color and texture to the garden with aquatic plants such as water lilies and water hyacinths. A raised pond with brick walls provides a classic home for goldfish and koi.

Running water features fall into one of three categories: spray fountains, waterfalls, and spill fountains. Spray fountains are most suitable for formal ponds and are made versatile by assorted heads that shoot water in massive columns or lacy mists. Waterfalls send a cascade toward the pond from a simple outlet pipe. Spill or wall fountains flow from the outlet into a pool or series of tiered pans or shelves. They're good choices for smaller gardens and can even stand alone, independent of ponds (see pages 296–299).

Placing the pond

The obvious spot for a pond is where everyone can enjoy it. But because children find ponds irresistible, the safest locations are in fenced backyards. Check with your local building department about any requirements for fencing with self-latching gates, setbacks from property lines, electric circuits for pumps and lights, and pond depth. Generally, for ponds less than 24 inches deep you will not need a building permit.

If you are planning to add plants or fish to your pond, first consider the microclimate in your garden. The pond must be protected from wind and be situated away from deciduous trees that shed leaves and twigs into the water. Don't choose a low-lying area that will constantly overflow in wet weather. The backyard isn't the only

Water trickles from a rustic spout into this rock-edged pond set with log stepping-stones.

place for a pond. The addition of moving water to a front patio or entryway cools the air and blocks the noise of passing traffic as well.

Often it's the border that harmonizes the pond with the surrounding landscape. The choices are many: a grass lawn; an adjoining bog garden or rock garden (often located at one end of a sloping site); native stones and boulders; flagstones laid in mortar; a wide concrete lip; brick laid in sand or mortar; redwood or other rot-resistant wood laid as rounds or upright columns; terra-cotta tiles; or railroad ties.

You can find flexible pond liners at garden centers or through mail-order catalogs. Although PVC plastic is the standard material, it becomes brittle with exposure to the sun. More UV resistant—but twice the price—are industrial-grade PVC and butyl-rubber liners. Some pool builders prefer EPDM, a roofing material available in 10- to 40-foot-wide rolls. Most liners can be cut and solvent-welded to fit odd-shaped water features.

Another option is a preformed fiberglass pond shell. A number of shapes and sizes are available, but many are too shallow to accommodate fish. Although these cost more than PVC-lined pools, they can be expected to last longer—up to 20 years.

A. Rock is the theme of this pond: stepping-stones lead up to the pond, and a bridge of stone slabs leads across it to the rock garden. A spray fountain tucked behind the juniper shoots water into the pond.

B. Properly designed, a constructed pond can become a "natural" feature. The plastic liner, circulating pump, and coping stones that form this pond are hidden by plants that thrive both in and around the pond.

C. The clean lines of this square pond are enhanced by the water lilies floating on its surface; only the burbling fountain breaks the horizontal plane. The pond's dark liner intensifies reflections and produces a mirror effect.

A SIMPLE POND

Outlet is 120 volts and powers pump

Plant shelf

Sand bed, 2 inches thick, cushions liner

Submersible pump circulates water to waterfall or fountain jet

Prefilter helps keep pump free of debris

Flexible liner follows shape of hole; tucks under flagstone edgings

Depth of 24 inches is best for plants and fish

Under the gaze of a garden gnome, a spill fountain sends water trickling down tiered rocks and into the small pool tucked at the end of this deck. The beautifully arranged rocks of the fountain are echoed in the stones that edge the border planting.

This fish fountain not only adds a playful touch, it recirculates and aerates the water so that plants and fish can thrive. It needs to run about 20 hours a week to do its job. Large coping stones anchor the pool's plastic liner.

Building a pond

Garden ponds range from complicated formal reflecting pools and deep, plant-filled koi ponds with sophisticated pumps and filters to simple ornamental styles with just a couple of water plants and a few goldfish. A do-it-yourselfer can easily build a pond like the one shown at left—much of the work lies in excavating the hole and adding a sand bed for cushioning. Complete step-by-step instructions are given on pages 394–395.

The sound and sight of water tumbling down a small stream and over a waterfall can add to the pleasure of a pond. To create a stream, mound up soil collected during the pond excavation, then form a waterway in the mound and cover it with a length of liner material. Stack broad, flat rocks like steps, overlapping and slanting down from one level to the next.

A submersible pump will circulate water from the pond to the head of the waterfall or stream. You can find a variety of pump sizes at garden centers or through mail-order pond suppliers. (The volume of water and the height of its lift determine the size of the pump required.) A built-in flow-reducing valve on the pump's outlet side will reduce the flow of water in the falls. Most pumps come with a small strainer on the intake side, but this can easily become clogged with debris. It's best to add a large prefilter, available from the same sources.

To power the waterfall or fountain pump, or any adjacent lighting, you'll need a 120-volt outdoor outlet with a ground fault circuit interrupter (GFCI) near the pond. You may need to get an electrical permit before installing a new outdoor outlet.

Installing a rigid liner

One of the easiest ways to add a water feature to your yard is with a rigid pond liner. (For a slightly more elaborate setup, see pages 394–395.) Buy one at a garden center or home center. To keep the water clean, install a simple submersible pump with a prefilter. If you buy a solar-powered pump, you won't have to run an electrical line.

Set the shell in position on the ground, and trace its outline by pouring a line of sand all around it (photo A). Dig a hole that is 2 inches deeper and wider than the liner, to accommodate a layer of sand. You will probably need to set the liner in the hole to discover where more digging is needed.

Cover the bottom with 2 inches of wet, well-packed sand; if the sand starts to dry out, moisten it with a hose set on "mist." Set the liner in the hole, and adjust it for level (photo B). Run water into the pond liner until it is about half full.

Add about 4 inches of moist backfill sand all around the liner, and tamp it firm. Check for level, add 4 more inches, and so on until the sides are filled. Add backfill to create a gentle slope away from the liner. Set flagstones all around the liner, positioned so they hide the liner's lip (photo C).

STREAMS AND WATERFALLS

If your property is without a natural stream that can be incorporated into your garden design, consider creating one. The style of your garden and home will guide your choice. Whether your property is in the country or the suburbs, formal or informal in character, you can still fulfill your wish for running water.

A waterfall may gurgle gently downward or cascade dramatically in a dead fall of 3 feet or more. After it is installed, you can change a waterfall's character by moving a boulder or two. Streams have irregular features that follow what appears to be nature's own design. Of course, the beauty of creating your own stream is that you can enhance what nature offers. Locate it in an area with a change of grade from high to low. Ideally, the water will follow a course marked by obstacles — rocks, ledges, or weirs (a notch through which water flows) — to change the pace and direction of the flow of water. You can position rocks to help the water cascade and fall in a pleasing manner over ledges and boulders. Create areas for it to pool along its descent. At the sides of the stream, well-placed naturalistic plantings will enhance the scene. The water will eventually collect in a pool at the foot of the stream, to be pumped back to the source through PVC piping camouflaged by plants or buried underground.

A

A. Small boulders form the basis for a waterfall and are strewn throughout this tranquil pool. An unseen pump circulates water.

B. If a yard slopes steeply, take advantage of the grade and install a high waterfall. This one has several small ponds. The entire structure is formed with plastic liner and boulders.

C. In this Minnesota yard, a well-designed stream flows down a gentle slope lined with daylilies, coreopsis, and tumbling plants. The stream base is a plastic liner set in a trench, then covered with rocks and gravel.

POOLS

I n recent years, swimming pools have been trimmed to fit home landscapes rather than overpower them. High operating costs and increased maintenance, coupled with smaller lots and smaller families, mean that most homeowners need to tailor a pool's size and design to their needs. So before you fall in love with a pool design, ask yourself a few questions.

Are you lap swimmers, or do you like to just soak in the pool? How much available space do you have? Don't rule out a pool because you think you don't have room; some can be shoehorned into tight sites and constructed on limited budgets.

The architectural maxim "form follows function" definitely applies to pools. Children need a wide, shallow area; lap swimmers require a long, straight section. Unless it will be used for diving, a pool need not be deeper than 4 to 5 feet. For lap swimming, one long axis, preferably 40 feet, will suffice; the width can be as little as 7 or 8 feet.

When deciding where to put your pool, you will need to study the sunlight patterns in your garden, at least through the swimming season. If winds regularly blow through your property, look for the most protected spot, or install plantings or other barriers to block the winds. A pool can be installed on a hillside if you use retaining walls, but installation is much simpler and less costly on level ground.

Because of its size, you may not be able to make your pool completely private. In general, however, the more secluded it is from neighbors and passersby, the more comfortable you'll be. Although the pool needn't be immediately adjacent to your house, there should be clear access from the pool to a changing room and bathroom. You'll also want it to be convenient to reach—and well lit—in the evening.

Plan for a paved area or a deck surrounding or adjoining the pool. As a rule, the poolside area should be at least equal to the area of the pool itself, and it should drain away from the pool. Install a nonskid surface that keeps as cool as possible and won't reflect light. It's best to isolate lawns and planting beds from the pool; otherwise, swimmers will drag grass and soil into the pool with each entry.

With the addition of boulders, flagstones, bridges, and other free-form edgings, naturalistic pools and adjacent spas can double as garden ponds. Two other intriguing options are the vanishing-edge pool, where the pool

A

A. Concrete forms most of the coping and patio surface around this formal pool and spa. Joint lines have been drawn in the concrete to give the impression of separate cut stones. A small section of decorative tiles adds just enough color. Water in the spa empties into a lower pool and is continually recirculated while the spa operates.

B. This rectangular swimming pool looks anything but boxy because it is surrounded with natural features. Shrubs, flowering plants, and stone retaining walls soften its edge. In the foreground, a garden pond with lily pads and stone edging sprouts marshy plants.

C. Three rows of dark blue tiles and one row of white tiles with a Spanish design decorate one side of this swimming pool. The tiles face a retaining wall that holds a flower bed and a statue. At rear, a waterfall flows through trailing vines.

merges with a surrounding view, and the "wade-in" pool, which helps swimmers, and especially children, enter the water gradually.

Pool equipment includes the pump, heater, and filter. You'll need to provide a concrete slab to support them, ideally hidden from sight and sound by a screen, shrubs, or a lushly planted trellis. Place the slab between 25 and 50 feet from the pool: any closer, and the noise may be overwhelming; any farther away, and you'll need larger equipment to pump water the extra distance.

Before building a swimming pool, look into the legal requirements set forth in deed restrictions, zoning laws, and building, health, and safety codes. Also, familiarize yourself with the building codes that apply to associated structures such as decks, fences, and overheads.

Constructing a pool

Pools can be built above ground or completely or partly in-ground. Fully in-ground pools are accessible from patio areas and fit best into most landscapes, but both aboveground and partly in-ground pools can be integrated into your garden's design.

For the structure, concrete (usually sprayed as gunite or shotcrete and reinforced with steel) combines workability, strength, permanence, and flexibility of design. Interior finishes include paint, plaster, and tile, in ascending order of cost. To keep the price down, save tile for details—edgings, step markers, and around the waterline.

Vinyl-lined pools are usually much less expensive than concrete because the liner is prefabricated and because the pool can be installed in as little as a few days. The liner generally rests on a bed of sand and is supported by walls made of aluminum, steel, plaster, concrete block, or wood. These walls can extend above grade, making them especially economical for sloping sites. Vinyl is not as durable as concrete, but leaks can be repaired.

Fiberglass pools consist of a one-piece rigid fiberglass shell supported by beds of sand. These pools are also fairly quick to install, but the choice of pool shapes and sizes is limited.

Some homeowners choose to start out with aboveground pools, such as the familiar vinyl-lined pool. Since no excavation is required, an aboveground pool can be easy to install and certainly costs less than an in-ground type. These installations, whether temporary or permanent, are most successfully integrated into a garden's design when recessed at least partly below grade and built with a surrounding deck or raised platform.

If you are inheriting an older pool with your new home, there are ways to update it. New edging (called coping) or a deck surround can dramatically improve the look of an old pool. Surrounding a pool with a new selection of plants can also transform its appearance and help merge the pool with the landscape. The addition of a spa or a waterfall is another way to give a pool new appeal.

Pool Safety

For pool owners with children—or with young visitors or neighbors—accidents remain a constant threat. That is why all swimming pools require protective barriers.

Although height requirements vary, most communities insist that properties with pools have a fence that completely encloses the yard (or the fence might surround three sides of the garden and connect to the house). The fence should have self-closing gates with self-latching mechanisms that are beyond the reach of young children.

Another fence, at least 5 feet tall, should enclose the pool or separate it from the house. If it has vertical bars, they should be no more than 4 inches apart, and the fence should have no horizontal pieces that could provide toeholds for climbing. The pool should be clearly visible from the house; panels of safety glass, clear acrylic, or see-through mesh can enhance the view.

All gates to the pool should be child resistant, self-closing, and self-locking. Areas immediately outside the pool fence should not have chairs or other objects that can be easily moved or climbed.

Doors and windows that lead from the house to the pool can be made more secure with additional locking mechanisms installed at least 5 feet above the floor. Options for sliding glass doors include locks for the top of the moving panel and its frame, automatic sliding door closers, or removable bars that mount to the frame.

A properly installed and approved safety cover is also critical. The safest types either have tracks mounted to the decking or fastening devices set in the pool deck (this type is especially good for odd-shaped pools). Never allow swimming in a partially covered pool; completely remove the cover before entering the pool.

SPAS AND HOT TUBS

Whether the focal point of a garden or a private retreat, a hot tub or spa has understandable appeal—an invigorating bath alfresco, enlivened by jets of water that accommodates both social and solitary soaks.

Hot tubs differ from spas in materials and form, not function. Both use virtually identical support equipment to massage bathers with hot, bubbling water, but hot tubs are large, straight sided, and barrel shaped and are made of wood.

Proponents of hot tubs appreciate wood—the way it feels, its aroma, and its natural appearance. They also prefer the generally deeper soak of tubs composed of redwood, cedar, teak, or other woods. These materials require careful maintenance, however. Too much chlorine or bromine can degrade wood; too little allows bacteria to grow. And wooden hot tubs must not be allowed to dry out or leaks can develop as the staves shrink.

Spas depart from the rustic simplicity of hot tubs, running the gamut of design choices from boxy portable models to installations of pool-sized proportions. The portable, or self-contained, spa is more like a home appliance—it doesn't have to be permanently installed and comes as a complete unit, ready to be plugged into a 120-volt outlet (or wired to a 240-volt circuit). Its support equipment is part of the package. A "skirt," typically of redwood, surrounds the shell.

In-ground types can be set into a hole dug into the ground or into an above-grade surface such as a deck. Shopping for an in-ground spa means choosing between a factory-molded shell made of acrylic reinforced with fiberglass or high-impact thermoplastics, or a more expensive, longer-lasting shell made of concrete.

Concrete spas can be custom designed, allowing for a virtually limitless range of shapes and sizes. They are also the most durable. Often adjuncts to swimming pools, concrete spas enjoy a longer season of use than swimming pools. After the pool has been closed for the cold season, the spa's hot, bubbling water keeps bathers comfortable while the leaves fall and the snow flies.

An offshoot of the spa industry is the increasingly popular "swim spa"—an elongated version of an in-ground spa. Strong hydrojets in swim spas create currents that allow bathers to swim for miles—without moving forward an inch.

Strictly symmetrical, the alignment of this circular spa, pool, and paving establishes a formal mood. A round brass bowl, transferring water from spa to pool, adds a finishing touch to the circular theme.

A

Spa logistics

A number of practical considerations will enter into your choice of a spa site. Take a careful look at the sun and wind patterns in your yard. Try to anticipate when you're likely to use the spa or tub; then find one or more sites where sun, shade, and wind will be to your liking at that time of day.

If the spa or tub will be the hub of social gatherings, if you plan to use it at night before retiring, or if you think you'll use it in the cold seasons, you'll want to install it near or on a patio or deck attached to the house. If you'd rather soak in seclusion, consider a site away from the house—perhaps a quiet, unused corner of your property.

Unless you choose a self-contained spa, plumbing and the spa's support system also govern placement. Heaters, pumps, and filters require connections to electric and gas lines. If you're using solar heating panels, which are usually placed on the roof, this will dictate a site near the house.

Regardless of where the spa or tub is located, you'll feel more comfortable if it is well hidden from passersby. Build an arbor or a gazebo around the spa, or screen it with live plantings or an arrangement of fences and walls.

You'll also need to provide a way of getting to the tub that's safe and comfortable for bare feet. A paved walk from the house would be ideal, with masonry or wood paving around the spa or tub itself.

Many spas come with built-in low-voltage lights. But you'll want to add additional lighting to illuminate steps, deck edges, and other potentially hazardous places.

Just as they do for swimming pools, local laws require that spas and tubs have secure covers to keep unsupervised children out of the water. Consult local zoning ordinances to find out what covers, fencing requirements, setback limits, and other equipment are required. Spa covers also save on electricity by retaining heat.

A. Like a swimming hole at the bottom of a wooded hillside, this spa is shielded by plants, including brilliant red azaleas, a fothergilla, and a blooming dogwood. A small waterfall from the spa flows into the swimming pool.

B. This bubbling hot tub invites fresh-air bathing in the perfect privacy of a jungle of greenery. Safe and comfortable underfoot, the wooden decking surrounding the tub contrasts cleanly with the plant foliage.

A SPA SURROUND

Overhead screens sun, weather, and wind

Privacy screen

Skirt hides the spa's support system. Built-up perimeter doubles as bench seating

Wooden decking provides insulation and absorbs moisture. Space decking boards for best drainage

Downlights increase safety at night

STEPS

In addition to their obvious practical function—as a transition between different levels or from one garden feature to another—steps can be an accent that sets the mood for an entire landscaping scheme.

Most dramatic are wide, deep steps that lead the eye to a garden focal point. A set of stairs can also double as a retaining wall, a base for planters, or additional garden seating space.

Materials influence step styles. Poured concrete and masonry block usually present a formal, substantial look. Unglazed tiles and concrete pavers have a similar effect. Natural materials such as stone and wood add an informal touch and fit into less structured gardens. Informal steps also have a simpler construction (see pages 392–393).

Matching the building material used in a patio or for garden walls helps unite steps to a garden's overall landscaping. On the other hand, contrasting materials draw attention to the steps and the areas of the garden they serve. Combining materials can create a transition between unlike surfaces. For example, you can link a brick patio to a concrete walk with steps made of concrete treads (horizontals) and brick risers (verticals).

Regardless of the type of material you use, always put safety first. Treads should be designed to provide safe footing in wet weather. And steps should be adequately lit at night with unobtrusive, non-glare path lights or fixtures built into risers or adjacent step walls (see pages 290–293).

Scale is another important consideration. Principal entries require steps that are inviting and that allow more than one person to climb them at one time. Service-yard steps, on the other hand, can be scaled down to fit their more limited use.

Your garden layout and the steps' function will influence your decision about width. Simple utility steps can be as narrow as 2 feet, but 4 feet is the usual recommended width for outdoor steps. To allow two people to walk side by side, steps should be at least 5 feet wide.

Ideally, the depth of the tread plus twice the riser height should equal 25 to 27 inches. For both safety and ease of walking, the ideal

These wide wooden steps, flanked by exuberant annual plantings, will easily accommodate two people walking side by side.

dimensions are a 6-inch riser with a 15-inch tread. Though riser and tread dimensions can vary, their relationship remains the same. Risers should be no lower than 5 inches and no higher than 8 inches. Treads should never be smaller than 11 inches. And all the risers and treads in any one flight of steps should be uniform in size.

To design your steps, work out your plan in detail on graph paper. Experiment with different combinations of risers and treads, widths, and configurations to achieve the necessary change of level and most pleasing design.

Soften the edges of a series of steps, and help walkers find them without difficulty, by placing containers or open beds along their borders. You can even add planting pockets within a wide series of tiers, as long as the greenery won't impede smooth travel.

If your slope is too steep for even 8-inch risers, remember that steps needn't attack a slope head-on: sometimes the most appealing solution is an L- or even a U-shaped series of multiple flights of steps. Break the runs with a wide landing between, using the transition area to house a reading nook, a rose bed, or a wall fountain.

Rarely will the steps fit exactly into a slope as it is. You may need to cut and fill the slope to accommodate the steps. If you have questions about your site, or if your steps will touch a public access area such as a sidewalk or be connected to a building, you should contact your local building department.

A. Paving bricks of various colors form a retaining wall and a stepped path that wanders through crabapples in bloom.

B. Massive slabs of cut limestone form each step. Smaller cut stones provide edging for the steps and retain soil for flower beds.

C. The beautiful grain and warm color of this plantation-grown teakwood is enhanced by the walkway's simple design.

D. These steps are made by framing with landscaping timbers, then laying flagstones in a bed of sand.

WALLS

Walls define space, provide privacy and security, edit views, screen out wind and noise, and hold elevated soil at bay. They bring an unmatched sense of permanence to a garden; in fact, some of the world's oldest structures are walls. Once you've determined a wall's function, you can choose its location, height, width, and degree of visual screening. You'll also need to select materials that coordinate with the style and design of your house and existing garden structures.

Among the typical materials for garden walls are bricks or blocks, uncut stone, and poured concrete. With bricks or blocks, you can choose a decorative pattern for laying the courses, incorporate a solid or openwork face, vary the thickness, and employ combinations of materials. Glass-block sections let light pass through, as do upper edgings of lath, lattice, and trellises.

In the hands of an experienced mason, stone can create walls that appear integral to a landscape. Stone that is prominent in your region will look the most natural in your garden. Poured concrete offers more design possibilities because surface texture and shape are established by wooden forms. Most of the work goes into constructing and stabilizing these forms; the actual "pour" is accomplished quickly.

Before beginning any wall, ask your local building department about regulations that specify how high and how close to your property line you can build, what kind of foundation you'll need, and whether the wall requires steel reinforcement. Many municipalities require a building permit for any masonry wall more than 3 feet high. Some may require that the wall be approved by an engineer.

Retaining walls

You can tame a gentle slope with a single low retaining wall or a series of garden steps that hold the surface soil in place. But if your slope is long and steep, consider building two or three substantial walls to divide it into terraces, which you can then enhance with plantings (see pages 388–391).

Engineering aside, you can build a retaining wall from any of the materials discussed above. Wood is another option for retaining walls, whether in the form of various-size boards or railroad ties or wood timbers set vertically or horizontally.

On a low, stable slope, you can lay uncut stones or chunks of broken concrete without mortar or footings. Fill the soil-lined crevices with colorful plantings.

New systems for building concrete-block retaining walls don't require you to mix a single bag of concrete. These walls are built with precast modules that stack or lock together via lips, pins, or friction. They are ideal for building 3- or 4-foot retaining walls (see page 391).

A. This low, lattice-style wall encloses a perennial garden, yet the spaces between the bricks allow air and light to pass through—and give passersby a glimpse of the plantings beyond.

B. The height of this mortared stone wall could make it seem forbidding if it were not for the graceful arched window opening into the garden.

C. A timber wall retains a steep bank planted with peonies, barberry, and English ivy.

Wall-building basics

Regardless of the type of wall you plan to raise, you will have to support it with a solid foundation, or footing. Poured concrete is about the best footing you can provide because it can be smoothed and leveled better than other materials. Usually, footings are twice the width of the wall and at least as deep as the frost line. But consult local codes for exceptions.

For very low walls (no more than 12 inches high) or for low raised beds, you can lay the base of the wall directly on tamped soil or in a leveled trench.

In most cases, a freestanding wall more than 2 or 3 feet high should have some kind of reinforcement to tie portions of the wall together and prevent it from collapsing. Steel reinforcing bars, laid with the mortar along the length of a wall, provide horizontal stiffening. Placed upright (for example, between double rows of brick or within the hollow cores of concrete blocks), reinforcing bars in poured concrete add vertical strength that can keep a wall from toppling under its own weight.

Special steel ties of various patterns are made for reinforcing unit masonry and attaching veneers to substructures. An example is shown on the facing page.

Vertical columns of masonry, called pilasters, can be tied into a wall to provide additional vertical support. Many building departments require that they be used at least every 12 feet. Also consider placing pilasters on either side of an entrance gate and at the ends of freestanding walls. When you're building the foundation of your wall, the footing will have to be twice the width of the pilasters.

A. This patio surface of concrete slabs is softened by occasional crevice plants. A dry-laid flagstone retaining wall holds a profusion of black-eyed Susans.

B. The pleasing texture of this mortared stone wall, set into a gentle slope, blends well with the surroundings and provides a perfect stage for the low-mounding plants growing above it.

A BRICK WALL

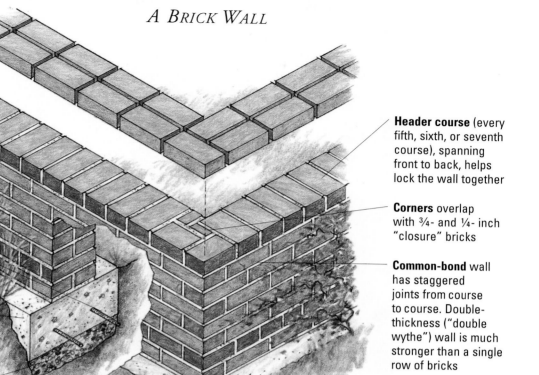

Reinforcing bars strengthen structure (check local codes)

Poured footing is typically twice wall's width and 12 inches deep (or as deep as frost line)

Gravel base ensures good drainage

Header course (every fifth, sixth, or seventh course), spanning front to back, helps lock the wall together

Corners overlap with ¾- and ¼- inch "closure" bricks

Common-bond wall has staggered joints from course to course. Double-thickness ("double wythe") wall is much stronger than a single row of bricks

A CONCRETE BLOCK WALL

Bond-beam block adds strength at top

Concrete block core is set with ⅜-inch mortar joints

Stone veneer set in mortar covers block core

Mortar

Wall ties help connect veneer to block core

Poured footing is typically twice wall's width and 12 inches deep (or as deep as frost line)

Reinforcing bars strengthen structure (check local codes)

LANDSCAPING WITH PLANTS

In a well-designed landscape, each plant has a planned effect. Whether star or supporting cast member, its color, texture, and form—even the plant's fragrance or fruit—play an important role in the garden scene. Trees, vines, and tall shrubs provide shade, privacy, and protection from wind. Perennials brighten beds and borders. Ground covers carpet the soil. Annuals give nearly instant color. And some of these plants attract wildlife, while others solve conditions of a problem site.

The challenge of landscaping is to place plants where their best qualities shine and can play off one another. Silvery foliage, for example, blends strong color combinations and illuminates the garden in moonlight. Spiky, tall grasses add movement to the garden as they shiver or sway to the rhythm of a breeze. Use the pages in this chapter to help create the garden of your dreams.

TREES

From spring's flowering dogwoods in the Missouri Ozarks to autumn's flaming sugar maples in the North Woods, trees define the Midwestern landscape. They're equally vital to the home garden. In fact, your first landscaping decision should be to choose your trees: their shade, shelter, screening ability, and framework affect not only living space but also all the other plants in the yard.

Trees are usually the most expensive individual plants you'll buy, but their cost is offset by their permanence. They can also help in energy conservation. In summer, a tree-shaded house requires less air-conditioning than a sun-drenched one. And if you plant deciduous rather than evergreen trees along the south side of the house, their leafless winter branches

---

Japanese tree lilac (Syringa reticulata) *adds graceful form to the garden throughout the year. In June, its branches are smothered with showy, fragrant, creamy white flowers. Handsome dark green foliage predominates during summer. In winter, its lustrous brown bark adds warm color to snowy landscapes.*

will allow sunlight into the home during the cold months of the year, reducing heating and lighting costs.

When you choose trees, think about the purpose you want them to serve. To block the sun, for example, select a tree that develops a sizable canopy, such as an ash or oak. For a screen, look for trees that retain branches on their lower trunks, like little-leaf linden or white pine; or combine trees that have bare lower trunks with shrubs or walls. (Note that evergreens are the trees to pick if you want a year-round screen.)

For a focal point, choose a tree with flowers, fruits, or especially attractive foliage or bark. Flowering crabapple, dogwood, and hawthorn, for example, provide spectacular color with both spring flowers and late-season fruit. 'Heritage' river birch has smooth, shiny, pink young bark; as the tree grows older, the bark curls in brown or blackish sheets. If it's foliage color you're looking for, you'll find choices ranging from countless shades of green to pale yellow to a red so deep it's almost black. And of course, many trees flaunt brilliant autumn leaf color: sugar maples, for example, turn from yellow to orange to red, while white oaks show burgundy and crimson.

For winter interest, plant a tree that has a striking bare silhouette, such as pagoda dogwood, or one with fantastically twisted, contorted twigs and branches, like Harry Lauder's walking stick (*Corylus avellana* 'Contorta'). Beautiful bark is also a plus in the winter garden; try 'Heritage' river birch, mentioned above, or amur choke-cherry, with glossy cinnamon brown bark.

For lovely looks as well as a bonus harvest of delicious fruit or nuts, choose a tree such as hickory, walnut, pawpaw, pear, or persimmon.

Tree characteristics

Tree silhouettes vary greatly from species to species (see facing page). Young nursery specimens don't always give a good idea of ultimate shape, though, so make sure you know what mature form to expect before you buy a tree.

All trees are classified as either deciduous or evergreen. Deciduous trees produce

TREE SILHOUETTES

Columnar Narrowly oval Cone shaped Globular Horizontally spreading Weeping

new leaves in spring, hold them through summer, then drop them in fall and remain bare in winter. Evergreens retain their leaves year-round. Needle-leafed evergreens include trees with needlelike foliage—fir, pine, and spruce, for example—and those whose leaves are actually tiny scales, such as arborvitae and juniper. These conifers (cone-bearing evergreens) look more or less the same in every season, though their color may change slightly during the cold months. They typically drop a few needles throughout the year. Broad-leafed evergreens, such as holly and rhododendron, have wide leaves similar to those of many deciduous trees, but they hold them all year. They thrive in only the southern part of the Midwest.

Matching the tree to the site

You've decided what role you want your trees to fill. Now, for best success, make your selection only from those trees that will flourish in your climate, easily surviving the area's lowest and highest average temperatures. Be sure, too, that the tree suits the garden site you have in mind. If you're selecting a tree for a poorly drained site, plant one that thrives in wet soil, such as bald cypress, swamp white oak, or river birch. If your soil is often dry, plant a drought-tolerant tree like a linden. If you long for a particular tree that is not perfectly suited to your environment, you can take steps to boost its chances of survival. For example, you might plant a borderline cold-hardy tree in a sheltered place near the house or a wall. Or locate a tree that prefers moist soil within easy reach of the hose.

PLANTING TREES

Take into account the ultimate height and growth rate of a tree before you buy it. You may be tempted to purchase a fast-growing species for quick shade or privacy, but if it overpowers its space, you'll be forced to remove it, prune heavily and often, or simply live with your mistake.

Trees known to have aggressive root systems or those that drop masses of fruit or leaves should be planted in the background, not near a pool, patio, or walk. Likewise, avoid putting trees with brittle wood in wind- or storm-swept locations. Instead, use them as specimens in protected locations and position them away from the house. Avoid trees that are particularly susceptible to pests or diseases. In most of the Midwest, for example, the European white birch often succumbs to borers. The hardy river birch, however, is virtually resistant to these pests.

A. Mature deciduous trees lend an established look and shade the front of the house in summer.

B. Flowering crabapple adds color to the front walk.

HOUSE

◀ NORTH

C. Needle-leafed evergreens screen the driveway year-round.

D. Semidwarf and standard fruit trees thrive when placed along south- and west-facing walls.

E. Flowering specimen tree adds beauty and gives privacy and shade.

SMALL PATIO TREES

A patio tree, like any other guest you invite into your garden, should be well mannered. Its roots should remain underground, rather than prying up paving or invading nearby flower beds. It shouldn't pepper the area with pollen or litter; it shouldn't attract pests or diseases. When fully grown, it should be small, ideally no taller than 40 feet—but at the same time, its canopy should be high enough to walk under and wide enough to cast shade for a bench or small table.

As long as you don't mind sweeping up autumn leaves, a small deciduous tree such as a Japanese tree lilac or miyabe maple works best. A disease-resistant flowering crabapple like 'Prairifire' or 'Donald Wyman', with tiny fruit that stays on the tree until eaten by birds in winter, is another good choice. Evergreens are not recommended: they often drop prickly needles, they cast

extremely dense shade, and they're typically rangy plants that require frequent pruning.

One of the best times to plant a patio tree is in April, when temperatures are cool and rains are likely. However, you can plant a container-grown specimen at any time during the growing season, as long as you water it deeply once a week in dry weather. The new tree should be small enough to lift without heavy equipment—typically no more than about 10 feet tall. Larger specimens may provide instant gratification, but they're often slower to put on new growth after transplanting than smaller ones.

Rabbits like to nibble on the bark of young trees, so protect the trunk with a loose collar of rabbit fencing. The collar should extend 1½ feet above the anticipated snowfall level. Remove the collar periodically to ensure that the trunk is pest free.

The distinctive rose-purple flowers of eastern redbud announce the arrival of spring in the Midwest. Reddish purple heart-shaped leaves soon follow, gradually turning dark green in summer, then yellow in autumn. Tiered and spreading branches, persistent seedpods, and dark, scaly bark provide winter interest.

Magnolia × soulangeana

Well-Behaved Patio Trees

Acer griseum
PAPERBARK MAPLE

Acer miyabei
MIYABE MAPLE

Amelanchier × grandiflora
APPLE SERVICEBERRY

Carpinus caroliniana
AMERICAN HORNBEAM

Cercis canadensis
EASTERN REDBUD

Cornus alternifolia
PAGODA DOGWOOD

Cornus mas
CORNELIAN CHERRY

Crataegus viridis 'Winter King'
GREEN HAWTHORN

Heptacodium miconioides
SEVEN-SON FLOWER

**Magnolia × soulangeana
(named selections)**
SAUCER MAGNOLIA

**Malus 'Prairifire' or
'Donald Wyman'**
FLOWERING CRABAPPLE

Prunus sargentii
SARGENT CHERRY

Syringa reticulata
JAPANESE TREE LILAC

Xanthoceras sorbifolium
YELLOWHORN

Caring for Landscape Trees

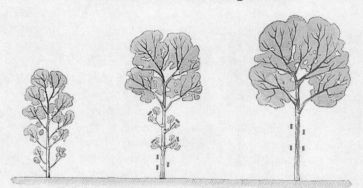

Forming a strong trunk. *A young tree develops a strong trunk faster if its lower branches are left on and allowed to grow for the first few years after planting. As the tree matures, shorten these lower branches to direct growth upward; eventually, you may remove them completely.*

Preserving the roots. *Strong, vigorous roots are vital to a tree's health: they sustain it and anchor it in the soil. If you install paving under the crown of an established tree, avoid solid materials, such as poured concrete, which keep air and water from reaching the roots. Instead, leave as much open soil as possible around the trunk and select a paving material or design that allows water to penetrate. Use loose materials, or set bricks or pavers in sand rather than cement.*

Any extensive soil removal around a tree (for construction of a retaining wall, for example) will take with it some of the roots, possibly weakening the tree. To preserve the existing grade beneath the tree, make elevation changes beyond the branch spread. Get professional advice for any soil-level change under the tree's branches.

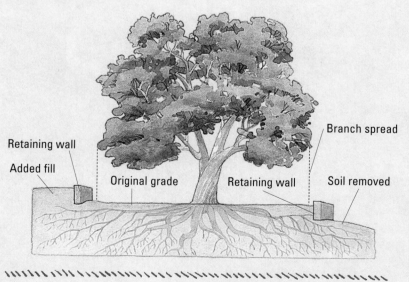

Retaining wall

Added fill

Original grade

Retaining wall

Branch spread

Soil removed

ENHANCING VIEWS

Trees are so valuable to any landscape that they should be incorporated into a view—or used to enhance it—whenever possible. They are wonderful for establishing a sense of perspective for distant vistas, such as a body of water or mountains, thus creating closeness and intimacy within a grand panorama. And city lights become magical and animated when seen through leafy, rustling branches at night.

Occasionally, however, trees interrupt key parts of a view and require selective pruning. Pruning to perfect a view must be carried out without endangering the health of the tree. Depending on how you wish to frame the view, several techniques will accomplish this goal: windowing, thinning, skirting up, or crown reduction. If you are not an experienced pruner, don't attempt to prune large trees. Hire a professional arborist who knows how to do the job properly. In many states, arborists must be licensed and must carry their own insurance; you can find an arborist by checking in the Yellow Pages under Trees, by asking for recommendations from friends, or by contacting the American Society of Arborists.

If you are skillful enough to remove a good-size tree limb, look for its branch collar—a raised lip at the junction of the trunk and the limb. Make a preliminary cut on the underside of the branch just beyond the collar. This will prevent the falling limb from tearing bark on the trunk. Then cut through the branch from the upper side. Avoid using pruning paints or tree sealant to seal the wound; these products have no effect on a tree's ability to resist infection.

If pruning alone won't open up views, consider having the trees removed. Keep some trees on the edges of your outlook, however, as these are the ones that frame the view.

Thinning. Selectively pruning the branches of a midrange tree can open up views, and gives a tree better wind tolerance. Do not prune the main limbs, but clear out bunches of foliage and the smaller branches that grow between them (below). Remove weak limbs and vertical water sprouts first, and any branches that are rubbing or crossing each other. Then you will have a better view of the overall branch shape and can prune selectively along the main limbs. As you work toward the ends of each main limb, prune less vigorously in order to leave a natural-looking, broad, and leafy top.

Windowing. Some trees that are close to a house or patio grow so densely that they block views of the surrounding landscape. By selectively removing some of the lateral branches (above), you can open up the tree, creating fully framed views—or windows—of whatever lies beyond. When you window a tree on one side, balance it with some pruning on the opposite side, even if both sides are not obstructing the view.

Skirting up. Removing some of the lower limbs (also known as limbing up) of a mid-range tree can reveal a view without ruining the lines of the tree (left). As a rule of thumb, don't skirt up more than half of the tree's height, less if possible. If the tree is top-heavy, thin it so that it doesn't look like a lollipop.

Crown reduction. To lower a tree's canopy, use a technique called crown reduction, which reduces the size of the tree while retaining its natural growth lines (right). Prune the tallest branches as far down to the trunk as possible but near small side branches that point in the same upward direction. If there are no such branches, track the tall limb down to one of its own upward-pointing, robust secondary branches. Cut just above this branch.

Trees vs. Power Lines

Before you plant a tree, take a minute to look overhead. If you see power lines, you can save the tree, the power company, and yourself some future grief by choosing a tree with a mature height of 25 feet or less.

Many beautiful small trees thrive in the Midwest (see page 205) and won't threaten power lines. Choose a disease-resistant flowering crabapple such as 'Adams', 'Prairifire', 'Red Jewel', 'Sugar Tyme', or 'Adirondack'. If you prefer an evergreen, opt for a dwarf Serbian spruce or other dwarf conifer—when mature, these are only a fraction as tall as their full-size relatives.

If you already have a large tree with branches reaching into the power lines, you have two choices: pruning the tree before the power company does or having the tree removed. A trained arborist should be able to thin or reduce the crown of the tree. By removing entire lateral branches and shortening others by cutting them back to a fork, the tree still retains a fairly natural shape. Reject any proposal to "top" the tree—that is, to cut off a large portion of the crown in an attempt to shorten the plant. Topping is disastrous, resulting in unsightly stumps and weak, fast-growing upright branches sprouting from every cut. Not only will the tree suffer and possibly become unstable, but new growth will soon threaten the lines again.

PLANTING UNDER TREES

A lawn won't thrive in the shade under mature trees but many colorful perennials do. Many plants that prefer partial shade will prosper beneath the branches of a tree such as pagoda dogwood or river birch. The dense canopy and surface roots of a Norway maple or sycamore, however, present a challenge. Plants beneath these branches must cope with heavy shade and dry soil caused by tree roots that quickly slurp up available water.

Barrenwort *(Epimedium)*, yellow archangel, and other ground cover plants that thrive in dry soil offer an attractive solution. You can also increase your choice of plants if you remove a few selected branches from the tree to allow more light and rainfall to reach the plants. Create interesting effects by combining plants of different foliage texture and color.

A. 'Hermann's Pride' yellow archangel *(Lamium galeobdolon)* lights up the shade with its variegated foliage. In spring, its yellow flowers brighten the garden. A good choice for dry shade beneath a tree, 'Hermann's Pride' grows in slowly enlarging clumps, unlike the rampant-spreading species.

B. Hosta and sedge *(Carex)* grow best in dappled shade and moist soil. Both are good choices for planting under an oak or other deep-rooted tree.

C. In filtered shade beneath high branches, deep pink hydrangea flowers add an attractive splash of bright color. Hosta, fern, and bishop's weed *(Aegopodium podagraria* 'Variegatum') add contrasting forms and colors.

A SHADE GARDEN

A profusion of shade-loving perennials flourishes in the dappled light beneath a pagoda dogwood. At the garden's edge, the foliage of a red-leaf Japanese barberry shrub adds summer-long color while casting welcome shade on a planting of Lenten roses. Throughout the growing season, perennials offer a parade of flowers in soft hues, accented by leaves of blue, gold, or green.

Planting area: 32' × 12'

The Plants

PERENNIALS

A. Alchemilla mollis
LADY'S-MANTLE **(2)**

B. Anemone × hybrida 'Honorine Jobert'
JAPANESE ANEMONE **(6)**

❉ **Cimicifuga simplex**
KAMCHATKA BUGBANE **(5)**

C. Arrhenatherum elatius bulbosum 'Variegatum'
BULBOUS OAT GRASS **(1)**

❉ **Iris sibirica 'Butter and Sugar'**
SIBERIAN IRIS **(3)**

D. Carex flacca (C. glauca)
BLUE SEDGE **(3)**

❉ **Hosta 'Lancifolia' (3)**

E. Carex morrowii expallida (C. m. 'Variegata')
VARIEGATED JAPANESE SEDGE **(3)**

❉ **Hosta 'Stiletto' (3)**

F. Digitalis purpurea (biennial)
COMMON FOXGLOVE **(5)**

G. Helleborus niger
CHRISTMAS ROSE **(5)**

H. Helleborus orientalis
LENTEN ROSE **(3)**

I. Hosta 'Gold Standard' (2)

J. Hosta sieboldiana 'Elegans' (1)

K. Lamium maculatum 'White Nancy'
DEAD NETTLE **(4)**

L. Thalictrum aquilegifolium
MEADOW RUE **(3)**

❉ **Astilbe 'Bressingham Beauty' (3)**

M. Thalictrum rochebrunianum 'Lavender Mist'
LAVENDER MIST MEADOW RUE **(3)**

❉ **Dryopteris goldieana**
GIANT WOOD FERN **(2)**

TREES AND SHRUBS

N. Berberis thunbergii 'Atropurpurea'
RED-LEAF JAPANESE BARBERRY **(2)**

O. Cornus alternifolia
PAGODA DOGWOOD **(1)**

P. Hamamelis × intermedia 'Arnold Promise'
WITCH HAZEL **(1)**

❉ **Hamamelis virginiana**
COMMON WITCH HAZEL **(1)**

❉ FOR COLDER REGIONS

PLANNING FOR FALL

From crimson-toned black gums in Ohio and Indiana to golden cottonwoods in the Great Plains, brilliant color splashes across the Midwestern countryside in autumn. Fall color gets noticed— and, increasingly, gardeners are looking for autumn-color specimens to add to home landscapes.

You'll find dozens of trees and shrubs from which to choose, including longtime favorites like sugar maple and red oak, beloved natives such as sassafras and Eastern wahoo *(Euonymus atropurpureus)*, and uncommon treasures like American smoke tree and fothergilla. For an unusual twist on autumn color, look to flowers— add a fall bloomer such as shrubby tube clematis, or seven-son flower, a small tree affectionately known in the Midwest as the crepe myrtle for the north.

Even the perennial border dresses for fall, with the gold and reddish purple foliage of plants such as peony, balloon flower, cushion spurge, and amsonia accenting fall flowers like bottle gentian and toad lily. And don't forget ornamental grasses; many offer showy flower plumes and colorful foliage as the year winds down.

Fall color is like a box of crayons: you pick the colors you want and create the combinations that suit you best. You might, for example, use brilliant yellows (honey locust, witch hazel, sweet birch) to separate clashing colors like pinkish red (from European spindle tree or coralberry) and orange red (from amur maple, mountain ash, serviceberry, or sumac). Remember that evergreens set off autumn colors and make them appear even more vibrant. And expect your garden to look a bit different every year—fall color varies, depending on the weather. Note, too, that color varies among plants within a single species, so it's best to buy a variety selected for dependable fall color, such as 'Autumn Jazz' viburnum or 'Autumn Splendor' painted buckeye.

A generation ago, Jack Frost got all the credit for the Midwest's colorful fall scenery, but today it's homeowners who deserve applause for the region's increasing fall color. Find what you like, make a note of it, and look for it in living color at your local nursery.

Like shining jewels, brilliant red rose hips sparkle against the multicolored autumn foliage of a hardy rugosa rose.

A. **Red sumac** and golden ornamental grasses create a serene setting in the soft glow of autumn sunlight.

B. **The foliage of fountain grass** arches gracefully over fall-blooming sedum.

C. **The brilliant scarlet foliage** of a red maple in fall dazzles a Midwestern landscape.

D. **A native hickory** shows off in autumn with dependable and long-lasting yellow foliage.

E. **Aster blooms** provide plenty of restful blues and purples in fall, contrasting beautifully with the season's predominant yellows, oranges, and reds.

TREES AND SHRUBS FOR THE WINTER GARDEN

You don't have to let cold winds and bitter temperatures extinguish your garden's beauty. With the right mix of trees and shrubs to provide texture and color, the sparkling snows and frosts of winter can transform an otherwise barren landscape into an enchanted garden.

Against the background of a winter sky, a snow-encrusted evergreen or the frosted limbs of a river birch provide delightful contrast and texture. For color, shrubs such as winterberry and Siberian or redtwig dogwood make striking seasonal standouts, as do deep green conifers—gorgeous with a dusting of white snow. Conifers can double as windbreaks; plant them along your garden's northwest corner to protect more delicate plants against winter's fiercest blasts. Good choices include spruce, pine, and white fir. A southern exposure, on the other hand, is the perfect spot for deciduous trees such as paperbark maple and Japanese tree lilac. Once they've shed their leaves, sunlight can freely enter the garden, bringing a little welcome warmth.

Take full advantage of your garden's winter features: plant trees and shrubs with striking bark, interesting branch structure, or vividly colored berries where you can easily see them from your windows, letting you enjoy the garden from indoors. And by all means, don't forget the birds: their liveliness and song can go a long way to brighten even the bleakest day. Keep feeders full and choose hardy specimen plants that provide food and shelter, such as juniper, yew, pine, hawthorn, and crabapple.

Achieving success in the winter garden is easy. The secret is to work in harmony with the season, staying open to all of nature's possibilities.

A. The rough, cinnamon-colored, peeling bark of a paperbark maple *(Acer griseum)* adds a warm touch in the winter garden and looks handsome against a backdrop of snow.

B. A generous mix of deciduous and evergreen trees and shrubs of varying densities and heights gives this snow-covered garden plenty of shape and visual interest.

C. The bright red stems of Siberian dogwood (*Cornus alba* 'Sibirica') bring welcome color throughout the winter.

D. Many ornamental grasses such as miscanthus remain erect throughout the year, adding their subtle beauty and color to the winter landscape.

Great Choices for Winter Gardens

EVERGREEN TREES

Abies concolor
CONCOLOR FIR

Chamaecyparis nootkatensis 'Pendula'
NOOTKA FALSE CYPRESS

Picea omorika
SERBIAN SPRUCE

Pinus cembra
SWISS STONE PINE

Pinus strobus
EASTERN WHITE PINE

DECIDUOUS TREES

Acer griseum
PAPERBARK MAPLE

Amelanchier arborea
SERVICEBERRY

Betula nigra 'Heritage'
HERITAGE RIVER BIRCH

Carpinus caroliniana
AMERICAN HORNBEAM

Cercis canadensis
EASTERN REDBUD

Cornus alternifolia
PAGODA DOGWOOD

Crataegus viridis 'Winter King'
GREEN HAWTHORN

Malus 'Prairifire'
FLOWERING CRABAPPLE

Prunus maackii
AMUR CHOKECHERRY

Salix matsudana 'Tortuosa'
CORKSCREW WILLOW

Syringa reticulata
JAPANESE TREE LILAC

Ulmus parvifolia
LACEBARK ELM

SHRUBS

Cornus alba 'Sibirica'
SIBERIAN DOGWOOD

Corylus avellana 'Contorta'
HARRY LAUDER'S WALKING STICK

Cotoneaster apiculatus
CRANBERRY COTONEASTER

Ilex × meserveae
BLUE HOLLY

Ilex verticillata
WINTERBERRY

Juniperus horizontalis 'Douglasii'
CREEPING JUNIPER

Taxus × media 'Tauntonii'
YEW

Thuja occidentalis 'Techny'
AMERICAN ARBORVITAE

TOP: *Corylus avellana* 'Contorta'
BOTTOM: *Ilex verticillata*

SHRUBS

I f your grandparents lived in the Midwest, chances are your childhood memories include the sweet scent of lilac blossoms and the "spring snowflakes" of falling spirea petals. Indeed, shrubs are a memorable part of the Midwestern landscape past and present, and an important part of your own home landscaping.

Shrubs are to the landscaper what throw pillows are to the interior decorator: the eye-pleasing "extra touch" that makes all the difference between bland and grand. These plants are terrific transition tools, filling that all-important eye-level gap between ground-level plantings and trees. They're also versatile

buffers, softening the hard lines of buildings, fences, driveways, and sidewalks. Take a closer look at landscapes you admire. Chances are, you'll see shrubs serving as the screens, frames, and backdrops that subtly, gently glue the picture together.

Set close to each other, shrubs form a living fence. Clipped boxwoods just a few feet high help define a formal garden. A staggered row of loose, flowery lilacs serves as a privacy screen. A hedge of thorny, dense shrubs, such as barberry or clipped hawthorn, makes an effective barrier. And don't forget to show off shrubs individually or in small groups: they are fine accents. A single

Vivid yellow-leaf barberries bring a beacon of light to this sunny border, complementing the pink flowers of dianthus. The colorful foliage persists throughout the growing season.

flowering specimen, such as viburnum or butterfly bush, can be an eye-catching focal point; a group of dwarf shrubs adds heft and structure to a mixed flower border.

Like trees, shrubs may be deciduous or evergreen. They grow in a variety of rounded, tapered, or fountainlike shapes. Many offer something extra—flowers, vivid fruit, or colorful foliage that gives them special seasonal appeal. In some cases, the blossoms are intensely fragrant; daphne and mock orange are two well-loved examples. And some shrubs, such as 'Royal Purple' smoke bush and 'Bonanza Gold' barberry, have foliage that is decorative throughout the growing season, not just in autumn.

From the hundreds of shrubs available, select those that best suit your garden—its soil, exposure, and available water. Azaleas and rhododendrons, for instance, thrive in the semishade beneath high-branching trees and prefer moist, well-drained acid soil. Shrub roses and lilacs, on the other hand, do best with bright light and a nearly neutral soil.

Considering size

It's difficult to imagine a shrub's ultimate size when you first bring it home from the nursery: newly planted, it almost always looks too small for the allotted space. Still, that yew now blotting out your neighbor's window was once a tiny mound just 2 feet high; that forsythia now looming over the walkway started life as a few wispy sprays. To save yourself hours of tedious pruning, keep each shrub's mature height and width in mind before you plant. Don't succumb to the urge to put it close to another shrub, a walk, or a doorway: unlike perennials, which are usually easy to transplant, your new shrub should be set out in its permanent home, a spot roomy enough to contain it comfortably as it puts on size. When the available spot is truly small, look for space-saving dwarf shrubs such as 'Minuet' weigela or 'Bronxensis' greenstem forsythia. And remember that annual flowers can do a beautiful job of filling gaps while you wait for newly planted shrubs to grow.

An old-fashioned favorite, Van Houtte spirea graces the land-scape with a springtime fountain of white blooms.

Pruning Needs

Most shrubs require some pruning to control size, maintain shape, and—in the case of most flowering shrubs—increase flower production. Prune spring bloomers such as forsythia, deutzia (shown above), and lilac as soon as blooms fade. Give summer bloomers such as panicle hydrangea, Japanese spirea, and potentilla a hard pruning in early spring. These shrubs produce flowers on the current year's growth; if they are allowed to grow unchecked, the quality and quantity of their flowers often suffer. Pruning encourages vigorous new shoots and buds. Spring pruning also ensures that the flowers of some tall summer bloomers, such as rose of Sharon, will remain low enough for you to see and enjoy.

Most deciduous shrubs send up new stems from the plant's base. To rejuvenate these plants and keep their vitality going, periodically remove the oldest and the weakest stems at their base (below left). Evergreens have a permanent framework of branches. Only dead or damaged branches need pruning (below right), though yews can be pruned more radically.

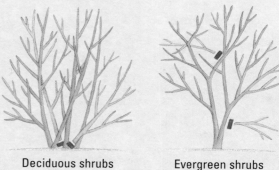

Deciduous shrubs   Evergreen shrubs

SHRUBS IN BORDERS

A border with both perennials and shrubs is a visual feast, more appealing than with either type of plant alone. Shrubs lend permanence to flowering borders that change with the seasons. In winter, shrubs may be the only source of visual interest. In other seasons, they can be focal points and accents or, conversely, serve as backdrops for showier plants. Shrubs that reflect the color or texture of nearby trees link the planting scheme to the surrounding landscape. The weight and substance of many shrubs contrasts with more delicate herbaceous plants. Flowering shrubs furnish color and many are fragrant, making them powerful attractants for birds and butterflies.

Select shrubs with a variety of foliage colors and blooms to keep the garden colorful in all seasons. The border at right uses ninebark, arrowwood viburnum, and spirea for bloom in spring, as well as Dyer's greenwood and 'New Dawn' rose for summer bloom. Throughout the growing season, shrubs also brighten the border with their colorful foliage. 'Dart's Gold' ninebark is yellow green from spring to early summer, while 'Goldmound' spirea's golden color persists all summer. In fall, the border is a blaze of color with pinkish red 'Rudy Haag' euonymus (or other noninvasive selection), orange-red fragrant sumac, and 'Autumn Jazz' viburnum's showy burgundy, orange, red, and yellow. A dark green juniper and an emerald green arborvitae play a supporting role during the summer, then take center stage in winter.

A. Viburnums prosper in the partial shade of this woodland border. Members of the most versatile and trouble-free group of shrubs, all viburnums have attractive flowers. Many kinds also grace the garden with colorful fruit and fall foliage.

B. A row of junipers serves as the perfect backdrop for golden privets and fountain grass in a border planned to give year-round interest. All are drought-tolerant plants that need little supplemental water once established.

C. Shrub roses dominate borders on both sides of a walkway. The bluish green leaves of sea kale (*Crambe maritima*) and sedum, each displaying masses of flowers in season, combine well with the silvery grasses (*Festuca* and *Miscanthus*) and the teal color of a garden shelter.

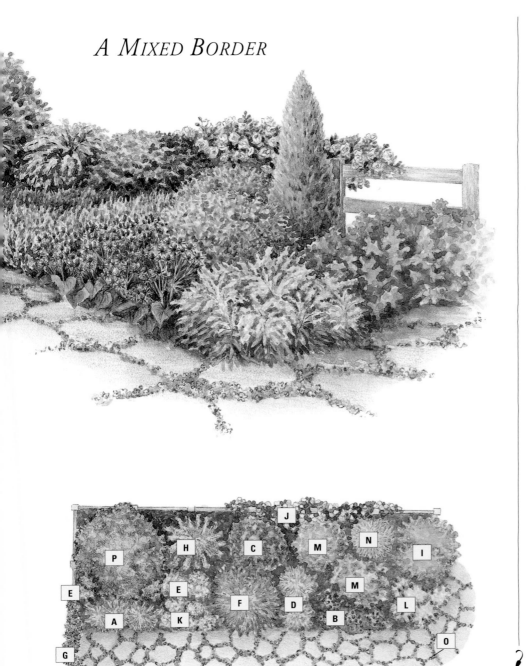

A MIXED BORDER

Planting area: 28' × 12'

The Plants

A. **Amsonia hubrechtii**
WILLOW BLUE STAR **(2)**

B. **Eryngium amethystinum**
AMETHYST SEA HOLLY **(4)**

C. **Euonymus alatus 'Rudy Haag'**
BURNING BUSH **(1)**

D. **Genista tinctoria 'Royal Gold'**
DYER'S GREENWOOD **(2)**

E. **Geranium macrorrhizum 'Ingwersen's Variety'**
BIGROOT CRANESBILL **(5)**

F. **Juniperus chinensis sargentii 'Glauca'**
JUNIPER **(1)**

G. **Lonicera sempervirens**
TRUMPET HONEYSUCKLE **(1)**

H. **Physocarpus opulifolius 'Dart's Gold'**
NINEBARK **(1)**

I. **Rhus aromatica 'Gro-Low'**
FRAGRANT SUMAC **(2)**

J. **Rosa 'New Dawn'**
ROSE **(1)**

K. **Scabiosa columbaria 'Butterfly Blue'**
PINCUSHION FLOWER **(5)**

L. **Solidago 'Golden Baby'**
GOLDENROD **(5)**

M. **Spiraea japonica 'Goldmound' (2)**

N. **Thuja occidentalis 'Emerald'**
AMERICAN ARBORVITAE **(1)**

O. **Thymus serpyllum**
MOTHER-OF-THYME **(MANY)**

P. **Viburnum dentatum 'Autumn Jazz'**
ARROWWOOD **(1)**

A TREASURE

Your grandfather may have spent hours fussing over leaf spot on his rose bushes—but don't think constant coddling is the price you'll have to pay to grow your own. Thanks to the efforts of plant breeders, you can now choose from a long list of disease-resistant roses. They bloom all summer long, too, not just in June like many older kinds. Some are star performers for Midwest landscapes.

SMALL HEDGES, EDGINGS. Floribunda roses bear large clusters of medium-size flowers atop compact, 2- to 5-foot-tall plants covered with glossy green leaves. Spaced 1½ to 2 feet apart, they make excellent hedges or edgings for garden paths. Dependable varieties include white 'Iceberg', pink 'Simplicity', yellow 'Sun Flare', and red 'Lilli Marleen'. The polyantha rose, a parent of many modern floribundas, carries abundant small flowers in big clusters. 'The Fairy' and 'Nearly Wild' are particularly attractive as hedges.

GROUND COVERS. These roses grow no taller than 2 feet and spread their canes widely, making them perfect for low raised beds and banks. Choose vigorous, disease-resistant ones such as 'Red Meidiland', with single flowers that bloom all season long.

FENCE DRAPES. Climbing roses ("leaners," really, because they don't cling to surfaces on their own) are particularly beautiful against weathered split rail fences. Easy-care types include red 'Blaze', pink 'Cl. The Fairy', and the deep pink shrub rose 'William Baffin'.

MIXED BORDERS. Some roses combine handsomely with perennials in mixed borders. 'Graham Thomas' (yellow English rose), 'Carefree Beauty' (coral pink shrub rose), and 'Henry Hudson' (double, white hybrid rugosa) all team up well with perennials such as catmint, cranesbill, lavender, and sage.

TRELLISES, ARBORS. Some climbing roses are quite vigorous and are at their best when supported on sturdy trellises or arches. Two excellent choices are 'New Dawn', with blush pink double flowers, and its offspring 'White Dawn'; they look romantic and old-fashioned, especially when trained against white latticework.

Succeeding with roses

Because winter temperatures drop to 0 degrees F and below in the Midwest, it's important to choose cold-hardy

OF ROSE GEMS

roses (see pages 220–221). Modern shrub types tolerate the region's bitter winters (and its blistering summers, too) much better than hybrid teas.

Whenever possible, purchase roses growing on their own roots rather than grafted roses. Even if cold weather kills the tops of own-root roses, they are apt to come back—and as the rose you want, not as the rootstock variety. If you buy a grafted rose, increase its chances of winter survival by burying the bud union (the swollen knob where the roots and the grafted top meet) 1 to 3 inches below ground; use the greater depth in the northernmost Midwest.

Plant roses where they'll receive at least 6 hours of sunlight each day. They also appreciate a spot protected from harsh winds, though they also need good air circulation. If you do plant in a windy location, you may want to tie the canes together in winter to protect them from breaking.

'Belle Story'

When you're looking for good advice about growing roses, think local. Talk to neighbors, consult with your Cooperative Extension Office, and visit nearby public gardens to see what grows well in your area. Contacting the American Rose Society (ARS) can be helpful, too. Composed of hundreds of local rose societies throughout the U.S., the ARS provides information to anyone interested in growing roses. It also rates every rose currently in commerce, on a scale of 1 to 10; those earning a score of 9 or 10 are designated "outstanding," while those with a score of 5 or lower are "of questionable value."

A. Full bloom in early summer. A cream-colored rose and a purple clematis entwine above brilliant pink peonies. With proper pruning of the rose and the clematis, the show repeats yearly.

B. Many different kinds of roses in a rainbow of colorful blooms thrive in Midwestern gardens. Here, a bucketful of freshly picked beauties awaits final cutting and arranging.

C. Large clusters of the ruffled, light pink blooms of 'Cl. The Fairy' cloak this sundial. A vigorous grower, this polyantha rose is a continuous bloomer with a compact, spreading habit.

What's Old Is New

Antique roses are those belonging to classes developed before 1867, the year the first hybrid tea rose was introduced. Variously categorized by parentage into albas, bourbons, Chinas, hybrid perpetuals, noisettes, moss roses, portlands, and early teas, their virtues have been rediscovered. They can be found where modern roses are sold, though specialist growers offer wider selections.

Some old roses bloom only in spring. They are superb for tumbling over a fence, filling in a mixed border, or providing a green backdrop for later-blooming flowers. Or, plant fragrant varieties in a corner of the vegetable garden. Repeat-blooming old roses (hybrid perpetuals, for example) are more suitable for highly visible areas.

Old roses range in habit from compact, 4-foot shrubs (China roses) to tall, 5- to 8-foot shrubs with opulent flowers (hybrid perpetuals). Some are vigorous, gangly shrubs with cup-shaped blooms (bourbons).

If you like the look of old roses but want something new, consider the modern English roses, which were created by British hybridizer David Austin. These vigorous and often disease-resistant roses were developed by crossing old roses with modern hybrid teas and floribundas. The resulting roses combine the form and fragrance of old roses with the repeat flowering and color range of modern hybrids. Plants vary from shrubs to shrubby climbers.

A. Old centifolia rose 'Fantin-Latour' spills over in midsummer with full, soft pink blooms. The shrub's sumptuous, fragrant flowers (inset) belie its tough, cold-hardy nature.

B. In fall, plump orange rose hips follow the blooms of a hybrid rugosa rose. Among many virtues, rugosas adapt to a wide range of soils and conditions. They are cold hardy, with handsome, disease-resistant, deeply veined leaves. Rugosa plants make excellent hedges.

C. Coral pink, semidouble blossoms of 'Carefree Wonder', the most famous of the Griffith Buck roses, spill over a path. Exceptionally disease resistant, this rose blooms spring through fall.

Roses for Cold Climates

WHITE

'Blanc Double de Coubert'
(HYBRID RUGOSA)

'Henry Hudson' (HYBRID RUGOSA)

'Madame Plantier' (HYBRID ALBA)

Rosa rugosa alba (SPECIES)

YELLOW

'Golden Wings' (SHRUB)

'Prairie Harvest' (SHRUB)

'Topaz Jewel' (HYBRID RUGOSA)

'William Baffin'

'Champlain'

RED TO DARK PINK

'Champlain' (SHRUB)

'F. J. Grootendorst'
(HYBRID RUGOSA)

'Hansa' (HYBRID RUGOSA)

'John Cabot' (SHRUB)

'Knock Out' (SHRUB)

'Roseraie de l'Haÿ'
(HYBRID RUGOSA)

'Rugosa Magnifica'
(HYBRID RUGOSA)

'William Baffin' (SHRUB)

PINK

'Belle Poitevine' (HYBRID RUGOSA)

'Carefree Beauty' (SHRUB)

'Carefree Wonder' (SHRUB)

'David Thompson'
(HYBRID RUGOSA)

'Delicata'
(HYBRID RUGOSA)

'The Fairy' (POLYANTHA)

'Fantin-Latour' (CENTIFOLIA)

'Frau Dagmar Hartopp'
(HYBRID RUGOSA)

'Great Maiden's Blush'
(ALBA)

'Jens Munk'
(HYBRID RUGOSA)

'Nearly Wild'
(FLORIBUNDA)

'Thérèse Bugnet'
(HYBRID RUGOSA)

DISPLAYING VINES

Lightweight wooden or metal trellises of different sizes can hold only lightweight climbers such as clematis. More sturdy are the types that have posts that can be anchored in the ground or in a large pot.

Freestanding trellises and arbors support permanent vines with hard, woody stems, such as grape or wisteria. The stems twirl up the posts, and the spreading foliage provides shade.

A sturdy wall bears the weight of heavy, vigorous growers such as trumpet vine or climbing hydrangea. Prune and tie to prevent the plants from sprawling.

VINES

Whether framing an entry, draping a pillar, scrambling over a tree stump, or just rambling along the ground, vines are the jewelry of the garden. Many have flowers in dazzling colors; some, such as sweet autumn clematis, honeysuckle, wisteria, and moonflower, add a sweet perfume as well.

Let vines blanket a fence or weave a delicate, lacy cover for a wall. A sturdy arbor supporting vines that cast cooling shade can become a haven for relaxing out of doors in warm weather. Because most annual vines grow fast, they're ideal for use as temporary screens. Shade a porch during summer by training moonflower or morning glory up lengths of twine or garden netting. Make a small deck or balcony more private by planting trailing vines such as black-eyed Susan vine in hanging baskets or other containers suspended from the eaves overhead.

Besides having a softening effect on walls, vines also greatly improve the appearance of other garden structures, such as lattice screens and gazebos. If necessary, tie the young vines to the structure with tree tape or strips of soft cloth until the stems begin to climb on their own. If your vines are clambering up vertical supports, they'll need less frequent clipping and training than vines trained horizontally. The latter tend to bloom more heavily, however, because their stems usually receive more sunlight.

Unlike its unruly cousins, native trumpet honeysuckle (Lonicera sempervirens) *decorates without taking over. Its tubular, bright orange-red flowers attract hummingbirds in spring.*

Vines Can Do Many Things

A. Soften a fence. Allow a vine such as the wisteria above, rambler rose, or trumpet honeysuckle to grow beside a fence and cascade its lavish flower sprays over the top. Another option is to use vines to hide an unsightly chain-link fence or disguise old or sagging wood. Vigorous growers such as clematis, honeysuckle, or silver lace vine easily weave through the open-worked fencing.

B. Create screens and boundaries. Quick climbers like morning glory or more permanent perennials such as the Boston ivy shown above or Virginia creeper can cover walls with color. Vines covering a boundary fence give privacy and increase the feeling of enclosure on the garden side, while the thick cover of greenery also serves as an attractive seasonal windbreak.

C. Highlight an entry. A vigorous vine such as the Dutchman's pipe shown below or English ivy creates welcome shade for the front porch. Or brighten the entry with colorfully blooming annuals such as hyacinth bean or cardinal climber or perennials like climbing hydrangea or perennial pea vine.

Choice Vines

PERENNIALS

Campsis radicans
TRUMPET VINE

Clematis × jackmanii
JACKMAN CLEMATIS

Clematis terniflora
SWEET AUTUMN CLEMATIS

Fallopia baldschuanica (Polygonum aubertii)
SILVER LACE VINE

Hedera helix
ENGLISH IVY

Hydrangea anomala petiolaris
CLIMBING HYDRANGEA

Lathyrus latifolius
PERENNIAL SWEET PEA

Lonicera × heckrottii
GOLDFLAME HONEYSUCKLE

Lonicera sempervirens
TRUMPET HONEYSUCKLE

Parthenocissus tricuspidata
BOSTON IVY

Wisteria floribunda
JAPANESE WISTERIA

ANNUALS

Cobaea scandens
CUP-AND-SAUCER VINE

Dolichos lablab
PURPLE HYACINTH BEAN

Ipomoea alba
MOONFLOWER

Ipomoea × multifida
CARDINAL CLIMBER

Ipomoea tricolor
MORNING GLORY

Thunbergia alata
BLACK-EYED SUSAN VINE

Lonicera × heckrottii

LAWNS

Throughout the suburbs and countryside of the Midwest, lawns are an integral part of the landscape, framing each house while also connecting it to the neighborhood. A lawn—often the simplest feature of a home landscape—serves as a foundation for the entire garden. And it need not be large to enhance the overall beauty of a property. A compact and well-designed grassy area is just as functional and handsome as an expanse of turf, and it requires much less work.

A well-tended lawn offers many assets to the home landscape. Pleasing to the eye and soft underfoot (yet durable enough to withstand foot traffic), a lawn offers an exemplary surface for entertaining, relaxing, and playing. It also helps show off other plants to their best advantage.

Lawn grass offers environmental benefits as well. It absorbs carbon dioxide and chemical pollutants such as sulfur dioxide and ground-level ozone from the atmosphere, and it releases oxygen. A lawn also stabilizes dust and pollen, muffles sound levels, and absorbs glare. A chemical-free lawn acts as a sponge, collecting surface water so that the underlying soil can filter out impurities and replenish underground aquifers with untainted water. Many songbirds are attracted by the "edge effect," where a lawn meets plantings of trees, shrubs, and flowers.

Lawns in the landscape

A lawn area needn't be square or rectangular. In a formal garden, for example, a small circle of lawn ringed by trees and flowers makes a beautiful centerpiece. A curved or kidney-shaped lawn directs the eye to a focal point, such as a specimen tree or sculpture. A grass path entices a visitor around a stand of shrubs to a private garden room beyond. And squares of turf alternated with paving create a striking patterned carpet for a seating area.

When designing a lawn, give serious thought to the amount of care grass requires. In a shady spot or on a dry slope, you may be better off planting a ground cover such as periwinkle or creeping juniper (see pages 228–229). If you prefer tending your plants to mowing the lawn, consider a low-maintenance grass such as buffalo grass (see pages 226–227).

Installing mowing strips around the perimeter of the lawn will also reduce the work required to maintain it. A ribbon of concrete, brick, or stone set slightly lower than lawn level will allow you to cut right to the edge of the grass. For quickest mowing, design your lawn with a simple shape, uninterrupted by plantings or decorative obstacles. To contain the lawn (as well as any plantings on the other side) invisibly, sink plastic or metal edgings in the ground along its border. If you plant a grass that spreads by stolons or rhizomes— such as bluegrass or zoysia—an edging 8 inches deep will keep the grass from invading nearby flower beds.

A

A. This narrow, curving lawn lends graceful lines that highlight flower borders filled with blooming coneflowers, bee balm, and other perennials. The relatively small grassy area, the deeply mulched perennials, and the edging strips between grass and flower beds keep mowing time and other yard maintenance to a minimum.

B. Many Midwesterners are opting for a meadow lawn filled with native wildflowers and grasses like the front yard shown here. This type of "lawn," first popularized by the Milwaukee environmental group The Wild Ones, offers summer-long color as well as a welcome habitat for birds and butterflies.

C. A lush carpet of green shows off flower beds and mixed borders to best advantage. The lawn flows around island flower beds, making it perfect for strollers who want to enjoy the flowers up close.

D. A buffalo grass lawn thrives in the dry Midwestern plains states with little or no supplemental watering. Spreading into a thick, durable carpet, this low-maintenance lawn seldom requires mowing.

Midwestern Lawn Grasses

 Buffalo Grass/Cool-Season Grasses
Cool-Season Grasses
Warm-Season Grasses/Transition Zone

The Midwest is famous for its extremes of weather. Temperatures can range from −50° to 100°F; annual precipitation may vary from 10 to 36 inches. For best success, any plant you choose for your garden will have to accept these variables—and that goes for lawn grasses, too. You'll also want to take into account the local soil, the amount of time you're willing to devote to maintenance, and, of course, your lawn's intended use: Will it be a play surface for children? A grassy "patio"? A manicured greenbelt between bright perennial borders?

Lawn grasses include cool-season and warm-season types. *Cool-season grasses* grow best in cool weather and slow down or go dormant in warm weather. Examples include Kentucky bluegrass, perennial ryegrass, tall fescues, and fine fescues. Though they're grown in much of the region, these grasses are best suited to the northern Midwest, where a mix of Kentucky bluegrass, perennial ryegrass, and creeping red fescue (one of the fine fescues) creates an attractive and durable lawn. *Warm-season grasses* grow best in warmer weather and go dormant or grow slowly in cool conditions; two examples grown in the Midwest are zoysia and buffalo grass. Warm-season grasses do well in the southern Midwest, a transition zone where cool-season grasses grade into or coexist with warm-season kinds. Use the map above to help you select the type of grass best suited to your region. For specific suggestions about lawn grass species or varieties for your area, check with your local nursery or Cooperative Extension Office.

CHOOSING THE RIGHT

*I*n all parts of the Midwest, a mix of Kentucky bluegrass, creeping red fescue, and perennial ryegrass is broadly adaptable, attractive, and quick to establish. For soils with a high pH and moderate salinity, try 'Dawson' or 'Ruby' creeping red fescue or plant a mix of creeping red fescue and hard fescue.

Where daytime temperatures remain at 90°F or above, and above 70°F at night, you might prefer zoysia or buffalo grass for a good, low-maintenance lawn. Or, for a more durable surface, try a blend (two or more varieties) of tall fescues. Buffalo grass also does well in the drier western plains.

Kentucky bluegrass is the Midwest's most commonly used cool-season grass. It mixes well with other cool-season grasses, tolerates cold and drought, and, thanks to a unique rhizome system, recovers well from physical, pest, and disease damage. It also provides a thatch cushion that protects the grass plants' crowns from wear and weather extremes (don't allow the thatch to exceed ½ inch thick, though). 'Park', 'Kenblue', and 'South Dakota Common' are the most drought tolerant and work best in mixes (two or more species). Varieties like 'Touchdown', 'NuGlade' (shade tolerant), 'Ram I', 'Nugget', and 'Baron' work best in blends and recover fastest from heat and cold damage.

A Kentucky bluegrass lawn can be grown from seed (though all varieties are slow to establish) or sod.

Perennial ryegrass varieties like 'Palmer', 'Repell', and 'Goalie' compete with Kentucky bluegrass for beauty, though a mix of ryegrass and bluegrass is more attractive and easier to maintain. Perennial ryegrass establishes in 10 to 14 days, acting as a "nurse" grass for the slower-germinating bluegrass. However, it often doesn't survive the cold, open winters in Canada or the northern regions of North Dakota, Minnesota, Wisconsin, and Michigan.

Tall fescue, once the "sow's ear" of grasses, is now a "silk purse" selection. Its varieties have the deepest root system of any cool-season grass, allowing the plants to draw up water and stay green long after other grasses have gone dormant. Varieties 'Amigo',

GRASS FOR YOUR LAWN

'Rebel Jr.', and 'Shenandoah II' grow as far north as the Dakotas and south to Oklahoma. 'Rebel II' and 'Rebel Jr.' are heat tolerant, winter hardy, and agreeable to close mowing. 'Amigo' takes full sun to partial shade and is the best choice for drier regions of the northern Midwest.

Fine fescues *comprise five species: chewings, strong creeping red, slender creeping, hard, and sheep fescues. If you want a low-maintenance lawn that's more than just moderately salt tolerant, select a variety of sheep fescue or hard fescue. Or try a mix of sheep and hard fescues for a low-maintenance, drought-tolerant lawn that stays green longer. For a prettier lawn, choose a slender creeping fescue such as 'Dawson', 'Marker', or 'Cindy'. The chewings fescues give aggressive cover, are disease resistant, and take close mowing; 'Jamestown II' and 'Dover' are excellent choices.*

Fine fescues are also added to seed mixes for lawns in shaded areas—beneath a tree canopy, for example, or under or beside a structure.

Zoysia grass, *when planted in the right location, is the ideal low-maintenance grass. In the southern Midwest, it provides a low-growing, luxurious, weed-free lawn that requires very little, if any, upkeep once established. Good varieties include 'Meyer' and 'Midwest'.*

Zoysia is slow to establish, especially if planted by the conventional method of plugging—planting small clumps (plugs) of grass. Sod provides an instant lawn, but it is extremely expensive.

Buffalo grass, *native to the prairie states from Kansas to the Dakotas and into Canada, is perfectly adapted to the rangelands of the Great Plains. It spreads by stolons—aboveground creeping stems that start new plants where they root—and, thanks to a very slow vertical growth rate (it typically reaches no higher than 4 inches), seldom needs mowing. Buffalo grass makes a good drought-tolerant, low-maintenance lawn. Like zoysia, it's typically grown from plugs. Popular varieties include 'Sharp's Improved', 'Plains', and 'Bison'.*

Seed, Sod, and Plugs

Though seeding a lawn means a season of fighting weeds, it's the least expensive method and offers you the broadest selection of grasses. Once established, a seeded lawn will have a more extensive root system and will generally be more disease resistant than a sodded one. For the seed species and varieties best suited to your location and soil, check with a local nursery or your Cooperative Extension Office. Opting for sod—strips or rolls of live grass plants that you lay down like carpeting—limits your choice of grasses since the grower typically selects a few varieties of one grass species to grow. However, sodding has no equal for instant gratification: mud one day, grass the next! Given 2 to 3 weeks of regular watering, the sod "knits" to the soil beneath. Be aware, though, that it's often grown on a high-organic soil (called peat sod) that can cause disease and drainage problems. Whenever possible, select mineral or dirt sod; these are more compatible with common garden soils. If peat sod is the only choice, commit to 2 years of annual core aeration—a process that entails extracting small chunks of sod from the lawn to improve the circulation of air, water, and nutrients in the soil.

Plugging (planting small pieces of sod) is the usual way to plant warm-season grasses; buffalo grass and zoysia are typically planted in this manner. Because they are spreading grasses, the voids usually fill in within a growing season. Plant the plugs as close as possible (a maximum of 12 inches apart). For other grasses, this method offers an alternative (albeit labor-intensive) way to establish a lawn when seeding is too unreliable and sod is too expensive.

When to plant. Seed cool-season grasses in late summer or early fall. The seed germinates quickly in the warm soil and grows during the cool of autumn. Any annual weeds that germinate at that time will be killed off by frost before they have a chance to reseed.

Plant warm-season grass plugs at any time in the growing season except late summer. The ideal planting time is in spring, as soon as the soil temperature reaches 70°F.

Mowing heights. Most cool-season grasses are mowed at 2½ to 3 inches; the latter is the best height for home lawns. A zoysia lawn can be mowed at about 1 inch.

Left to right: Tall fescue, creeping red fescue, chewings fescue, zoysia, and buffalo grass

LAWN ALTERNATIVES

Though lawn grass is probably the most widely used ground-covering plant, it's just one option among many. Ground covers of all types are both decorative and functional, playing several important roles in the garden. They frequently lay the foundation for an entire landscape, unifying diverse plantings of perennials, shrubs, and trees. As a living mulch, these plants conserve moisture, smother weeds, and insulate the soil from extremes of hot and cold. A ground cover is also a good choice for carpeting a slope, the space under a tree, or any other area where a lawn would be difficult to establish and maintain. And there are many ground covers that offer the bonus of colorful flowers or showy foliage or both.

So many choices

Some ground covers, such as creeping juniper and moss phlox, do best in full sun. Others, like pachysandra and epimedium, thrive in the shade. Pachysandra is a favorite for its ease of care, though it does need moist, humus-rich, acid soil. Three outstanding choices are 'Green Sheen', with shiny foliage, 'Silver Edge', with leaves margined in silver, and 'Green Carpet', a compact plant with smaller leaves.

Periwinkle, one of the most popular and widely planted ground covers, is also one of the most versatile, performing well in dappled sun or shade and retaining its attractive green leaves throughout winter. Like pachysandra, it demands little upkeep, and it even stays healthy in deep shade and dry soil (beneath trees, for example), where lawn grasses typically falter. Selections worthy of attention include 'Bowles' Variety', with dark green foliage and lavender-blue flowers; 'Sterling Silver', sporting cream-edged leaves; and 'Blue and Gold', bearing bright blue blooms and foliage margined in golden yellow.

Carpet bugleweed also flourishes in sun or partial shade, displaying its blue, purple, or white flower spikes against a blanket of attractive foliage. Two of the most popular varieties, both with vivid blue blossoms, are 'Catlin's Giant', with large bronze-purple leaves, and 'Burgundy Lace', with foliage marbled in maroon, cream, and green.

Many other ground cover plants thrive in the Midwest. From the widely planted choices described on the facing page, select those that will work best in your garden.

Mounds of blue, pink, and white spring flowers cover low mats of creeping phlox in a sunny space. Even after the flowers fade, the needlelike foliage provides an attractive ground cover to surround the stepping-stones.

Japanese spurge carpets the shady ground under a tree with its glossy green foliage. A popular low-maintenance spreader, Japanese spurge also lights up dark areas in spring with its greenish white flower spikes.

GROUND COVERS FOR SUN OR SHADE

NAME	EXPOSURE	BLOOMS	DESCRIPTION/LANDSCAPE USES
Ajuga reptans 'Burgundy Lace' ('Burgundy Glow') Carpet bugleweed	Full sun or partial shade	Late spring to early summer	Leaves in bright combination of maroon, cream, green; vivid blue flowers on upright, 6-in. stems. Spreads very fast, particularly in moist areas; will grow into the lawn unless curbed. Easy to divide and transplant. (to −40°F)
Cornus canadensis Bunchberry	Partial shade	Late spring to early summer	Deciduous woodland plant, 6 to 9 in. high. Tiny true flowers surrounded by four white bracts; small scarlet berries at summer's end. Slow growing. Good choice for small areas. (to −50°F)
Epimedium × rubrum Red barrenwort	Partial to full shade	Late spring to early summer	Semievergreen, slow-spreading plant to 1 ft. high. Red-tinted new foliage in spring; attractive crimson-and-yellow blooms. Good under trees and shrubs. (to −30°F)
Geranium 'Johnson's Blue' Cranesbill	Full sun or partial shade	Summer	Semievergreen; most popular blue perennial geranium. Large violet-blue blooms cover plant most of summer. Good for massing at front of border. To 1½ to 2 ft. tall and twice as wide. (to −30°F)
Geranium macrorrhizum Bigroot cranesbill	Full sun or partial shade	Early summer	Semievergreen; reaches 8 to 10 in. high, 2 ft. wide. Good choice for large areas or borders in sun or light shade. Fragrant leaves have good fall color. Bears magenta pink flowers. (to −30°F)
Hedera helix 'Thorndale' English ivy	Full sun to full shade		Vigorous evergreen plant; dark green leaves with whitish veins. Without snow cover, leaves may be scorched by cold, dry winds. Best protected under trees or shrubs. Attractive with spring bulbs. One of the hardiest selections. (to −20°F)
Hosta 'Ground Master'	Partial to full shade	Late summer	Deciduous. Medium green leaves have creamy yellow margins that fade to white. Pale lavender flowers. Spreading plant to 10 in. high; ideal for mass plantings. Not recommended for dry sites. (to −40°F)
Juniperus horizontalis 'Bar Harbor' Creeping juniper	Full sun		Dense, spreading, gray-green carpet to 1 ft. tall, 6 to 8 ft. wide. Young leaves are needlelike, older ones resemble scales; both turn purplish in winter. Best in well-drained, dry, or sandy soils. (to −40°F)
Lamium maculatum 'Pink Pewter' Dead nettle	Partial to full shade	Late spring to fall	Highly recommended for shady areas; grows 8 in. high. Beautiful silver leaves thinly margined in green; delicate pink blooms all summer. Somewhat drought tolerant. Deciduous in colder regions. Spreads fast to fill in large areas. (to −30°F)
Mitchella repens Partridgeberry	Partial shade	Summer	Foot-tall native of eastern U.S. Trailing stems root at nodes, spreading to form a mat. Glossy dark green leaves have prominent white veins. Whitish flowers; attractive bright red berries. Prefers moist, well-drained, organic, acid soil. (to −30°F)
Pachysandra terminalis 'Green Carpet' Japanese spurge	Partial to full shade	Spring	Dense, glossy deep green foliage makes a mat 8 to 10 in. high. Greenish white, very fragrant flowers bloom at stem tips early in season. This and other named selections are excellent in dense shade under mature trees. (to −30°F)
Persicaria affinis 'Superba' Dwarf Himalayan fleeceflower	Partial shade	Summer	Tough plant with leathery green leaves that turn an attractive bronzy red in fall. Short spikes of pale pink blooms turn reddish with age. Good on slopes, under shrubs. (to −40°F)
Phlox subulata 'Candy Stripe' Moss phlox	Full sun	Spring	Newer selection; evergreen to semievergreen. Produces blooms striped in white and rose pink. Grows to 6 in. high; popular edging or rockery plant for small areas. (to −40°F)
Rhus aromatica 'Gro-Low' Fragrant sumac	Full sun or partial shade	Spring	Deciduous. Vigorous, mounding shrub to 2 ft. high; ideal for tough sites. Aromatic glossy green leaves turn orange, then reddish purple in fall; the sunnier the site, the better the fall color. Very drought tolerant. (to −30°F)
Thymus serpyllum 'Pink Chintz' Mother-of-thyme	Full sun	Summer	Attractive clusters of pink blooms cover 3-in.-high mat of evergreen foliage. Leaves are fragrant when rubbed or walked on. Best in well-drained, neutral to alkaline soil. Tolerates moderately fertile soils and hot, dry conditions. (to −30°F)
Vinca minor Periwinkle	Partial to full shade	Spring to early summer	Extremely reliable and useful; produces thick, 4- to 6-in.-high mat of shiny dark green foliage. Good in dry shade. Attractive periwinkle blue flowers. Takes sun in cool climates if watered well. Cut back after bloom for denser growth. (to −30°F)

THE GARDEN

Color is the garden's mood. Form is its geometry. Texture its touch. Together, they make the garden a sensory experience, defining how it *feels* to us from the first moment we see it. By learning a few basics, you can make sure your garden creates the sensation you want.

Designing with color

Would you like your garden to feel calm and peaceful? Then fill it with *cool colors*—blues, purples, and greens—shown on the right side of the color wheel. If, on the other hand, you prefer a garden that sizzles with excitement and energy, fill it with *warm colors*—red, orange, and yellow—those on the left side of the color wheel. Warm colors are also great for accents and focal points. Against green or another color-quiet background, they combine well with each other. Individually, each pairs well with blue.

Visible from afar, warm colors dominate the garden when viewed up close. Cool colors tend to disappear with distance or in the dim light of evening, making the garden look washed out. You can solve the problem without compromising the tranquility of a cool-color border by adding just a few plants in warm colors to the mix.

To make a bold statement, pair *contrasting colors*—those that lie directly opposite each other on the color wheel. For example, try combining purple and yellow, blue and orange, or red and green. These con-

A. Pairing the contrasting colors of yellow coreopsis blooms with those of blue-purple mealycup sage makes the flowers of both look more vivid.

B. Visible from a distance, the warm colors of red, yellow, and orange of blanket flower, bee balm, and butterfly weed demand attention.

C. These cool-color blooms of purple-and-white pansies backed with green foliage generate calm and serenity.

D. The silvery leaves of lamb's ears, shown here with the bright yellow blossoms of cushion spurge *(Euphorbia polychroma),* soften or resolve color conflict in the garden.

E. The intense blue flower spikes of lupine blend easily with pink, red, and white blooms.

COMPOSITION

trasting colors serve to intensify each other. You can also make a *harmonious* composition by adding a close neighbor of one of the contrasting colors—say, purple and yellow with the latter's neighbor yellow orange.

If you're a beginner, resist the urge to plant one flower of every color you find at the garden center. Instead, plant masses of single colors that ease into each other. To make designing your garden easier, choose a favorite color or combination of colors as the basic theme, then add other plants with foliage or flowers that are harmonious within the color theme. But remember: there are no rules for garden design that can't be broken. The most important thing is that the combinations you choose please you. Like all other forms of art, the beauty of a garden is in the eye of the beholder.

The arbiters of color

White, gray, and silver are the garden peacemakers, mellowing the heat of competing warm colors, enlivening the tranquility of cool colors, and bridging or blending all the colors in the garden. It's hard to have too much white, gray, or silver in any garden. Blue also combines or mixes well with any other color. The rarest color found in plants, blue is an asset wherever it is used. Just a few blue blossoms can be an effective buffer between clashing colors such as orange and magenta. Make lavish use of all these garden diplomats to separate colors that often collide, such as pink and yellow.

Garden Greens

Green is the mainstay of the garden, providing a handsome backdrop for any color of flower. Variations in green can also create a dramatic accent.

Dark green
Dark green foliage, whether used as a background or in combination with other plants, adds rich texture and a settled, mature look to the garden. A dark green background also gives a feeling of depth to a planting.

Yellow green
Yellow-green foliage is handsome as a foil, backdrop, or spotlight. It brightens more sedate colors like deep purple or blue and adds a "sunny" spot in shady gardens. Yellow green is a lively backdrop for marine blue flowers, such as forget-me-nots.

Blue green
Blue-green foliage adds a calming effect, much like a pool of water, and blends easily with all other plant colors. Planted against a backdrop of dark green or among warm-colored flowers, it also can serve as a focal point.

Gray green
Frosty gray- or silver-green foliage can be used to cool down hot colors or highlight cool ones. It's also an attractive accent as the single color of a border. Gray-green foliage takes on a special luminescent quality in the evening, especially in moonlight.

A. **The contrasting textures** of feathery celosia blossoms, large daisies, narrow-leafed grasses, and bold canna foliage create drama in this garden border.

B. **In this garden vignette,** sedum is paired with feather reed grass to highlight the radically different textures of the two plants.

Applying texture

Texture isn't as readily apparent as color when you first glimpse a garden, but it's just as important. A garden filled with only fine-textured, small-leafed plants would be boring. One filled exclusively with plants of coarse, bold foliage would be overwhelming. By choosing plants that have contrasting textures, you can create striking effects. Like color, texture helps set the mood of the garden. For example, an emphasis on bold, coarse-textured plants creates drama. Using fine-textured plants as the dominant partner in the mix creates a more restful landscape.

Leaf shape and size are an important part of texture. The typically small, narrow leaves of a fern, for example, have a fine texture. The wide, sometimes-pleated leaves of a hosta have a coarse texture. Marrying the two in a shady border makes an eye-pleasing combination. You could also create a stunning scene simply by planting hostas of different shapes and sizes, from those with large, spoonlike leaves to others with narrow, dagger-shaped foliage.

The way the leaf surface feels to the touch is another important part of texture. A perennial such as bergenia has glossy leaves; the foliage of lamb's ears is soft and fuzzy. Foliage may also be crinkled, spiny, fleshy, cushiony, or hairlike. Consider the texture that flowers add to the garden, too. The dainty texture of baby's breath blooms or the airy sprays of moor grass, for example, contrasts nicely with the large, lush blooms of roses or lilies.

Considering form

The shape, or form, of a plant plays an important part in garden design. When planning your landscape, consider each plant's characteristic growth habit, whether rounded, spiky, columnar, sprawling, fountainlike, or weeping. Use plants of contrasting shapes to balance and complement each other. By massing similar plants, you can accentuate their shape. Weeping specimens are best used as a focal point to call attention to their unusual form.

In addition to the overall shape of a plant, consider the shape of the flowers. Combine plants with contrasting flower form, whether spire, disk, globe, daisy, or plume, to add visual interest to the garden.

C. **Tall spires of gayfeather** (foreground) stand out against a backdrop of flat-clustered yarrow blooms and daisylike coneflowers and sunflowers.

Size, a part of form, also deserves careful consideration. Otherwise, a plant may be out of proportion with the garden or require continual pruning to be pleasing to the eye. When planning a border, the time-honored rule of thumb dictates "tall in back, short in front." That's still good advice. But when you're creating a garden vignette, don't be afraid to break the rule. Small plants clustered around a taller, bulkier plant in the foreground, for example, could show off the contrast of forms and serve as an attractive accent.

D. **A combination of plants** in a single color accentuates form. Here, lavender, lamb's ears, and cardoon are combined in a silvery green composition.

E. **Narrow columns** of arborvitae are a harmonious backdrop for the broader spreading shape of a dwarf Alberta spruce.

233

LANDSCAPING WITH PERENNIALS

Trees, shrubs, and vines give form to the landscape, but perennials give it pizzazz. Today's palette of perennials offers an array of colors, textures, shapes, and sizes to choose from. They are prized because they come back after winter dormancy to bloom year after year.

Most perennials take a few years to get established. They vary in the length of time they can grow in one spot before blooming declines, signaling that it's time to rejuvenate the plants by digging them up and dividing the roots. But perennials are a great way to repeat some of your favorite landscape elements without starting from scratch every year.

Perennials are available to suit every location and site. Some like sun, some shade. Some thrive in moist soil, others in dry. Most perennials die down to the ground after the first hard frost, then come back from their roots

the following spring. A few, such as Lenten rose and coral bells *(Heuchera)*, retain their leaves through the winter in much of the Midwest. Deadheading—the removal of spent flowers—encourages repeat bloom of many kinds of perennials and improves the plants' appearance.

A border composed entirely of perennials provides a spectacular display and an engaging challenge for the gardener who wants to orchestrate plantings for color and form. Borders can take just about any shape—kidney, circular, or rectangular. They can be islands, surrounded by paving or lawn, making it easy to view plants from all sides. Or they can take the classic form of a double border that flanks two sides of a walk or lawn.

Many gardeners like to create mixed borders, which can include small trees and shrubs, bulbs, roses, ornamental grasses, annuals, and perennials. But the

This colorful border combines pink coneflowers (Echinacea) *and yellow black-eyed Susans* (Rudbeckia) *with ornamental grasses for sharp contrast. Rustling grasses, evergreens, and the dried flowers of perennials will provide winter interest.*

AN EASY-CARE PERENNIAL BORDER

perennials are the mainstays, supplying successive color throughout much of the year, extending the time that the border remains attractive, and lending it enormous variety in color and form.

Getting started

In the course of buying perennials, you can easily spend more than you expected. But with careful planning and selective shopping, you can stay within your budget. For example, you'll get better value from a plant such as coneflower *(Echinacea)* or coreopsis that gives a lengthy flowering period than from one with a brilliant but short-lived display. The border shown above contains 13 perennials: four coreopsis, two coneflowers, four catmints, one Russian sage *(Perovskia)* and two scabiosas. All are easy to grow, with blooms that last for many weeks.

For the longest possible period of bloom, buy plants before they flower or when they are just starting to bud. Small plants are usually a better value. In most cases, when perennials are transplanted from 1-gallon containers, quarts, and 4-inch pots, the less-expensive plants in the smaller containers will catch up to the growth of the 1-gallon plants within six weeks. If plant roots are allowed unimpeded growth and never experience being root-bound—as plants in larger containers sometimes do—they will establish and grow swiftly, without transplant shock.

Moreover, it pays to shop around. The cost of the same 4-inch container plant may triple between one nursery and another—a big difference in cost when you want to fill an entire border with flowers. But don't sacrifice quality for price. Starting with a robust plant will pay off for years to come.

Coreopsis verticillata 'Moonbeam'   *Hosta* 'On Stage'   *Echinacea purpurea*

BLOOMS ALL SEASON

For waves of color throughout the growing season, choose an assortment of spring- and summer-blooming plants. This border plan, designed in English country–garden style and featuring a variety of sun lovers, makes it easy. A rugosa rose and two white-flowered shrubs—deutzia and mock orange—anchor the composition.

Spring-flowering perennials such as columbine, iris, peony, and oriental poppy give way to the summer blooms of queen of the prairie, hollyhock mallow, catmint, veronica, and other flowers in tones of blue and pink. White Shasta daisies and phlox and pale yellow kniphofia provide accents, while the silvery gray foliage of lamb's ears brightens the border throughout the seasons.

A. Color and texture rule in this summer border filled with pink and yellow coneflowers *(Echinacea* and *Ratibida)* and purple Russian sage *(Perovskia)*. Bright zinnias and verbenas, both annuals, complement the perennial show.

B. The late-summer blooms of showy sedum *(Sedum spectabile)* are enhanced by the bright blue foliage of blue oat grass *(Helictotrichon sempervirens)*. A spring-blooming dogwood *(Cornus)* and the colorful foliage of purple-leafed smoke tree *(Cotinus coggygria)* provide further interest.

C. Catmint *(Nepeta)* delivers a long season of interest in the border with its lavender-blue flower spikes and gray-green foliage. When blooming begins to wane, cut back part way for another flush of flowers.

A SPRING–SUMMER SHOW

Planting area: 20' × 8'

The Plants

A. Anchusa azurea 'Loddon Royalist' **(2)**

B. Aquilegia McKana Giants
(McKana hybrids)
COLUMBINE **(1)**

C. Campanula glomerata 'Joan Elliott'
CLUSTERED BELLFLOWER **(3)**

D. Campanula persicifolia
'Telham Beauty'
PEACH-LEAFED BLUEBELL **(6)**

E. Chrysanthemum maximum
(Leucanthemum × superbum)
'Esther Read'
SHASTA DAISY **(2)**

F. Delphinium elatum 'Lord Butler'
CANDLE DELPHINIUM **(3)**

G. Deutzia gracilis
SLENDER DEUTZIA **(1)**
❄ Potentilla fruticosa 'Abbotswood'
SHRUBBY CINQUEFOIL **(1)**

H. Filipendula rubra 'Venusta'
QUEEN OF THE PRAIRIE **(3)**

I. Geranium himalayense
LILAC CRANESBILL **(1)**

J. Iris 'Papillon'
SIBERIAN IRIS **(3)**

K. Iris 'Vanity'
BEARDED IRIS **(3)**

L. Kniphofia 'Primrose Beauty'
RED-HOT POKER **(1)**
❄ Hemerocallis 'Hyperion'
DAYLILY **(2)**

M. Malva alcea 'Fastigiata'
HOLLYHOCK MALLOW **(3)**

N. Nepeta × faassenii
CATMINT **(3)**

O. Paeonia 'Festiva Maxima'
PEONY **(1)**

P. Papaver orientale 'Allegro'
ORIENTAL POPPY **(1)**

Q. Philadelphus × virginalis
'Minnesota Snowflake'
MOCK ORANGE **(1)**

R. Phlox maculata (P. carolina)
'Miss Lingard'
CAROLINA PHLOX **(3)**

S. Phlox subulata 'White Delight'
MOSS PHLOX **(6)**

T. Platycodon grandiflorus mariesii
BALLOON FLOWER **(4)**

U. Rosa rugosa 'Thérèse Bugnet'
ROSE **(1)**

V. Stachys byzantina 'Silver Carpet'
LAMB'S EARS **(2)**

W. Veronica austriaca teucrium
'Crater Lake Blue'
SPEEDWELL **(3)**

❄ FOR COLDER REGIONS

CASUAL ELEGANCE

From the Ohio River valley to the High Plains, Midwestern cottage gardens brim with flowers in a mix of shapes, sizes, and colors. You'll find sturdy natives growing side by side with pass-along plants from other gardeners. The effect is charming and informal. Hollyhocks and bee balm look just right against the weathered shingles of a lakeside cottage. Around a prairie home, coneflowers and butterfly weed mingle with peonies descended from plants carried by pioneers on their move westward. Goldenrod and asters dazzle the eye in fall.

Traditional English cottage gardens are enclosed with stone walls, but gardeners in the Midwest often substitute with a hedge or fence. The only "rule" of a cottage garden is a seeming lack of plan, complete with random and volunteer plantings. Besides perennials, it often holds herbs and dwarf fruit trees, as well as scrambling vines. Self-seeding flowers weave in and out among the more permanent specimens, tying an otherwise jumble of flower textures and forms together into a cohesive garden. Love-in-a-mist, Cupid's dart, forget-me-not, love-lies-bleeding, and kiss-me-over-the-garden-gate are just a few self-seeders with romantic names that make themselves at home in a cottage garden. Larkspur, nicotiana, Johnny-jump-ups, and sweet alyssum take root wherever conditions suit them. And many perennials reseed themselves as long as the garden isn't too heavily mulched in fall or early spring.

A. Self-seeding annual love-in-a-mist *(Nigella damascena)* blooms amidst perennial, bright pink flowers of campion *(Silene)*. The blue flowers add a cooling effect to the garden on a hot summer day. Seedlings tend to choose ideal conditions, and their surprise appearances add spontaneity to the garden.

B. An exuberant cottage garden blooms with roses, pinks, and self-seeding columbines. Evergreens add summer background and winter interest.

C. A rambler rose on an arbor provides a perfect background to show off a colorful mix of blooming perennials. The reds and golds demand attention.

A Cottage Garden

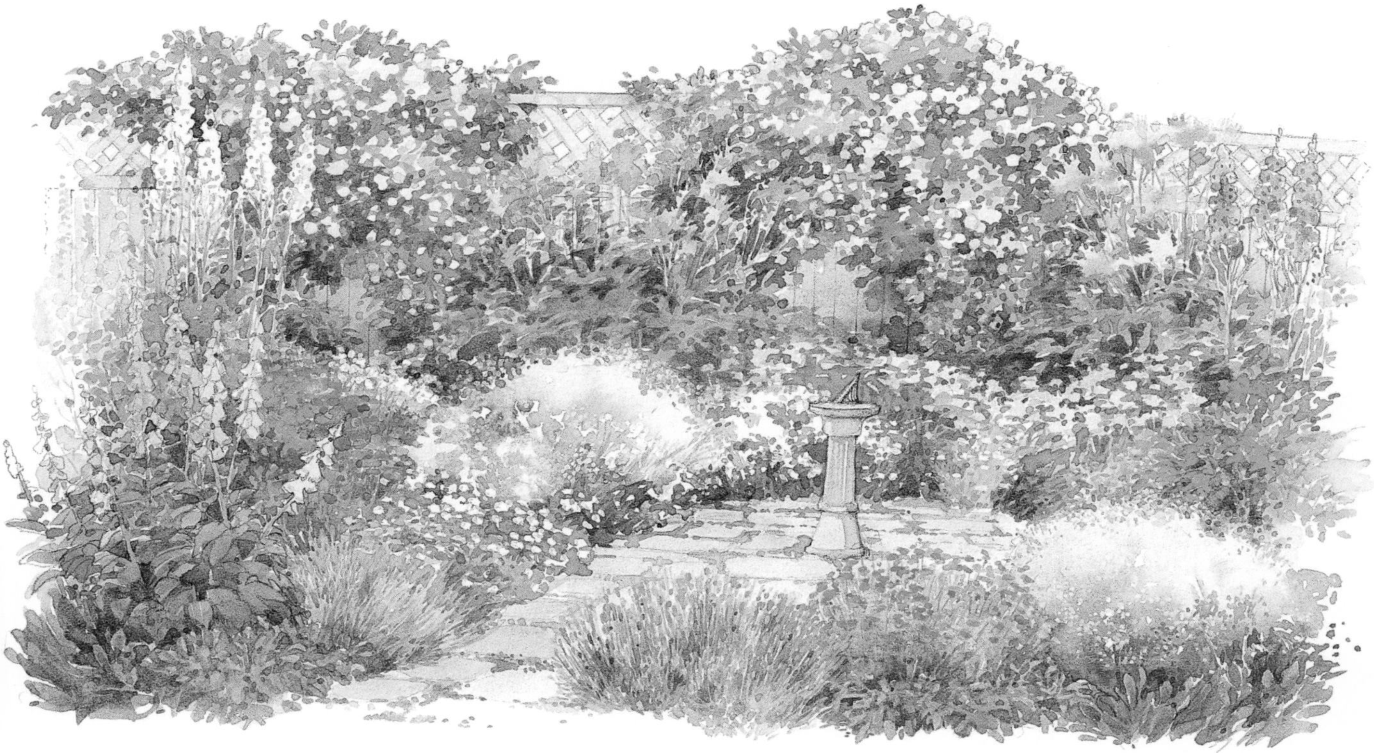

The Plants

A. Astrantia major 'Alba'
MASTERWORT **(9)**

B. Campanula glomerata 'Alba'
CLUSTERED BELLFLOWER **(6)**

C. Convallaria majalis
LILY-OF-THE-VALLEY **(12)**

D. Delphinium elatum 'Galahad' (5) and 'Summer Skies' (4)
CANDLE DELPHINIUM

E. Digitalis purpurea Excelsior Hybrids
FOXGLOVE **(7)**

F. Filipendula rubra 'Venusta'
QUEEN OF THE PRAIRIE **(3)**

G. Gypsophila paniculata 'Bristol Fairy'
BABY'S BREATH **(6)**

H. Lavandula angustifolia 'Hidcote'
ENGLISH LAVENDER **(6)**
❄ **Scabiosa columbaria 'Butterfly Blue'**
PINCUSHION FLOWER **(6)**

I. Linum perenne
PERENNIAL BLUE FLAX **(14)**
❄ **Penstemon 'Prairie Dusk'**
BEARD TONGUE **(6)**

J. Monarda didyma 'Marshall's Delight'
BEE BALM **(4)**

K. Nigella damascena 'Persian Jewels'
LOVE-IN-A-MIST **(19)**

L. Rosa gallica 'Versicolor' ('Rosa Mundi')
ROSE **(1)**
❄ **Rosa 'Carefree Wonder'**
ROSE **(2)**

M. Rosa 'New Dawn'
ROSE **(2)**
❄ **Rosa 'William Baffin'**
ROSE **(2)**

N. Viola × wittrockiana Imperial Impressions Mix
PANSY **(24)**

❄ FOR COLDER REGIONS

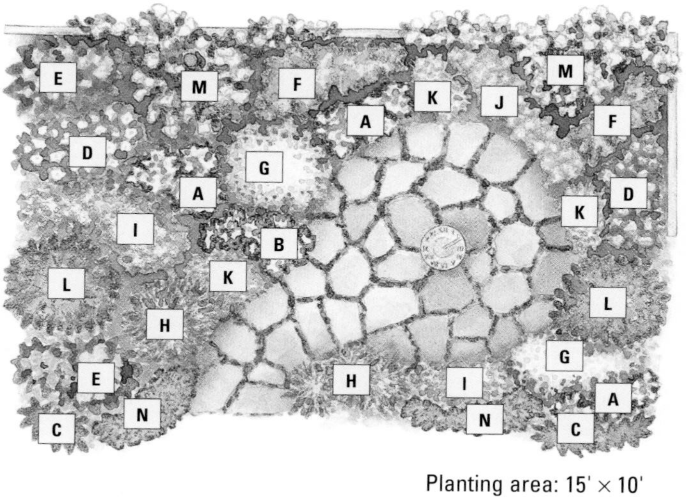

Planting area: 15' × 10'

JEWELS OF THE PRAIRIE

Talk about hardy! The wildflowers and colorful grasses that originally covered the Midwest withstood blizzards, droughts, fires, and trampling herds of buffalo. No wonder so many gardeners are bringing some of these beautiful natives back into home landscapes.

Sporobolus heterolepis and Asclepias

Prairie flowers tough enough to compete successfully with native grasses need no coddling in the garden, where they provide a kaleidoscope of color throughout the seasons. In early spring, the single lavender blooms of pasque flower *(Pulsatilla patens),* South Dakota's state flower, open above their low, clumping plants. Soon after, the deep blue flower spikes of false indigo *(Baptisia minor)* appear.

In midsummer, giant red-violet blossom spires top Kansas gayfeather *(Liatris pycnostachya).* Drooping yellow petals surround the prominent brown centers of gray-headed coneflowers *(Ratibida pinnata).* Butterflies float and dart around vivid orange butterfly weed *(Asclepias tuberosa).* Bright purple flower clusters appear on fountainlike plants of purple prairie clover *(Petalostemon purpureum),* a legume that adds nitrogen to the soil.

Petalostemon purpureum

Veronicastrum virginicum

Oenothera macrocarpa

Baptisia minor

Many prairie gems bloom for months. Deep blue blooms cover tiny prairie skullcap *(Scutellaria resinosa)* throughout the summer. Sprawling Missouri primrose *(Oenothera macrocarpa, O. missouriensis)* blooms all summer, too, flaunting its many showy, saucer-shaped yellow blooms. A profusion of cup-shaped, wine red flowers of poppy mallow *(Callirhoe involucrata)* stand above their creeping plants, blooming continuously for several months from spring through midsummer.

Echinacea purpurea

In fall, lavender-blue blossoms cover 3-foot-tall smooth asters *(Aster laevis),* one of the latest-blooming prairie wildflowers. And as the flowers bow out, prairie grasses dominate the landscape. Indian grass *(Sorghastrum nutans),* topped with silky seedheads, turns orange or yellow. The russet red of little bluestem *(Schizachyrium scoparium),* Willa Cather's beloved "red grass," persists throughout the winter. Fine-textured switch grass *(Panicum virgatum)* turns from burgundy or gold to beige, adding its subtle beauty to the winter landscape.

Prairie paradise. Above a sea of grasses, the feathery plumes of prairie smoke *(Geum triflorum)* produce a rose pink mist. Woody rhizomes help this tough native wildflower compete successfully with grasses and survive weather extremes.

Callirhoe involucrata

Silphium laciniatum

Asclepias tuberosa

Liatris pycnostachya and Rudbeckia hirta

WILDFLOWERS

Rattlesnake master, sneezeweed, and tickseed—these are just a few of the many wildflowers that grow in the Midwest. With their evocative names and brilliant colors, wildflowers offer the gardener a chance to bring pioneer history, Native American lore, and ecological conservation into the garden.

Wildflowers are the perfect subjects for a miniature meadow. A 4- to 8-foot border of coneflowers, butterfly weed, and asters creates a cheery transition between lawn and woods. You can also grow patches of these natives between ground covers. Or designate a corner of your yard as a "wild" patch where children can play among the blooms.

Although wildflowers seem right at home in a naturalistic meadow, don't be afraid to include them in a formal border. Good candidates are coneflowers *(Echinacea)* and lance-leaf coreopsis. And feel free to intersperse native species and their modern hybrid offspring—such as spike gayfeather *(Liatris spicata)* and its varieties 'Alba', 'Floristan Violett', and 'Kobold'—with exotic garden flowers.

Specialty seed companies offer regional mixes of showy Midwestern natives to sow into meadows. You can also create your own mix by buying and mixing seeds of the native flowers you prefer. But make sure to mix grasses and forbs (plants other than grasses) in the seed mix to create a true meadow effect.

Prairie natives such as purple coneflower (Echinacea) *and black-eyed Susan* (Rudbeckia) *are drought tolerant. Mainstays of the Midwestern prairie for hundreds of years, these tough plants need no supplemental water to survive in the home landscape.*

Planting a Meadow

Site preparation is the most important step in establishing a prairie meadow. First choose a sunny site, then take the time to prepare the soil as for any garden. Eliminate all existing vegetation by applying a broad-spectrum herbicide such as glyphosate (Roundup or Kleenup), by cultivating, or—if you're willing to delay planting for a full growing season—by smothering. If the area you select for wildflowers is

part of a lawn, using a sod cutter to remove the top several inches of grass and soil provides a quick way to prepare the soil.

The least expensive way to start a meadow is by broadcasting seed. To establish firm contact with the soil, roll the soil after seeding, then mulch with weed-free straw. If you prefer, you can start by plugging small grass and wildflower plants into a prepared bed at 1-foot intervals. Never gather plants or take cuttings or seeds from plants in the wild. Many native plant species are in danger of extinction, and others are threatened.

After planting, small areas must be kept weeded. When seeds ripen at the end of the growing season, cut back the wildflowers and allow the seeds to fall to the ground. Maintain large meadows by mowing once a year in autumn. In early spring, periodic burning— nature's own method of maintaining a meadow—is an option in some open areas. Without mowing or burning, young trees and vines such as bittersweet (Celastrus) would soon shade out the other plants.

A SELECTION OF WILDFLOWERS

	NAME	EXPOSURE	BLOOMS	DESCRIPTION/LANDSCAPE USES
WHITE, YELLOW ▼	*Baptisia lactea* White false indigo	Full sun	Late spring to early summer	Grows 3 to 5 ft. tall, bearing many clusters of sweet pea–shaped blooms. Likes sandy soil. Good cut flower; seedpods can be harvested for dried arrangements. (to –30°F)
	Coreopsis lanceolata Lanceleaf coreopsis	Full sun or partial shade	Late spring to late summer	Grows to 2 ft. tall. Prolific bloomer, producing golden yellow flowers nonstop through summer. Good cut flower. (to –30°F)
	Solidago rigida Stiff goldenrod	Full sun	Fall	Grows 2 to 5 ft. tall. Clusters of bright yellow blooms attract butterflies; birds favor seeds. Effective in groupings. (to –30°F)
RED, ORANGE ▼	*Aquilegia canadensis* Canada columbine	Full sun or partial shade	Midspring to early summer	Grows 2 to 3 ft. tall. Five-spurred scarlet blooms with yellow inner petals attract hummingbirds. Ideal in perennial border, cottage garden, or bright woodland planting. (to –40°F)
	Asclepias tuberosa Butterfly weed	Full sun	Summer	Drought-tolerant plant to 3 ft. tall bears beautiful clusters of bright orange blooms that attract butterflies. Good cut flower; seedpods can be harvested for dried arrangements. (to –30°F)
	Lobelia cardinalis Cardinal flower	Full sun	Summer to fall	Bog plant grows 2 to 4 ft. tall; much valued for tubular blooms in brilliant red. Flowers attract hummingbirds, are excellent for cutting. (to –30°F)
	Ratibida columnifera Mexican hat	Full sun	Early summer to early fall	Drought-resistant plant to 2½ ft. tall. Bears large, daisylike blooms with conical center and drooping, red-on-yellow, pure yellow, or brownish purple petals. Nice cut flower. (to –40°F)
PINK, VIOLET, BLUE ▼	*Amorpha canescens* Lead plant	Full sun or partial shade	Late summer to early fall	Shrub to 3 ft. tall. Leafstalks and aromatic leaflets are grayish white. Spikes of sweet pea–like blooms are violet with orange anthers. Good in mixed border. (to –50°F)
	Aster laevis Smooth aster	Full sun	Late summer and early fall	Clump-forming plant to 3 ft. tall. A choice blue aster, bearing lavender-blue blossoms with yellow centers. Use in border, naturalized garden. Good cut flower. (to –30°F)
	Echinacea angustifolia Narrow-leaf purple coneflower	Full sun	Summer	Durable perennial to 3 ft. tall. Vivid pinkish purple blooms have conical orange-brown center. Ideal in perennial garden. (to –30°F)
	Eryngium yuccifolium Rattlesnake master	Full sun	Summer to early fall	Semievergreen plant to 4 ft. tall, with spiny, sword-shaped bluish gray leaves. Handsome pale blue flowers with gray-green bracts match foliage. Prefers moist, well-drained soil. (to –30°F)
	Filipendula rubra Queen of the prairie	Full sun or partial shade	Summer	Grows to 5 ft. tall. Bears peachy pink plumes; good cut flower. Ideal in perennial border, as screen. Likes moist soil. (to –40°F)
	Liatris aspera Rough blazing star	Full sun	Late summer to early fall	Grows to 6 ft. tall. Has bottlebrush-type flowers. Blooms attract butterflies and are excellent for cutting. (to –30°F)
	Monarda fistulosa Bergamot	Full sun or partial shade	Summer to early fall	Bushy, clump-forming plant reaches 4 ft. tall. Lilac to pale pink flowers with purple-tinged bracts attract bees and butterflies. Excellent in a border or wildflower meadow. (to –40°F)

Coreopsis lanceolata

Asclepias tuberosa

Ratibida columnifera

Monarda fistulosa

WATER-THRIFTY FAVORITES

When dry weather comes to the heartland, water restrictions often aren't far behind. Traditional garden borders soon show the strain. Many drought-tolerant mainstays of Western gardens can also take withering conditions in the Midwest, as long as they're planted in well-drained soil. Otherwise, the Midwest's inevitable downpours and heavy snowfalls would rot the plants' roots.

Once their roots are established, many fine plants thrive in both wet and dry weather. Star performers include plants that have evolved to endure climate extremes, such as bush cinquefoil, sweetshrub, Adam's needle, coreopsis, and prairie grasses like switch grass and prairie dropseed.

Many unthirsty imported plants come from the Mediterranean region, southern Africa, Central and South America, Australia, and other parts of the world where hot, dry summers are the norm. Yarrow, artemisia, junipers, and many herbs all flourish in sunny, rarely watered locations.

To create a flower border that will need little irrigation after the first year—thus saving you water, time, and money—choose a well-drained site and fill it with groups of dry-climate perennials and flowering shrubs. Such plantings are particularly appropriate in areas that are difficult to water, such as steep slopes.

A. Many native perennials are tough and drought tolerant. Here, variously colored butterfly weeds (*Asclepias*) and purple coneflowers (*Echinacea*) brighten a traditional border. Both are excellent wildlife plants.

B. Among the medicinal and culinary herbs are many that are drought tolerant. Often fragrant, their scent concentrates when their essential oils are not diluted by watering the plants. This herb garden includes lamb's ears (*Stachys*), yarrow (*Achillea*), and lavender cotton (*Santolina*).

C. For an unthirsty combination, plant black-eyed Susans, showy sedum, and ornamental grasses in a sunny spot in well-drained soil.

A WATERWISE BORDER

The Plants

A. **Achillea filipendulina 'Coronation Gold'**
FERNLEAF YARROW (2)

B. **Achillea 'Moonshine'**
YARROW (7)

C. **Asclepias tuberosa**
BUTTERFLY WEED (7)

D. **Catananche caerulea**
CUPID'S DART (6)

E. **Coreopsis lanceolata**
LANCELEAF COREOPSIS (3)

F. **Echinacea purpurea 'Magnus'**
PURPLE CONEFLOWER (4)

G. **Erigeron compositus 'Alpine Snow'**
FERNLEAF FLEABANE (3)

H. **Euphorbia polychroma**
CUSHION SPURGE (7)

I. **Geranium × oxonianum (G. endressii) 'Wargrave Pink'**
CRANESBILL (2)

J. **Liatris spicata 'Kobold'**
SPIKE GAYFEATHER (5)

K. **Pennisetum alopecuroides 'Hameln'**
FOUNTAIN GRASS (2)
❄ **Sporobolus heterolepis**
PRAIRIE DROPSEED (2)

L. **Penstemon grandiflorus 'Prairie Jewel'**
BEARD TONGUE (3)

M. **Perovskia 'Blue Spire'**
RUSSIAN SAGE (8)

N. **Rosa rugosa 'Frau Dagmar Hartopp'**
ROSE (1)

O. **Stachys byzantina 'Big Ears'**
LAMB'S EARS (5)

❄ FOR COLDER REGIONS

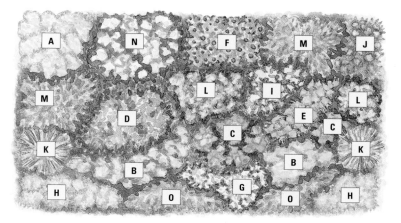

Planting area: 11' × 6'

BULBS

Some of the best-loved garden flowers, such as tulips and daffodils, arise from bulbs—or from corms, tubers, tuberous roots, or rhizomes. Although traditionally associated with spring, some bloom in late winter, summer, or fall, making bulbs ideal for single displays and for mixed borders.

Bulbs are inexpensive, and to get a good splash of color, you should plant them by the dozens. Bulbs that multiply and spread from year to year, such as grape hyacinths, can be naturalized under trees or in meadows.

In naturalized settings, grassy cover disguises bulb foliage, which must be left until it has yellowed and can easily be pulled away. In formal gardens, overplant newly planted bulbs with annuals such as pansies or forget-me-nots. The flowers will bloom simultaneously, but the long-blooming annuals will camouflage wilting bulb foliage.

Plant hardy spring-flowering bulbs like tulips and daffodils in fall along a walkway or path. Wait until after the last spring frost before planting tender summer bulbs such as cannas and caladiums. For an ongoing source of cut flowers, plant gladiolus at 4-week intervals in spring and early summer. You can also enjoy special bursts of late-season color if you plant autumn-flowering crocus and colchicum bulbs in late summer or early fall.

A. While snow still lingers, bright crocus blooms ignore the cold and chase away doldrums for winter-weary gardeners. These dependable tiny bulbs, ideal for edging walks and borders, slowly multiply for an increasingly beautiful display.

B. Stretch the bulb season through midsummer with fragrant 'Black Dragon' lilies. Rose-purple on the outside with a yellow throat, the fragrant blooms are borne in massive clusters on each sturdy stem.

C. A study in elegance, these stately white tulips stand out against a backdrop of green. Because many tulips don't give a repeat performance the following spring, gardeners typically remove the bulbs when the flowers fade and replace them with warm-weather annuals.

A Springtime Show

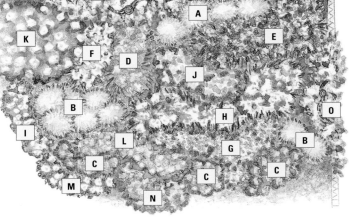

Planting area: 14' × 9'

The Plants

A. Artemisia 'Huntington' (4)

**B. Artemisia schmidtiana
'Silver Mound'**
WORMWOOD **(8)**

**C. Hyacinthus orientalis
'Blue Giant' (12) and
'Gipsy Queen' (16)**
HYACINTH

❄ **Scilla siberica
'Spring Beauty'**
SIBERIAN SQUILL **(30)**

D. Iris 'Beverly Sills'
BEARDED IRIS **(5)**

E. Iris sibirica 'Orville Fay'
SIBERIAN IRIS **(6)**

F. Iris sibirica 'White Swirl'
SIBERIAN IRIS **(3)**

G. Myosotis sylvatica
FORGET-ME-NOT **(15)**

**H. Narcissus 'Cheerfulness' and
Hemerocallis 'Happy Returns'**
DAFFODIL **(40)** AND DAYLILY **(7)**

I. Primula vulgaris
PRIMROSE **(15)**

**J. Primula vulgaris hybrids
(several colors)**
PRIMROSE **(20)**

**K. Rosa rugosa
'Blanc Double de Coubert'**
ROSE **(1)**

L. Tulipa 'Apricot Beauty'
TULIP **(18)**

M. Viola × wittrockiana 'Cornetto'
PANSY **(10)**

**N. Viola × wittrockiana
Imperial Antique Shades**
PANSY **(24)**

O. Wisteria frutescens 'Nivea'
AMERICAN WISTERIA **(2)**

❄ **Wisteria macrostachya**
KENTUCKY WISTERIA **(2)**

❄ FOR COLDER REGIONS

ANNUALS

Flowering annuals and biennials provide quick, showy color that can bring instant drama to a quiet corner of the garden. Annuals complete their entire life cycle, from seed germination to flowering and death, in less than a year; biennials develop roots and foliage during their first year, then bloom and die in their second year. In spring and early summer, and again in fall, nurseries offer a good selection of annuals in flats or small containers. Many are also easy to start from seed, and seed packets begin showing up on store racks as early as February.

Many annuals are prized for their season-long bloom—from spring until frost, in some cases. Use them to fill gaps between shrubs and young perennials and to occupy the empty spots left after bulbs bloom and their foliage dies back. Display them in pots and window boxes for splashes of color. Train annual vines such as morning glory, sweet pea, hyacinth bean, or nasturtium onto a fence or through a sturdy shrub. And don't forget the annuals valued for their foliage, such as multicolored coleus, silver dusty miller, and even delicious purple basil. In a formal bed or border, make a large single-color grouping of each type of annual; in an informal planting, mixed colors are most appropriate.

Put annuals to work to brighten up difficult spots and to stretch the garden season. Sunflowers, zinnias, and portulacas, for example, thrive in hot, dry sites, while begonias, impatiens, and caladiums provide plenty of midsummer color in shady places. And for color in early spring and late fall, depend on annuals that can survive subfreezing temperatures, such as pansies and ornamental cabbage.

A. Late spring. Golden California poppies shine above lavender moss verbena *(Verbena tenuisecta)* and pink and purple petunias. In warmer parts of the Midwest, poppies and petunias can be started easily from seed in a sunny spot in the garden.

B. Contrasting colors. In this annual garden, purple heliotrope and salvia blooms cool down the fiery orange plumes of celosia and complement its form. These dependable bedding plants all thrive in a sunny site.

C. Sizzling hues. During the hottest months, bright red zinnias, cosmos, and cannas add zing to a border bursting with annuals. Deadheading the spent blooms regularly keeps flowers going until frost.

AN ANNUAL PARADE

	NAME	EXPOSURE	DESCRIPTION
▼ COOL COLORS	*Ageratum houstonianum* Floss flower	Full sun or partial shade	Powder-puff blooms in blue, mauve blue, or white. Height varies from 6 in. to 3 ft.; use shorter varieties for borders, taller ones in cottage gardens.
	Begonia × *semperflorens* Wax begonia	Full sun or partial shade	Compact (6- to 12-in.) mounds of green or bronze-tinted succulent leaves. White, pink, red, or bicolored blooms; double forms available. Good in mass plantings.
	Catharanthus roseus Madagascar periwinkle	Full sun	Phloxlike blooms in white, pink, rose, or lilac on 1- to 2-ft.-tall plants. Needs well-drained soil; takes hot, dry conditions.
	Cleome hasslerana Spider flower	Full sun	Reaches 4 to 6 ft. tall. Distinctive lilac, white, or pink flowers have a spidery look. Best in background, as summer hedge, against a fence. Self-seeds.
	Impatiens walleriana Busy Lizzie	Partial or full shade	Single or double blooms in cool pinks, magenta, lavender, white; also many red and orange shades. Good as mass planting, in hanging baskets, containers. Grows 6 in. to 2 ft. tall.
	Lobelia erinus Bush or trailing lobelia	Partial or full shade	Bushy types best in border; trailers excellent as edging in window boxes or containers. Both types grow 3 to 6 in. high, bloom in blue, purple, lilac, wine red, or white.
	Lobularia maritima Sweet alyssum	Full sun	Trailing, to 1-ft. plant. Bears clusters of tiny, honey-scented white flowers; there are also varieties in shades of purple and pink. Use in borders, between stepping-stones, in containers or hanging baskets. Self-seeds.
	Nicotiana × *sanderae* Flowering tobacco	Full sun or partial shade	Funnel-shaped blooms in white, lavender, purple, lime, red, or rose. Tolerates most soils. Some are fragrant at night; white-blossomed types are often more fragrant than others. Grows to 2 ft. high.
	Petunia × *hybrida*	Full sun or partial shade	Upright to trailing plants, 6 in. to 2 ft. high. Trumpet-shaped, single to double flowers in blue, purple, white, red, pink, even yellow; also some bicolors. Good for bedding, borders.
	Salvia farinacea 'Victoria' Mealycup sage	Full sun	Upright grower to 3 to 4 ft. Medium green leaves; spikes of blue flowers. Good as vertical accent. Cut the blooms for fresh or dried arrangements.
▼ WARM COLORS	*Mimulus* × *hybridus* Monkey flower	Full sun or partial shade	Bushy, upright plant to 1 ft. Funnel-shaped blooms in orange, red, or yellow, with red, maroon, or purple spotting. Use as mass planting, in borders, containers, hanging baskets, or beside ponds.
	Pelargonium × *hortorum* Geranium	Full sun or partial shade	Hundreds of selections vary in height (from 3 in. to 3 ft.), leaf shape, leaf markings. Single or double flowers in white or shades of orange, red, pink, rose, purple. Deadhead for continued bloom.
	Tagetes erecta, T. patula African or French marigold	Full sun	Tough plants 6 in. to 3 ft. tall; colors include orange, yellow, maroon, cream, bicolors. Use shorter types at front of border, taller kinds in background. Said to repel nematodes and other pests. Deadhead to keep bloom going.
	Zinnia angustifolia	Full sun	Compact plant to 16 in. high bears masses of round blooms in orange, white, pink. Grows like a ground cover. Resists powdery mildew; tolerates drought.

Cleome hasslerana

Lobelia erinus

Mimulus × *hybridus*

Tagetes patula

PLANTS WITH

T he heart of the early Midwest was its field crops, but the region's soul has always been its flower gardens. Midwestern farm wives planted sun-loving flowers in front of homes surrounded by white picket fences or arrayed them in neat rows adjoining huge vegetable gardens. Garden phlox, pink, tuberose, and other fragrant blossoms were cut and gathered by the armload for vases indoors. Easy-to-dry flowers like cockscomb and immortelle filled the bloomless void during the long, hard winters. Planted in rows, hollyhocks served as a quick-growing flowering screen—and the blossoms also provided the makings for pioneer dolls, with a bud for the head and an open flower for a billowing skirt. Families found relief from the hot summer sun on front porches shaded by quick-growing vines of Dutchman's pipe and enjoyed protection from drying winds afforded by bridal wreath spireas and lilacs.

When the pioneers settled the Midwest, they brought with them prized seeds and roots to plant in their new gardens. Passed down through generations, many of these old-fashioned favorites still survive. Today, in fact, "old" is one of the newest Midwestern landscaping trends. Heritage gardens, featuring a potpourri of delightful and almost-forgotten shapes, colors, and scents, are the region's living legacy. Annuals like kiss-me-over-the-garden-gate, larkspur,

A. Early homesteaders counted on hollyhocks *(Alcea rosea)* for a living screen of lush greens and bright, cheery blooms. Self-seeding biennials, hollyhocks flower in their second year.

B. Old-fashioned spider flowers *(Cleome)* are easy to grow from seed. They add beauty and diversity not typically found in a garden filled with only purchased bedding plants.

C. Delightful heart-shaped blooms dangle in spring from arching stems of a bleeding heart *(Dicentra)*. One of the Midwest's hardy perennials, bleeding heart thrives in shade.

A Past

love-in-a-mist, and spider flower, all easy to grow from seed but seldom offered as bedding plants, are reappearing in Midwestern landscapes. Perennials like bellflower, bleeding heart, and balloon flower are adored for the uncommon shapes of their blossoms. Peonies, old garden roses, and bearded irises, so tough that many still bloom in long-abandoned farmyards, are finding renewed favor. And biennials such as sweet William, standing cypress, and money plant have come back to grace gardens once again.

In creating heritage gardens, we both honor our roots and enjoy the beauty of the hardy plants that stood up to the hot summers, cold winters, and constant winds our forebears found here. The plants you choose should be well loved and a part of the Midwest's history. One of the best sources for these old-time plants is a friend or neighbor who grows a family heirloom. And as demand for these plants increases, garden centers and specialty mail-order suppliers are expanding their offerings. The Flower and Herb Exchange in Decorah, Iowa, publishes a yearbook filled with sources for rare, old-fashioned favorites.

D. The familiar and intoxicating fragrance of lilac blossoms *(Syringa × persica)* lingers in the memory of just about anyone who grew up in the Midwest. Exceptionally easy to grow in this region, lilacs require a cold winter for best bloom.

E−F. Midwestern treasures. Settlers brought fragrant double-pink peonies and bearded irises with them to plant in the gardens of their new prairie homes. Tough and adaptable, these perennials still flourish throughout the region.

251

HERBS

Gardeners have known the culinary and medicinal value of herbs for thousands of years. Today, herbs are equally valued as adornments—planted in a kitchen window box, mixed with other plants in a scented garden, or used as a low hedge along a garden path. Most herbs are easy to grow in full sun and many develop a more intense flavor and fragrance when given little water.

Formal herb gardens, created by growing herbs in intricate geometrical designs, have been popular for centuries. If you decide to grow herbs in a formal design, expect to spend more time maintaining such an orderly garden than you would an informal border. Choose from several different types of formal herb gardens. "Sundial" gardens are composed of flowering herbs that open at different times of the day. Intricate "knot" gardens create twining patterns with neatly clipped, compact herbs and shrubs. In the knot garden shown below, plants with varied foliage textures and tones create the geometrical design, and brightly colored calendula blossoms fill in the corners. Formal gardens require precision in planting: begin hedges with small plants spaced close together and place herb plants according to a carefully designed pattern.

The compact, informal herb garden shown at right pairs foliage with flowers to look good while also delivering snippets of herbs for flavoring soups, salads, and grilled meats. Fragrant cheddar pink and catmint bloom along the path. The rose-covered obelisk and pots filled with lemon verbena, scented geraniums, and various culinary herbs add structure to the informal design.

A KNOT GARDEN

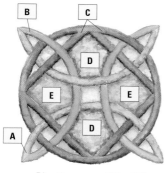

Planting area: 12' × 12'

The Plants

A. Artemisia abrotanum
SOUTHERNWOOD **(28)**

B. Berberis thunbergii 'Bonanza Gold'
JAPANESE BARBERRY **(18)**

C. Buxus microphylla 'Wintergreen' (B. m. koreana 'Wintergreen')
BOXWOOD **(36)**

D. Calendula officinalis (dwarf, cream)
POT MARIGOLD **(24)**

E. Calendula officinalis (dwarf, yellow)
POT MARIGOLD **(24)**

A Fragrant Corner

The Plants

A. Artemisia dracunculus
FRENCH TARRAGON **(2)**

B. Dianthus gratianopolitanus
CHEDDAR PINK **(4)**

C. Heliotropium arborescens
COMMON HELIOTROPE **(4)**

D. Nepeta × faassenii
CATMINT **(4)**

**E. Ocimum basilicum
'Dark Opal'**
PURPLE BASIL **(4)**

F. Rosa 'Lavender Lassie'
ROSE **(1)**

G. Thymus serpyllum 'Album'
MOTHER-OF-THYME **(10)**

**H. Thymus vulgaris
'Orange Balsam'**
THYME **(2)**

I. IN STRAWBERRY POT:

Origanum majorana
SWEET MARJORAM **(1)**

Rosmarinus officinalis
ROSEMARY **(1)**

Salvia officinalis 'Compacta'
GARDEN SAGE **(1)**

Satureja hortensis
SUMMER SAVORY **(1)**

Thymus × citriodorus 'Aureus'
VARIEGATED LEMON THYME **(3)**

J. IN URN:

Aloysia triphylla
LEMON VERBENA **(1)**

Pelargonium odoratissimum
SCENTED GERANIUM (APPLE) **(2)**

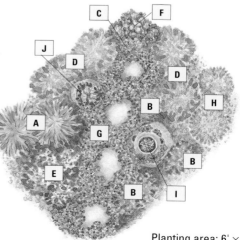

Planting area: 6' × 8'

FRUITS AND VEGETABLES

The Midwest has a long-standing reputation for its productive food gardens. Modern innovations such as the breeding of space-saving plant varieties and the use of raised beds help make today's food gardens compact and attractive, too. Many gardeners mix edibles with flowering perennials and annuals. Using vegetables as ornamentals in the landscape allows you to enjoy small amounts of home-grown produce without a big commitment of time and garden space.

Keep in mind that many vegetable and perennial blossoms, including those of squash, violas, and daylilies, are edible and quite tasty, fresh or cooked. They add bright color and zing to foods from salads to soufflés.

The colors and textures of leafy greens such as Swiss chard enliven borders, while plants like rhubarb and blueberries add structure. Long-lived vegetables such as cabbages can fill decorative containers. Herbs, with their distinctive fragrances and interesting colors, can line pathways.

For the best effect when mixing vegetables and flowers, cluster plants in groups of three or more. Vary plant heights and add accents such as fennel or dill. To avoid a busy look, repeat a few of the dominant plants throughout the bed.

Many vegetables and fruits, such as broccoli and apples, require extra attention to control insect pests and diseases. Others, especially root crops like beets and carrots, are virtually maintenance free. Do not plant disease-susceptible ornamentals—those that require spraying—with edible plants.

A. Heirloom vegetables ready for harvest contrast with the bright blossoms of edible flowers. The handsome blue-green leaves of leek (foreground) take center stage.

B. A river of gold signet marigolds winds among blue-green and red cabbages, curly-leafed savoy cabbages, and smoky-colored kale, blurring the line between decorative and edible.

C. Brussels sprouts and lettuces create a luxuriant tapestry of leaf shapes and colors punctuated by bright marigold and red salvia blooms.

An Abundant Garden

Planting area: 15' × 30'

The Plants

A. **Allium schoenoprasum**
CHIVES **(3)**

B. **Apples, columnar* (3)**

C. **Asparagus
'Conover's Colossal' (6)**

D. **Beans, pole
'Kentucky Wonder' (3)**

E. **Blueberries: 'Patriot'* (2)**

F. **Broccoli
'Early Purple Sprouting' (4)**

G. **Brussels sprouts
'Rubine Red' (2)**

H. **Cabbage
'Early Jersey Wakefield' (4)**

I. **Hemerocallis 'Happy Returns'**
DAYLILY **(7)**

J. **Hyssopus officinalis**
HYSSOP **(3)**

K. **Kale
'Dwarf Blue Curled Scotch' (4)**

L. **Laurus nobilis**
SWEET BAY **(1)**

M. **Lettuce: 'Black-Seeded
Simpson' (4), 'Great Lakes' (4),
and 'Red Sails' (4)**

N. **Ocimum basilicum
'Purple Ruffles'**
PURPLE BASIL **(2)**

O. **Peppers, sweet
'Blushing Beauty' (3)**

P. **Petroselinum crispum
'Gigante d'Italia'**
ITALIAN PARSLEY **(6)**

Q. **Raspberries: 'Heritage' (3)**

R. **Rhubarb: 'German Wine' (1)**

S. **Shallots: 'Odetta's White' (12)**

T. **Squash, summer
'Ronde de Nice' (2)**

U. **Strawberries: 'Tristar' (12)**

V. **Tomatoes: 'Brandywine' (2)**

W. **Tropaeolum majus**
GARDEN NASTURTIUM **(4)**

X. **Viola tricolor**
JOHNNY-JUMP-UP **(6)**

* PLANT AT LEAST TWO VARIETIES
FOR POLLINATION.

ORNAMENTAL GRASSES

The tall grasses that once covered the Midwest are coming home again, finding their way into prairie-style plantings as well as formal landscapes. Practical additions to home gardens, these versatile plants offer beauty and grace while requiring only minimal care.

Like many other perennials, most ornamental grasses grow in clumps that enlarge slowly. In flower borders, they make good companions for irises, daylilies, and plants with softly spired or daisylike flowers. A few, such as ribbon grass *(Phalaris arundinacea)*, spread by rhizomes and can be invasive. But if planted where their rhizomes can be contained, they can make wonderful ground covers.

Massed in groups, clumping grasses such as blue oat grass and switch grass can have the same color impact that shrubs would provide. For an effective hedge or screen, use one of the taller kinds, such as feather reed grass.

In a large garden, fill wide borders with tall, airy-textured grasses in interesting colors. In a smaller space, use ornamental grasses as accents. If you have a pond, try planting a moisture-loving sort such as purple moor grass *(Molinia caerulea)* near the water's edge to create a natural-looking scene.

Most ornamental grasses are long lived. Consult the chart at right for help in finding several excellent selections for your garden.

Pretty in fall, a medley of grasses colors the landscape beneath a fiery sugar maple. Containers filled with blue fescue and annual red fountain grass boost these shorter grasses to new heights.

AN ORNAMENTAL GRASS SAMPLER

	NAME	EXPOSURE	BLOOMS	DESCRIPTION/LANDSCAPE USES
TO 2 FEET	*Alopecurus pratensis* 'Aureus' Yellow foxtail grass	Full sun or partial shade	Spring to summer	Green leaves striped gold; short foxtail-like tan flower spikes early in season. Mass at front of border. (to −30°F)
	Deschampsia cespitosa 'Northern Lights' Variegated tufted hair grass	Full sun or partial shade	Late spring to summer	Striking green-and-cream leaves; foliage pinkish early in season and in cool weather. Tall, gold to greenish gold flower spikes turn straw colored in winter. Good massed. (to −20°F)
	Festuca glauca 'Elijah Blue' Blue fescue	Full sun or partial shade	Late spring to early summer	Clump of intensely blue foliage; excellent massed as edging for borders. Violet-blue flower spikes age to tan. (to −40°F)
	Sesleria caerulea Blue moor grass	Full sun or partial shade	Spring	Tufted clump of narrow, metallic blue-gray leaves; bluish purple flower spikelets. Use as accent at front of border. (to −30°F)
	Sporobolus heterolepis Prairie dropseed	Full sun	Late summer to fall	Elegant prairie native has emerald green foliage, cloud of scented, airy flowers. Leaves turn golden in fall. Extremely drought tolerant. Excellent as a border. (to −40°F)
2 TO 4 FEET	*Chasmanthium latifolium* Northern sea oats	Full sun to full shade	Summer	Upright clump of bamboolike green leaves that turn yellow in late fall. Silvery green flowers like flattened clusters of oats on tall spikes; turn copper in fall. Good for cutting. (to −20°F)
	Helictotrichon sempervirens 'Sapphire' Blue oat grass	Full sun	Late spring to summer	Vivid blue foliage in rounded clumps; tan flower spikes. Ideal massed or as accent in border. Effective with purple- or silver-leafed plants. (to −40°F)
	Panicum virgatum 'Heavy Metal' Blue switch grass	Full sun or partial shade	Summer to early fall	Excellent, popular variety with erect form, bright metallic blue foliage, and pinkish flowers. Leaves turn yellow in fall. Excellent as accent. Species is a prairie native. (to −40°F)
	Schizachyrium scoparium 'The Blues' Little bluestem	Full sun	Late summer	Compact plant with upright blue leaves, pinkish plumes. Ideal for massing or naturalizing. Foliage turns bronzy orange in fall; plumes turn coppery. Species is a prairie native. (to −30°F)
4 TO 6 FEET OR MORE	*Calamagrostis × acutiflora* 'Karl Foerster' Feather reed grass	Full sun or partial shade	Summer	Forms arching clump of medium green leaves. Upright, pinkish bronze plumes age to buff, last through winter. Plant as a specimen or group as a screen. Handsome accent in fall. (to −30°F)
	Miscanthus sinensis 'Purpurascens' Flame grass	Full sun or partial shade	Late summer to fall	Purplish green leaves turn reddish orange in fall. Upright, pinkish tan flower plumes. Use in mass plantings or as specimen; good in front of dark evergreens. (to −30°F)
	Miscanthus sinensis 'Silberfeder' Silver feather miscanthus	Full sun or partial shade	Late summer to fall	Fine-textured grass with green leaves; silvery to pinkish plumes last through winter. Good as specimen or in mixed or perennial border. (to −30°F; requires winter protection in some areas)
	Molinia caerulea arundinacea 'Skyracer' Tall moor grass	Full sun or partial shade	Summer to fall	Impressive grass with gray-green leaves. Blossom spikes are carried on tall arching stems. Use as specimen, massed at back of border, or in front of conifers. Golden fall foliage. (to −30°F)
	Sorghastrum nutans Indian grass	Full sun	Summer	A prairie native. Erect bluish green leaves. Reddish gold seedheads are handsome dried. Use at back of border. (to −30°F)

Miscanthus sinensis 'Silberfeder'   *Helictotrichon sempervirens*   *Panicum virgatum*   *Calamagrostis × acutiflora*

GRASSY BORDERS

Though a solitary clump of ornamental grass can create a focal point among other garden plants, you can enliven an entire border—or a whole garden—by skillfully combining several or even a dozen kinds of grasses. Massed grasses in bold hues bring color and excitement when you mix them with more traditional border plants such as flowering perennials and shrubs. Incorporating grasses with other types of plants imitates nature, softening the appearance and bringing harmony to the garden by unifying the other plantings. You can use grasses to separate flower colors that would otherwise clash. Grasses also look right at home planted around a pond, in a rock garden, or as a transition between mowed lawn and woodland.

Plant small grasses in groups, larger ones as accents. Or combine tall grasses with large, bold perennials such as Joe Pye weed *(Eupatorium purpureum)* and queen of the prairie *(Filipendula rubra)* to capture the feel of a walk through the tall-grass prairie. Taller grasses show off especially well when backlit by early morning or evening light, and the slightest breeze makes them wave softly to and fro. Many ornamental grasses have flowers that can add striking or subtle color and texture to the garden. And some of these offer blooms that can be cut for fresh or dried arrangements. In winter, the grasses add interest to the garden. The photographs at left present some particularly showy grasses, illustrating ways to combine them with other plants.

A. Feather reed grass *(Calamagrostis)* provides excellent contrast with spiky yucca leaves and showy sedum flower clusters. These easy-care plants are seldom bothered by pests or diseases, and all three thrive in the heat of a typical Midwestern summer.

B. A feathery clump of variegated bulbous oat grass *(Arrbenatherum elatius bulbosum* 'Variegatum'), with its frosty white—edged foliage, lights up this perennial border. The variegated leaves contrast handsomely with the darker gray-green foliage of dianthus in the foreground.

C. Fountainlike foliage of miscanthus grasses provides a perfect backdrop for a sea of black-eyed Susans *(Rudbeckia)* in late summer. Ornamental grasses swaying in a breeze bring welcome movement to the garden.

A WALK AMONG THE GRASSES

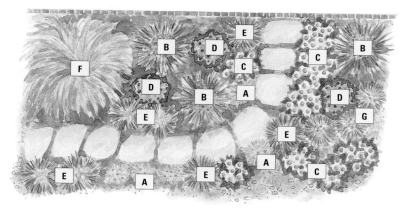

Planting area: 9' × 18'

The Plants

A. Alopecurus pratensis 'Aureus'
YELLOW FOXTAIL GRASS **(6)**

**B. Calamagrostis × acutiflora
'Karl Foerster'**
FEATHER REED GRASS **(3)**

C. Echinacea purpurea 'White Swan'
CONEFLOWER **(8)**

D. Helenium 'Moerheim Beauty'
SNEEZEWEED **(3)**

**E. Helictotrichon sempervirens
'Sapphire'**
BLUE OAT GRASS **(7)**

F. Miscanthus sinensis 'Silberfeder'
SILVER FEATHER MISCANTHUS **(1)**

**G. Schizachyrium scoparium
'The Blues'**
LITTLE BLUESTEM **(3)**

DWARF CONIFERS

Conifers are finding new homes in Midwestern gardens, thanks to dwarf varieties that mature at 6 feet or lower. Like their larger relatives, these pint-size specimens offer year-round color as well as interesting texture and form. But unlike full-size trees, they won't grow into towering sentinels that can dominate—and sometimes swallow up—a landscaped garden.

Based on their height at maturity, conifers are divided into four size classes: miniature (plants remain under 3 feet at age 10); dwarf (3 to 6 feet tall after 10 years); intermediate (6 to 15 feet); and large (taller than 15 feet). Though any but the largest size is suitable for gardens, dwarfs are ideal—they're big enough to make an impact, yet small and slow growing enough not to overshadow their neighbors. In winter, a light dusting of snow turns the tiny trees into a magical presence.

Typically sold in 1- or 5-gallon pots, dwarf conifers come in a variety of forms. Some are upright; others cascade or sprawl near the ground. Some are slim and columnar, others broad and rounded. Foliage covers a range of colors, including gold, green, and blue; you'll also find some types with variegated needles.

Use dwarf conifers to dress up an entryway, or plant one as a specimen tree or shrub in a rock garden. Cluster several hardy selections in a large pot for a low-maintenance, year-round container "forest." The more colorful choices can beautifully anchor a perennial planting or provide contrast in a mixed border, though it's important to consider the seasonal hues of nearby plants. For example, a golden dwarf spruce might be a handsome focal point in a winter landscape—but if it's planted amid pink roses, its yellow needles might clash with the rose blooms in summer.

A. Hardy and evergreen, creeping yellow junipers, a bright green pine, and a blue spruce provide color contrast throughout the year. Dwarf plant size allows close planting and offers the perfect scale in a rock garden.

B–D. Choice specimens with excellent compact form include **(B)** *Picea pungens glauca* 'Globosa', rounded with whitish blue foliage; **(C)** *Picea omorika* 'Nana', pyramidal with bicolor needles; and **(D)** *Pinus mugo* 'White Bud', with mounding habit and dark green foliage.

Colorful Conifers

GREEN FOLIAGE

Picea omorika 'Nana'
SERBIAN SPRUCE

Pinus mugo 'Sherwood Compact'
MUGHO PINE

Thuja occidentalis 'Hetz Midget'
AMERICAN ARBORVITAE

Tsuga canadensis 'Cole's Prostrate'
PROSTRATE CANADA HEMLOCK

GOLDEN FOLIAGE

Chamaecyparis pisifera 'Filifera Aurea Nana'
GOLD THREADLEAF FALSE CYPRESS

Juniperus horizontalis 'Mother Lode'
CREEPING JUNIPER

Picea glauca 'Rainbow's End'
WHITE SPRUCE

Thuja occidentalis 'Rheingold'
GOLDEN AMERICAN ARBORVITAE

BLUE FOLIAGE

Abies concolor 'Compacta'
CONCOLOR FIR

Juniperus chinensis 'Blue Alps'
CHINESE JUNIPER

Picea pungens 'Montgomery'
COLORADO SPRUCE

Pseudotsuga menziesii 'Fletcheri'
DOUGLAS FIR

E. A colorful palette. Top picks for the Midwest in this group include, at far left, blue-green *Pinus strobus* 'Blue Shag', steel blue *Abies balsamea* 'Nana'; in the center, *Juniperus squamata* 'Blue Star' (left), *Thuja occidentalis* 'Hetz Midget' (right); and at bottom left to right, golden *Juniperus horizontalis* 'Mother Lode', gold and orange *Thuja occidentalis* 'Rheingold', and slate blue *Picea pungens* 'Montgomery'.

E

ROCK GARDEN PLANTS

Like picture postcards of nature, rock gardens simulate boulder-strewn mountain slopes or rocky coastal bluffs dotted with small flowering or evergreen plants. Columbines and tulips only 2 inches tall and tiny pines and junipers that top out at just 1 foot are some of the plants that thrive in Midwestern rock gardens. Other favorites include rockcress, creeping sedums, hen and chicks, snow-in-summer, and soapwort *(Saponaria)*.

True alpine plants grow on high mountain slopes, spending winters beneath a blanket of snow. Low and ground hugging, they send deep roots into rocky crevices. Many sport brilliantly colored and often surprisingly large blossoms. Fortunately for Midwestern gardeners, many of these plants prosper at elevations far lower than their native habitats, provided that soil is well drained. And small flowering bulbs, perennials, and dwarf shrubs native to windy and dry-summer areas of Asia, Europe, and other parts of the world prosper in rock gardens throughout the Midwest.

With its naturally brisk drainage, a hard-to-mow slope makes an ideal site for a rock garden. Remember that small rock garden plants are best seen at close range; set them in around stone steps or along the tops of low retaining walls to show their flowers and foliage to best advantage. In a larger rock garden, dwarf conifers and small contorted shrubs can be used to dramatic effect.

Local rocks, all of the same composition, make the most natural-looking garden. Rather than spacing them evenly, arrange them in groups to mimic a hillside with rocky outcroppings. Bury the rocks about halfway, tilting them so water runs back into the soil rather than down the slope. Lay the rocks with the grain of each one running in the same direction.

After planting, cover the ground with a mulch of gravel or stone chips to preserve soil moisture and keep down weeds.

A. Bright pink, ball-shaped flowers stand atop tiny tufts of sea thrifts' *(Armeria maritima)* grassy green foliage. Thriving in light, well-drained soil, this perennial is a rock-garden star.

B. In this sunny garden, creeping phlox *(Phlox subulata)* carpets the rocks in brilliant pink. After flowering, plants should be cut back halfway to promote dense foliage.

C. A bank of white blossoms and silvery leaves in June earns *Cerastium tomentosum* its common name, snow-in-summer. A rapid spreader in moist, fertile soil, it's better behaved in the dry, well-drained soil of a rock garden.

A MINIATURE MOUNTAINSIDE

The Plants

A. **Arabis caucasica 'Flore Plena'**
WALL ROCKCRESS **(3)**

B. **Arctostaphylos uva-ursi 'Vancouver Jade'**
BEARBERRY **(2)**

C. **Armeria maritima 'Rubrifolia'**
SEA THRIFT **(5)**

D. **Artemisia schmidtiana 'Silver Mound'**
WORMWOOD **(1)**

E. **Aurinia saxatilis 'Sunny Border Apricot'**
BASKET-OF-GOLD **(1)**

F. **Cerastium tomentosum columnae**
SNOW-IN-SUMMER **(3)**

G. **Festuca glauca 'Elijah Blue'**
BLUE FESCUE **(2)**

H. **Geranium dalmaticum**
CRANESBILL **(3)**

I. **Juniperus squamata 'Blue Star'**
JUNIPER **(1)**

J. **Oenothera macrocarpa (O. missouriensis)**
MISSOURI PRIMROSE **(3)**

K. **Penstemon pinifolius 'Mersea Yellow'**
PINELEAF PENSTEMON **(3)**

L. **Picea pungens 'Montgomery'**
COLORADO SPRUCE (DWARF) **(1)**

M. **Scutellaria resinosa**
PRAIRIE SKULLCAP **(1)**

N. **Sedum 'Vera Jameson' (1)**

O. **Veronica spicata incana**
SILVER SPEEDWELL **(3)**

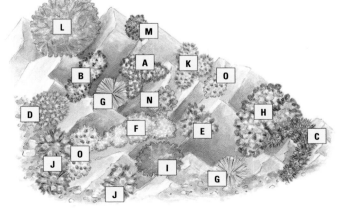

Planting area: 10' × 14'

SUCCULENTS

With their fleshy, water-storing leaves, succulents are a practical choice for many Midwestern landscapes. They're also a designer's delight, with their myriad shapes, colors, and textures that create an exciting palette.

Sedum, one of the most versatile of garden plants, is particularly valued for the many shades and shapes its foliage and blossoms bring to the landscape. Among creeping species, leaf color ranges from the blue gray of *Sedum cauticolum* to the red-edged green of *S. spurium* 'Dragon's Blood' to the green, white, and pink of *S. s.* 'Tricolor'. *S.* 'Vera Jameson', a taller selection, has maroon-tinged leaves. Sedum's flowers offer plenty of variety, too, coming in a color range that includes pink, red, gold, yellow, or white. *S.* 'Autumn Joy' in particular is prized for its blooms: rosy pink in midsummer, they deepen to a red bronze in fall, then finally turn to golden brown in winter.

Drought-tolerant yucca plants with their bold, spiky foliage add drama to the garden. Their towering blossom stalks provide a striking vertical accent. A collection of low-growing hen and chicks creates a kaleidoscope of colors and intriguing shapes. The paddle-like stems and yellow flowers of prickly pear offer interesting contrast. For the greatest impact, mass succulents in groups, choosing a different leaf color and shape for each cluster of plants.

Tough, cold-hardy succulents tolerate almost any well-drained soil and, once established, cope well with drought. To create a garden bed you won't have to water in dry weather, combine them with ornamental grasses and other unthirsty perennials, such as artemisia, blanket flower, lamb's ears, and yarrow.

A. This handsome foursome requires little or no watering. The pink-mauve flowers of 'Autumn Joy' sedum cut a cheerful swath in this bed of yucca, blue fescue, and hen and chicks.

B. Sedums are favored for their cold hardiness. Here, a variegated form of *Sedum kamtschaticum* dominates a rockery.

C. Low, dense prickly pear cactus shows off the delicate bright green foliage and white blooms of *Baptisia alba* (white false indigo). Baptisias adapt to almost any well-drained soil.

D. An old-fashioned favorite, tiny hen and chicks comes in many colors and shapes. Their thick, fleshy leaves assure the plants' survival in dry weather. After flowering, the "mother hen" dies, but the "chicks" continue to multiply.

Hardy Succulents

Opuntia compressa (O. humifusa)
PRICKLY PEAR
Mat-forming plant; thick, fleshy,
padlike leaves

Opuntia polyacantha
PLAINS PRICKLY PEAR
Same as *O. compressa,* but with
prominent downward-pointing spines

Sedum 'Autumn Joy'
Green leaves, pink-mauve flowers

Sedum cauticolum
Blue-green foliage, pink flowers

Sedum floriferum 'Weihenstephaner Gold'
Green leaves, gold flowers

Sedum 'Frosty Morn'
Gray-green leaves, white flowers

Sedum kamtschaticum
Green leaves, yellow-gold flowers

Sedum kamtschaticum 'Variegatum'
Dark green leaves with white markings

Sedum 'Matrona'
Gray-green leaves, pink flowers

Sedum sexangulare
Green leaves, yellow flowers

Sedum spectabile 'Brilliant'
Blue-green leaves, red flowers

Sedum spurium 'Dragon's Blood'
Red-edged leaves, red stems and flowers

Sedum spurium 'Tricolor'
Green, white and pink leaves, red stems,
pink flowers

Sedum 'Vera Jameson'
Maroon-tinged leaves, pink flowers

Sempervivum arachnoideum
COBWEB HOUSELEEK
Fleshy leaves in compact rosettes densely
covered with white hairs

Sempervivum tectorum
HEN AND CHICKS
Fleshy leaves in compact rosettes

Yucca filamentosa 'Bright Edge'
Swordlike leaves broadly edged in rich
yellow

Yucca glauca
Sharply pointed gray-green swordlike
leaves

Yucca gloriosa 'Golden Sword'
Swordlike leaves with prominent central
gold stripe

THE NATURALIZED GARDEN

Explorers like Lewis and Clark marveled at the beauty and diversity of the Midwestern landscape, filling their journals with descriptions of wetlands, woodlands, prairies, and plains. They found a landscape that had been shaped by prehistoric glaciers and floods, by fires and winds. The plants that survived were tough, holding their own against extremes of weather and aggressive neighbors in native communities of trees, shrubs, and vines, or grasses and flowers. Both hardy and pretty, these natural landscapes are, indeed, worth re-creating in our own backyards.

Why do we find undisturbed forests and prairies so beautiful? Perhaps because nature's plan doesn't use lawnmowers or tape measures. In forests, countless trees, shrubs, vines, and flowers grow together in a seemingly random pattern. Prairies, too, are dense blends of many plant species. There's no reason why we can't reproduce these natural designs in at least part of our home landscape, creating a feast for the eyes, ears, and soul.

A naturalized garden invites exploration. Plants spill over onto meandering paths, often growing in clusters rather than as single specimens. The sound of gurgling water and singing birds, the fragrance of flowers, and the motion of waving grasses and fluttering butterflies delight the senses.

Whether native or adapted to the Midwest, the plants in a naturalized garden should echo the surrounding countryside. In the southern half of the region, an understory of redbuds in a landscape duplicates the springtime blossom show of wild-growing trees. In a northern garden, bugbane, goat's beard, and other cold-hardy perennials thrive in the shade under native oaks and birches. In a Great Plains garden, prairie grasses and drought-tolerant flowers like poppy mallow and goldenrod seem most at home.

"We cannot all live in wilderness," wrote Minnesota naturalist Sigurd F. Olson, "but we can, no matter where we spend our lives, remember the background which shaped this sense of the eternal rhythm." Home landscaping is a way for most of us to reconnect every day with what Olson called our "primeval background," a place where land and the elements dictate the plan. "Problem" sites offer an opportunity to add diversity to the landscape. A poorly drained area, for example, is a perfect place for meadowsweet and turtlehead. On a steep slope, aggressive plants like variegated ribbon grass and bishop's weed are an asset, not a liability. And plants matched to their site seldom suffer problems. Pesticides and fungicides aren't needed. Beneficial insects, earthworms, and birds thrive and increase. Fallen leaves enrich the soil.

"Everyone," wrote the famed Midwestern landscaper Jens Jensen, "is entitled to a home where the sun, the stars, open [areas]... trees... smiling flowers, are free to teach an undisturbed lesson of life." In creating a natural landscape, you can enjoy such an oasis of serenity in your own backyard.

A. **This sunny meadow** filled with bright yellow sunflowers and lavender bergamot *(Monarda fistulosa)* blossoms is an extension of the countryside.

B. **A rustic birdhouse** creates the perfect accent for a naturalized garden.

C. **Indian grass** surrounded by blooming black-eyed Susans *(Rudbeckia hirta)* and sunflowers *(Helianthus)* mirrors the prairie.

D. **Bright red blooms** of bee balm *(Monarda didyma)* attract a hummingbird.

E. **Backed by a limestone bluff** and swift-running creek, this Missouri garden bursts with blooms of bleeding hearts, Virginia bluebells *(Mertensia pulmonarioides),* and violets. A "window" cut into the undergrowth gives a view of the creek and connects the garden to its natural setting.

FINISHING TOUCHES

A garden's personality comes from more than its plants and structures. Much depends on the gardener's knack for adding finishing touches—a copper lantern, a brightly glazed pot, a collection of folk-art birdhouses. From a teak bench to a lacy hammock or a well-placed boulder, these decorative elements can create a focal point in your garden, complement a grouping of foliage and flowers, or simply delight the eye.

Luckily, garden accessories have never been as plentiful and as varied as they are today. Furniture is available in a variety of styles, umbrellas come fitted with lights or with canvas walls that block the wind, and birdbaths range from rustic to sculptural in form. Resourceful gardeners are turning humble boulders into striking sculptures and adding flair with birdhouses, statuary, outdoor lighting, and painted fences. Giving your garden a distinctive look is as simple as letting your imagination lead the way.

BIRDBATHS

If you set a birdbath out in your garden, it's a sure bet feathered visitors will come flocking—especially on warm summer days. Birdbaths run the gamut from simple to elaborate. Some are simple bowls that sit on the ground or atop pedestals or hang from chains. Others are designed as much for the people who watch the birds as for the birds themselves. You can also display eye-catching birdbaths as garden art.

Once birds discover your garden bath as a reliable source of water—placed in the right spot,

kept filled and clean—your garden will come alive with their color, music, and activity. You'll discover the quiet pleasure of watching sparrows, cardinals, and other songbirds swoop into the bath for a splashing good time. Squirrels can also delight you with their antics as they attempt to take advantage of your birdbath.

A dip cools birds in summer, and it can help them keep warm in winter. Frequent bathing insulates birds by keeping their feathers clean and fluffed. So keep the birdbath filled and ready for whatever flies your way.

Birdbath Basics

Keep it shallow but roomy. *Ideally, baths should be 2 to 3 inches deep and 24 to 36 inches across. The sides should slope gradually.*

Consider materials. *Some materials like plastic are too slippery for birds and can crack with age. Metal dishes, if used, should be of stainless steel or other rust-resistant material.*

Keep it clean. *Use a strong jet of water from the hose to clean the bowl. If the bottom is dirty, scrub it.*

Keep it safe. *Put the birdbath next to shrubs or trees that provide cover and escape routes. Place ground-level baths where they have 10 to 20 feet of open space around them—but no more, or you'll leave damp birds exposed to hawks, owls, and cats.*

Keep it moving. *Running water attracts birds. Some baths come with built-in fountains, or you can add a small fountain by adding a submersible pump with a spray head.*

Keep it from freezing. *In cold climates, add a heating element in winter to keep the bath water thawed.*

G

A. What bird could possibly pass up the opportunity to take a dip in this cobalt-blue birdbath?

B. This fanciful stone bowl, embellished with salamanders, can rest on a pedestal or a boulder.

C. As much sculpture as birdbath, this copper basin stands out against a fountain of ornamental grasses.

D. This homemade bath is a glazed terra-cotta saucer resting atop a pot.

E. A steel sundial encircles the copper basin in this dual-purpose structure.

F. A yellow toy sailboat adds a whimsical touch to this birdbath—a cast-concrete bowl, perched atop a tree stump.

G. Suspended near a window, this glazed stoneware bath provides a delightful show of songbirds.

BIRDHOUSES

Like weather vanes and sundials, birdhouses can be as artistic as they are functional. They come in many styles, from gaily painted wooden antiques to sleek metal models. However delightful they may look to you, you'll want to make sure the birds find them attractive as well.

Only cavity-nesting birds (those that nest in tree hollows) use birdhouses. This group includes bluebirds, chickadees, nuthatches, swallows, and wrens. The type of birdhouse you install determines the kinds of birds you'll attract, but this is a most inexact science—a birdhouse may be intended for a wren or a bluebird, but it will be fair game for any birds of similar size.

Small birds, such as chickadees, nuthatches, and most wrens, prefer a hole that's 1⅛ inches across. Medium-size birds, such as bluebirds, swallows, and purple martins, need a nest box with a hole 1½ inches wide. White-breasted nuthatches need a 1¼-inch opening.

Larger birds, such as flickers and kestrels, take boxes with 2½-inch entry holes. Flickers usually like to dig out their own nests, but sometimes you can attract them with a large nest box. Fill it with wood chips; they'll dig it out.

A. This fanciful flying-stork birdhouse doesn't fool many birds.

B. Attached to a wooden post and camouflaged by a clematis vine, this inviting house is ready to host a family of birds.

C. Built to Audubon specifications, these sleekly designed birdhouses sit atop tall poles.

Birdhouse Basics

To keep birdhouses safe *from raccoons and cats, mount the houses atop metal poles. If you want to put a birdhouse in a tree, hang it from a branch.*

Keep houses away *from feeders (the mealtime bustle makes nesting birds nervous).*

Face the entrance *away from the prevailing weather, and remove any perch your birdhouse came with (it's unnecessary, and house sparrows may sit on it to heckle birds inside).*

Birdhouses *should be made from materials that insulate well, such as 1-inch-thick wood (plastic milk bottles and milk cartons are too thin and have poor ventilation; heat can bake chicks inside or make them fledge too early).*

Nest boxes *(shown below) need a side or top that opens for easy cleaning, drain holes on the bottom, and, in hot summer areas, ventilation holes high in the sides.*

If you put up *more than one, keep houses well separated and out of sight of one another. Houses must be up before migrant birds start returning in late February, looking for nest sites soon after they arrive.*

D. This wren house has a 1⅛-inch entry hole and a short chain to minimize swinging.

E. A chickadee house mimics the birds' favored hollow conifer.

F. This terra-cotta "bird bottle" accommodates wrens, sparrows, and swallows.

G. Made of metal, this bird condo can house a flock.

H. A bluebird nest box with a 1½-inch entry has a removable side for easy cleaning at season's end.

STONE

From the native limestone of Indiana to the granite of Minnesota, gardeners in the Midwest have a wealth of stone to choose from. As a material for walls, paths, ponds, benches, and ornamentation, stone adds warmth, strength, and unique character to the garden.

Quarries, construction materials suppliers, and nurseries can supply huge boulders and slabs or stone of more manageable size such as potato rock, pebbles, and flagstones. Before you buy, consider what size is appropriate for your site. Once placed, a large boulder will be difficult to move. It is wise to work with a landscape architect, designer, or contractor with experience in installing stone. If you have a sloping lot, a landscape professional can also ascertain the ability of the site to hold the stone securely.

Boulders are great for decorating streams, waterfalls, and pond borders, but remember that rock that is in contact with water should be hard and durable. Limestone and sandstone are not good choices, as they flake and deteriorate; their particles can clog pumps.

A. Blending beautifully with the naturally occurring rock nearby, these flat stepping-stones make a functional and organic pathway.

B. The horizontal and vertical forms of these large boulders seem to mirror the growth habits of the plants and trees sharing this planting bed.

C. A large stone slab anchors the serenity of this Japanese sand garden. Its solid form and texture contrast with the sand and small-leafed azalea.

Boulder Basics

Try to work with rock made available in your region. It will be relatively inexpensive and more likely to suit your landscape.

At the rock yard, flag the rocks you want with colored tape. Figure out exactly where each will go in the garden—and which side will go up (taking snapshots of the rocks can help you place them at delivery time).

Most rock is sold by the ton, though some is also sold by shape (slabs and columns, for example). If you want rocks covered with moss or lichen, expect to pay extra, but beware: moss doesn't always survive the move from supplier to backyard patio.

Don't put large rocks on top of small ones. Unless you do it artfully, the large rocks will look unstable. Rocks with flat tops are useful as informal benches or for holding container plants.

Allow for the settling of large rocks (the amount can be significant).

Rocks look better with time. Scars from transport and handling disappear, and lichen will grow on them if you live where the air is relatively unpolluted.

Artificial boulders offer a lighter-weight alternative, but they can be more expensive. Typically made of concrete over metal lath, they're shaped, colored, and textured to look like the real thing.

FURNITURE

There's an enduring graciousness to outdoor furniture. It evokes images of rolling lawns, intimate gardens, and lemonade in the afternoon. But deciding which furniture to buy can be a challenge.

Many styles are available, in materials that include teak, woven willow, and cast iron. Rustic furniture blends well with natural surroundings. Contemporary styles are available to complement patios and decks. Still other outdoor "furniture" comes not from a showroom but from a gardener's imagination—well-placed boulders, stones, or wooden planks can also provide outdoor seating.

Manufactured lounges, chairs, and tables are often designed in sets, with pieces priced individually or in a grouping. In general, wooden furniture is more expensive than that of cast resin or metal.

Whichever type you choose, keep in mind that outdoor furniture must withstand the elements—sun, rain, insects—and heavy wear and tear from people and pets. Deck and patio furniture can be stored or covered over the winter, but check with the manufacturer if you plan to leave benches, chairs, or other items in the garden year-round.

A. A rustic willow-and-redtwig highback chair and table nestle among a natural planting of coneflowers and Queen Anne's lace.

B. This brightly painted Adirondack chair adds personality and color to the garden.

C. **A sense of tranquility** surrounds this shaded arbor swing and fountain tucked among ferns, liriope, begonias, and impatiens.

D. **The warm colors** of gladiolas and ornamental peppers in terra-cotta pots accentuate this cedar bench displayed against a stone ledge.

E. **A clean white porch swing** sparkles among cascading geraniums.

F. **An inviting secluded seating area** uses brilliant begonias and salmon-colored geraniums to accentuate the warm brick of the patio and the patina of the wood furniture.

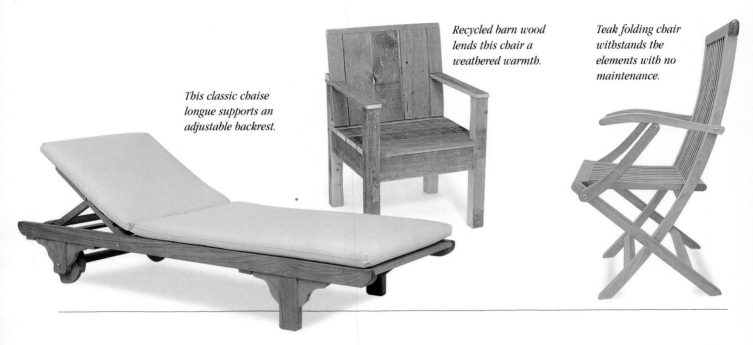

This classic chaise longue supports an adjustable backrest.

Recycled barn wood lends this chair a weathered warmth.

Teak folding chair withstands the elements with no maintenance.

Furniture Materials

With so many styles available, the choice of garden furniture can bewilder even decisive shoppers. One good way to narrow the field is to narrow your range of materials.

METAL. If you like heavy metal but your budget doesn't, you can buy cast aluminum or steel that looks like wrought iron. Also consider enameled or powder-coated aluminum-frame furniture. It won't rust, and it's durable and lightweight.

WOOD. Teak and redwood are favored for their beauty, strength, and resistance to insects and rot. Other woods include jarrah, a member of the eucalyptus family that performs and weathers like teak; Honduran cedar, the pink-brown wood with the distinctive "cigar-box" smell; and jatroba (also known as courbaril), a tight-grained wood from the West Indies and Central and South America. (To avoid depleting natural supplies, purchase only plantation grown or recycled wood.)

Willow is less durable, but a yearly application of water sealer will extend its life. As woods weather, they turn gray unless you seal them with marine varnish or semitransparent stain.

SYNTHETICS. Wicker and rattan made of natural fibers are less durable and are better suited to sheltered patios or enclosed porches. Synthetic wicker looks and feels like natural wicker, but it is made of cellulose, resin, or latex-coated fibers and is undaunted by weather. The quality, texture, and color of plastic or resin furniture are improving, and tables and chairs made from these materials are colorful and inexpensive outdoor furnishings.

Matching table-and-chair set is of rolled steel. Perforations on the seat prevent water from pooling.

This teak armchair brings a flourish to formal settings.

Both bistro chair (left) and teak steamer chair (below) fold for storage.

Wicker's natural flexibility creates a chair with the right amount of give.

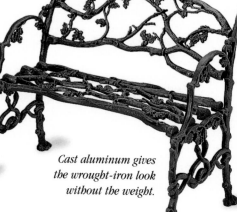

Cast aluminum gives the wrought-iron look without the weight.

This stately cedar chair recalls design elements of the Arts-and-Crafts movement.

Joinery 101

When shopping for outdoor furniture, pay close attention to the joinery. A good joint—where a chair leg or arm meets the seat, for example—looks nearly seamless. And it is strong: it gives a chair, bench, or table the strength needed to withstand weight and lateral movement.

The photographs at right show three types of quality joinery on wooden furniture. Brass hexagonal head bolts and barrel nuts (top) reinforce joints at critical points. Mortise-and-tenon joints held in place with dowels (middle) create a strong interlocking bond. Screws and blocking join and reinforce a redwood chair (bottom).

GARDEN ART

Like icing on a cake, the right garden art, in the right place, can transform an ordinary garden into a magical and intriguing place. An outdoor sculpture can serve as a visual surprise among riotous blooms or as a focal point that adds interest to a quiet foliage background.

The key to selecting and displaying garden art effectively is to begin with pieces that fit your garden's style. Gardens that are more formal will benefit from pieces that are symmetrical and ornate, made of classic materials of stone or metal. Gardens that are more modern in style call for bolder and more colorful shapes. Antique pieces work well in gardens with heritage plants, and, for casual gardens, a whimsical piece of folk art can add a playful touch.

Shopping for garden art is half the fun. For larger, more expensive pieces, look in outdoor sculpture galleries or inquire through a museum. Major metropolitan areas and small towns known to be artists' havens usually have at least one such gallery. Some artists also sell directly from their studios or will create a piece for you.

Specialty garden shops, interior-design and gift stores, and mail-order catalogs offer a good selection of garden art in a more modest price range. Sundials, birdhouses, wall plaques, colorful gazing balls, and wood, stone, or metal sculptures are available in many styles through these sources. And great garden treasures are always awaiting discovery in salvage yards, antique shops, and thrift stores.

A. **A metal sunflower** stands proudly amid a brilliant mass of cosmos and zinnias.

B. **This friendly stone hedgehog** from England peers out of a purple crown of 'The President' clematis in this St. Paul, Minnesota, garden.

C. **A burnished rooster weather vane** is happy to wake up every day amid a field of coneflowers.

D. **Crotons, nicotiana, and bougainvillea** tumble out of a wooden cart in this Minneapolis garden.

E. **Fall's bounty** decorates two friendly scarecrows.

A. **An armillary sphere** and axial arrow made of copper mark the hours in a garden full of gooseneck loosestrife.

B. **A colorful painted chair** and drying basket set off their bright jewel tones against a backdrop of red coleus in this Nebraska garden.

C. **Salvia 'Mainacht'** and bright shrub roses are the foreground for a simple sundial displayed against viburnums.

Display Basics

Size and shape of a garden piece determine its placement. Large sculptures can sit on the ground, stand on a pedestal or platform, or take center stage in a fountain or pool. Large pieces are usually best viewed against a uniform background. For smaller pieces, the specific plants or other objects nearby become an important part of the display.

Grouping is crucial. Too many pieces scattered though a garden make it look cluttered. Arrange them too close together, and they lose their unique impact.

Keep the backdrop simple. No matter where you put garden art, make sure the surroundings are simple enough to display it properly. Hedges, fences, walls, and masses of green plants work well as backgrounds.

Keep scale in mind. A large piece requires plenty of space to prevent it from dwarfing its neighbors. A small piece can get lost in a jungle of foliage.

Use your imagination. If the piece is too big to move from place to place, walk around your garden and imagine it placed in various locations. Make sketches or take photographs if necessary to aid your imagination. If the piece is smaller, you can place it in various locations to see where it looks best. Be sure you have the right place for your garden art before you buy.

D. An old tractor seat and grain scoop become a strutting turkey in this Missouri garden.

E. A larger-than-life scholarly frog is sure to evoke a chuckle from garden visitors seeking a quiet reading corner.

F. Silver water "bubbles" add a playful touch to a water garden, whether inside or outside the pool.

GARDEN ART FOR ALL SEASONS

G arden art can be changed with the seasons or it can remain as a fixed, reliable feature despite falling leaves, blowing snow, driving rain, or howling winds.

Seasonal garden art can add variety and interest to your garden. A playful way to celebrate the seasons in the garden is to change artistic features and plants to correspond with changing seasons or seasonal holidays. Folk art, garden signs, banners, and containers are all available in seasonal themes. Seasonal garden art can also include natural or temporary elements to enhance the art itself, unlike permanent pieces that need to be created from sturdy materials.

In fall, gourds and pumpkins echo the colors of the autumn leaves and complement a wooden witch or a plump metal turkey. Winter provides a wealth of evergreens to be dressed up with berries, lanterns, and bows. A colorful snow sprite or elf can be displayed against a snowy background. In spring, bright wildflowers can surround a stone bunny or spill from a woven basket. Summer's green colors invite painted wooden creatures to sun themselves beneath grasses and on top of stone walls. Or the red, white, and blue of the Fourth of July can become a theme for choosing art and flowers.

Garden art that is meant to be appreciated year-round should be seasonless—a ceramic dragonfly floating above a snowbank doesn't make much sense, but a simple stone obelisk transcends the change of seasons. Place temporary seasonal pieces where they can be enjoyed from a window or on the approach to your home. Keep in mind that the setting for the art will change if the background plants are deciduous.

A. A **bikini-clad green frog** enjoys a sunny day on an arched bridge over a lily-covered pond.

B. A **folk-art flag** surrounded by salvia, coleus, and petunias in patriotic colors celebrates the season of summer fireworks.

C. **Autumn's rich colors** are captured in the red well pump and fallen leaves, with pumpkins and mums adding seasonal flair.

D. **Season's greetings** are extended in this garden with bright ribbons on a snow-covered basket filled with evergreens.

A WHIMSICAL GARDEN

What gardener can resist a garden that appeals to the child in all of us—one that is whimsical and tiny and intriguing and totally impractical and perfect? Such a garden was created by Craig Bergmann and Associates for a recent Chicago Flower and Garden Show. Their Wind in the Willows garden was based on Kenneth Grahame's beloved book of the same name. Using plants grown especially for the garden, the designers successfully created the illusion of an English garden peopled with woodland creatures without actually showing the characters themselves. Foxgloves and skunk cabbage are scattered along a river bank. Ratty's little home, built into a berm at the base of an old stump, has a planted roof of diminutive "meadow" flowers.

Underlying the charm of The Wind in the Willows garden is the use of scale to create places that evoke a sense of mystery or intrigue. The garden is intended to be used by the creatures who inhabit it, not the humans who observe it. Paths are winding and circuitous, and rooms and furnishings are built for the tiny creatures and their friends. By creating the illusion that the spaces were connected by unseen paths, these designers created a sense of mystery and stirred the viewers' desire to see more. The absence of the characters is one more appeal to onlookers' curiosity.

The Wind in the Willows garden can inspire us to take our garden planning beyond the everyday human scale into the realm of the imagination and consider many delightful possibilities as yet unrealized.

A. A tiny wheelbarrow, the perfect size for its imaginary users, nestles among lilies and foxgloves.

B. Ratty's miniature cottage is tucked into the suckers of an old willow and is surrounded by trailing clematis, primroses, foxglove, and other English garden flowers.

C. Mole's house is just down this woodsy path through bleeding heart and foamflower.

D. Tea for three is set in miniature at a tiny moss-covered table and chairs beneath a bleeding heart.

HAMMOCKS

The world slows down when you stretch out in a hammock. Suspended and supine, you notice more keenly the pleasures of summer—the soft air brushing your cheek, a swaying view into the branches of a tree, chirping birds, the scent of sun-warmed flowers.

Today's hammocks have evolved well beyond the trusty versions made of cotton rope. New synthetic materials are softer, more comfortable, and more durable than traditional materials. The variety of colors and patterns can be easily coordinated with contemporary outdoor furniture. And sizes now run the gamut from a cozy single to king-size.

If your garden lacks trees or posts at just the right distance apart to hang a hammock (12 to 15 feet), look for a model with a sturdy frame made of wood, aluminum, or other material. Check home-supply stores, outdoor-furnishings dealers, and mail-order companies to find just the right hammock; then kick back and relax.

A. The classic cotton rope hammock comes in various lengths and widths. This one is large enough for two people.

B. Quilted and padded for comfort, this hammock is covered with an acrylic fabric that resists fading and mildew.

C. A variation on the theme, this hammock chair is suspended from a single 36-inch oak crossbar. Its plump cushions are covered in washable acrylic.

D. This Brazilian-style hammock of handwoven and crocheted cotton thread is finished with a lacy fringe.

E. A hybrid hammock like this one combines fabric for comfort with rope for air circulation around the legs.

F. The delicate look of this multicolored Mayan hammock belies its strength—it contains almost 2 miles of string.

D

Hammock Basics

Synthetic rope hammocks *are usually made of durable, soft-spun materials such as polyester that resist moisture and come in a range of colors. As with a hammock made of cotton rope, this type will imprint its pattern on your arms and legs if you lie on it for a while.*

Cloth hammocks *are often made of the same fabric that covers contemporary umbrellas and outdoor chairs. It's strong and mildew resistant, and it stands up to harsh sun.*

Screen or mesh hammocks *are made of a shadecloth-type material that is soft, allows good air circulation, can be cleaned easily, and is water and stain resistant.*

Quilted hammocks *are typically made of two layers of weather-resistant polyester with batting between.*

Most hammocks *come with sturdy metal chains, S-hooks, and oversize threaded hooks you can attach to posts. Some suppliers sell these separately. Frames enable you to place a hammock almost anywhere — on a deck or patio or in the middle of a lawn. Other hammock extras include storage bags, canopy tops, and add-on wheels for the frames.*

E

F

A

LIGHTING

B

Well-chosen and carefully placed lighting can create many moods in your garden, from drama to romance.

Outdoor lighting allows you to accentuate certain areas of the garden and leave others in shadow to enhance the mystery. It can also visually enlarge rooms inside your house. If you peer out at an unlighted garden at night, your windows seem like dark mirrors. Landscape lighting makes the windows transparent again, and your home feels more spacious because the eye is drawn outdoors.

Good lighting has a practical use, too. Lights can illuminate a driveway, make paths safe for walking, and brighten dark areas to discourage intruders.

Lighting can be subtle, dramatic, and anything in between. Lighting a pond under water or silhouetting a single shrub or tree can add ethereal magic to a nighttime garden. Carefully placed lights can even mimic the play of moonlight and shadows. Consider the many options shown on the following pages and add hours of enjoyment to your garden after dark.

Lighting Basics

Outdoor lighting fixtures can be either decorative or functional, or both. Decorative lights—lanterns, hanging and post- or wall-mounted units, path lights, and strip lights—add some light, but they're primarily meant to be seen and to create an ambience.

A functional fixture's job is to light the garden without being seen. The less visible these fixtures are, the more successful your lighting will be.

Backlighting a lacy shrub makes it glow delicately.

Path lights can flank walks or be placed high under eaves.

Sidelighting dense trees defines their form.

"Grazing" lights aim upward to highlight architecture.

Uplighting trees reveals their form; their canopy reflects the glow.

Shadowing magnifies plant silhouettes on walls.

"Moonlighting" casts soft pools of light below trees.

A. The warm glow of path lights extends a welcome to the well-lit front porch of this Missouri home.

B. This low-voltage, hand-crafted copper lantern hangs from a curved staff.

C. Cleverly placed strip lighting—recessed in a notch on the underside of the cedar deck railing—provides a soft illumination that invites guests to relax and enjoy the night-time scene.

Standard Current or Low Voltage?

Outdoor lighting can be powered by standard 120-volt current or by low-voltage systems with transformers that reduce 120-volt household current to 12 volts.

Standard current

Well suited for large projects or for lighting tall trees with a bright beam of light, standard-voltage fixtures are often better built and longer lasting than low-voltage models. However, they're also larger, harder to hide, more costly to install, more difficult to move, and harder to aim.

Any standard-voltage installation requires a building permit, and codes require that circuits be wired through ground-fault circuit interrupters (GFCIs). Wires must be encased in rigid conduit unless they're at least 18 inches underground, and all junctions must be encased in approved outdoor boxes.

Low voltage

The advantages of low-voltage fixtures are many, including energy conservation, easier installation, and better control of light beams. Also, some fixtures are solar powered.

On the down side, these fixtures are often merely staked in the ground and can be dislodged easily. They're also expensive, and the number of lamps that can be attached to one transformer is limited.

A. Because it's lightweight, this low-voltage copper cylinder is easy to hang from trees.

B. Graceful lines mark this Craftsman-style copper lantern.

C. A "mushroom" path lamp lights the way for safe passage.

D. This two-tiered pagoda stands tall among shrubs.

E. Unobtrusive and ideal for "grazing," this low-voltage unit casts light upward.

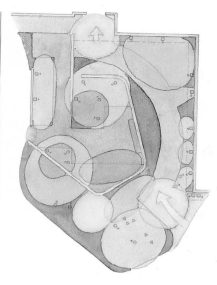

F. This wall-mounted decorative spot provides a vertical shaft of light.

G. The swivel spot casts a narrow beam wherever you need it.

H. When mounted on a wall or ceiling, this low-voltage square spot supplies a pale glow.

I. Designed to illuminate steps and decks, this 12-volt light measures only 3½ inches across.

J. Placed under water, this low-voltage unit may be aimed upward at statues, plants, or small waterfalls.

K. This flush-mounted light tucks beneath steps, staying out of harm's way.

Light Placement

Whether your garden is large or small, start by determining how much of it you want to light. Most lighting designers divide the garden into three zones: a foreground, which is usually given midlevel brightness; a middle ground, with low-level light and an interplay of shadows; and a background—often the brightest of all—to draw the eye through the garden.

The concept plan above shows these different zones. Pathways are marked, and entryways are shown by arrows. Individual lights are indicated by triangles (tree mounts), circles (ground lights), and squares (wall mounts); arrows show the direction of the light they will cast. Fine-tuning for placement and brightness should be done under actual conditions.

Lighting should never be spotty. It should define, not disguise. For example, uplighting gives the mantle of a tall tree a dramatic form, but it can also make the treetop appear to hover, ghostlike, above the earth. To visually anchor the trunk, also illuminate the trunk near ground level.

Finally, be aware of how your lights may affect your neighbors. Some communities have ordinances regulating "light trespass." Timer-controlled lighting is available on many fixtures.

PORTABLE LIGHTING

Special occasions, such as holidays, outdoor parties, or the change of seasons, often call for temporary lighting that can be put into place almost instantly. A variety of lanterns are available, from hurricane lamps that burn oil to glass-sided lanterns that house candles. Classic New Mexican luminarias—open paper bags that contain votive candles set in sand—are now made in metal and ceramic and have been electrified. Tiny hat lights, hot peppers, or pumpkins on strings can bring a festive atmosphere to a patio or deck. Lanterns on stakes can add drama along the path to a gate or door.

A sampling of lights you might find in stores and catalogs that sell home accessories is pictured here. Keep in mind that selections change from year to year.

No matter which lantern you choose, you'll need to place it with care; this is especially true for lanterns with open flames. Unless snow covers the ground around them, avoid placing lanterns along a path or among foliage, where they can pose a fire hazard. Also, make sure that they're sturdy and will not topple in a breeze. Avoid putting metal lanterns that could become hot near dry plant material.

A. The charm of a wagon wheel and split rail fence is heightened by seasonal lights in this Illinois landscape.

B. Galvanized steel-hat lights dance across a patio.

C–G. Variations on the hurricane-lamp theme, these lanterns protect candles from evening breezes. All are glass and metal, except for the terra-cotta "beehives" (E).

H. Four lights nestled at the top of the center pole of this umbrella cast a warm glow on those dining or relaxing on the terrace.

I. The glow of candles adds to the ambience of this moonlit garden in St. Paul, Minnesota.

J. A cast-iron Japanese lantern casts a flickering glow across night gardens.

WATER FEATURES

Few things fascinate us as water does—silent and still or tumbling joyfully over cascading rocks. The quiet music of burbling, trickling, or splashing water brings a certain tranquility to a space; even the smallest water feature can calm the surroundings and soothe the soul. The sounds of water can mask unwanted noise, creating a sense of the countryside in urban and suburban gardens. As a bonus, moving water attracts all sorts of wildlife, from birds to squirrels to bullfrogs.

A pleasing water feature can be as modest as a wall-mounted fountain that trickles water into a basin or as elaborate as a 6-foot granite sculpture that sends a graceful arc of water into a pool. You can convert a wooden planter box, metal basin, or large pot into a small, informal water feature (see page 299). Simply coat the inside of a wooden container with asphalt emulsion or epoxy paint, or use a liner of heavy-gauge plastic sheeting. If you're using an unglazed pan or clay pot, coat the interior with asphalt emulsion, epoxy, or polyester resin. Simply drop in a submersible pump to create a fountain, and add water.

A. This beautifully detailed lead-gray cistern and fountain is actually made of molded plastic. Filled with water-loving plants and surrounded by a rainbow of coleus foliage, it brings a touch of formality to a deck garden.

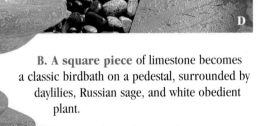

B. A square piece of limestone becomes a classic birdbath on a pedestal, surrounded by daylilies, Russian sage, and white obedient plant.

C. This galvanized watering can spouts a gentle arc of water into a half barrel. A small submersible pump in the barrel sends water up through clear plastic tubing to a hole drilled near the top of the can. The can is held in position with a length of heavy nylon cord running from its handle to a nearby fence.

D. Water spouts from pebble-covered pumps in this checkerboard-style garden oasis.

E. This cast-stone fountain mounts on a garden wall.

F. An English birdbath fountain of cast stone is fitted with a plug-in pump. Water bubbles out from the orb's top.

A. This traditional cascading fountain is enlivened by bright blue floating water "bubbles" and the blue chair cushion.

B. Elements of traditional Japanese water gardens are combined to form a water feature enhanced by carefully chosen and managed plants.

C. Water tumbles over stones into a calm lily-covered pond that clearly belongs to Paige.

D. An antique hand pump turns a simple barrel into an easy-to-manage water garden.

C

A Pond in a Pot

You can create your own simple water feature. All you need is a glazed ceramic pot at least 30 inches in diameter, without a drainage hole, or a half barrel or other large container fitted with a heavy plastic liner. Fill the container about two-thirds full with water, then add plants, such as miniature water lilies, cattails, or rushes, each in its own pot (set plants on inverted pots to raise them). Then fill the rest of the tub with water.

Mosquito fish (gambusia) or goldfish will control mosquito larvae and will also feed on the algae in the pot. You will need about six fish for a 30-inch container. If you are not using fish, put in a submersible pump to create a burbling fountain.

Unless you have an area indoors, such as a greenhouse, where you can overwinter the container, you will have to empty the pond and retire it until spring. Return the fish to a deep pond, discard the plants and the plastic liner, and clean the pot and the pump.

D

CHOOSING CONTAINERS

When choosing a container for your garden, begin by deciding whether it is to be the focal object or serve as a quiet background for the display of interesting plants. A container can blend in with its surroundings or stand out by virtue of its contrasting color, material, or form.

You can select a variety of container styles for your garden, but there should be some similarity among most of the containers to avoid too much visual distraction.

Containers should be of a size consistent with the scale of the garden and its structures. If you choose containers that are too small, they will be lost in the background. Small containers are also difficult to maintain because they lack moisture-holding capacity. Choosing a smaller number of larger containers creates a stronger visual impact.

Before you choose a container, you should decide on its placement and the type of plants you intend for it. If you will want to move the container, make sure it is light in weight, or place it on skids or wheels. The soil mix you use should also be light if moving the container is important. Heavy, rich soil mixes encourage overly lush growth.

Be prepared to water some containers daily or even twice a day in extremely hot or windy conditions. To ease this task, locate containers near a source of water, or install permanent drip lines to large pots. Good drainage is essential in all containers, either through a drainage hole or by building a layer of gravel or stone in the bottom.

Containers for year-round use in the Midwest must be able to withstand freezing and thawing without cracking. Choose sturdy materials if your container must stand up to the weather. Removing the soil and plants during winter helps to alleviate cracking and will extend the life of your pot.

A. Primary, hot colors of gazania, euryops, dahlias, lilies, and sunflowers contrast with the bright blue glaze of this container, displayed against a toned-down-blue fence.

B. A graceful ceramic basket filled to overflowing with 'Princess Blue' and yellow violas adds a bright spot of spring in this St. Louis garden.

C. A steel blue campfire coffeepot is brightened for spring by luscious watermelon-colored pansies.

D. Window boxes overflowing with petunias, kingfisher daisy *(Felicia bergeriana),* and the red tassel flowers of love-lies-bleeding *(Amaranthus caudatus)* brighten the porch of this home.

E. Fully glazed, these painted Italian terra-cotta jardinieres feature a grapevine design. Choosing a plant with a mounding habit shows off the pot's design to best advantage.

F. This example of container gardening at its best on a deck in Illinois uses a variety of sizes, shapes, and locations to grow plants in layers.

G. This trio of terra-cotta containers includes a Cretan jar, an Italian urn with glazed interior, and an Italian fluted flowerpot.

CHARM IS IN THE DETAILS

Much of the subtle charm of a garden lies in its details. Paying attention to these details enhances a garden's personality in a way that the use of plants alone cannot.

The traditional pineapple symbol of welcome in colonial Williamsburg still appears in many gardens, but you can opt for more obvious and personal invitations. Carved stones or painted wood or metal signs can be placed at the main entrance to the garden or point the way to a more hidden path. Don't be afraid to add a little humor or fun to your garden. Make your garden your own with just the right personal touch.

Fasteners on the garden gate, finials on the fence posts, or brass hose guides can add a pleasing touch to any garden. Or your details may be less evident, such as the careful selection of just the right flat stones to place at the end of a downspout, the use of a section of old iron fence as a trellis for a peavine, or the choice of a translucent dragonfly that floats on a copper stake above a perennial bed.

By definition, details are not the focal point of the garden, but they can provide great pleasure when selected in thoughtful counterpoint to a garden's themes. Searching for just the right detail can continue the adventure of gardening long after the main plan is accomplished.

A. An Adirondack chair and bicycle planter in this St. Louis garden are framed by bright impatiens.

B. A welcome stone invites visitors to descend these stone steps into a lush Minnesota woodland garden.

C. Bright sunflowers tower over an artistic stick figure perched on a painted picket fence in St. Catherines, Ontario.

D. A tiny garden sign framed in flowers is displayed among succulents and fine-textured plants.

E. A simple stepping-stone repeats in its cast surface the pattern of the landscape carpeted with fallen leaves.

REGIONAL PROBLEMS AND SOLUTIONS

Across the Midwest, the seasonal extremes of winter, with its frost and snow, and summer, with its searing heat and periods of drought, can create problems for even the most experienced gardeners. The local landscape, whether forest, prairie, city, or rural plain, brings its own special challenges. Whether one must search out plants that thrive in lower temperatures or in wide-open, windswept locations, protect seedlings from hungry deer, or provide cover from the hot sun, every regional problem brings an opportunity for a new approach to gardening in the Midwest. Thoughtful landscape design and careful maintenance can help a gardener overcome special problems and find a level of satisfaction in creating beauty where previously there was none.

REGIONAL PROBLEMS

Winter cold

With the exception of those in a small section of Missouri's Bootheel, Midwestern gardeners can expect winter low temperatures to fall below 0°F every year. Bitterly cold temperatures of −20°F or colder are common in the northern areas. With such extreme cold, the growing season is short. In northern areas, the number of frost-free days may be as few as 90 in a cold year, and the more temperate areas typically see around 200 frost-free days per year. Annual flowers and vegetables must mature quickly or risk premature death by fall frosts. Perennial flowers, trees, and shrubs must be adapted to the chill to survive from one year to the next. Where winter snow cover is unreliable, gardeners must mulch perennial plants to protect tender root systems.

The regional winter temperatures map at right shows the moderating influence of the Great Lakes in the region. Winter temperatures don't dip quite as low near the lakes. Snow cover is more constant in the snow belt next to the lakes, enabling gardeners near these large bodies of water to grow slightly more tender species.

Gardens in the southwestern area of the Midwest often fall victim to fickle late-winter weather. Far from the moderating influence of oceans or the Great Lakes, temperatures fluctuate widely. As snowfall melts away and exposes barren brown earth, the heat of the strengthening late-winter sun may bring several days of springlike 70°F weather, only to be followed by another chill arctic blast rolling in from the Canadian prairies. Plants that begin their growth cycle too quickly during the warm spells will suffer freeze injury when the cold returns. (See pages 314–317 for tips on preparing plants for winter.)

WINTER TEMPERATURES

 Extreme cold; winter lows of −20°F or colder for most years

Fluctuating winter temperatures

Areas of both fluctuating winter temperatures and extreme cold

Summer heat, humidity, and drought

Temperature extremes are the norm in the Midwest. Not only is winter bitterly cold, but summer can be blistering hot. The south-western areas typically endure 45 or more days of temperatures above 86°F annually. Plants begin to languish in the heat because photosynthesis shuts down at high temperatures. Instead of putting on new growth, heat-stressed plants use up stored energy reserves simply to survive. Other sections of the Midwest get hot weather, too; it just doesn't last as long. Northeastern Minnesota, northern Wisconsin, upper Michigan, and the Great Lakes shores are the best places to escape the heat.

"It's not the heat, it's the humidity," say residents of the corn belt. High temperatures and high humidity may be perfect for grow-ing corn, but they are uncomfortable for humans. Many plants are stressed by the combination of heat and humidity as well, and fun-gal diseases thrive in warm, humid conditions. A gardener must be alert to potential disease development and practice preventive maintenance. Increasing air circulation to more quickly dry plant surfaces, using trickle or drip irrigation to keep foliage dry, water-ing early in the day so plants dry off before evening, and planting disease-resistant plants are some of the tested techniques for thwarting plant diseases.

SUMMER TEMPERATURES

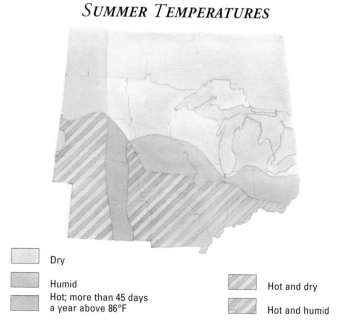

☐ Dry	
☐ Humid	▨ Hot and dry
☐ Hot; more than 45 days a year above 86°F	▨ Hot and humid

Most summer rainfall in the Midwest comes from Gulf of Mexico moisture carried northward by prevailing southerly summer winds. In the rain shadow of the Rocky Mountains, west of the 100th meri-dian (central Kansas, Nebraska, and the Dakotas), conditions are consistently drier than in the rest of the region. Gardeners here must grow plants that use little water or irrigate to keep plants alive. Other areas of the region experience dry periods as well. Enough rain falls "on average" to sustain plant growth without supple-mental watering, but it never seems to come at the right time. An intense downpour may be followed by a month or more with only an occasional sprinkle. Growing native plants adapted to the peri-odic dry cycles helps, but any gardener in the Midwest should be prepared for watering moisture-starved plants during the inevitable dry cycles. (See pages 328–329 for tips on protecting plants from the sun.)

Wetlands, poor drainage, and flooding

Glaciers formed the landscape of the Midwest, creating a combina-tion of relatively flat plains, and lakes scooped out by the advancing ice. As the glaciers retreated northward, runoff water from melting ice carved out rivers and valleys and created temporary lakes dammed by the ice. On a grand scale, historical Lake Agassiz cov-ered much of North Dakota, northwest Minnesota, and Canada. Here, the old lakebed creates a broad, flat plain with little change in elevation for miles on end. With little slope and clay soils, poor soil drainage is common.

The lake country of Minnesota, Wisconsin, and Michigan was created by glacial scooping action. Where shallow depressions formed, plant life gradually converted lakes to bogs filled with decaying organic matter. The process continues today. Shallow lakes become marshes, marshes become bogs, and bogs become organic muck soils. These sites have high water tables and poor

WETLANDS

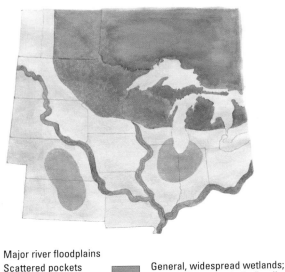

 Major river floodplains

Scattered pockets of poor drainage

General, widespread wetlands; poor drainage, periodic flooding

drainage. Gardeners in these locations must grow plants adapted to constantly wet soil conditions.

The gently sloping plains in Kansas and Nebraska have glacial depressions that never formed permanent lakes but are seasonally wet. These "prairie pockets" form standing water in late winter and spring but dry out in summer and fall. They are important waterfowl nesting habitats, but they pose a challenge for gardeners who must deal with the seasonal wet and dry cycles.

Gardeners in river-bottom floodplains, such as those along the Mississippi, Missouri, and Ohio Rivers, face similar boom-or-bust water cycles. Flooding of bottomlands is common during the spring snowmelt runoff; dry conditions prevail in the summer. Periodic flooding and silt deposition make river bottomlands very productive

garden sites, but local residents must learn to cope with the flooding. Many communities have constructed dikes and levees to protect large areas from river surges. However, in historical floods, such as in the spring of 2001 or the summer deluges of 1993, the levees must be supplemented with temporary sandbag dikes to hold back excess water. Sump pumps may be used in low areas to pump the water up to the flooded river stage.

Away from the major floodplains, Midwestern gardeners with streams or creeks near their property may need to be alert for flash flooding during intense summer thunderstorms. Plants tolerant of both standing water and drought are needed in these lowlands.

Wind

Wide-open expanses of prairie, mile upon mile of wheat, corn, and soybeans, and scattered stands of trees along rivers and streams and in small towns combine to define much of the rural Midwestern landscape. With no major mountains to break the force of winds, and with few trees to slow airflow, winds stream across the landscape unabated. The Great Plains and Central Prairies feel the brunt of the wind's force. And Chicago is known as the Windy City for good reason!

The Midwest is a weather battleground. Tornado Alley, stretching from Kansas into Iowa, is the result of periodic collisions of cold, dry air masses from the northwest with warm, moist gulf air. Even when the weather front results simply in thunderstorms rather than tornadoes, straight-line winds and wind-driven rain can flatten tender plants. Newly planted trees and taller perennial flowers may need staking to keep them upright. Another option is to plant them in a protected location out of the full force of the wind.

A gardener may have to create shelter from the wind by planting a windbreak. Several rows of shrubs and trees on the windward side of the property can create a pocket of relatively calm air around the home. In most sections of the Midwest, the winter wind

This riverside park in LaCrosse, Wisconsin, was flooded by the Mississippi River in the spring of 2001.

WIND

 Areas of high winds

blows primarily from the northwest; a windbreak on the north and west sides of the property creates relief from arctic blasts. (See pages 334–335 for more tips on protecting plants from wind and for a list of plants recommended for windbreaks.)

Alkaline and acidic soils

The Midwest has a split personality when it comes to soil pH. In the western half of the region, where evaporation is equal to or greater than precipitation, soils tend to be alkaline (high pH). The eastern half of the region is more likely to have neutral (pH 7) or acidic (low pH) conditions.

Part of the explanation for the regional split comes from the parent soil material. Soils in the Great Plains mostly derive from calcareous soils that are high in alkaline calcium carbonate. The granite and sandstone parent materials of Great Lakes soils are more acidic. The Mississippi and Ohio River watershed soils are mainly calcareous in origin but are neutral or acidic rather than alkaline, because water also plays a big role in determining pH. Where rainfall is abundant, soils become acidic as the rainfall percolates through the soil and leaches away alkaline bases. Plant growth also contributes to acidification of soils. In areas of greater rainfall, plant growth is greater, and soils become more acidic from the decay of organic matter.

The best way to determine the pH of your garden soil is to have it tested. Check with your local Cooperative Extension Service for laboratories that will test garden soils. Many localized factors can affect site-specific pH. High levels of organic matter tend to lower pH. Groundwater from limestone aquifers will raise pH. Subsoil brought to the surface during home construction will likely be of higher pH than native topsoil.

Most garden plants grow best in slightly acidic soils, from pH 6.0 to 7.0. Some, such as blueberries and azaleas, require more acidic conditions; others, such as juniper and yucca, tolerate alkaline soils. If soil pH is too acidic for the plants you want to grow, pulverized limestone or wood ashes may be added to raise the pH. Powdered forms of limestone will change the soil reaction quickly; coarsely ground material may take years to change pH. If your soil's pH is too high, elemental sulfur, ammonium sulfate, or iron sulfate may be needed to lower it. Avoid using aluminum sulfate to lower pH, as it can cause aluminum toxicity in plants. The amount of acidifying agent or limestone required depends on the existing pH of the soil and the soil texture. Sandy soils require the least material to effect a change; clay soils require the greatest amount. (See pages 126–127 for more information on soils.)

SOILS

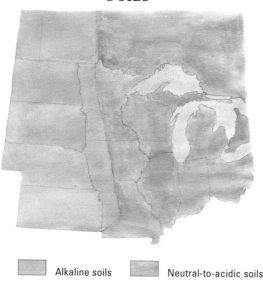

☐ Alkaline soils   ☐ Neutral-to-acidic soils

Roadside Pollution

Airborne particulates—small particles of dust and debris from cars, trucks, and buses—can sometimes harm plants growing close to busy streets or highways. When the particulates settle on plants, they reduce the amount of light that reaches the leaves and provide breeding grounds for insect pests such as mites. To help keep roadside plants healthy, wash them off frequently with strong jets of water from a hose. Thoroughly rinse both the top and the bottom surfaces of leaves.

Smog-damaged plants exhibit various symptoms, depending on the species, the growing conditions, and the growing season. Leaves may become yellow or bleached; the needles of conifers may discolor and drop off, leaving the plant half-bare. (See page 327 for more on smog.)

MANAGING WETLANDS

Water in a fountain or a pond can add an extra dimension to a garden, but water that stands in puddles and saturates the soil can be a problem. Poor drainage and saturated soil can cause root rot and may suffocate plants not adapted to such conditions. Because excess water displaces the oxygen in the soil, it deprives plant roots of that essential element. And without oxygen, most plants cannot fuel photosynthesis; eventually they die.

Many gardens have a patch where the runoff water from storms collects and the soil stays wet longer than elsewhere on the property. However, a wet, boggy area that rarely—if ever—dries out is another matter. In that case, you have several options.

AMEND CLAY SOIL. Clay soil is dense and drains slowly. If rainfall is heavy, or if there is a lot of water seeping into the area, clay will remain soggy for a long time. Lighten the soil with organic amendments, such as well-rotted manure and compost, to promote aeration and drainage.

RISE ABOVE THE PROBLEM. If the ground is always moist but not boggy, you can surmount the problem by building a raised bed. The height to which you need to go depends on what you intend to plant. Shallow-rooted annuals and perennials can make do with an 8- to 10-inch soil depth; deep-rooted plants, including trees and shrubs, may need as much as 2 or 3 feet. A low raised bed can support itself, especially if you plant around the edge to hold the soil in place. For deeper raised beds, provide retaining walls, and be sure to include drainage holes at the bottom if the sides have no gaps for water to seep through.

CHANNEL EXCESS WATER. There are several methods for channeling excess water to a convenient place for disposal. Flexible drainpipes attached to downspouts are easy to install. Bury the pipe, allowing it to resurface at a spot where the water can run off safely. Another option is a channel of drain tiles, which are also positioned underground. You'll need to dig a trench sloped at a rate of 2 inches for every 8 feet of length. Then lay down a 2-inch-deep layer of gravel, and top with tiles set end to end. Cover the tile joints with landscape fabric to keep out soil and debris, and finish with a 4- to 6-inch layer of gravel. You can either leave the channel as is or cover it with another

MANAGING EXCESS WATER

Streambeds of river rock can channel water to a drain. Landscape to make attractive.

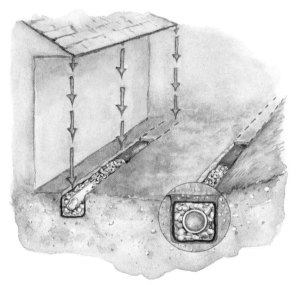

Drainage trenches lined with gravel hold perforated flexible drainpipes.

Catch basins drain water away from low areas through pipe to street or storm drain.

A. In this marshy garden, cream-colored sedges *(Carex)* mimic the texture of the maiden grass *(Miscanthus sinensis* 'Gracillimus') behind the timbers. Bright red hardy hibiscus and Joe Pye weed *(Eupatorium purpureum)* add color contrast to the garden, while giant silver grass *(Miscanthus* 'Giganteus') provides a backdrop.

B. A small rowboat placed on a "stream" of sedges *(Carex)* spanned by a rustic wooden bridge provides a creative and attractive solution to a low wet spot in the landscape.

A pool of standing water surrounded by bog plants turns a potential eyesore into a garden gem. Here, white-flowering primrose *(Primula)* combines nicely with the bold blue-green foliage of *Hosta sieboldiana* 'Elegans' and the grassy foliage of Siberian iris.

layer of landscape fabric and soil to better disguise the drainage channel in the landscape.

PLANT A BOG GARDEN. Transform a liability into an asset by turning a muddy spot of standing water into a beautiful bog garden. Some garden plants, such as hosta, astilbe, and many iris, get along in normal soil but really prosper when given continual moisture. There are a host of other beautiful plants that prefer wet conditions. See the list at right for some ideas.

BUILD A BOARDWALK. Create easy, comfortable access through your bog or water garden with a boardwalk built just above the level of the wet ground. The wood surface is pleasing underfoot, and the dry path offers an opportunity to view up close particularly choice plants and wildlife that would normally remain remote.

If you yearn for a bog garden but don't have a suitable environment, you can create one. Dig out the soil to a depth of 12 to 18 inches (the depth depends on the plants you want to use), line the hole with heavy plastic that is punctured in a few places for slow drainage, backfill the hole, water well, and plant. Because it isn't a natural bog, you'll need to watch for signs of drying out and water as necessary.

Plants for bog gardens

Acorus calamus
SWEET FLAG

Aronia
CHOKEBERRY

Aruncus dioicus
GOAT'S BEARD

Asclepias incarnata
SWAMP MILKWEED

Astilbe

Athyrium filix-femina
LADY FERN

Caltha palustris
MARSH MARIGOLD

Carex
SEDGE

Cephalanthus occidentalis
BUTTONBUSH

Chelone
TURTLEHEAD

Clethra alnifolia
SUMMERSWEET

Cornus stolonifera
REDTWIG DOGWOOD

Eupatorium purpureum
JOE PYE WEED

Hibiscus moscheutos
HARDY HIBISCUS

Hosta

Ilex verticillata
WINTERBERRY

Iris (some)

Larix
LARCH

Ligularia dentata

Lobelia cardinalis
CARDINAL FLOWER

Miscanthus sinensis
JAPANESE SILVER GRASS

Myosotis sylvatica
FORGET-ME-NOT

Myrica pensylvanica
NORTHERN BAYBERRY

Osmunda regalis
ROYAL FERN

Physocarpus opulifolius
EASTERN NINEBARK

Pontederia cordata
PICKEREL WEED

Rodgersia podophylla

Sagittaria latifolia
ARROWHEAD

Salix
WILLOW

Sorbaria sorbifolia
URAL FALSE SPIREA

Taxodium distichum
BALD CYPRESS

Thalictrum
MEADOW RUE

Trollius × cultorum
GLOBEFLOWER

Typha latifolia
COMMON CATTAIL

Veronicastrum virginicum
CULVER'S ROOT

Viburnum trilobum
AMERICAN CRANBERRY BUSH

Purple Loosestrife and Other Invasive Plants

Throughout much of the Upper Midwest, wetlands cloaked in broad bands of purple are a common sight. The blooms of purple loosestrife (Lythrum, shown above) may be beautiful, but the plant is an environmental menace. It has an aggressive growth habit, spreading rapaciously and choking out indigenous flora until it becomes the sole occupier of extensive wetland areas. It is not a source of food to native wildlife, and it poses a severe threat to waterfowl habitats.

Hybrid varieties such as 'Morden Pink' have been thought to be infertile and therefore to present no danger of spreading seed throughout the wild. But recent research shows these hybrids to be highly fertile when crossed with others or with wild purple loosestrife.

Although well adapted to boggy garden sites, purple loosestrife of any type should not be planted because it poses a danger of spreading into the wild. In fact, many states in the Midwest have made it illegal to plant the species, which was introduced to North America from Europe almost 200 years ago. Possible substitute plants include obedient plant (Physostegia virginiana), purple coneflower (Echinacea purpurea), and spike gayfeather (Liatris spicata). In addition to their pretty flowers, these substitutes produce seeds enjoyed by songbirds.

Many other plants introduced to the Midwest have become invasive in certain habitats. Some with a history of spreading beyond their cultivated bounds include those listed at right.

BUCKTHORN (Rhamnus) *These shrubs tolerate a wide range of soil types and sunlight conditions. Birds spread their seeds throughout wetlands, woodlands, and prairies. Once established, buckthorn shades and crowds out native shrubs and herbs.*

DAME'S ROCKET (Hesperis matronalis) *Dame's rocket sets a prolific amount of seed and, where conditions suit its spread, quickly escapes backyard cultivation. This plant is now so firmly established throughout woodlands, wood edges, and roadsides that many people are surprised to discover that it is an introduced plant.*

GARLIC MUSTARD (Alliaria petiolata) *This plant, originally imported as an herb by early settlers of the Midwest, has now escaped cultivation into woodlands, where it chokes out native plants of the forest floor.*

HONEYSUCKLE (Lonicera) *Both the shrub honeysuckle (Lonicera maackii) and vining Japanese honeysuckle (Lonicera japonica) pose problems to native plants in woodlands. Birds spread seeds from the plants' red berries throughout their range. Japanese honeysuckle can climb and drape itself over existing shrubs, effectively smothering*

TOP: Garlic mustard
BOTTOM: Honeysuckle

them. These honeysuckles also release chemicals into the soil that are toxic to other plants, enabling the invaders to establish a solid stand.

KUDZU (Pueraria lobata) *Heralded as a "miracle plant" but with a notorious history in the South, kudzu is now making its way into the Midwest. This vine has a legendary growth rate; it strangles large trees, shrubs, and almost anything else in its path. Kudzu now has become established as far north as northern Illinois and southern Michigan.*

MULTIFLORA ROSE (Rosa multiflora) *Originally touted as a foolproof plant for living fences, the thuglike nature of multiflora rose is now readily evident on abandoned farmland and pastures, in fencerows, and in woodlands and prairies. This thorny shrub spreads from seed and suckers, rapidly forming impenetrable thickets.*

FROST AND SNOW

The Midwest is a region of seasonal changes. Crisp, snowy winter days dissolve to reveal the pastel promises of spring. Hot summers gracefully give way to the unrivaled hues of autumn. But winter holds dangers for the garden—arctic air, unpredictable frosts, and heavy snows and ice storms threaten plant survival. Even hardy plants sometimes require protection against the Midwestern winter.

Preparing for winter

Sunny days combined with cold nights and frigid wind—a hallmark of Midwestern winters—can spell trouble in the garden. As the ground thaws and refreezes, perennials, especially newly planted ones, may be heaved out of the ground, exposing tender roots to frost damage. Sun, wind, and cold temperatures hasten evaporation from soil and leaf surfaces, causing dehydration. When the elements remove more moisture from leaves than the roots are able to replace, plants experience a condition known as winterkill.

Young trees are vulnerable to sunscald, which occurs when sunny winter days warm the trees' tender bark above the freezing point. Cold nighttime temperatures then refreeze the bark and the wood beneath it. This cycle of warming and freezing causes cells under the bark to die and the bark to split when growth resumes the following year.

To protect your garden from winter damage, you would be wise to take the following precautions before the first frost:

PRECONDITION PLANTS. Finish transplanting at least a month before a hard freeze is expected; this gives the plants' roots time to anchor themselves in the ground. Avoid fertilizer applications late in the growing season: they can stimulate new, tender growth that won't harden off before winter sets in, leading to stem dieback. Wait to prune shrubs or trees until they have gone completely dormant in the fall—or, better yet, wait until late winter to do your pruning. Trimming late in the season stimulates growth just when the plants are preparing to enter dormancy.

KEEP PLANTS HYDRATED. As winter approaches, make sure you water the garden if rainfall is insufficient to keep the soil moist. Pay particular attention to evergreens, both broadleaf and needled types. Without adequate soil moisture, their foliage will turn brown. Continue to water as needed throughout fall and winter when the temperature rises above freezing and conditions are dry. Newly planted evergreens in exposed, windy locations may benefit from an antidesiccant spray applied just as the ground freezes for winter.

MULCH. Mulching helps keep soil at an even temperature. This prevents the alternating freezing and thawing that can cause plants to

Plants such as these 'Sunburst' squashes and other annuals cannot survive a hard spring frost.

Tree limbs weighed down by ice storms may easily break if you try to clear them. Allow the ice to melt instead.

A layer of mulch prevents weeds from spreading during the growing season and protects tender perennials through the winter.

heave out of the ground, damaging roots. After the ground freezes, apply a 4- to 6-inch layer of loose organic material, such as shredded leaves, straw, or chopped cornstalks, around the base of plants to insulate them through the winter.

PROTECT FROM SUN. Young trees, especially thin-barked maples, lindens, and fruit trees, are susceptible to sunscald. Apply a commercial tree wrap to susceptible trees in late fall, after the trees have gone dormant and freezing temperatures have arrived. Remember to remove the wrap before growth begins in the spring to prevent girdling of the trunk and to avoid creating a haven for insects and diseases under the wrap.

SHIELD FROM WIND, HEAVY SNOW, AND ICE. To prevent heavy, wet snow from breaking upright branches of small conifers, wrap them with a spiral of cloth strips, or make a tent from bamboo stakes covered with burlap to shelter the plants from snow and wind. Better yet, plant evergreens only in locations where winter winds and heavy snow are not likely to cause damage. If ice forms on the branches of trees or shrubs, do not try to break it off; you may damage the plant.

USE PLANT-FRIENDLY DE-ICERS. Salts used to melt snow and ice on roads and walkways can accumulate in the soil nearby and damage plants growing there. If the soil is well drained, heavy irrigation in spring may help leach out salts and reduce damage to plants. If you have sensitive plants located near a road where salt spray may be a problem, tack a burlap screen to stakes between the road and the plants to create a protective shield. To control ice on hardscapes, apply sand, kitty litter, or urea fertilizer rather than salt. If you must use salt, try calcium chloride or magnesium chloride rather than the more damaging sodium chloride. Never pile salty snow around the base of plants.

Special situations

In most of the Midwest, some plants, such as roses (except hardy shrub roses), require extra precautions. In the warmer areas, a mound of soil and mulch around the canes is adequate winter protection for hybrid tea roses. In colder areas, the most reliable means of overwintering hybrid teas, climbers, and tree roses is to bury them in a trench (see illustration, bottom right). Tie the canes together to make them easier to handle. With a spade or shovel, dig a hole as long as the rose is tall. Dig the hole wide enough and deep enough to accommodate the entire rose. Start digging away from the base of the rose and work toward it. Use a spading fork to loosen the soil around the roots and shank or trunk. With the help of the spading fork, push the rose over into the trench. Hold it in place with several wire loops, and cover it with several inches of soil. After the soil freezes, mulch the buried plant.

Other gardens

WATER GARDENS. Water gardens come in a variety of sizes and shapes. Shallow pools and those with straight sides should be drained for the winter or heated with a tank heater to prevent ice damage, which may occur when the water freezes and expands. If

Winter Protection

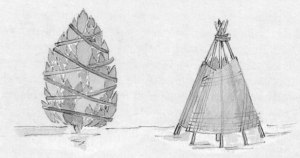

Snow. To prevent heavy, wet snow from breaking upright branches, wrap conifers with a spiral of cloth strips (left). A tent of bamboo stakes covered with burlap (right) also shelters plants from snow.

Mulch. Avoid pruning roses in fall, except for long canes that may be whipped by winter winds. Unless temperatures fall below −15°F, mounding soil and mulching provide adequate protection for hybrid roses. After plants are exposed to several nights of temperatures around 20°F, mound soil 9 to 12 inches high around base of plant. Place wire cylinder around plant, and fill 2 feet deep with shredded leaves or other mulch.

Minnesota Tip Method. In colder regions, in late fall dig a trench longer and deeper than the entire plant. Tie rose canes together. Loosen soil around the roots, and ease the rose into the trench with a spading fork. Peg the plant in place with wire pins, cover with a layer of soil, and mulch heavily.

you're draining the pool, remove the plants to a protected area, such as a greenhouse or basement. If the pond has sloped sides and is at least as deep as the frost line in your area, there is no need to fear ice damage to the pool itself. The entire pool will not freeze solid; as the surface water freezes, the sloped sides will allow for expansion of the ice. Still, the pool must be properly prepared for winter (see facing page).

CONTAINER GARDENS. After the first killing frost, move clay and ceramic pots indoors. Dig up tender rhizomes, tubers, and bulbs, and store them in a cool, dry place. Some planters, such as wooden ones, can tolerate temperature fluctuations. If such a planter is to be left outside, mulch it heavily or partially bury it in the ground to better insulate it against winter cold.

Preparing for the thaw

Late winter and early spring bring some of the greatest dangers to the garden. Fluctuating warm and cold temperatures can be as damaging to plants as extreme cold in midwinter. Keep mulch in place as long as possible in spring to insulate against sudden temperature changes. But watch for new growth beginning under the mulch. Once perennials start to sprout, the mulch should be pulled away to keep it from smothering the new growth.

Spring temperatures can be quite warm during the day, and the timing of the last freeze is unpredictable. At this time of year, the garden is vulnerable to a particular type of freeze that occurs in isolated spots on clear, still, dry nights. A radiation freeze happens when the warmth that was stored in the ground during the day rises quickly and is replaced by cold air.

Young plants set out in the spring are most susceptible to radiation freezes. To protect plants, cover them with floating row cover fabric, plastic, burlap, or newspaper to slow the loss of heat and insulate them against the cold.

A. Burlap fencing acts as a screen against drying winter winds for these deciduous and evergreen shrubs.

B. To protect broadleafed evergreens from winter sun damage, use wooden stakes wrapped with burlap to shield the plants from afternoon sun.

C. Resting under a layer of mulch 4 to 6 inches deep, these raised beds have been prepared for winter. The beds will also warm quickly in the spring and may be planted earlier than flat beds.

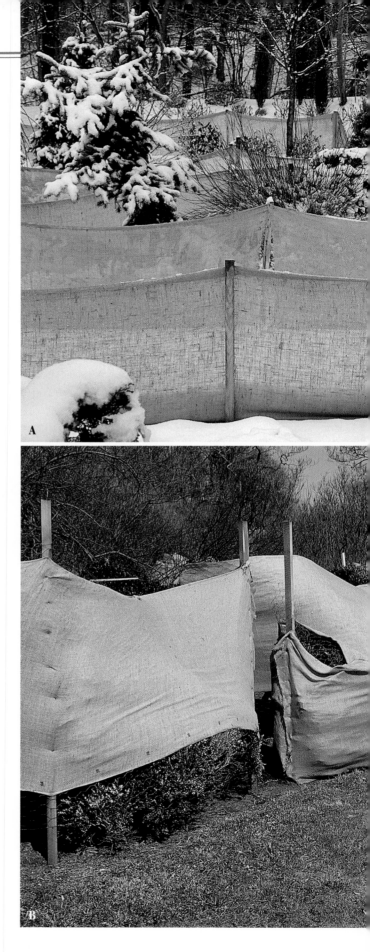

WINTERIZING A WATER GARDEN

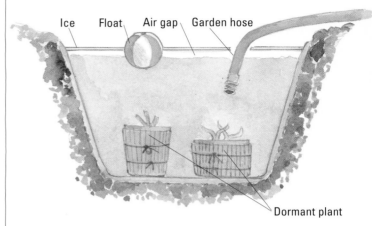

Ice Float Air gap Garden hose

Dormant plant

To overwinter plants, you need water deeper than ice will form, typically 2 feet deep; in the northern Midwest, ice can be 3 or 4 feet deep. In colder regions, it may be simplest to drain the pool and relocate plants to water tanks indoors. To over-winter plants outdoors, lower them to bottom of pond, below ice line. As long as rootstocks do not freeze, plants should survive. If ice covers surface for more than 2 weeks, create an opening for air exchange by chopping a hole in the ice and siphoning out some water to create an air gap, or insert a livestock tank heater to keep a section of the water ice free.

PROPER MULCHING TECHNIQUE

When mulching, avoid piling mulch directly against tree and shrub stems, as this encourages rot and other diseases. Instead, keep mulch pulled away from the trunk or stem—in the shape of a bagel rather than mounded like a muffin. Don't mulch any deeper than necessary; that would only encourage winter pests and inhibit air and water from reaching plant roots. A 2- to 6-inch layer of mulch provides the benefits without the drawbacks of excessive mulch.

ANIMAL PESTS

Awhite-tailed deer, her neck arching to pluck a leaf from a branch; a furry brown rabbit on a well-manicured lawn, nibbling at spring's first delicate shoots—these images evoke idyllic snapshots of the Midwestern landscape. Lovely, unless the animals in those snapshots happen to be feasting on your real-life garden. The deer and her family can decimate a garden in one evening, and, although the rabbits may take longer, they too will eradicate entire plants. Some gardeners want to look out their windows and see wildlife on the property, but no one wants to give over a garden to the animals completely; so the question becomes, how do you create a landscape that both meets your goals for the garden and keeps it safe from ravenous wildlife?

First, before landscaping a new garden, consult your neighbors and your local Cooperative Extension Service to find out which animals are common in your area and what their favorite plants seem to be. Next, decide how far you are willing to go to protect your garden. Some simple techniques can be effective—a pet dog can sometimes scare away deer and rabbits, for example—but truly hungry animals are difficult to deter completely. For some pests, you will need to use traps, repellents, or barriers.

Raccoons. These nocturnal bandits raid fishponds and muddy garden pools and dig holes in lawns and garden beds in their search for grubs. Raccoons overturn garbage cans and strew refuse around. They eat many fruits and vegetables, especially corn and melons.

Woodchucks (groundhogs). Large herbivores, these animals dig burrows up to 50 feet long with multiple rooms and entrances. The tunnels alone cause extensive lawn damage, but these pests also gnaw on the bark of fruit trees and can consume entire vegetable gardens.

Moles and voles. Moles do the garden a service by eating larvae and other bugs; rarely do they eat garden plants. But they dig tunnels below the surface, leaving burrows for voles to inhabit. Voles, one of the worst garden pests, eat plants, seeds, bulbs, berries, and bark.

Pest-proofing your garden

RACCOONS. If your water garden contains fish, protect it with electric fences that can be turned on at dusk and off at dawn, and provide places in the pond for fish to hide. Control grubs in lawns with parasitic nematodes. Don't throw kitchen waste into the compost or leave pet food outdoors. Secure garbage cans. Harvest ripe fruits, and keep fallen fruit picked up. Prune back tree limbs or woody vines that overhang the house.

WOODCHUCKS (GROUNDHOGS). Traps and fences are available. Bait the trap with fruit. Any fence should be at least 3 feet high and extend 2 feet below the ground. Woodchucks like cover, so clear any tall grass near the garden.

Deer. The most notorious garden pests, these hungry animals live around many communities, especially on the edge of wild land. They eat prized garden plants, especially vegetables and roses. Deer like to browse; they establish trails and feed mainly at dawn and dusk.

Wild rabbits. Wherever residential neighborhoods adjoin woods or meadows, these little opportunists dart into gardens to eat young seedlings and tender shoots as well as summer flowers, shrubs, and young-tree bark. They're a threat to vegetable gardens, too.

Squirrels. Familiar sights in most neighborhoods, squirrels bury acorns or other nuts in pots, lawns, and flower beds—then leave them to sprout. They also nibble on corn, bulbs, fruit, bark, and shoots. They love seeds and will wreak havoc on bird feeders.

MOLES. Traps, repellents, and other products are available. Line planting holes and raised beds with wire mesh. Castor bean oil is an effective repellent for moles. You may need to apply it a couple of times during the growing season to keep them at bay. Attempting to rid lawns of moles by eliminating grubs is not a good solution. Moles will eat grubs, but their primary diet is earthworms. The benefits of earthworms far outweigh the potential damage from moles.

VOLES (MEADOW MICE). Traps are available and may work well when used in large numbers. Line planting holes and raised beds with wire mesh. Eliminate possible food sources, such as vegetables left in the garden at the end of the season. Wrap a plastic guard or a piece of mesh extending below the soil around the base of young trees to protect the bark.

DEER. Planning a deer-proof garden is challenging. The density of the deer population and how hungry they are—especially in winter—often determine what and how much they eat. Try planting some of the plants listed on pages 322–323. If you prefer to use a fence, it must be at least 7 feet tall or be electrified to act as a deterrent.

RABBITS. Clean up thickets and brush piles, which rabbits use as nests. Protect vegetable gardens with fences of wire mesh that are at least 2 feet above ground and 6 inches below, with openings smaller than 1 inch. Loosely wrap the trunks of young trees with wire mesh or plastic cylinders. Cats also prove excellent deterrents.

SQUIRRELS. Protect the soil around container plants and bulbs with fine wire mesh. In early spring, drape bird netting over grapevines, roses, deciduous fruit trees, and berry bushes. If live traps are used—and trapping is against the law in some areas, so check in your local jurisdiction—be cautious when releasing the animals. Wear heavy gloves, cover the cage, and step back when opening it.

Pest Protection

A deer fence may be the only way to keep these animals out of the garden. It must be at least 7 feet tall.

Mesh fences should be at least 2 feet above ground and 6 inches below ground to stop rabbits, voles, and moles.

Tree guards of hardware cloth or plastic prevent rabbits and voles from gnawing on the tender bark of young trees.

Nets of string or nylon encircling the canopy of a young fruit tree can foil birds and squirrels during harvest season.

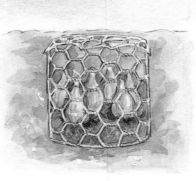

A wire basket set inside the planting hole is an effective barrier, keeping tender bulbs out of reach of voles.

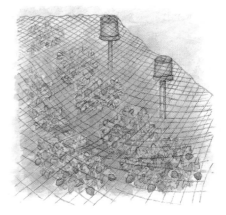

Nylon netting stretched across sticks or PVC pipes keeps birds and deer away from seedbeds and kitchen gardens.

A. A high fence wound through trees and shrubs melts into the background but manages to protect this garden of blooming woodland shrubs and herbaceous perennials—such as variegated Solomon's seal (*Polygonatum odoratum* 'Variegatum')—from marauding deer.

B. Japanese silver grass *(Miscanthus sinensis),* a deer-resistant grass, is a focal point in this garden.

Pest control methods

Various methods are used to keep animal pests out of the garden, including barriers, repellents, habitat alteration, and traps. Any of these methods can be effective. However, if you are unwilling to use a lethal trap or to kill a trapped animal humanely, trapping is not recommended. Many pests carry viral diseases that may be transmitted to humans. Releasing a pest in another location will reduce the food supply available to that species in that area and possibly burden another garden with the problem you are trying to solve.

METHOD OF CONTROL

ANIMAL	TYPE OF FENCING	TREE GUARDS	REPELLENTS USED	TYPE OF TRAP	ENVIRONMENTAL CHANGES
Raccoons	Electric fence for ponds			Live	Eliminate food sources. Prune tree limbs. Provide cover for fish
Woodchucks	Fence at least 3' above and 2' below ground			Live	Clear garden of tall grass
Moles	Line planting beds with wire mesh		Castor bean oil	Lethal	Eliminate food sources. Keep lawn mowed. Adopt a cat
Voles	Line planting beds with wire mesh	Plastic or mesh extending below ground		Lethal	Eliminate food sources. Keep lawn mowed. Adopt a cat
Deer	At least 7' high or electrified		Commercial repellents applied regularly, especially after rain		Try using plants deer avoid
Rabbits	Use a small-meshed fence 2' high and 6" below ground	Plastic or wire mesh extending below ground	Commercial repellents applied regularly, especially after rain	Live	Clean up thickets and brush piles. Adopt a cat or dog
Squirrels		Netting over bushes and fruit trees. Use wire mesh on planters	Commercial repellents applied regularly, especially after rain	Live	Apply metal squirrel guards to trees

Deer-Resistant Plants

Very few ornamentals are absolutely invulnerable to deer, but some appear to be the food of last resort. The list at right includes plants that are known to be poisonous, and therefore less appealing, and plants that have been reported either in studies or anecdotally as being deer resistant. This list is only a guideline, however: what deer find distasteful one year or in one area, they may find irresistible at another time or in another location. The best method for finding deer-resistant plants for your area is trial and error. Plants with thorns (but not roses) or spiny projections, such as holly and barberry, are the most deer resistant, so you may want to start with these. Check with your local Cooperative Extension Service for a list of locally adapted plants to round out your deer-resistant garden.

In a garden filled with deer-resistant plants, pink astilbe colors the foreground, blooming against the white-flowered backdrop of black snakeroot (*Cimicifuga racemosa*).

GRASSES

Calamagrostis × acutiflora
FEATHER REED GRASS

Chasmanthium latifolium
NORTHERN SEA OATS

Festuca glauca
BLUE FESCUE

Miscanthus sinensis
JAPANESE SILVER GRASS

Miscanthus sinensis 'Purpurascens'
FLAME GRASS

GROUND COVERS

Ajuga

Asarum
WILD GINGER

Nepeta × faassenii

Cerastium tomentosum
SNOW-IN-SUMMER

Convallaria majalis
LILY-OF-THE-VALLEY

Duchesnea indica
MOCK STRAWBERRY

Epimedium
BARRENWORT

Lamium maculatum
DEAD NETTLE,
SPOTTED NETTLE

Pachysandra terminalis
JAPANESE SPURGE

Vinca minor
PERIWINKLE

Waldsteinia fragarioides
BARREN STRAWBERRY

PERENNIALS

Achillea
YARROW

Aconitum
MONKSHOOD

Allium
FLOWERING ONION

Aquilegia
COLUMBINE

Artemisia
MUGWORT, SWEET ANNIE,
WORMWOOD

Asclepias tuberosa
BUTTERFLY WEED

Astilbe

Chionodoxa luciliae

Cimicifuga racemosa
BLACK SNAKEROOT

Coreopsis
TICKSEED

Dianthus
PINK

Digitalis purpurea
FOXGLOVE

Echinacea purpurea
PURPLE CONEFLOWER

Echinops
GLOBE THISTLE

Galanthus
SNOWDROP

Geranium
CRANESBILL

Helleborus
LENTEN ROSE,
CHRISTMAS ROSE

Hyacinthus orientalis
COMMON HYACINTH

Iris

Kniphofia
RED-HOT POKER

Lavandula
LAVENDER

Liatris spicata
SPIKE GAYFEATHER

Monarda didyma
BEE BALM

Narcissus
DAFFODIL

Nepeta
CATMINT

Paeonia
PEONY

Perovskia atriplicifolia
RUSSIAN SAGE

Pulmonaria
LUNGWORT

Ranunculus
BUTTERCUP

Saponaria ocymoides
SOAPWORT

Scilla sibirica

Sedum

Solidago
GOLDENROD

Stachys
LAMB'S EARS, BETONY

Tanacetum vulgare
TANSY

Teucrium
GERMANDER

Thymus
THYME

Verbascum
MULLEIN

Veronica
SPEEDWELL

Yucca

SHRUBS

Berberis
BARBERRY

Buxus
BOXWOOD

Ceanothus americanus
NEW JERSEY TEA

Chaenomeles
FLOWERING QUINCE

Cornus kousa
KOUSA DOGWOOD

Cornus stolonifera
REDTWIG DOGWOOD

Cotoneaster

Forsythia

Hamamelis
WITCH HAZEL

Ilex
HOLLY, INKBERRY, WINTERBERRY

Juniperus
JUNIPER, EASTERN RED CEDAR

Kerria japonica
JAPANESE ROSE

Ligustrum
PRIVET

Sambucus
ELDERBERRY

Spiraea

Symphoricarpos
CORALBERRY, SNOWBERRY

Viburnum

Weigela florida

TREES

Betula
BIRCH

Catalpa

Cotinus coggygria
SMOKE TREE

Fraxinus
ASH

Ginkgo biloba
MAIDENHAIR TREE

Gleditsia triacanthos
HONEY LOCUST

Juniperus
JUNIPER

Larix
LARCH

Liquidambar styraciflua
SWEET GUM

Liriodendron tulipifera
TULIP TREE

Ostrya virginiana
IRONWOOD

Picea
SPRUCE

Robinia pseudoacacia
BLACK LOCUST

Syringa
LILAC

Taxodium distichum
BALD CYPRESS

Tsuga canadensis
CANADA HEMLOCK

VINES

Campsis radicans
TRUMPET VINE

Celastrus scandens
AMERICAN BITTERSWEET

Fallopia baldschuanica
SILVER LACE VINE

Parthenocissus
BOSTON IVY,
VIRGINIA CREEPER

Vitis
GRAPE

PLANT ALLERGIES

Itchy eyes, near-constant sneezing, a runny nose—to many allergy sufferers, this is how spring, summer, and fall are defined. Wind-borne pollen causes about 60 percent of all allergy problems, and most of it comes from trees and summer-blooming grasses. You may opt to stay indoors during the worst of the allergy season, or you could try planting low-allergen plants in your garden.

Seasonal allergies affect millions of Americans annually. Trees—especially oaks, maples, and birches—are the major culprits in spring; grasses trigger midsummer problems; and weeds, such as ragweed, bring on symptoms from late summer until the first freeze. In addition, some plants cause an itchy skin condition called contact dermatitis when they touch the skin.

Reducing pollen

The very nature of wind-borne pollen makes it difficult to escape. You can't replace all the trees and shrubs growing in your neighborhood or eliminate the pollen-rich grasses growing along the roadsides. But you can choose plants for your own garden that are known not to produce wind-borne pollen. By replacing wind-pollinated plants with those pollinated by insects, you can greatly reduce the allergens in your garden.

What to plant?

Happily, the most colorful flowering plants don't produce airborne pollen. Petunias and pansies, for example, are low-allergen plants, as are peonies and daylilies. This is because nature uses color to entice insects. Foraging bees, for example, respond to blue and yellow above all other colors. Fragrance also attracts pollinators, so another advantage to planting insect-pollinated plants is the rich perfume they exude.

Planting nonallergenic trees and shrubs likewise will reduce pollen in the garden. If possible, you should also eliminate or min-imize hedges and lawns: many are allergenic, and they can trap pollen and mold spores.

Among the plants listed on the facing page are those that produce little pollen as well as some of the most notorious troublemakers. In addition, there is a list of plants known to cause contact dermatitis in some people. An allergist can tell you about your particular sensitivity to plants and may recommend other nonallergenic plants suitable for planting in your area.

Tips for a sneeze-free garden

DISPATCH WEEDS REGULARLY. Many weeds are highly allergenic. Keep them mowed, hoe them, or pull them out by hand before they bloom, or spray them with an herbicide.

TRIM GRASSES. Lawn grasses are among the most common sources of allergies. Mow your lawn frequently at the proper height so that seed heads don't form. Keep grass growing vigorously with regular water and fertilizer to prevent it from going to seed. Try to avoid mowing the lawn yourself. If grass causes your allergies to flare up too much, replace the lawn with a substitute ground cover.

USE A RAKE. Nothing makes dust, pollen, and fungal spores spread faster than leaf blowers. Try a rake instead.

GARDEN WHEN POLLEN COUNTS ARE LOW. Weather reports often include the pollen count for the day. Concentrate your gardening efforts on days when pollen counts are low. This will vary with the season, weather patterns, and time of day—late morning and early afternoon usually have lower pollen counts than the early morning or evening.

CONSIDER OTHER CAUSES. Fungal spores, dust mites, and animal dander cause many allergies, particularly in fall. Consult an allergist to identify the cause of your symptoms before you undertake any relandscaping.

Aster

Philadelphus coronarius

Juniperus chinensis

Allergenic plants

TREES AND SHRUBS

Acer
MAPLE, BOX ELDER

Alnus
ALDER

Betula
BIRCH

Carya
HICKORY, PECAN

Fraxinus
ASH

Juglans
WALNUT, BUTTERNUT

Juniperus
JUNIPER,
EASTERN RED CEDAR

Liquidambar styraciflua
SWEET GUM

Maclura pomifera
OSAGE ORANGE

Morus
MULBERRY

Pinus
PINE

Platanus
SYCAMORE, PLANE TREE

Populus
COTTONWOOD, POPLAR, ASPEN

Quercus
OAK

Salix
WILLOW

Ulmus
ELM

ANNUALS AND PERENNIALS

Amaranthus
LOVE-LIES-BLEEDING,
AMARANTH

Ambrosia
RAGWEED

Artemisia
WORMWOOD, SWEET ANNIE,
MUGWORT

Aster

Carex
SEDGE

Dendranthema grandiflora
CHRYSANTHEMUM

Helianthus
SUNFLOWER

Tagetes
MARIGOLD

Zinnia

Liquidambar styraciflua

Plants that can irritate the skin

Angelica archangelica
ARCHANGEL

Anthriscus
QUEEN ANNE'S LACE, CHERVIL

Dictamnus albus
GAS PLANT

Euphorbia polychroma
CUSHION SPURGE

Heracleum
COW PARSNIP, HOGWEED

Ruta graveolens
RUE

Toxicodendron
POISON IVY, POISON OAK,
POISON SUMAC

Aesculus parviflora

Nonallergenic plants

TREES

Aesculus
HORSECHESTNUT, BUCKEYE

Catalpa

Cercis canadensis
EASTERN REDBUD

Chionanthus virginicus
FRINGE TREE

Cladrastis kentukea
YELLOW WOOD

Cornus
DOGWOOD

Crataegus
HAWTHORN

Ginkgo biloba

Koelreuteria paniculata
GOLDENRAIN TREE

Liriodendron tulipifera
TULIP TREE

Magnolia

Malus
APPLE, CRABAPPLE

Prunus
CHERRY, PLUM, APRICOT, PEACH

Pyrus
PEAR

Sorbus
MOUNTAIN ASH

SHRUBS

Amelanchier
SERVICEBERRY, JUNEBERRY,
SHADBLOW

Aronia
CHOKEBERRY

Berberis
BARBERRY

Buddleja davidii
BUTTERFLY BUSH

Calycanthus floridus
CAROLINA ALLSPICE

Caryopteris × clandonensis
BLUE-MIST SPIREA

Chaenomeles
FLOWERING QUINCE

Clethra alnifolia
SUMMERSWEET

Cotoneaster

Deutzia gracilis
SLENDER DEUTZIA

Forsythia

Hamamelis
WITCH HAZEL

Hibiscus
HARDY HIBISCUS,
ROSE OF SHARON

Hydrangea

Kolkwitzia amabilis
BEAUTY BUSH

Lonicera
HONEYSUCKLE

Mahonia aquifolium
OREGON GRAPE HOLLY

Myrica pensylvanica
NORTHERN BAYBERRY

Philadelphus coronarius
MOCK ORANGE

Rhododendron
AZALEA, RHODODENDRON

Rosa
ROSE

Spiraea

Viburnum

Weigela florida

POLLUTION

Gardens in the Midwest are subjected to a variety of pollutants. In urban areas, smog and air pollution can affect the growth and appearance of plants.

In many cases, gardeners themselves are the source of the problem through inappropriate fertilization, pesticide application, and landscape maintenance practices. For instance, fertilizers are salts; if used excessively, they can damage or even kill sensitive plants. In addition, surface and groundwater contamination may result from overfertilization. In winter, salt on the roads and sidewalks can cause problems similar to fertilizer burn on plants. Indiscriminate pesticide use endangers the gardener applying the chemical and threatens to build resistance to the pesticide in the pest for which control is targeted.

Fertilizers and water contamination

It is unfortunate that so many garden publications refer to fertilizer as plant food; it gives the wrong impression that fertilizer must be constantly applied for plants to survive. Plants make their own food through photosynthesis. Fertilizer is a nutritional supplement, to be used when plants aren't getting enough of the necessary nutrients through the soil in which they are grown.

Excessive use of fertilizers is bad for plants for several reasons. Overfertilized plants put on lush growth that makes them more susceptible to disease and insect pests. Sensitive growing tips of plants may be damaged by the fertilizer salts, causing leaf browning and root damage.

Improper fertilization can also lead to problems for the environment. Nitrogen is very water soluble, and it moves readily through the soil dissolved in water. Eventually it gets into groundwater aquifers, the source of drinking water for many Midwesterners. High nitrate content in drinking water leads to health problems, especially for pregnant women and young children. Areas of the Midwest with limestone bedrock are especially susceptible to groundwater contamination. Cracks in the limestone allow soil water to bypass the filtering action of clay and sand particles, in essence creating a direct link from your fertilizer spreader to your water supply.

Excess phosphorus also causes problems. Though it doesn't move readily through the soil, phosphorus adheres tightly to soil particles and washes into surface waters whenever soil erosion occurs. High phosphorus levels in lakes leads to increased aquatic plant life.

Salts and de-icers

The salt used by local road crews and by homeowners to melt snow and ice on roads and walkways can accumulate in soil and damage plants. Sodium chloride, a common de-icing salt, not only dehydrates plants, but also destroys soil structure. Gypsum counteracts the soil structure breakdown, but washing away excess salt by deep, frequent watering in the spring may be needed to reduce the salt content.

As an alternative to salt, apply sand, kitty litter, or urea fertilizer to paved areas to control ice. Or, for complete environmental safety, consider using calcium magnesium acetate (CMA) as a de-icer. It is as effective as salt, is no more corrosive than tap water, and it biodegrades. The drawback is that it costs up to 30 times more than salt.

For plants growing near roadways and subject to airborne salt spray, consider erecting a salt spray barrier. Before the ground freezes for winter, drive stakes or fence posts into the ground between the plants and the roadway. Staple or tack burlap screening

Tips for Responsible Fertilizer Use

Fill fertilizer spreaders on hard surfaces, where spills can easily be cleaned up.

Wash off fertilizer spreaders on lawns or in the garden rather than on hard surfaces, to prevent excess fertilizer from entering storm drains.

Leave a buffer zone of unmanaged grasses or natural vegetation along shorelines of lakes, rivers, and streams.

Avoid overwatering, to prevent leaching of fertilizers.

Avoid applying fertilizer to natural drainage areas or on hard surfaces in the yard.

Use smaller amounts of fertilizer. Applying some in a slow-release form makes gradual quantities of the fertilizer available to plants.

Recycle grass clippings on the lawn to reduce the need for supplemental fertilizer.

Never apply fertilizer to frozen ground.

Roadside plants along winter's roads can be harmed by salt spray from passing vehicles.

to the stakes to catch the spray before it can reach the plants. It also helps to plant salt-tolerant species in the salt-spray zone.

Pesticides

According to the EPA, homeowners use ten times the amount of pesticides per acre as the average farmer. Homeowners also are likely to apply them indiscriminately and incorrectly. Fortunately, there are many steps you can take to reduce pesticide use without sacrificing your yard to diseases or hordes of marauding insects.

MAKE CERTAIN A PROBLEM EXISTS. Observe the plants in your yard on a regular basis. Get to know the good bugs from the bad. Over 90 percent of all insects are either benign or beneficial. Just because bugs are crawling on your petunias doesn't mean it's time to reach for the sprayer. By frequently scouting for pest problems, you are more likely to catch them in their early stages while they are still easy to manage. If you check plants infrequently, the problem you see now may not be what caused the original damage.

SET AN ACTION THRESHOLD. Most plants can tolerate some damage from insects or diseases. A healthy, well-established oak tree can stand up to heavy defoliation from gypsy moths with no long-term consequences. However, if the tree is under stress from a recent drought, previous defoliation, or a confined root system, defoliation may send it into a state of decline from which it will never recover. Consider that the complete elimination of insect pests may not be in your best interests; if the pests are gone, so are their natural predators.

USE PREVENTIVE ACTION. Many pest problems can be kept in check by matching the plant to the right environment. Nature is full of checks and balances; only when the scale tips in favor of the pest will problems develop. Such practices as proper watering to alleviate drought stress, pruning to open tree canopies for better air circulation, and removing diseased plants promptly can keep problems from becoming widespread.

ENCOURAGE THE BENEFICIALS. Natural predators, such as lady beetles (also called ladybugs) and parasitic wasps, help keep pests at bay. Spraying at the wrong time may reduce the predator popu-

lation and encourage a population explosion of the pest. Naturally occurring diseases for insects, such as *Bacillus thuringiensis (Bt)* for caterpillar control, milky spore *(Bacillus popillae)* for Japanese beetle control, or the protozoan *Nosema locustae* for grasshoppers, are low-toxicity ways to keep pests in check.

USE LOW-TOXICITY CHEMICALS. If you must use a pesticide, consider low-toxicity products that do not remain in the soil or water for long. Insecticidal soaps and horticultural oils are quite effective on soft-bodied insects and mites, yet are extremely safe to use.

OBSERVE PROPER TIMING. Less pesticide is needed when it is applied at the proper time. Insects are more sensitive to insecticides just after they hatch than when nearly fully grown. Weeds in the seedling stage are less tolerant of herbicides than mature plants. For broadleaf lawn weeds such as dandelions, fall treatment is more effective than spring treatment.

Air pollution

Smog stresses plants. It breaks down the natural wax coating on leaves, so plants are left without their natural protection from water loss during droughts.

Motorists in St. Louis, Chicago, and Milwaukee are familiar with higher summer gasoline prices due to the EPA requirement for reformulated gasoline during the summer smog season. Burning fossil fuels in automobiles releases sulfur and nitrogen. These elements in their oxide form, along with ozone, are responsible for smog. Ozone has a tendency to travel—up to 120 miles away from the source—so small towns and suburbs are not guaranteed an air pollution–free life.

Gardeners who carpool to work, take public transportation, or ride their bikes can feel good about helping reduce air pollution. But gardeners also need to be aware that gas-powered lawn mowers, string trimmers, leaf blowers, and other equipment contribute significantly to air pollution. Often these lawn tools are not tuned to burn fuel as cleanly as cars, so for their size they outpollute cars. In addition, it is estimated that millions of gallons of fuel are spilled annually while filling gasoline-powered lawn equipment. Use a funnel to direct fuel into the tank, and take care not to overfill.

SUN

The sun is a powerhouse that fuels plant growth. But too much sun can damage plants and make the outdoors unbearable for people as well. Summer sun also heats up houses, making additional air conditioning necessary, which raises electric bills and overtaxes the region's supply of power. Fortunately, there are some easy ways you can reflect or block the sun's heat.

Plant protection

Plants that are adapted to the climate in which they are grown are seldom damaged by the sun if they are well maintained and well irrigated. But seedlings or plants that have recently undergone changes in growing conditions, such as transplanting or heavy pruning, can be harmed or even killed by strong sun. Signs of such damage include scorched leaves, especially at the edges, leaf drop, blistered fruit, and split or cracked bark.

Consider sun patterns when you choose sites for trees and shrubs. Plants that face south, southwest, or west, or those that receive plenty of afternoon sun, are in the most danger of sunburn. And those that are placed beside heat-reflecting driveways and patios or that are in exposed positions are more vulnerable to sun damage.

Seedlings of flowering annuals and perennials need protection from the sun until they can establish their roots in the ground. This is especially true if they have been planted during warm weather. Methods of protecting young plants are shown on the facing page. You can also "harden off" seedlings for a week or so by exposing them to increasing intervals of time outdoors.

The bark of young trees and severely pruned trees is sensitive to sunburn, especially when the sun is at a low angle in the winter sky. Strong sunlight can kill exposed bark, causing it to split. Wrap thin-barked, newly planted trees with a commercial tree wrap the first winter or two after planting. Remove the wrap before growth begins in the spring, and reapply it in late fall if the bark is not yet corky. When pruning, avoid removing more than 25 percent of the branches in a tree during any one year. The remaining branches will help shade the area where branches were removed, preventing sunburn as well as minimizing stress to the tree from loss of limbs.

A floating row cover of lightweight cloth protects plants against both excess sun and cold. In summer, it filters sunlight, saving seedlings and young transplants from the scorching rays of the sun. In winter, it prevents heat from escaping from the bed.

SUN PROTECTION

Plant grafted trees with the bud union (where the tree has been grafted onto the rootstock) away from afternoon sun.

A bamboo mat or window shade can guard a tree trunk from sun. Remove as soon as conditions improve.

Hot spells

Periods of intense heat in late spring and early summer can hit plants when they are at a vulnerable stage. They are still producing tender new growth and haven't yet become conditioned to hot, dry weather. Take the following steps to protect them.

WATER THOROUGHLY. Plants wilt slightly on warm summer days because their leaves lose water faster than their roots can take it up. During the night, the plants recover—if their roots have water to absorb. After an extremely hot day, make sure that water is available to the whole root zone (usually the entire area beneath the leaves of herbaceous plants or several times the width of branches for trees and shrubs). When you irrigate, give plants plenty of water; don't just sprinkle. Don't assume, when water starts to puddle on the soil surface, that the root zone is thoroughly wet. Most soils can't absorb water as quickly as a hose can supply it. Let the water soak in; come back and water several times until you are certain the water has penetrated deep into the root zone. If you're uncertain, use a soil sampling tube (sold in garden centers) to check water penetration. Thorough watering encourages roots to grow deep.

Mulching helps soil retain moisture and cools roots near the surface. For shallow-rooted plants, such as azaleas, blueberries, and begonias, mulch is essential. Apply an organic material such as shredded bark or wood chips in a layer 2 to 4 inches thick around the root zone of these plants.

SPRINKLE NEW PLANTS. When temperatures begin rising toward 100°F, it is important to cool off plants and protect them from direct sunlight. Newly planted flowers and vegetables need the most help. Sprinkle overhead throughout the hottest part of the day. As the water evaporates, it helps cool the plants.

Soil in containers dries out quickly. Moving planters and pots into the shade can be easier than trying to keep them wet during periods of extreme heat.

A sturdy frame of 2 by 2s supports 4-inch lath. Wire sections together at top; move as needed to shield young plants.

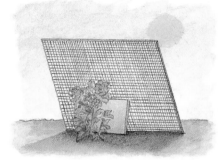

A lightweight window screen can provide temporary shade for new plantings. Prop it against a stake or board.

Making a Portable Plant Screen

A portable plant screen does a good job of shading a bed of seedlings or transplants. Prefabricated lattice, sold at home-improvement stores in panels of various sizes, makes a quick and easy screen; you can use the panel whole or cut it to fit the garden bed. Drive in 1- to 1½-foot-long 2-by-2 stakes at the corners of the bed and at the midpoint of each side. Tack horizontal slats made of 1-by-2 lumber on top of the stakes; then rest the lattice on top of the slats. You can also prop up a lattice panel on the south side of a planting bed, where it will provide both shade and protection from wind.

WATERWISE GARDENING

If Mother Nature would only cooperate, most Midwestern gardeners wouldn't need to worry about drought and water conservation. With the exception of the High Plains of Kansas, Nebraska, and the Dakotas, average rainfall throughout the growing season is enough to sustain plant growth. Unfortunately, it

doesn't come in regular doses. Some years or parts of the year may be wet and others dry. Recurring drought and water restrictions are a familiar scenario for Midwesterners, who need to plan landscapes that are as water-thrifty as possible.

By following the fundamental principles for a waterwise garden discussed here, you will not only have the pleasure of knowing that you are a responsible gardener, but also be rewarded with a garden that requires far less maintenance. By choosing drought-tolerant plants adapted to your region, improving your soil, and mulching regularly, you will save countless hours of weeding, mowing, trimming, and watering your plants.

USE WATER-CONSERVING PLANTS. Some plants need a lot of water to survive; others perform better with less. You can find water-thrifty trees, shrubs, flowering plants, ground covers, and grasses for your garden. Some provide seasonal color; others, year-round green. The key is to choose plants that are well adapted to the natural conditions of your area. Consider choosing native plants accustomed to periodic dry cycles. Consult your local Cooperative Extension Service for recommended plants for your region.

GROUP PLANTS WISELY. Place thirsty plants together and drought-tolerant plants elsewhere. Then put the plants that need regular watering on a separate irrigation system and watering schedule.

IRRIGATE EFFICIENTLY. Make sure that your watering practices and devices use water as efficiently as possible. Information on choosing an irrigation system can be found on the following pages; installation guidelines appear on pages 396–397. Avoid runoff, which wastes water. Water your plants only when needed, not by the clock or calendar. Water deeply and less often to encourage deep rooting.

IMPROVE YOUR SOIL. Before planting trees, shrubs, and perennial flowers, incorporate organic matter in a wide area around the plant, not just in the planting hole. Roots will spread farther in the

improved soil, and you will improve the soil's ability to resist evaporation and retain moisture.

MULCH. Place a layer of organic material over soil and around plants. Mulch greatly reduces moisture loss through evaporation, reduces weed competition, and slows erosion.

CONTROL WEEDS. These garden intruders consume water needed by more desirable plants.

LIMIT TURF AREAS. A lawn requires more irrigation than most other landscape plants. Limit its size to just what you need for your purposes, and choose a grass, grass mix, or grass blend adapted to your climate (see pages 226–227). Consider replacing at least part of your lawn with hardscape materials or alternative plants.

MAINTAIN YOUR GARDEN. Raise mower heights during the heat of summer. Keep plants pest free, adequately fertilized, and properly pruned to minimize their stress. Stressed plants often require more water. Tighten faucet handles so they don't drip. Check irrigation systems regularly for proper functioning.

PROVIDE SHADE. Use shade trees, shrubs, and trellises to shade hardscapes and sections of the yard where heat builds up. Cooler plants lose less water.

A. This midsummer combination of lamb's ears *(Stachys byzantina),* sedum 'Autumn Joy', black-eyed Susan *(Rudbeckia fulgida sullivantii* 'Goldsturm'), and feather reed grass *(Calamagrostis × acutiflora)* brightens up a sunny, dry garden border.

B. Ornamental grasses such as maiden grass *(Miscanthus sinensis* 'Gracillimus') and fountain grass *(Pennisetum alopecuroides),* and sedums 'Brilliant' and 'Autumn Joy' are tough plants that do well in dry landscapes. Their dried foliage and stems provide interest through fall and winter as well.

C. The billowing lavender blossoms and gray-green foliage of Russian sage *(Perovskia atriplicifolia)* contrast nicely with this upright line of feather reed grass *(Calamagrostis × acutiflora).*

CHOOSING AN IRRIGATION SYSTEM

An irrigation system should fit the lay of your land and the arrangement of your plants. But you should also choose a system that doesn't demand more time than you have to spend in the garden. Choose wisely, and watering becomes a leisurely and rewarding process, with healthy, good-looking plants. Choose poorly, and watering becomes a dreaded task, an obligation that takes away from the joys of gardening. Worse, a poorly designed irrigation system results in unhealthy plants and a lot of wasted water.

A wealth of equipment—from microsprinklers to automatic timers to soil moisture sensors—can help you water your garden efficiently, even when you're busy or out of town.

The most common irrigation devices are pictured on these pages; for step-by-step instructions on installing drip and sprinkler systems, see pages 396–397.

Hoses

A hose can make the task of watering easy or difficult. If you buy an inexpensive type that is prone to kinking, you'll spend more time cursing than watering. But if you purchase a durable, kink-free type, it will last much longer and work more efficiently.

Unreinforced vinyl hoses are inexpensive and lightweight, but they are also the least durable and the most prone to kinking. Reinforced vinyl hoses are less likely to kink and are lightweight—important if you have to move the hose around a lot. Rubber hoses, which have dull surfaces, are the heaviest and toughest types. They kink in hot weather but work well in cold weather. Reinforced rubber-vinyl hoses are flexible, kink resistant, moderately heavy, and durable.

Hoses are sold by length and by inside diameter (½-inch, ⅝-inch, and ¾-inch hoses are common). Though the difference in hose diameter may seem slight, the water volume each carries varies greatly. If you have low water pressure, or if you must run

your hose uphill, you'll need all the pressure and flow you can get. Buy the largest-diameter, shortest hose that is practical for your situation.

Hose-end sprinklers

These come in a variety of forms, from large impulse sprinklers that can cover hundreds of square feet to small bubblers ideal for watering shrubs or containers. Choose models with a spray pattern that matches the areas you'll be watering. If you have clay soil or sloping ground that is slow to absorb water, select models that apply water slowly to avoid wasteful runoff.

The down side of hose-end sprinklers is that they have to be moved around by hand to cover large areas and that they deliver water unevenly; some areas they cover get wetter than others. To get an idea of how much and how evenly your sprinklers apply water, place five identical straight-sided cups randomly in the area of coverage. Run the sprinklers for 15 or 30 minutes, then measure the water accumulated in each

A. Soaker hose with factory-drilled holes lets water slowly drizzle out.

B. Water from emitter line spreads slowly through soil to irrigate grass roots.

C. Porous polyvinyl tubing soaks soil at high pressure; at low pressure, water seeps.

D. Delivery tubes for irrigation systems range from (left to right) ½-inch-diameter tube to spaghetti tube and two soaker tubes.

E. Other components of an irrigation system include (left to right) emitters, minisprinklers, and piping that leads from the water source.

F. Hose on facing page is a good-quality, reinforced type that bends without kinking.

cup. The cups nearest to and farthest from the sprinkler will probably have the least water. In any case, both the amount of water and the unevenness of the distribution will give you an idea of how long to run the sprinklers (use timers so you don't forget the sprinklers are on) and how to move them so that patterns overlap and everything is watered evenly.

Soaker hoses

One of the simplest and least expensive ways to water plants is with soaker hoses. Unlike sprinklers or a complete drip irrigation system, they attach to hose bibbs quickly and with little fuss.

Of the two types of soaker hoses available, one applies a fine spray, the other small droplets. Both are generally sold in 50- and 100-foot lengths.

Perforated plastic emits streams of water from uniform holes drilled along one side. The hose can be used face down, so water goes directly into the soil, or turned up for broader coverage. Output depends on pressure and how far you run the hose. This type of soaker hose is very useful for irrigating narrow areas of lawn or bedding plants, or around the bases of trees that need slow, deep irrigation.

Ooze tubing is made from recycled tires. The water seeps out of tiny pores. It requires a filter to prevent clogging, and applies water slowly—as little as 4 gallons per minute per 100-foot length. If you don't use a pressure regulator, turn on the water until it seeps out of the pores. If you see pinhole sprays, turn down the pressure. To prevent mineral deposits from clogging tubing, bury it 2 to 6 inches deep or cover with mulch.

This tubing can be used like perforated plastic pipe, or it can be run out in rows (spaced about 2 to 3 feet apart) to irrigate large beds.

Drip irrigation

For any size garden and all kinds of plantings except lawns, drip irrigation is the most efficient way to get water down to plant roots. Drip irrigation applies water at slow rates so that it can be absorbed without runoff. Because the water is applied directly where it is needed, it results in greater conservation and fewer weeds.

Even though a drip irrigation system may look intimidating, it is easy to install, even for a beginner. The key is good planning and design. Laying out the water lines requires only cutting with pruning shears and punching holes for emitters.

Start your design with a detailed drawing of your garden, including the positions and spacing of plants. Learn the water needs of your plants. Are they drought tolerant, or do they need frequent irrigation? If you are starting a new garden, group the plants according to their water needs.

Rough out your plan on paper, and take it to an irrigation-supply store for some expert help with the design and installation of your system.

Rigid-pipe sprinkler systems

Traditionally used for watering lawns, underground pipe systems with risers for sprinkler heads remain the best method for watering medium-size to large lawns and low-growing ground covers. For the greatest water savings, however, use drip irrigation for trees, shrubs, perennials, annuals, and vegetables. With a good electronic controller, both of these systems can be run automatically.

The basic components of a rigid-pipe system are shown on page 396. Residential water lines seldom have enough pressure to service the house and water the entire garden at one time. Unless you have only a small area to water, you'll need to divide your sprinkler system into several circuits, each serving only part of the lawn or garden and operated by its own valve. You then operate one circuit at a time to avoid exceeding the maximum flow rate for your water supply. Valves can then be operated by an automatic controller.

Automated irrigation

An automatic sprinkler system is the most efficient way to water. Manufacturers now offer a dazzling array of equipment that can make it work even better.

CONTROLLERS. Electronic controllers are far more accurate than mechanical timers —and most have useful features that mechanical timers do not offer.

Controllers capable of daily multiple cycles reduce runoff. When water is applied faster than the soil can absorb it, some will run off the property. If you have this problem, set a repeat cycle to operate the sprinklers for 10 or 15 minutes at, for example, 4:00, 5:00, and 6:00 A.M.

Dual- or multiple-program controllers let you water a lawn on a more frequent schedule than that needed for ground covers, shrubs, and trees.

SPRINKLERS. New low-precipitation-rate nozzles reduce runoff, improve spray uniformity, and allow a large area to be irrigated at one time. They are particularly useful on sloping ground or on soil that absorbs water slowly.

MOISTURE SENSORS. Linked to an electronic controller, a moisture sensor in the open air or in the ground takes the guesswork and day-to-day decisions out of watering. Sprinklers equipped with moisture sensors won't go on if it's raining or if the ground is sufficiently moist.

F

WIND

Excessive winds create havoc in the garden. During summer thunderstorms, delicate plants may be flattened by strong winds. In winter, winds sweeping off the plains make outdoor activities uncomfortable and dangerous for humans; windchill temperatures of −30° to −100°F can freeze exposed skin in minutes. Landscape plants don't feel windchill, but they do suffer drying and desiccation when winter winds are strong.

Gardeners in windy regions of the Midwest have several options to make their yards more hospitable for humans and plants alike. On large properties, shelterbelts or windbreaks can slow the wind. In more confined spaces, fences or hedgerows will do the same. Tall plants and newly planted trees may need staking to keep them upright on sites that are exposed to heavy winds.

Windbreaks and shelterbelts

Trees reduce wind speed by increasing the resistance to wind flow. An isolated tree or stand of trees acts almost like a solid barrier to wind, forcing the wind over or around it. Although barriers increase the wind speed around the barrier, a properly designed windbreak can reduce wind speed on the lee side by up to 75 percent. The amount and area of wind reduction is affected by the height and density of the planting. Generally, a windbreak protects an area from 10 to 15 times the average height of the tallest plants in the windbreak. A denser windbreak provides more wind reduction close to the planting, but the area of protection is less. For most sites, the greatest benefit comes from a windbreak that allows some air through.

In rural settings or on large estates where space is not a factor, the windbreak should have at least six rows of plants—a row of dense shrubs on the windward side, two rows of conifers, two rows of broadleaf trees, and another row of shrubs on the leeward side. In urban areas with space limitations, even a single row of plantings can be used to slow the wind. The windbreak should be placed to protect the garden and home during the winter—typically north and west of the home, as most winter winds in the Midwest come from the northwest.

Broadleafed and needled evergreens planted on the lee side of the windbreak will be less likely to develop brown foliage through the winter from drying winds.

An added bonus of windbreaks is their ability to trap snow. Snow makes a wonderful insulator; tender perennials planted in the snow-deposit area are more likely to survive the harsh winter weather. In the High Plains, the extra moisture trapped from the melted snow will be a boon to young plants during the growing season as well.

Staking a Tree

New tree plantings on windy sites will need temporary staking to prevent wind from blowing them over. Trees up to 2 ½ inches in diameter will need two stakes; those from 2 ½ to 4 inches will require three stakes equally spaced around the tree. Select stakes at least as tall as the tree's lowest branches, plus 18 inches. Position the tree so that the side with the most branches faces into the wind, to counteract the tree's natural tendency to grow away from the wind. Wrap a 2-inch-wide nylon band with grommets at each end around the trunk of the tree 5 feet from the ground, and attach the band to the stakes with wire run through the grommets. The band should be attached loosely enough to allow free movement of the tree but tightly enough to prevent it from blowing over. Remove the stakes and nylon bands after one growing season.

Tall-growing perennial flowers also need staking on windy sites. Surrounding the flower bed with shrubs helps reduce the wind problem. Individual plant stakes should be slightly shorter than the plant's height. Wood, plastic, or bamboo stakes are commonly used. Tie plants to the stake using a figure 8 or double loop, with one loop around the plant and the other loop around the stake. Other types of flower supports include tomato cages, poultry netting, or small tree branches used as a trellis.

Wind barriers

Where space is limited, gardeners can use a wooden fence as a windbreak. As with a windbreak planting, a solid fence is less effective than one that allows some wind to penetrate. Try a louvered, board-on-board, or spaced-board pattern rather than a solid design.

If a full-yard windbreak is impractical, wind-sensitive plants may be screened individually by tacking burlap to stakes that surround the plant. Leave the top of the barrier open to lessen heat buildup and to promote air exchange.

Wind-tolerant plants

Perhaps the best solution on windy sites is to grow plants that tolerate the wind. Avoid broadleafed evergreens that will desiccate, and tall herbaceous flowers that will be flattened by wind. Choose low-growing flowers and ground covers to add color to the yard. Also avoid fast-growing trees and shrubs. Instead, plant trees and shrubs with slow to moderate growth rates; slow-growing plants have stronger wood.

An effective windbreak of cottonwood *(Populus deltoides)*, green ash *(Fraxinus pennsylvanica)*, Russian olive *(Elaeagnus angustifolia)*, and lilac *(Syringa vulgaris)*.

Woody plants for windbreaks

TREES

Abies
FIR

Acer tataricum ginnala
AMUR MAPLE

Alnus
ALDER

Celtis occidentalis
HACKBERRY

Crataegus
HAWTHORN

Fraxinus
ASH

Gleditsia triacanthos
HONEY LOCUST

Juniperus
JUNIPER,
EASTERN RED CEDAR

Maclura pomifera
OSAGE ORANGE

Picea
SPRUCE

Pinus
PINE

Prunus
PLUM, CHERRY

Quercus
OAK

Thuja occidentalis
AMERICAN ARBORVITAE

SHRUBS

Amelanchier
SERVICEBERRY, JUNEBERRY

Berberis
BARBERRY

Caragana
PEASHRUB

Cornus
DOGWOOD

Cotoneaster

Elaeagnus
RUSSIAN OLIVE

Ligustrum
PRIVET

Myrica pensylvanica
NORTHERN BAYBERRY

Philadelphus coronarius
MOCK ORANGE

Prunus
SAND CHERRY, PLUM,
NANKING CHERRY

Rhus
SUMAC

Ribes
CURRANT

Sambucus
ELDERBERRY

Shepherdia argentea
SILVER BUFFALOBERRY

Sorbaria sorbifolia
URAL FALSE SPIREA

Spiraea

Taxus
YEW

Viburnum

LANDSCAPE PLANS

The first step in planning a garden is to have a vision of what yours should be. Search through gardening books and visit local gardens to sample styles until you find one that complements your house and surroundings. Once you have your garden style in mind, think about the many uses for your garden. Do you need a place to entertain, a children's recreation area, a pool, or a vegetable patch? You can meet many different needs with a good design. Plan your layout on paper, and then select plants that are appropriate for your growing conditions.

Whatever the size, shape, or style of your garden, it will be your unique place of refuge and relaxation, so it should reflect your personality and needs. The following pages provide some specific plans and plant choices to help inspire you to create your own special garden that meets your individual needs.

The Plants

A. Acer platanoides 'Olmsted'
NORWAY MAPLE

B. Acer rubrum 'October Glory'
RED MAPLE

C. Amelanchier alnifolia
SASKATOON SERVICEBERRY

D. Cotoneaster horizontalis Perpusillus
ROCKSPRAY COTONEASTER

E. Crataegus × mordenensis 'Toba'
TOBA HAWTHORN

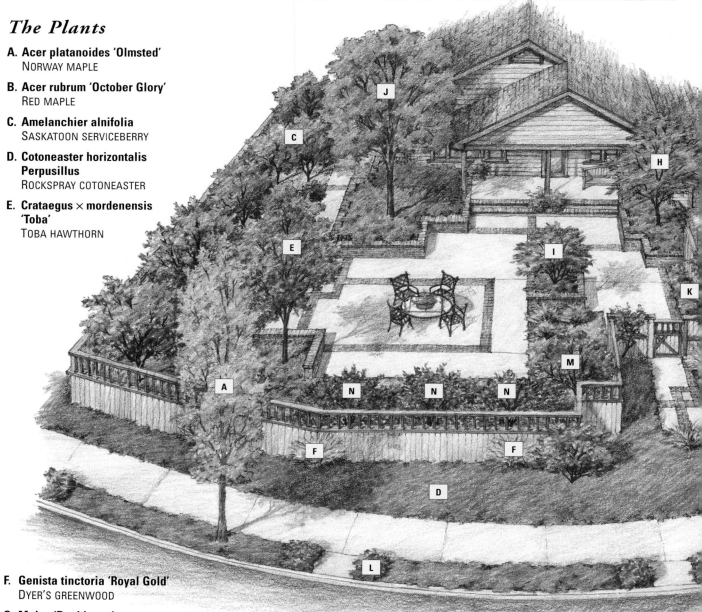

F. Genista tinctoria 'Royal Gold'
DYER'S GREENWOOD

G. Malus 'Doubloons'
FLOWERING CRABAPPLE

H. Prunus cerasifera 'Newport'
MYROBALAN PLUM

I. Prunus × cistena 'Minnesota Red'
PURPLE-LEAF SAND CHERRY

J. Quercus rubra
RED OAK

K. Rosa rugosa 'Charles Albanel'
RUGOSA ROSE

L. Scabiosa columbaria 'Butterfly Blue'
PINCUSHION FLOWER

M. Spiraea trilobata 'Fairy Queen'

N. Syringa vulgaris 'Monge'
LILAC

FRONT-ENTRY GARDENS

The garden plans on these two pages show what is possible when a front garden is reclaimed for private use. Above, a 5-foot-high fence and entry gate create a private, enclosed area. Visitors entering the gate are treated to a series of garden rooms until they reach either the patio or the front door. The first garden room is just inside the gate and contains a ground cover rugosa rose with fragrant red double flowers. The second transition is at the front door steps, where the deep purple leaves of the Newport myrobalan plum continue the color theme.

A red oak and hawthorn tree provide shade for the patio during the morning hours. In spring, white flowers on the serviceberry and crabapple highlight the driveway and side garden. A few weeks later, new blooms add more color when the blue perennial pincushion flower, the small golden genista, and the purple-red lilac flower along the fence. In fall, oak,

A Second Entry Garden

The same property is shown below with an alternative plan. Here the landscape architect has created a low-maintenance design filled with shrubs, perennials, ground covers, and stone accents.

This garden design preserves a small, oval traditional lawn in the center. Surrounding the lawn are dense plantings that act as a living fence for the residents. The property lines are well defined by the dense, upright eastern arborvitae and the black chokeberry.

The Plants

A. Acer × freemanii 'Celebration'
RED MAPLE (HYBRID)

B. Aronia melanocarpa 'Autumn Magic'
BLACK CHOKEBERRY

C. Cornus stolonifera 'Kelseyi'
REDTWIG DOGWOOD

D. Euonymus alatus 'Compacta'
BURNING BUSH (DWARF)

E. Forsythia 'Meadowlark'
FORSYTHIA

F. Fraxinus pennsylvanica 'Patmore'
GREEN ASH

G. Geranium macrorrhizum 'Bevan's Variety'
BIGROOT CRANESBILL

H. Geranium sanguineum striatum
BLOODY CRANESBILL

I. Hemerocallis 'Catherine Woodbury' ('Woodbery')
DAYLILY

J. Heuchera micrantha 'Bressingham Bronze'
PURPLE ALUM ROOT

K. Juniperus chinensis 'Blaauw'
CHINESE JUNIPER

L. Juniperus horizontalis 'Prince of Wales'
CREEPING JUNIPER

M. Pachysandra terminalis 'Green Carpet'
JAPANESE SPURGE

N. Potentilla fruticosa 'Goldfinger'
SHRUBBY CINQUEFOIL

O. Prunus × cistena 'Crimson Dwarf'
PURPLE-LEAF SAND CHERRY

P. Rhododendron 'PJM'

Q. Rhus aromatica 'Gro-Low'
FRAGRANT SUMAC

R. Ribes alpinum 'Compactum'
COMPACT ALPINE CURRANT

S. Spiraea japonica 'Golden Princess'
GOLDEN JAPANESE SPIREA

T. Thuja occidentalis 'Techny'
AMERICAN ARBORVITAE

U. Vinca minor 'Gertrude Jekyll'
PERIWINKLE

NORTH ▲

red maple, and serviceberry are all ablaze throughout the garden. The crabapples and large hawthorn tree provide late-season interest with colorful fruit.

A low ground cover planting of cotoneaster ties together the sidewalk area and the driveway with a display of pinkish white blooms in summer, bright red fruit in fall, and a herringbone branching pattern in winter. This plant truly provides four-season interest.

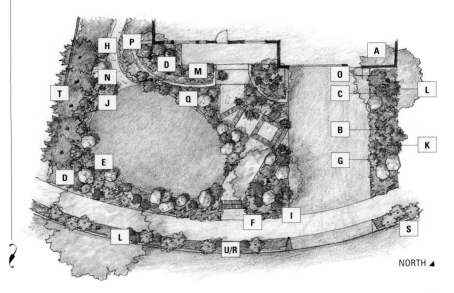

NORTH ▲

A NARROW GARDEN

Narrow gardens, found in many side yards, are design challenges because of their shape. A long, narrow garden often includes a tall fence, leaving stark, flat walls that are difficult to keep in scale, soften, and make attractive. The surrounding structures may reduce the amount of sunlight that reaches the ground-level plants—the sun might reach the garden floor only for a short time at midday. In this garden, the designer has met these challenges through careful plant selection and optimum use of all horizontal and vertical spaces. The result is an attractive garden in an intimate space that is only 6 feet wide.

The key to this garden is the successful use of trailing, narrow, or climbing plants that soften the hard structures with their different textures. A natural flagstone walk slows the pace of visitors as they step from stone to stone, careful not to tread on the low native partridgeberry ground cover planted between each stone. Formal and informal styles mix through the use of the fountains and natural plant combinations. The sound of splashing water helps mask sounds of the outside world.

French doors from the living room open onto the garden and offer a view of the main attraction of the garden—symmetrical decorative wall fountains. The two fountains are framed by delicate green foliage and the seasonal blooms from several shrubs and vines. Hardy 'PJM' evergreen rhododendrons will bloom with bright lavender-pink flowers in the spring. Later in the summer, the single, light pink flowers of the 'Max Vogel' Japanese anemone will appear. Lush hydrangea, moonseed vines, and ferns hide some of the boundary fence and integrate the raised planter with the in-ground plantings.

In fall, round, white hydrangea blooms will attract attention in this narrow garden full of colorful foliage. One of the fall highlights is the bright red leaf color of the amur maple.

In winter, the hydrangea seed heads add an interesting effect while covered in snow. The bigleaf winter creeper has large, dark green, glossy leaves that will show well against the snow. The extra protection of the house and fence will help reduce winterburn on this plant. Also providing winter interest is the evergreen ground cover Japanese spurge.

The Plants

A. Acer tataricum ginnala 'Flame'
AMUR MAPLE

B. Anemone × hybrida 'Max Vogel'
JAPANESE ANEMONE

C. Dryopteris marginalis
MARGINAL WOOD FERN

D. Euonymus fortunei 'Vegetus'
BIGLEAF WINTER CREEPER

E. Hydrangea arborescens 'Annabelle'

F. Impatiens walleriana
(Swirl series) 'Coral'

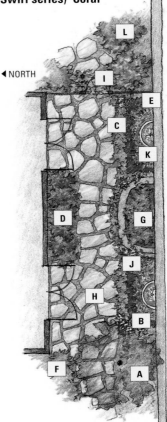

◄ NORTH

G. Menispermum canadense
COMMON MOONSEED

H. Mitchella repens
PARTRIDGEBERRY

I. Pachysandra terminalis
'Green Carpet'
JAPANESE SPURGE

J. Rhododendron 'PJM'

K. Tsuga canadensis 'Minuta'
CANADA HEMLOCK (DWARF)

L. Viburnum × burkwoodii 'Chenault'

GARDENS FOR SMALL SPACES

In a small space, the challenge for the garden designer is to keep everything in the right scale. For this courtyard garden plan as well as the deckside retreat and grassy glade plans on the following pages, container plants, vertical vines, and narrow trees all effectively integrate with wood, stone, and cement paving to create a unified design.

The courtyard garden maximizes a small area by creating two distinct "rooms." The secluded dining area is almost totally enclosed with plants. A 'Princess Kay' plum, planted in a hole cut through the concrete slab, has fragrant white double blooms in spring and reddish purple leaves in fall. Brick planters contain hosta, flowering shrubs, bright yellow daylilies, perennial switch grass, and a durable coral-colored peony. More color and foliage are provided by golden yellow French marigolds, a tropical palm,

red geraniums, crinkled hair grass, and red petunias. Comfortable seating and an elegant dining table add interest to this private garden.

The deckside retreat (see page 344) features a cedar deck made of 2 by 4s arranged in a pattern inspired by a Japanese fan. The lawn area also uses this shape. Although the deck takes up almost half of the 20-by-40-foot backyard, it minimizes garden maintenance and is an ideal area for garden parties. Decorative containers of herbs and perennials tie in the deck with the garden and bring the garden closer to the house. A built-in seating area on the edge of the deck faces a modern stone fountain in the southwest corner and a river birch with salmon-colored bark that darkens to orange-brown and eventually peels off in sheets. The fountain utilizes three basalt columns.

The Plants

A. Berberis thunbergii 'Atropurpurea Nana'
RED-LEAF JAPANESE BARBERRY (DWARF)

B. Chamaedorea elegans
PARLOR PALM

C. Deschampsia flexuosa 'Tatra Gold'
CRINKLED HAIR GRASS

D. Festuca glauca 'Elijah Blue'
BLUE FESCUE

E. Hemerocallis 'Ida's Magic'
DAYLILY

F. Hosta 'Invincible'

G. Lonicera japonica 'Halliana'
JAPANESE HONEYSUCKLE

H. Paeonia lactiflora 'Coral Charm'
PEONY (HERBACEOUS)

I. Panicum virgatum 'Heavy Metal'
BLUE SWITCH GRASS

J. Pelargonium (Century series) 'Red'
GERANIUM

K. Petunia × hybrida (Celebrity series) 'Red'

L. Prunus americana (P. nigra) 'Princess Kay'
WILD PLUM

M. Salvia coccinea 'Lady in Red'
ORNAMENTAL SAGE

N. Tagetes patula (Disco series) 'Golden Yellow'
FRENCH MARIGOLD

O. Viburnum trilobum 'Alfredo'
AMERICAN CRANBERRY BUSH

The grassy glade design (see page 345) has the same property dimensions as the deckside retreat but includes some easy-care plants such as mugho pine, trumpet vine, ornamental grasses, and drought-tolerant succulents. Evergreens and a fence along the garden's perimeter provide privacy. Flowering vines on a trellis mask the view to a service area and block the view to the neighbors' second-story balcony. The change in elevation from the step-down patio makes the garden appear larger. Interesting features in this garden include natural stones among the planting beds, an accent sculpture along the back fence, and a recirculating waterfall spilling into a tranquil pool.

THE COURTYARD GARDEN

NORTH ▶

A DECKSIDE RETREAT

Garden view from house

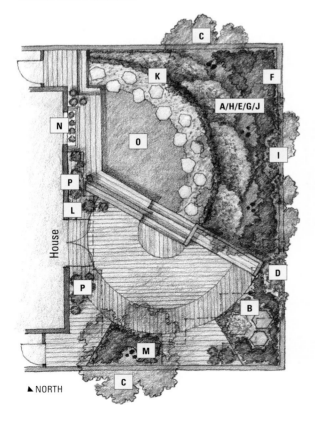

▲ NORTH

The Plants

A. Anemone blanda 'White Splendor' GRECIAN WINDFLOWER

B. Asarum europaeum EUROPEAN WILD GINGER

C. Betula nigra 'Heritage' RIVER BIRCH

D. Clematis 'Hagley Hybrid'

E. Crocus speciosus 'Alba', C. vernus 'Snow Storm'

F. Euonymus fortunei 'Sarcoxie' WINTER CREEPER

G. Gaultheria procumbens WINTERGREEN

H. Heuchera micrantha 'Palace Purple' PURPLE ALUM ROOT

I. Parthenocissus tricuspidata BOSTON IVY

J. Trillium sessile WAKE ROBIN

K. Viola sororaria 'Freckles' VIOLET

L. ANNUALS: Ipomoea batatas 'Blackie' SWEET POTATO VINE; **Pelargonium 'Contrast'** GERANIUM; **Tagetes tenuifolia 'Lemon Gem'** SIGNET MARIGOLD; **Thymophylla tenuiloba** DAHLBERG DAISY

M. BULBS: Narcissus 'Golden Cheerfulness', DAFFODIL, **N. 'Thalia'; Tulipa tarda** TULIP

N. HERBS: Melissa officinalis 'Aurea' GOLDEN LEMON BALM; **Thymus vulgaris 'Silver Posie'** SILVER-EDGE GARDEN THYME

O. LAWN: Kentucky bluegrass mix

P. PERENNIALS: Coreopsis verticillata 'Moonbeam'; Rudbeckia hirta Becky Mix BLACK-EYED SUSAN

A Grassy Glade

Garden view from house

The Plants

A. Berberis koreana
KOREAN BARBERRY

B. Campsis × tagliabuana 'Mme Galen'
TRUMPET VINE

C. Diervilla lonicera
DWARF BUSH HONEYSUCKLE

D. Helictotrichon sempervirens
BLUE OAT GRASS

E. Juniperus chinensis 'Obelisk'
CHINESE JUNIPER

F. Lonicera japonica 'Halliana'
JAPANESE HONEYSUCKLE

G. Lonicera sempervirens 'John Clayton'
TRUMPET HONEYSUCKLE

H. Miscanthus sinensis 'Kleine Silberspinne'
JAPANESE SILVER GRASS

I. Pachysandra terminalis 'Green Carpet'
JAPANESE SPURGE

J. Pinus mugo mugo
MUGHO PINE

K. Sedum 'Autumn Joy', S. telephium 'Herbstfreude', S. t. 'Orpine'

L. Syringa reticulata 'Ivory Silk'
JAPANESE TREE LILAC

M. LAWN: Kentucky bluegrass mix

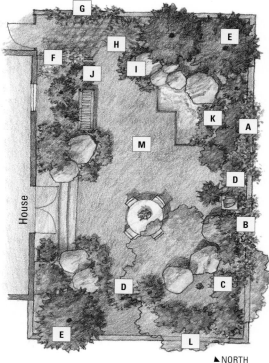

▲ NORTH

A GARDEN FOR CUTTING

The objective of this garden is to harvest bouquets by the dozens from early spring to the first snowfall. Not only are traditional cut flowers being grown in the perennial beds, but even the trees and shrubs have been selected to provide material for fresh or dried floral arrangements.

Most of the cutting plants are grown in the large perennial and bulb beds flanking the grape arbor. Tightly clipped feverfew outlines these beds and adds formality to the lawn area. Beyond the beds, through the grape arbor, are two raised beds filled with perennial and annual statice to harvest in the summer for dried arrangements. Beyond the statice is a lattice pavilion, which is the support for scarlet trumpet honeysuckle vines. Along the perimeter of the property are fruit trees, pussy willow, climbing roses, little-leaf linden, and alder. Each of these can contribute fresh flowers and fruit for seasonal arrangements.

Spring favorites for harvesting in this garden include tulips, daffodil, and pussy willow. Summer ushers in blooms on the roses, mock orange, honeysuckle, elderberry, dogwood, pin cherry, yarrow, and many more. In fall, the colorful foliage and fruit of the 'Concord' grape, 'Flame' willow, viburnum, and mountain ash are prized for floral arrangements. In winter, the catkins on the alder, tendrils on grapevines, and purple stems of the raspberry are ideal for brightening up a room.

This garden will produce armloads of fresh or dried blooms for arrangements. Harvest flowers in the early morning when they are freshest. Immediately place the stems in a bucket of water that is protected from the sun. Cut the stems again when they are placed in the final arrangement. Flowers or seeds that are harvested for drying should be hung upside down and protected from the sun. The drying room (such as an attic) or area should be warm and dry.

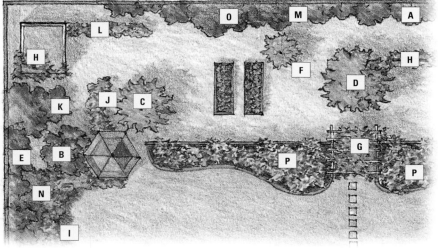

NORTH ◢

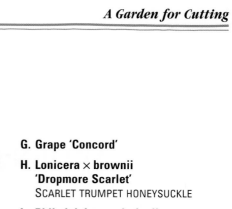

G. **Grape 'Concord'**

H. **Lonicera × brownii 'Dropmore Scarlet'**
   SCARLET TRUMPET HONEYSUCKLE

I. **Philadelphus × virginalis 'Minnesota Snowflake'**
   MOCK ORANGE

J. **Raspberry 'Heritage'**

K. **Rosa 'Alexander Mackenzie', R. 'Champlain', R. 'David Thompson', R. 'Frontenac', R. 'Henry Kelsey', R. 'John Franklin', R. 'Morden Ruby', R. 'Stanwell Perpetual'**
   ROSE (SHRUB)

L. **Rosa 'John Cabot', R. 'William Baffin'**
   ROSE (CLIMBER)

M. **Salix discolor**
   PUSSY WILLOW

N. **Salix 'Flame'**
   WILLOW

O. **BORDER:** AMERICAN FILBERT; ARROWWOOD VIBURNUM; BLACK CHOKEBERRY; ELDERBERRY; GRAY DOGWOOD; LEAD PLANT

FLOWER BEDS

P. **ANNUALS:** ANNUAL CLARY SAGE; ANNUAL COSMOS; ANNUAL DELPHINIUM; BACHELOR'S BUTTON; BELLS-OF-IRELAND; BLUE SAGE; COCKSCOMB; COREOPSIS; DAHLIA; GLOBE AMARANTH; LOVE-IN-A-MIST; LOVE-LIES-BLEEDING; MALLOW; PINCUSHION FLOWER; POT MARIGOLD; PRAIRIE GENTIAN; ROCKET LARKSPUR; SNAPDRAGON; STATICE; STOCK; STRAWFLOWER

BULBS, HARDY: DAFFODIL; TULIP

BULBS, TENDER: DAHLIA; GLADIOLUS

PERENNIALS: BELLFLOWER; BLANKET FLOWER; BLEEDING HEART; CAMPION; COLUMBINE; DAYLILY; DELPHINIUM; DIANTHUS; FEVERFEW; GAS PLANT; GLOBE THISTLE; HOSTA; LADY'S-MANTLE; LAMIUM; MONKSHOOD; OBEDIENT PLANT; PEONY; PURPLE CONEFLOWER; SPEEDWELL; YARROW

The Plants

TREES

A. **Cornus alternifolia**
   PAGODA DOGWOOD

B. **Pinus strobus**
   EASTERN WHITE PINE

C. **Prunus pensylvanica**
   PIN CHERRY

D. **Sorbus decora**
   SHOWY MOUNTAIN ASH

E. **Tilia cordata 'Greenspire'**
   LITTLE-LEAF LINDEN

SHRUBS AND VINES

F. **Alnus incana 'Aurea'**
   GOLDEN GRAY ALDER

A FOUR-SEASON GARDEN

In a northern climate with well-defined seasons, it makes sense to plan the garden to showcase natural displays during every season of the year. In the garden design featured here, plants were chosen that have bright flowers, fruit, seeds, foliage color, or interesting bark or other contrasts of texture during specific times of the year.

The most overlooked (and most critical) time to consider four-season interest is during winter. Here, the winged stems of the burning bush and the textured bark of the river birch will stand out in a snowy season. The wind will blow the plumes of the ornamental grasses and show movement because of their placement in front of the evergreen pine. Spring will come alive with purple crocus, yellow daffodil, and apricot tulip bulbs blooming through the front of the shrub border. The yellow catkins of the filbert and the yellow spiderlike blooms of witch hazel are other interesting features during early spring. In late spring, the double white lilacs will fill the garden with a sweet perfume.

Visitors can sit on the bench and absorb the sights and scents of summer with pleasure. The evergreen rhododendron will come into bloom just before the yellow flowers of the coreopsis. Summer will also bring the almost-pure-white trumpet blooms of the hosta, which will draw visitors to the back of the garden.

Fall brings brilliant color to the garden from the burning bush, mountain ash, and bayberry berries. A surprise feature at this time is the autumn crocus blooms. These large pink double flowers appear mysteriously without any foliage. Their coarse leaves will show themselves in spring and then die back in preparation for the spectacular fall blooms.

The Plants

A. Andropogon gerardii
BIG BLUESTEM

B. Betula nigra 'Heritage'
RIVER BIRCH

C. Corylus americana
AMERICAN FILBERT

D. Euonymus alatus 'Compacta'
BURNING BUSH (DWARF)

E. Hamamelis virginiana
COMMON WITCH HAZEL

F. Helictotrichon sempervirens
BLUE OAT GRASS

G. Heuchera micrantha 'Chocolate Ruffles'
PURPLE ALUM ROOT

H. Hosta sieboldiana 'Elegans'

I. Juniperus sabina 'Broadmoor'
SAVIN JUNIPER

J. Miscanthus sinensis 'Purpurascens'
FLAME GRASS

K. Myrica pensylvanica
NORTHERN BAYBERRY

L. Pachysandra terminalis 'Green Carpet'
JAPANESE SPURGE

M. Pinus densiflora 'Umbraculifera'
TANYOSHO PINE

N. Pinus resinosa
RED PINE

O. Rhododendron 'Boule de Neige' (evergreen)

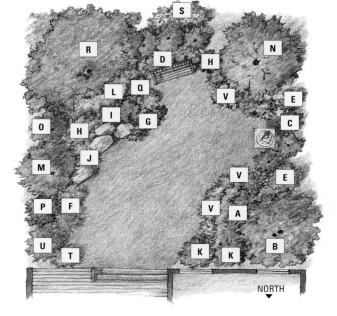

**P. Rhododendron
'Pink and Sweet'**
AZALEA (DECIDUOUS)

Q. Sedum 'Autumn Joy'

R. Sorbus americana
AMERICAN MOUNTAIN ASH

**S. Syringa vulgaris
'Miss Ellen Willmott'**
LILAC (DOUBLE WHITE)

T. Thuja occidentalis 'Caespitosa'
AMERICAN ARBORVITAE

**U. Viburnum trilobum
'Compactum'**
AMERICAN CRANBERRY BUSH

**V. BULBS: Colchicum autumnale
'Roseum Plenum'** AUTUMN
CROCUS; **Narcissus 'Dutch
Master'** DAFFODIL; **Tulipa
'Apricot Beauty'** TULIP

**PERENNIALS: Aster ericoides
'Pink Cloud'; Coreopsis
verticillata 'Moonbeam'**

NORTH

A GARDEN FOR WILDLIFE

A wildlife garden that provides the appropriate food, shelter, and water can attract numerous butterflies and moths, chipmunks, squirrels, birds, frogs, hummingbirds, bats, and many more creatures.

Butterflies require a flat surface on which to land and plenty of pollen or nectar to eat. Aster, yarrow, and blanket flower are ideal for them. Bright, bold colors attract butterflies to these nectar-rich plants. Here, an open area next to the pond provides a warm, sheltered location so they can "puddle" in the moist sand nearby.

Birds need plants that will provide plentiful nectar, seeds, or berries. Red pines will give birds the winter shelter they need. In summer, the deciduous shrubs offer protection, and many are a food source as well. The fruit of the mountain ash, bearberry, and serviceberry are prized as food by various birds.

A wildlife garden is always full of surprises and has a natural, untamed look. Do not be too quick to tidy up fallen leaves or to prune spent flowers. Leave these for the wildlife to use for shelter or food.

The Plants

FOR BUTTERFLIES AND MOTHS

A. Achillea × taygetea
YARROW

B. Asclepias tuberosa
BUTTERFLY WEED

C. Aster amellus 'Violet Queen'

D. Chelone obliqua
TURTLEHEAD

E. Gaillardia × grandiflora 'Mandarin'
BLANKET FLOWER

F. Hesperis matronalis
DAME'S ROCKET

G. Liatris spicata 'Kobold'
SPIKE GAYFEATHER

H. Malva moschata 'Rosea'
MUSK MALLOW

I. Phlox paniculata 'Orange Perfection'
GARDEN PHLOX

FOR BIRDS

J. Agastache 'Pink Panther'
HYSSOP

K. Amelanchier alnifolia
SASKATOON SERVICEBERRY

L. Amelanchier alnifolia 'Regent'
SASKATOON SERVICEBERRY (DWARF)

M. Arctostaphylos uva-ursi
BEARBERRY

N. Cornus stolonifera 'Kelseyi'
REDTWIG DOGWOOD

O. Eleutherococcus sieboldianus
FIVE-LEAF ARALIA

P. Gleditsia triacanthos inermis 'Imperial'
HONEY LOCUST

Q. Helianthus annuus 'Valentine'
SUNFLOWER

R. Lobularia maritima 'Carpet of Snow'
SWEET ALYSSUM

S. Lonicera periclymenum 'Graham Thomas'
WOODBINE

T. Pinus resinosa
RED PINE

U. Sedum × 'Bertram Anderson'

V. Sorbus aucuparia 'Cardinal Royal'
EUROPEAN MOUNTAIN ASH

W. Typha minima
DWARF CATTAIL

X. Viburnum acerifolium
MAPLELEAF VIBURNUM

FOR OTHER WILDLIFE

Y. Nymphaea 'Chromatella'
HARDY WATER LILY

Many pesticides that control destructive weeds, insects, or diseases in the garden will also harm beneficial creatures. Investigate the toxicity of pesticides before using them, and consider the use of natural pest control methods instead. Be sure to follow the manufacturer's directions for application. Many gardeners now avoid using pesticides altogether.

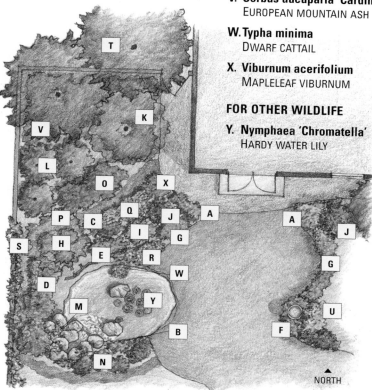

NORTH

A KITCHEN GARDEN

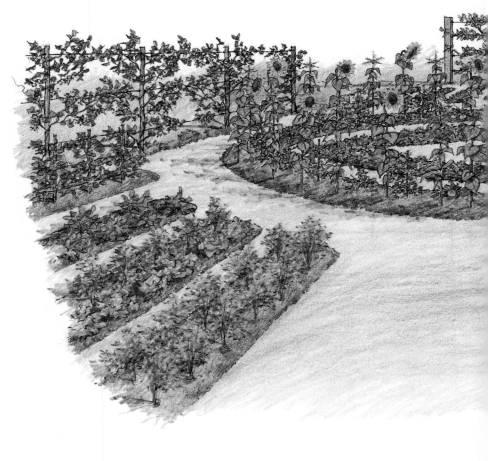

In a plot just 40 by 60 feet, more than three dozen different herbs, vegetables, fruit trees, and vines coexist in this attractive garden.

The garden has been designed so that vegetables can be harvested throughout most of the growing season. Early peas, lettuces, and radishes can be planted as soon as the soil can be cultivated. Summer harvesting starts with rhubarb and continues with many berry crops, beans, beets, peppers, tomatoes, summer squash, and corn. At the end of summer, the sunflowers, carrots, eggplant, beets, melons, and cabbage are ready for harvesting. The winter squash, turnips, and onions are harvested later in the fall and stored for use during the winter.

To conserve space, semidwarf apple trees, which rarely reach more than 8 feet tall, are trained to grow along fences. Two types of apples, blooming at the same time, have been selected for good cross-pollination. They can be harvested without a ladder. The grapes, blackberries, and raspberries are trained in the same fashion. Heavy-gauge wire is run horizontally between 4-by-4 posts to support the plants.

Two concentric semicircular beds located in the sunny center of the garden are filled with herbs, bush and staking tomatoes, and peppers. Corn and sunflowers become living stakes for the melons to climb. The mounded beds will heat up earlier in the spring, so these plants can have an earlier start.

Tall pole beans are located so that they will not shade the summer squash nearby. A compost bin is located behind the espaliered apple trees for any garden refuse. The finished compost is an excellent mulch for the garden when applied in the fall.

The Plants

A. APPLES: 'Cortland', 'McIntosh'

B. BEANS, BUSH: 'Goldkist' (yellow), 'Provider' (green)

C. BEANS, POLE: 'Kentucky Runner'

D. BEETS: 'Chioggia', 'Golden Beet', 'Red Ace'

E. BERRIES: Blueberry 'Darrow', 'Northland'; Raspberry 'Heritage'; Strawberry 'Sweet Delight'

F. CARROTS: 'Earlibird Nantes', 'Nevis'

G. CORN: 'Earlivee'

H. EGGPLANT: 'Black Bell', 'Dusky'

I. GRAPES: 'Marchal Foch' (red, midseason), 'Seibel de Chaunac' (blue, late)

J. GREENS: Lettuce 'Buttercrunch', 'Skyline'; Swiss chard 'Bright Lights'

K. Helianthus annuus 'Mammoth Russian', H. a. 'Teddy Bear' SUNFLOWER

L. HERBS: BASIL; DILL; ENGLISH THYME; FRENCH TARRAGON; GREEK OREGANO; PARSLEY; PURPLE SAGE; SWEET MARJORAM

M. MELON: 'Earliqueen' (muskmelon)

N. ONIONS: 'Ailsa Craig Exhibition', 'Norstar'

O. PEPPERS, HOT: 'Big Chile'

P. PEPPERS, SWEET: 'Ace' (green), 'Lipstick' (red), 'Purple Bell' (purple)

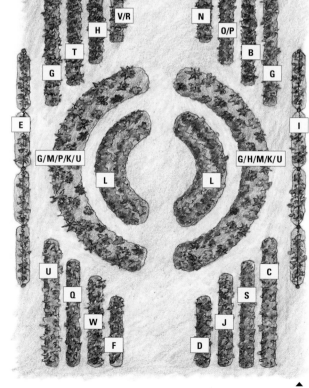

Q. **POTATOES:** 'Kennebec', 'Yukon Gold'

R. **RADISHES:** 'Cherriette', 'White Icicle'

S. **SQUASH, SUMMER:** Crookneck 'Yellow Crookneck'; Green zucchini 'Raven'

T. **SQUASH, WINTER:** Buttercup 'Black Forest'; Butternut 'Waltham Butternut'

U. **TOMATOES:** 'Beefmaster', 'Brandywine', 'Sweet Million' (staking); 'Sungem' (bush)

V. **TURNIPS:** 'Purple-Top White Globe', 'Seven Top'

W. **PERENNIAL AND LATE CROPS:** Rhubarb 'Victoria'; Cabbage 'Roulette', Cauliflower 'Snow Crown', Leeks 'Laura'

NORTH

A CONTAINER GARDEN

For plant lovers with only a small patio or balcony in which to garden, container-grown plants offer many possibilities. Dwarf fruit trees, shrubs, perennials, annuals, and tropicals can easily grow in containers. Even some vegetables, such as patio tomatoes, miniature cucumbers, lettuce, and cabbage, are easily grown in a container or hanging basket. Having a container garden offers the additional benefit of being able to rearrange or replace plants at any time to give the garden a different look.

The container garden shown here can be adapted to a roof-top, balcony, or ground-floor patio. Benches and large planter boxes can be permanently built-in or left freestanding to move on a whim.

Container possibilities are almost as varied as plant choices. The traditional terra-cotta pot is a favorite because it stabilizes larger plants (as do concrete urns) so that they do not blow over. Wooden planters can be custom built to any size. Many unusual containers can be used to grow plants—galvanized washtubs, wooden barrels, work boots, or an old wheelbarrow. The options are almost endless.

In this garden, a lath structure has been constructed to add sun protection so that shade-loving plants can be grown. The lathing also allows a hardy vine, such as the Virginia creeper shown here, to be grown over the structure, and hanging baskets can be hung from its beams. Below the lath, shade-loving begonias, impatiens, and browallia all thrive.

Plenty of colorful plants are used as vertical accents throughout this garden design, including spike gayfeather and the ornamental grasses. During winter, the evergreen foliage of the Norway spruce will be attractive next to the billowing seed heads of the big bluestem grass.

Except for the palm and annuals, most of the plants in this design are winter hardy for larger containers. Plants in containers are more susceptible to damage from drying winds, frost heaving, and low temperatures because they are raised above ground level. To increase the odds for winter survival, water plants well during the fall, group pots together for protection, use the largest containers available, and select as many cold-hardy plants as possible.

F. **Howea forsteriana**
   KENTIA PALM

G. **Liatris spicata**
   SPIKE GAYFEATHER

H. **Miscanthus sinensis 'Purpurascens'**
   FLAME GRASS

I. **Nymphaea 'Rembrandt'**
   HARDY WATER LILY

J. **Parthenocissus quinquefolia**
   VIRGINIA CREEPER

K. **Petunia × hybrida (Carpet series) 'Red'**

L. **Picea abies 'Emsland'**
   NORWAY SPRUCE

M. **Pontederia cordata**
   PICKEREL WEED

N. **Prunus × cistena**
   PURPLE-LEAF SAND CHERRY

O. **Sedum telephium 'Orpine'**

P. **Stachys byzantina**
   LAMB'S EARS

Q. **Tropaeolum majus 'Hermine Grasshof'**
   NASTURTIUM

R. ANNUALS FOR SHADE: **Browallia speciosa 'Blue Bells'** BUSH VIOLET; **Impatiens walleriana (Accent series) 'Red'**

S. ANNUALS FOR SUN: **Coleus × hybridus 'Bronze Pagoda'**; **Pelargonium 'Blazonry'** GERANIUM

T. FERNS: **Athyrium filix-femina** LADY FERN; **Dryopteris marginalis** MARGINAL WOOD FERN

U. HANGING BASKETS: **Caladium bicolor 'Little Miss Muffet'**; **Scaevola aemula** FAN FLOWER

V. PERENNIALS FOR SHADE: **Astilbe simplicifolia 'Aphrodite'**; **Heuchera micrantha 'Palace Purple'** PURPLE ALUM ROOT

The Plants

A. **Andropogon gerardii 'Champ'**
   BIG BLUESTEM

B. **Andropogon gerardii 'Roundtree'**
   BIG BLUESTEM

C. **Begonia 'Can-Can'**

D. **Dianthus barbatus**
   SWEET WILLIAM

E. **Genista tinctoria 'Royal Gold'**
   DYER'S GREENWOOD

A FAMILY GARDEN

Designing a garden so that it meets the needs of a growing family is a real challenge. Often, many different interests must be satisfied by creating separate areas within the garden. Mom may want a quiet place for relaxation in the evening after the children have gone to bed. Dad may want a barbecue and entertainment area for weekends. Children and pets will need a large play area. Other priorities might include a vegetable garden, flower beds, a children's playhouse, or a swimming pool.

This garden, which is a mere 55 by 65 feet, addresses all these family needs. A covered patio table has been placed close to the barbecue area so that adults can easily serve an outdoor meal and entertain during warm weather. The lawn area is large enough to play a game of croquet, bocce, or badminton or a game of fetch with the family pet.

Herbs such as basil, garlic chives, and thyme are conveniently located near the patio doors for quick, fresh harvests. Nearby are honeysuckle vines that will fill the warm summer air with a delightful fragrance. An enclosed vegetable garden is tucked behind the swimming pool. The surrounding fences create a microclimate that will warm this area faster than others; one advantage will be early tomato harvests.

This garden design gives careful consideration to the safety needs of children. A large play structure, constructed from a kit, was installed in the northwest corner of the property. An attractive soft, shredded cedar mulch was placed under the structure to cushion any falls and help prevent injuries. The nearby poplar tree will provide some shade for children late in the day. The swimming pool was enclosed with a decorative fence for safety.

G. **Euonymus alatus 'Compacta'**
BURNING BUSH (DWARF)

H. **Hemerocallis 'Daiquiri'**
DAYLILY

I. **Hydrangea paniculata 'Pink Diamond'**

J. **Limonium latifolium**
SEA LAVENDER

K. **Lonicera × brownii 'Dropmore Scarlet'**
SCARLET TRUMPET HONEYSUCKLE

L. **Lonicera japonica repens 'Red Coral'**
JAPANESE HONEYSUCKLE

M. **Luzula sylvatica**
GREATER WOODRUSH

N. **Lysimachia clethroides**
GOOSENECK LOOSESTRIFE (NONINVASIVE)

O. **Pachysandra terminalis 'Green Sheen'**
JAPANESE SPURGE

P. **Parthenocissus quinquefolia**
VIRGINIA CREEPER

Q. **Populus × canescens**
GRAY POPLAR

R. **Vinca minor 'Bowles' Variety'**
PERIWINKLE

S. **Weigela 'Minuet' (dwarf)**

T. **HERBS:** BASIL; GARLIC CHIVES; OREGANO; SWEET MARJORAM; THYME

The Plants

A. **Acer rubrum 'Morgan'**
RED MAPLE

B. **Alchemilla mollis**
LADY'S-MANTLE; **Astrantia major**
GREATER MASTERWORT

C. **Aruncus dioicus 'Kneiffii'**
DWARF GOAT'S BEARD

D. **Celtis reticulata**
SUGARBERRY

E. **Cornus stolonifera**
REDTWIG DOGWOOD

F. **Echinacea purpurea 'Magnus'**
PURPLE CONEFLOWER

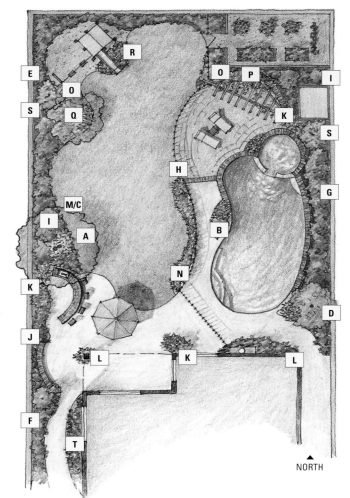

NORTH

A SHADE GARDEN

In a region that is known for open spaces, expansive views, and plenty of warm summer days, shade is a treasured commodity. Many larger Midwestern gardens contain mature native or ornamental trees that cast significant shade below. However, as trees grow, shady areas expand as well, and sun-loving plants often struggle with the decreased light levels. Lawns, annuals, perennials, and shrubs may have fewer blooms or be less resistant to pests and diseases with increased shade. The best strategy to deal with this problem is to renovate the garden and select plants that will thrive in a shady environment.

Many gardeners who are more familiar with sunny conditions are frustrated with shade and believe that only annual impatiens flower in the shade. However, the garden design above is proof that an interesting garden that includes plenty of blooms can be created for a shady site. Color and foliage contrast need not be lost just because there are trees overhead.

Defining the perimeter of this garden are several large oak trees that will cast morning shade. A red maple will shade the patio and part of the southern section, with the house shading a good portion of the garden during the afternoon as well. Interconnecting beds circle the perimeter of the garden under the large shade trees. The shrubs under these oaks, such as kerria, weigela, and sorbaria, were selected because they tolerate the shade and still bloom during the summer. These shrubs will also provide winter interest with their twig color and branching structure when seen against a backdrop of snow.

The spring-blooming perennials (Bethlehem sage, Virginia bluebells, and Lenten rose) all have attractive foliage during the remainder of the season. Lush ferns will contrast with the spiky foliage of the Japanese water iris. Fall attractions in this garden include displays of fruit and seed heads from the oaks and snowberry, as well as white blooms from the eupatorium shrubs.

The Plants

A. Acer rubrum 'Embers'
RED MAPLE

B. Adiantum pedatum
MAIDENHAIR FERN

C. Dicentra eximia 'Adrian Bloom'
FRINGED BLEEDING HEART

D. Dicentra 'Spring Morning'
BLEEDING HEART

E. Diervilla lonicera
DWARF BUSH HONEYSUCKLE

F. Dryopteris filix-mas
MALE FERN

G. Dryopteris marginalis
MARGINAL WOOD FERN

H. Epimedium × rubrum
RED BARRENWORT

I. Eupatorium rugosum (Ageratina altissima) 'Chocolate'
WHITE SNAKEROOT

J. Gleditsia triacanthos inermis 'Sunburst'
HONEY LOCUST

K. Helleborus orientalis
LENTEN ROSE

L. Heuchera americana 'Persian Carpet'
PURPLE ALUM ROOT

M. Hosta 'Ginko Craig'

N. Hosta 'Zounds'

O. Iris ensata 'Continuing Pleasure'
JAPANESE IRIS

P. Iris laevigata 'Variegata'
JAPANESE WATER IRIS

Q. Kerria japonica 'Golden Guinea'
JAPANESE ROSE

R. Matteuccia struthiopteris
OSTRICH FERN

S. Mertensia pulmonarioides
VIRGINIA BLUEBELLS

T. Pachysandra terminalis 'Green Sheen'
JAPANESE SPURGE

U. Phlox divaricata 'Fuller's White'
WOODLAND PHLOX

V. Prinsepia sinensis
CHERRY PRINSEPIA

W. Pulmonaria saccharata 'Sissinghurst White'
BETHLEHEM SAGE

X. Quercus gambellii
GAMBEL OAK

Y. Quercus macrocarpa
BUR OAK

Z. Quercus muehlenbergii
CHINQUAPIN OAK

AA. Rhododendron 'PJM'

BB. Rhododendron 'Spicy Lights'
AZALEA (DECIDUOUS)

CC. Sorbaria sorbifolia
FALSE SPIREA

DD. Symphoricarpos albus
COMMON SNOWBERRY

EE. Viburnum acerifolium
MAPLELEAF VIBURNUM

FF. Weigela 'Minuet' (dwarf)

◄ NORTH

MATERIALS AND TECHNIQUES

You have analyzed your garden site, sketched a plan, and chosen the right plants for your microclimates. Now it's time to lay some bricks and pound a few nails. You are sure to have a few questions. What kind of lumber is best for my trellis? How should I lay out a gravel pathway? Should I mix my own concrete or use ready-mixed?

Whether you are using wood or brick or trying new materials such as plastic or molded concrete pavers, the step-by-step instructions in this chapter should be of interest to you. Should you do all the work yourself or seek professional help? Although do-it-yourself projects can be satisfying and economical, some projects may take more expert knowledge than you have or require tools you don't know how to use. If you do decide to do it yourself, be sure to read the safety guidelines at the end of this chapter.

LUMBER

The following overview of lumber products, fasteners, and finishes should get you started with the basics for your deck, fence, overhead, step, or raised-bed project. Then, step-by-step directions illustrate the most common wood garden projects: an attached deck (see pages 366–367), a basic board fence (see pages 368–369), and a freestanding overhead (see page 370).

Lumberyard tools and materials

Because wood comes in so many sizes, species, and grades, a visit to a lumberyard can be a daunting experience for the beginning do-it-yourselfer. Busy salespeople may not be very helpful if you are unfamiliar with basic building terminology, so it's a good idea to familiarize yourself with the terms you'll need to know for your projects *before* asking an employee for help.

As a rule, softwoods are much less expensive, easier to tool, and more readily available than hardwoods. In fact, nearly all outdoor construction is done with softwoods. Hardwoods such as oak, hickory, and poplar are generally used for indoor projects.

SPECIES. Woods from different trees have specific properties. Redwood and cedar heartwoods (the darker part of the wood, cut from the tree's core), for example, have a natural resistance to decay. This characteristic, combined with their beauty, makes them attractive candidates for decks and natural-finish lath roofing. But these woods are expensive and can easily run double the cost of a structure built from pressure-treated pine, the most common decking lumber.

If a structural member will be painted, you can use untreated pine, hemlock, or fir. But pressure-treated lumber can also be painted.

Pressure-treated timbers serve well as edging for raised beds or steps and for building gates and decks; use construction-grade lumber—typically spruce, pine, or fir—for framing a garden shed or greenhouse. From left to right above: pressure-treated 6 by 6 and 4 by 4; landscaping timber; construction-grade 2 by 6; cedar and construction-grade 1 by 4s; pressure-treated and construction-grade 2 by 2s.

LUMBER GRADES. Wood is sorted and graded at a lumber mill according to several factors: natural growth characteristics (such as knots), defects resulting from milling errors, and commercial drying and preserving techniques that affect each piece's strength, durability, and appearance. A stamp on the lumber identifies its moisture content and its grade and species, as well as the mill that produced it and the grading agency. In general, the higher the grade, the more you will have to pay.

Structural lumber and timbers are rated for strength. The most common grading system includes the grades Select Structural, No. 1, No. 2, and No. 3. For premium strength, choose Select Structural. Often, lumberyards sell a mix of grades called No. 2 and Better. Other grading systems, used typically for 2 by 4s, classify wood as Construction, Standard, and Utility or as a mixture of grades called Standard and Better.

Redwood is usually graded for its appearance and the percentage of heartwood versus sapwood it contains: Clear All Heart is the best and the most expensive. B Heart, Construction Heart, and Merchantable Heart, in descending order of quality, are typical grades of pure heartwood; lesser grades are likely to contain more knots, splits, and other flaws.

Cedar grades, starting with the highest quality, are Architect Clear, Custom Clear, Architect Knotty, and Custom Knotty. These grades don't indicate if the wood is heartwood or sapwood. Light-colored cedar will rot if not regularly treated with a sealer.

BUYING LUMBER. Draw up your project, listing every board you will need. Boards generally come in lengths of 6 feet, 8 feet, 10 feet, and up to 18 feet or 20 feet. If you need a piece 8 feet 2 inches, for example, you need to buy a 10-foot board.

NOMINAL SIZES. Remember that a "2 by 4" does not actually measure 2 by 4 inches. Its *nominal size* is designated before it is dried and surface planed; the finished size is actually 1½ by 3½ inches. Likewise, a nominal 4 by 4 is actually 3½ by 3½ inches.

Rough lumber is usually closer to the nominal size because it is wetter and has not been surface planed. If exact measurements are critical, be sure to check the actual dimensions of any lumber you are considering before you buy it.

DEFECTS. Lumber is subject to a number of defects due to weathering and milling errors. When choosing lumber, lift each piece and look down the face and edges for any defects. The most common problems are cupping and bowing—warps and hollows on the board. In addition, be on the lookout for problems such as rotting, staining, splits, and missing wood or untrimmed bark along the edges or corners of the piece, called wane. Also look for insect holes and reservoirs of sap or pitch.

PRESSURE-TREATED LUMBER. For all structural elements that will not be visible, use pressure-treated lumber, which resists rot better than any other alternative. You can also use pressure-treated lumber for visible structures, but many people find cedar, redwood, or plastic lumber worth the extra cost.

Use lumber rated "ground contact," or with a chromium copper arsenate (CCA) level of 0.40 or greater; lumber with less treatment may rot. CCA is toxic, but it bonds firmly to wood fibers. You might get a rash from the sawdust, and you should keep children away while cutting this lumber. But once the wood is installed and dried and the sawdust is swept away, pressure-treated lumber is safe.

Green pressure-treated lumber is unattractive and dries to an ugly gray color. However, you can use a special product to clean and stain this wood to a surprisingly attractive finish. Brown-treated lumber comes fairly close to the look of redwood and is just as rot-resistant as green-treated lumber.

Plastic Wood

A number of companies now offer decking and other components made of plastic or a plastic-wood composite. Plastic wood is easy to cut and install, extremely durable, and ecologically sensitive, since it is made primarily of recycled materials.

Not all plastic wood products are equal. Some older types have colors that fade after a summer in the sun; newer products are more colorfast. Ask your dealer about durability, and *inspect decks in your area that were made with plastic decking to see how they have worn. Some are smooth, but others mimic the wear on a deep-grained wood.*

Some companies offer plastic decking only; others also sell easy-to-assemble fencing and railing components. As of yet, plastic wood is not available for structural elements such as joists, posts, and beams.

All the visible parts of this deck—the decking, the railing, and the bench, are made of a plastic-wood composite that mimics the color and grain of natural wood but requires no maintenance other than sweeping or mopping.

FASTENERS AND HARDWARE

Nails, screws, and metal framing connectors are essential for constructing sturdy outdoor structures. The hardware you would typically need for a garden project includes the following.

NAILS. Hot-dipped galvanized, aluminum, or stainless steel nails are essential for outdoor construction because they resist rust. Common and box nails are similar, but the former have a thicker shank, making them more difficult to drive but increasing their holding power. Both types are sold in boxes (weighing 1, 5, or 50 pounds) or loose in bins. Standard nail sizes are given in "pennies" (penny is abbreviated as "d," from the Latin *denarius*). The higher the penny number, the longer the nail. Equivalents in inches for the most common nails are as follows:

4d = 1½ in.   6d = 2 in.   8d = 2½ in.
10d = 3 in.   16d = 3½ in.   20d = 4 in.

Choose nails that have a length two or three times the thickness of the material you will be nailing through.

DECK SCREWS. Although more expensive than nails, coated deck screws have several advantages over nails: They don't pop out as readily, their coating is less likely to be damaged during installation, and their use eliminates the possibility of hammer dents in the decking. Moreover, they are surprisingly easy to drive into soft woods, such as redwood and cedar, if you use an electric drill or screw gun with an adjustable clutch and a Phillips screwdriver tip. Screws are not rated for shear (or hanging) strength, so use nails, lag screws, or bolts to fasten joists to beams or ledgers and posts to beams.

For decks, choose screws that are long enough to penetrate joists at least as deep as the decking is thick (for 2-by-4 or 2-by-6 decking, buy 3-inch screws). Screws are sold in small boxes, by the pound, or, at a substantial savings, in 25-pound boxes.

The heavy-duty lag screw, or lag bolt, has a square or hexagonal head and requires a wrench or a ratchet and socket to tighten it.

FRAMING CONNECTORS. The photo at right shows several framing connectors. Galvanized metal connectors can help prevent lumber splits caused by toenailing (nailing at a 45-degree angle) two boards together. Be sure to attach connectors with the nails specified by the manufacturer.

To eliminate visible fasteners, deck clips can be nailed to the sides of decking lumber and secured to joists. In addition to remaining hidden between the deck boards, these clips also elevate the boards slightly above the joist, discouraging the rot that wood-to-wood contact may breed. However, the clips are more expensive to buy and more time-consuming to install than nails or screws.

BOLTS. For heavy-duty fastening, choose bolts. Most are zinc-plated steel, but aluminum and brass ones are also available. Bolts go into predrilled holes and are secured by nuts. The machine bolt has a square or hexagonal head that must be tightened with a wrench. The carriage bolt has a self-anchoring head that digs into the wood as the nut is tightened. Expanding anchor bolts, also called lag shields, allow you to secure wooden members to a masonry wall.

Bolts are classified by diameter (⅛ to 1 inch) and length (⅜ inch and up). To give the nut a firm bite, select a bolt ½ to 1 inch longer than the combined thicknesses of the pieces to be joined. Use a washer at either side to keep the nut or bolt head from digging into the wood.

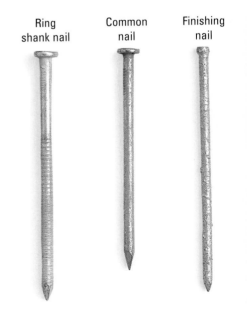

| Ring shank nail | Common nail | Finishing nail |

Framing connectors and hardware, clockwise from top far right: post anchors, deck post tie, earthquake straps, rigid tie corner, joist hangers, rigid flat tie, and decorative post tops.

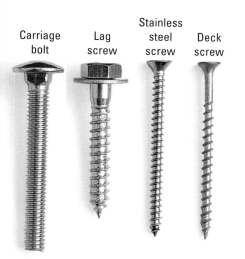

Carriage bolt | Lag screw | Stainless steel screw | Deck screw

Wood Finishes

Structural elements that contact soil or are embedded in concrete do not require a finish. But to protect other parts of a structure and to preserve its beauty, apply a water repellent, a semitransparent stain, or a solid-color stain.

Finishes change a wood's color or tone and may mask its grain and texture. Whatever product you choose, it's best to try it on a sample board first to be sure you like the look. Always read labels: some products should not be applied over new wood; others may require a sealer first.

Water repellents, also known as water sealers, help prevent decking from warping and cracking. Clear sealers don't color wood, but they allow it to gradually fade to gray; some types come in slightly tinted versions. You can buy either oil- or water-based versions, many of which include UV-blockers and mildewcides.

Don't use clear-surface finishes such as spar varnish or polyurethane on outdoor lumber. In addition to their high price, they wear quickly and are very hard to renew.

Semitransparent stains contain enough pigment to tint the wood's surface with just one coat while permitting the natural grain to show through. They are available in both water- and oil-based versions. In addition to traditional grays and wood-tone stains, you'll find products for "reviving" a deck's color and for dressing up pressure-treated wood.

Solid-color coverings include both deck stains and deck paint. The stains are essentially paints; their heavy pigments cover the wood's grain completely. Usually, any paint color can be mixed into this base. Even though these products are formulated for foot traffic, you'll probably have to renew them frequently. A word of caution: Don't choose stains or paints intended for house siding; they won't last.

Shown here, from top to bottom, are unfinished pressure-treated pine, clear sealer with UV protection, tinted sealer, semitransparent redwood stain, and gray solid-color stain.

BUILDING A LOW-LEVEL DECK

A low-level, house-attached deck helps extend the indoor living space. It is also a manageable and economical do-it-yourself project. Before you begin, review the advice given on pages 158–161 and check your local building codes. This type of deck can be completed over the course of a few weekends, but it will require the labor of at least two people.

Think ahead about benches or other items that may need to be integrated with the deck's framing. Be sure the completed deck will be at least 1 inch below adjacent access doors. If you're planning a freestanding deck, substitute an extra beam and posts for the ledger shown; extra bracing at the corners may also be necessary. For other deck plans, see Sunset's *Complete Deck Book*.

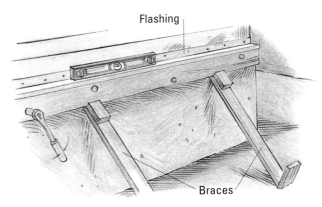

1. Determine the position of the ledger and prop it into place with 2-by-4 blocks or braces. Drill staggered holes for lag screws every 16 inches, then fasten ledger in place, making sure it is level. To prevent rot, either space the ledger off the wall with blocks or washers, or add metal flashing, as shown.

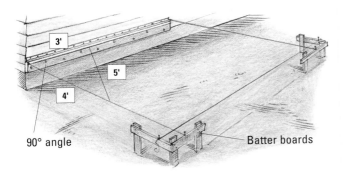

2. Strings attached to the batter boards mark the outline of the deck's framing. Anchor the batter boards 2 feet or so beyond the corners. String mason's line from the ledger to the boards. Use the "3-4-5" method to check for square, and adjust the lines as needed.

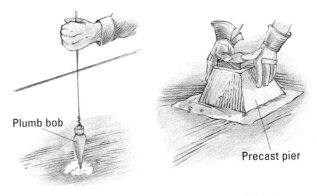

3. Dangle a plumb bob from mason's lines to mark footings. Dig holes to depths required by code; add gravel, then fill with concrete (see page 368). Push piers into the concrete, level their tops, and let concrete set overnight.

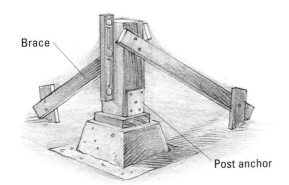

4. Unless piers have integral post anchors, add them now. Measure and cut posts—for this design, a joist's depth below the top of ledger. Check plumb on two sides of each post, temporarily brace each in place, and fasten to piers.

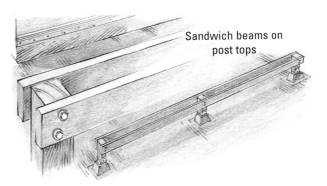

5. Position 2-by beams on each side of post tops, as shown. After leveling them with post tops, clamp them in place. Drill staggered holes, then fasten each beam to posts with bolts or lag screws.

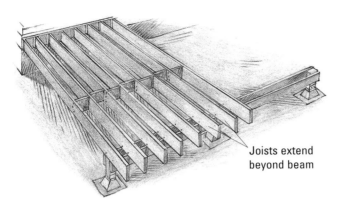

Joists extend
beyond beam

6. Position joists at predetermined span intervals, and secure
to ledger with framing connectors, as shown. Set them atop
beams, and toenail in place. Add blocking as required. Add
posts for any railings or benches, or for an overhead anchored
to deck framing.

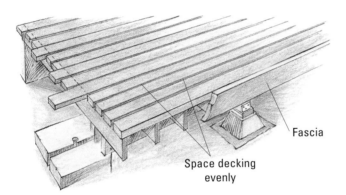

Fascia

Space decking
evenly

7. Align decking boards atop joists, staggering joints (if any).
Space boards, leaving about ³⁄₁₆ inch—or the thickness of
a 16d nail—for drainage. (Note: This spacing is not necessary
for pressure-treated wood.) Fasten decking to joists with 16d
galvanized nails or deck screws. Trim edges with circular saw.

4-by-4 post

8. Build the railing. Finish decking ends and edges as desired
with fascia boards or other trim. If you're planning benches,
planters, steps, or railings that aren't tied directly to the substructure, add them now.

Decking Patterns

*Decks are designed from the top down, so one of your
first decisions will involve selecting a decking pattern.
The design you choose may affect how the deck's substructure is built. For a house-attached deck similar to
the one shown, it's often simplest to run decking boards
parallel to the house wall. Generally, the more complex
the decking pattern, the smaller the joist spans and the
more complicated the substructure that supports it.*

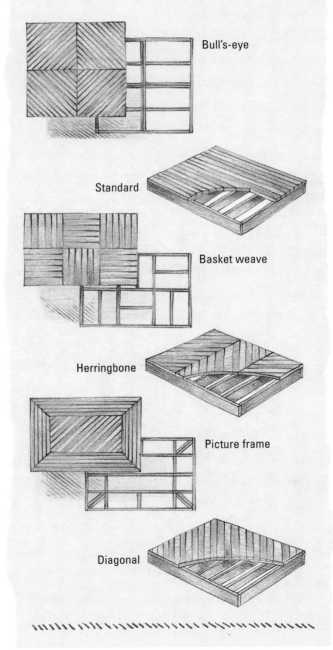

Bull's-eye

Standard

Basket weave

Herringbone

Picture frame

Diagonal

BUILDING A BOARD FENCE

In general, fence building is a straightforward task. The hardest part is digging the postholes; the tools shown on page 369 will make this easier. There are many design variations, but the procedure outlined below is a good one for putting up a basic board fence.

Before you set a post or pound a nail, check your local building and zoning codes, as they may influence style, material, setback, and other factors. Then tackle the building stages: plotting the fence, installing posts, and adding rails and siding.

For fences from 3 to 6 feet tall, plan to set posts at least 2 feet deep—12 inches deeper for end and gate posts. For taller fences, the rule of thumb for post depth is one-third the post length. You can either dig postholes to a uniform depth or cut the posts once they are in the ground. Once the posts are installed, the rest of the job is easy, especially when you have one or two helpers.

If you're planning to hang a gate, too, see pages 164–165 for construction and design pointers.

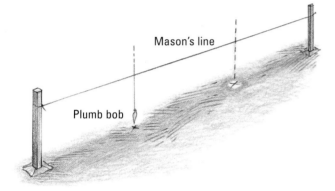

1. First, mark each end or corner post location with a stake. Run mason's line between the stakes, as shown. With chalk, mark remaining post locations on the line. Using a level or plumb bob, transfer each mark to the ground and drive in additional stakes. Then dig holes 6 inches deeper than post depth, making them 2½ to 3 times the post's diameter.

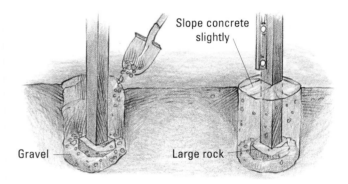

2. Place a rock at the base of each hole and add 4 to 6 inches of gravel. Place a post in a hole and shovel in concrete, tamping it down with a broomstick or capped steel pipe. Adjust the post for plumb with a level. Continue filling until the concrete extends 1 or 2 inches above ground level, and slope it away from the post to divert water.

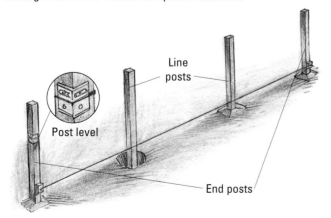

3. To align posts, first position two end or corner posts so their faces are parallel, then plumb them and set them permanently. Use spacer blocks and a mason's line to locate line posts, spacing each a block's thickness from the line. After setting posts in fresh concrete, you have about 20 minutes to align them before concrete hardens. Let cure for 2 days.

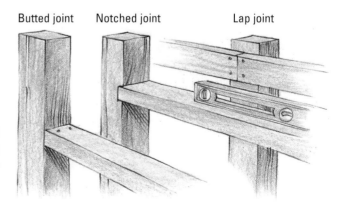

4. Brush on wood preservative where rails and posts will meet. Then fasten one end of each rail; check level with a helper and secure the other end. You can butt them against the post and toenail them, notch them in (cut notches before installing posts), or lap them over the sides or top of each post. If making lap joints, plan to span at least three posts for strength.

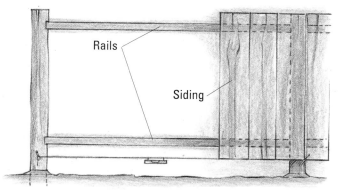

Rails

Siding

5. Cut siding boards to the same length. Stretch and level a line from post to post to mark the bottom of the siding. Check the first board for plumb, then secure it to rails with galvanized nails three times as long as the board's thickness. Add additional boards, checking alignment as you go.

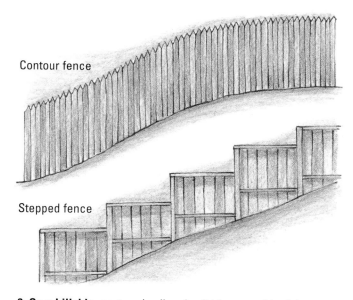

Contour fence

Stepped fence

6. On a hillside, post-and-rail and solid fences with pickets or grape stakes make good contour fences. Board, louver, basket-weave, and panel styles work better for stepped fences, which are more difficult to build. For both kinds, make sure that the bottoms of boards 6 inches or wider are cut to follow the contour of the hillside; otherwise, gaps will remain.

Digging Postholes

Don't attempt to dig a posthole using a shovel or spade—the hole will be too wide. Two handy tools are shown below.

Posthole, or clamshell, diggers (below left) work in hard or rocky soil. Spread the handles to open and close the blades, which trap soil. This tool is difficult to use for holes more than 3 feet deep as the sides of the hole interfere with the spreading of the handles.

A power auger, also known as a power digger or earth drill, is recommended whenever you have more than a dozen holes to dig. You can rent models for operation by one or two people (a two-person model is shown below right), and they may be freestanding or vehicle mounted. Every so often, pull the auger out of the hole to remove the dirt; a posthole digger or a small spade may also be required.

When you turn the handle of a hand-operated auger, the pointed blades bore into the soil, scraping it up and collecting it in a chamber. Once the chamber is full, remove the auger from the hole and empty out the soil. This tool works best in loose soil.

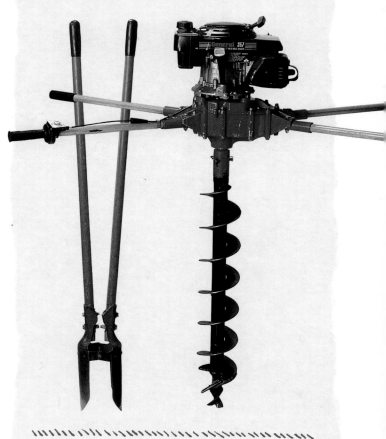

BUILDING AN OVERHEAD

An overhead is essentially a garden structure with a roof, such as an arbor or a pergola, that provides shade or a place for plants to climb. Building an overhead is similar to building a deck, although you'll probably spend a lot more time on a ladder. These illustrations outline the sequence for erecting a freestanding overhead. For a house-attached overhead, see the facing page.

If your overhead will span an existing patio, you can set the posts on footings and piers located outside the edge of the patio, or break through the existing paving, dig holes, and pour new concrete footings (and, if necessary, add piers). If you're planning to install a new concrete patio, then you can pour footings and paving at the same time, embedding the post anchors in the wet concrete.

1. Precut posts to length (or run a level line and cut them later). Set posts in anchors embedded in concrete footing or atop precast piers. Hold each post vertical and nail anchor to it.

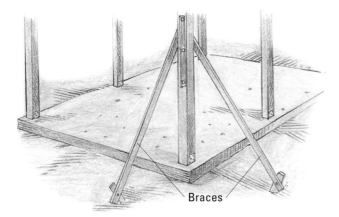

Braces

2. Continue to put up posts, plumbing each post with level on two adjacent sides. Secure each in position with temporary braces nailed to wooden stakes that are driven into ground.

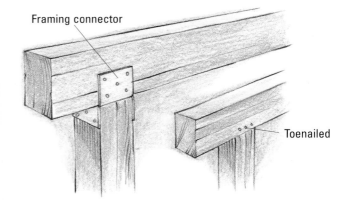

Framing connector

Toenailed

3. With a helper, position a beam on top of posts. Check that posts are vertical and beam is level (adjust, if necessary, with shims); then secure beam to posts.

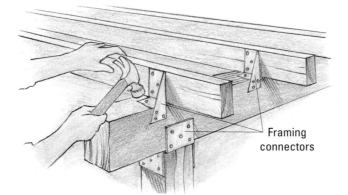

Framing connectors

4. Set and space rafters on top of beams, and secure them with framing connectors (shown) or by toenailing to beams. For extra strength, install bracing between posts and beams.

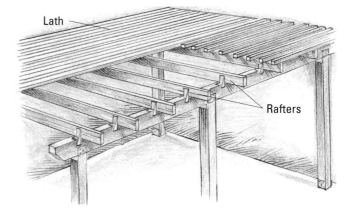

Lath

Rafters

5. Cover rafters with lath, either 1 by 2s or 2 by 2s. Space the lath for plant support or to achieve a specific amount of shade (see facing page).

Overhead alternatives

Although most overheads employ the same basic components (posts, beams, rafters or joists, and some type of roofing), there are many different ways to assemble them. Each, however, must conform to spans determined by local building codes, so be sure to check them before you start to build.

To attach an overhead to your house, you will need to install a ledger, much like a deck ledger (see page 366). Usually made from a 2 by 4 or a 2 by 6, the ledger is typically lag-screwed—either to wall studs, to second-story floor framing, or to the roof. If the house wall is brick or stone, however, you'll need to drill holes and install expanding anchors to bolt the ledger in place.

Rafters can be set on top of the ledger or hung from it with anchors, joist hangers, or rafter hangers. If your overhead's roof will be flat, simply square up rafter ends. Sloped rafters, however, require angled cuts at each end, plus a notch (as shown at right) where rafters cross the beam.

You can also opt for a solid roofing material such as shingles, siding, or even asphalt. If you leave the structure uncovered, treating it with a preservative or other finish can add years to its life.

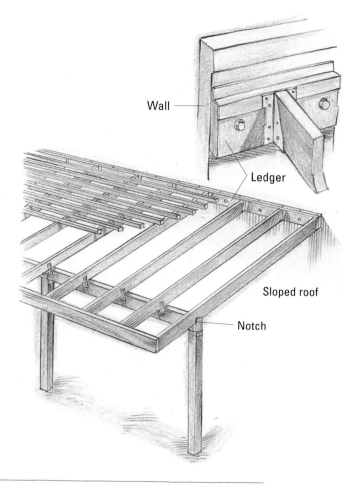

Wall

Ledger

Sloped roof

Notch

Designing for Shade

If you desire an open effect or plan to cover the overhead with vines, the rafters can act as a roof. For more protection, add wood laths or louvers, arranged in a lattice pattern or placed at right angles to the rafters. Vary the wood thickness and spacing to cast the shade you desire—thin lath laid flat won't cast as much shade as thicker stock. The direction in which you run the lath depends on the time of day you need the most shade. If you want midday shade, run the lath east to west; for more shade in the morning and early evening, run the lath north to south.

Experiment with the width, spacing, and direction of overhead members by temporarily nailing different sizes to the rafters and observing the effect for a few days.

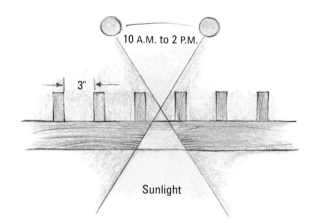

10 A.M. to 2 P.M.

3"

Sunlight

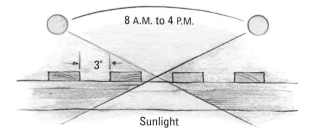

8 A.M. to 4 P.M.

3"

Sunlight

The same boards set 3 inches apart, but at different angles, will affect the extent of shade cast below an overhead. Lath or boards laid on edge diffuse early-morning and late-afternoon sun but let in plenty of light at midday (above). The same members laid flat (left) allow in more sun in the early morning and late afternoon but block more midday sun.

MASONRY

This section will guide you through the world of masonry materials and explain the basic techniques for building paths, patios, and walls. Although some stonework requires years of training, these basic masonry projects can be successfully completed by a do-it-yourselfer. The key is to proceed with patience.

However, you should seek advice from your local building department or garden supplier about the best concrete mix, brick types, or base treatment for use in your climate and soil. Speak with your neighbors about the masonry materials they have successfully used in their gardens, and browse through local offerings of masonry products before buying—new products constantly appear.

Loose stones and gravel can be used alone or with other stones of various sizes to create paths—or they can be seeded into concrete to create an exposed aggregate finish.

Shopping for stone

Stone is particularly appealing because it is a natural material, and most types are very durable. But the availability of stone types, shapes, sizes, and colors varies by locale, and stone's primary drawback is that it can cost up to five times as much as concrete or brick. Geography dictates price: the farther you live from the quarry, the more you'll have to pay. Some dealers sell stone by the cubic yard, which simplifies ordering; others sell it by the ton. Most suppliers can help you calculate how much you need based on a square-foot estimate.

STONES FOR PAVING. Stone tiles are precut in square or rectangular shapes; these are fairly uniform in thickness and easy to lay in a grid pattern. Cleft stones have random widths and thicknesses.

Granite is valued for its hardness and durability, so it may be worth its often steep price. Marble is not only expensive, but it is often too soft for outdoor use. Sandstone, limestone, and other sedimentary stones are popular choices; they are more porous than other types and usually have a chalky or gritty texture. Slate, a fine-grained metamorphic rock that is dense and smooth, is also an excellent choice for paving.

Flat flagstones and cut stone tiles are ideal for formal settings. Technically, flagstone is any flat stone that is either naturally thin or split from rock that cleaves easily. It blends well with plants and ponds or other water features. Furthermore, flagstone is one of the few paving materials that can be set directly on stable soil. However,

outdoor furniture and objects with wheels sometimes get caught on its irregular surface. Also, some types of flagstone become dirty easily and are difficult to clean.

Fieldstone, river rock, and pebbles are less expensive than flagstone or cut tiles. These water-worn or glacier-ground stones produce rustic, uneven pavings that make up in charm for what they may lack in smoothness underfoot. Smaller stones and pebbles, for example, can be set or seeded into concrete (see page 378); cobblestones can be laid in concrete or on tamped earth to cover an entire surface; or narrow mosaic panels of very small stones can be used to break up an expanse of concrete or brick.

For economy, good drainage, and a more casual look, don't forget gravel or crushed rock, both of which can provide material for garden paving. Gravel is collected or mined from natural deposits; crushed rock is mechanically fractured and graded to a uniform size. Frequently, gravels are named after the regions where they were quarried.

When choosing a gravel, consider color, sheen, texture, and size. Take home samples, as you would paint chips. Keep in mind that gravel color, like paint color, looks more intense when it is spread over a large area.

STONES FOR WALLS. There are two broad classes of stonework that work well for walls: rubble (untrimmed) and ashlar (trimmed). In addition, partially trimmed pieces such as cobblestones can create attractive effects.

The stones used in rubble walls are often rounded from glacial or water action; examples (often igneous in origin) include granite and basalt river rock and fieldstone. Since they are difficult to cut, it's usually easier to search for rocks that are the size you need. Rubblestone is frequently the cheapest kind available.

Fully trimmed ashlar stone is laid much like brick. The flat surfaces and limited range of sizes make formal coursing possible and require less mortar than does rubblework.

Ashlar stone is usually sedimentary in origin; the most commonly available type is sandstone. When a tougher igneous stone, such as granite, is cut and trimmed for ashlar masonry, costs are likely to be quite high.

Larger, flat stones are extremely versatile in the garden: use flagstones to create a walkway or terrace, or stack them to form a low decorative wall.

Artificial Rock

Rocks and boulders can lend a rugged texture to a residential landscape. However, big boulders can be hard to find and difficult to transport and install. In some gardens, the site conditions or the landscape design make it impossible to install them. Some homeowners are therefore turning to artificial rocks that are shaped, textured, and colored to resemble their natural counterparts.

One rock-forming method starts with a boulder-shaped frame of reinforcing bar. Wire mesh or metal lath is secured to the frame, then several layers of concrete are applied to the shell. To recreate the cracks and fissures of natural rock, the still-wet concrete may be carved with tools or embossed with crinkled aluminum foil, clear plastic wrap, or custom latex molds cast from actual rock formations.

Another popular rock-forming technique calls for latex models to be cast on real rocks. The models are sprayed with a mixture of concrete and strands of fiberglass or polypropylene. When the mixture dries, the forms are removed. The end product is a thin but sturdy panel with a rock-textured veneer. The models yield identical panels, which can be joined together horizontally or vertically so the viewer is not aware of the repeated shape.

True rock is often a pastiche of colors and may also be flecked with lichen or specks of soil. To imitate this look, installers color the concrete by brushing, spraying, or splattering on layers of diluted acrylic stains.

Artificial rocks offer other landscaping opportunities: they can form steps, waterfalls, and pockets for plants, lights, or ponds. Moreover, they can be used to hide pumps and electric or water lines as well as mask retaining walls.

Because of labor and materials, the cost of artificial rock is usually slightly higher than that of real stone or boulders.

These wide, slightly curved steps and low retaining walls are made of artificial cast stone formed directly on the hillside.

BRICK

Brick is one of the most weather resistant and enduring materials for outdoor projects. A brick patio is a good do-it-yourself job, but a brick wall is best left to a mason.

Two kinds are used for most garden construction: common brick and face brick. Most paving is done with common brick. People like its warm color and texture, and it is less expensive than face brick. Common brick is more porous than face brick and less uniform in size and color (bricks may vary up to ¼ inch in length). Choose common bricks with fairly smooth surfaces; rough surfaces collect water that can freeze and crack bricks.

Face brick, with its sand-finished, glazed surface, is not as widely available as common brick. More often used for facing buildings than for garden projects, this brick makes elegant formal walls, attractive accents, edgings, header courses, stair nosings, and raised beds—all outdoor projects where its smoothness will not present a safety hazard when it is wet.

The warm, variegated tones of the brick walkway above are especially attractive after a rainfall.

Used brick has uneven surfaces and streaks of old mortar that are attractive in an informal pavement. Imitation-used or "rustic" brick costs about the same as genuine used brick but is easier to find; it is also more consistent in quality than most older brick.

Low-density firebrick, blond colored and porous, is tailor-made for built-in barbecues and outdoor fireplaces. It provides interesting accents but doesn't wear as well as common brick.

The standard brick is about 8 by 4 by 2⅜ inches thick. "Paver" bricks, which are solid and made to use underfoot, are roughly half the thickness of standard bricks. All outdoor bricks are graded according to their ability to withstand weathering. If you live in a region where it regularly freezes and thaws, choose common bricks rated SX or face bricks rated SW, which means they can stand up to severe weather conditions. To calculate the quantities of brick you'll need for a project, visit a building supplier first, and be sure to have your measuring tape in hand.

A. **This natural-brick patio** and pierced-block wall define the courtyard space. Large pots with ferns, as well as overhanging trees, keep it woodsy and cool.

B. **A display of brick** (right column and below) includes rough common bricks in a range of colors, smoother face bricks for accents and edgings, bullnose types (with rounded edge) for stairs and capping walls, used or faux-used bricks, and precut bricks for patterns (such as triangle shown).

B

PAVERS

Pavers are an ideal material for do-it-yourself masonry projects. They are easy to install and available in many sizes, colors, and textures. And you'll have a choice ranging from simple 12-inch squares to interlocking pavers in a variety of shapes.

Use square pavers to form part of a grid or even a gentle arc. Squares or rectangles can butt together to create broad, unbroken surfaces, or they can be spaced apart and surrounded with grass, a ground cover, or gravel for textural interest.

Interlocking pavers fit together like puzzle pieces. They are made of extremely dense concrete that is mechanically pressure formed. Laid in sand with closed (butted) joints, they create a surface that is more rigid than brick. No paver can tip out of alignment without taking several of its neighbors with it, and the surface remains intact even under substantial loads. Some interlocking shapes are proprietary, available at only a few outlets or direct from distributors. To locate these, check the Yellow Pages under Concrete Products.

Modern cobblestone blocks are very popular for casual gardens; butt them tightly together and then sweep sand or soil between the irregular edges.

Turf blocks, which leave spaces for plants to grow through, are designed to carry light traffic while retaining and protecting ground-cover plants. This special type of paver allows you to create grassy patios and driveways or side-yard access routes that stand up to wear.

Cast-concrete "bricks," available in classic terra-cotta red as well as imitation-used or antique styles, have become increasingly popular as substitutes for the real thing because, in many areas, they're significantly less expensive.

Some landscape professionals cast their own pavers in custom shapes, textures, and colors: adobe, stone, and imitation tile, for example. You can also make forms and pour your own pavers, but they won't be as strong as standard pressure-formed units.

A. Precast pavers allow you to experiment with designs and shapes; many imitate tile, brick, or adobe. The assortment shown here includes interlocking puzzle-like shapes, stepping-stones, and turf blocks.

B. Side-laid natural bricks and pavers combine to form a patio bordered with easy-to-tend hostas.

C. Large pavers laid as a path help to make the most of this narrow side yard in St. Louis. Hostas and annual impatiens hug the walkway.

A–D. Four basic concrete finishes: broomed (A), travertine (B), semismooth (C), and exposed aggregate (D).

E. These steps of exposed aggregate and lumber, flanked by plantings of two types of juniper, provide safe and comfortable footing even when wet.

CONCRete

Though sometimes disparaged as cold and forbidding, poured —or, more accurately, cast—concrete is even more variable in appearance than brick. Used with well-made forms, it can conform to almost any shape. Furthermore, it can be lightly smoothed or heavily brushed, surfaced with handsome pebbles, swirled or scored, tinted or painted, patterned, or molded to resemble another material. And if you eventually get tired of the concrete surface you have chosen, you can use it as a foundation for a new pavement of brick, stone, or tile set in mortar.

Concrete does have certain disadvantages. In some situations, it can be hot or glaring or seem harsh or simply boring. And, if smoothly troweled, concrete can become slick when wet. Moreover, once its dry ingredients are combined with water, you have to work quickly before the mix hardens. A mistake could require an extensive and perhaps costly redo.

To enhance its appearance and improve traction, concrete paving is usually given some surface treatment. For example, you can spray it with a hose jet or sandblast it to uncover the aggregate, or you can embed colorful pebbles and stone in it. These finishes, generally known as exposed aggregate, are probably the most popular contemporary paving surfaces.

Other ways to modify a standard steel-troweled concrete surface include color dusting, staining, masking, acid washing, and salt finishing. Concrete can also be stamped and tinted to resemble stone, tile, or brick. The patterns simulate either butted joints or open ones, which can then be grouted to look like masonry units.

A standard slab for pathways and patios should be 4 inches thick. In addition, you will have to allow for at least a 2-inch gravel base in areas where frost and drainage are not problems, and a 4- to 8-inch base where they are likely to be cause for concern.

Forms for concrete are built in the same way as for wood edgings. For standard paving, you will need 2 by 4s on edge for forms and 12-inch 1 by 3s or 2 by 2s for stakes. If you plan to leave the lumber in place as permanent edgings and dividers, use rot-resistant redwood, cedar, or pressure-treated lumber. For curved forms, choose tempered hardboard, plywood, or, if they will be permanent, redwood benderboard.

Be prepared to reinforce a concrete area more than 8 feet square with 6-inch-square welded wire mesh; install it after the forms are ready (see pages 386–387). If you're not sure whether your slab will need reinforcement, consult the building department of your local home-supply center or a landscape professional.

If you have never worked with concrete before, have at least one professional on site to help and advise you. Troweling concrete to a smooth surface within the timeframe that it's workable is a skill that takes many months to learn.

Hard facts about concrete

Although many people think concrete is just "cement," it is actually a combination of portland cement, sand, aggregate (usually gravel), and water. The cement, which is a complex, finely ground material, undergoes a chemical reaction when mixed with water and becomes a kind of "glue" that binds everything together. It also gives the finished product its hardness. The sand and aggregate act as fillers and control shrinkage.

Buying bagged, dry, ready-mixed concrete is expensive but convenient, especially for small jobs. The standard 90-pound bag makes ⅔ cubic foot of concrete, enough either to fill a typical posthole or to cover a 16-inch-square area 4 inches deep.

If your project is fairly large, order materials in bulk and mix them yourself, either by hand or with a power mixer. For small projects, hand mixing is less complicated but requires significant exertion. Large forms that must be filled in a single pour will warrant a power mixer, which can be rented.

Use this formula to make regular concrete (the proportions are by volume):

1 part cement	2¾ parts aggregate
2½ parts sand	½ part water

Some dealers also supply trailers containing about 1 cubic yard of wet, ready-mixed concrete (about enough for an 8-by-10-foot patio). These trailers have either a revolving drum that mixes the concrete or a simple metal box that holds the concrete. Both types are designed to be hauled behind a car.

For a large patio, plan to have a commercial transit-mix truck deliver enough concrete to allow you to finish your project in a single pour. To locate concrete plants, look in the Yellow Pages under Concrete, Ready Mixed.

Molded Concrete

To create the look of stones by using concrete, you can dig holes or build shaped wooden forms and fill them with concrete. The resulting pads—with spaces in between for planting—can be textured, smoothed, or embedded with aggregate. Commercial forms are also available, as shown below.

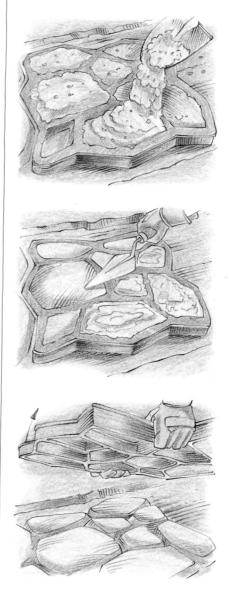

Plastic forms can be used to lay a path of concrete "flagstone." Place the form on a clean, level surface; use a trowel to fill the mold with concrete (top), and smooth the top (center). When the concrete can hold its shape, remove the mold (bottom).

LAYING BRICK IN SAND

With careful preparation and installation, a brick-in-sand path or patio will prove to be as durable as bricks set in mortar. In addition, if you decide to change the surface later, you need chip out only one brick to remove the rest in perfect condition.

Typically, a bed of 1½- to 2-inch-thick sand or rock fines (a mix of grain sizes) is prepared, and the bricks are laid with closed joints. If drainage is poor in your garden, you may also need to add a 4-inch gravel base (in areas where the ground freezes, 6 to 8 inches is advisable). A layer of landscape fabric will suppress the growth of weeds.

To hold both the bricks and the sand firmly in place, build permanent edgings around the perimeter (see page 385). Install the edgings first; they serve as good leveling guides for preparing and laying the bricks. If you have a lot of cutting to do, or shaping of complex angles (along curved edgings, for example), rent a brick saw from a masonry supplier or tool rental outlet.

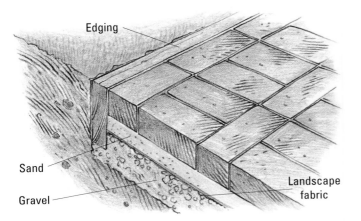

1. This typical brick-in-sand patio includes a gravel bed, a layer of landscape fabric, packed sand, and rigid edgings, which hold the bricks in place. Install edgings first.

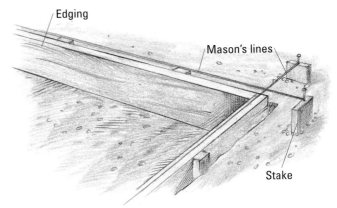

2. String mason's lines from stakes to serve as guides, first to mark edgings at the desired level and slope. Later, edgings can serve as a reference for leveling sand and bricks.

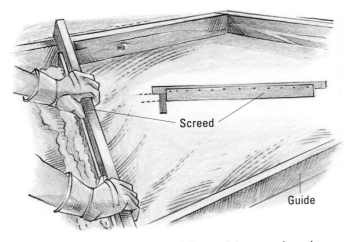

3. Lay down a 1½- to 2-inch-thick layer of dampened sand and level it with a bladed screed, as shown. If necessary, use a temporary guide on which to rest one end of the screed.

4. Another mason's line will help align courses. Begin at one corner; lay bricks tightly against one another, tapping each into place with a hand sledge or mallet. Check level frequently.

Concrete pavers can also be laid in sand, much like bricks. With interlocking types, alignment is nearly automatic. After laying these units, it's best to make several passes with a power-plate vibrator to settle them. You can probably rent a vibrator locally; if not, you can use a heavy drum roller or hand tamper instead. Then spread damp, fine sand over the surface; when it dries, sweep it into the paver joints. Additional passes with either the vibrator or the roller will help lock the pavers together.

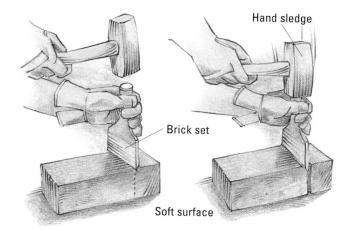

5. To cut bricks, score a line on all four sides (left); make the cut with one sharp blow (right). To cut angles, "nibble" at the waste area in several passes, a little at a time.

6. Throw damp, fine sand over finished pavement, let dry for a few hours, and then sweep it with a stiff broom into joints. Spray lightly with water, so that the sand settles completely.

Brick Patterns

When choosing a brick pattern (also known as a bond), consider the degree of difficulty involved in laying it. Some bonds require not only accuracy but also a lot of brick cutting. The patterns shown below are some of the most popular; the jack-on-jack and running bond are the simplest to lay.

Jack-on-jack

Running bond

Basket weave

Half basket

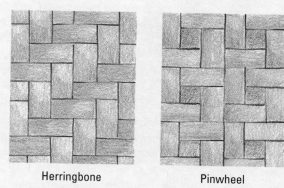

Herringbone

Pinwheel

LAYING MASONRY IN MORTAR

For the most permanent masonry surface, set stones, bricks, or tiles in a mortar bed over concrete that is at least 3 inches thick. If it is an existing slab, it must be clean and in good condition. Ask a concrete dealer whether you need to use a bonding agent for mortar on an existing or new concrete surface. A mortared stone wall must be set atop a concrete footing that is deeper than the frostline in your area (see page 387).

Although the instructions here are for laying a flagstone path, they are applicable to any masonry unit—ceramic tile, brick, or broken concrete—that you wish to set in mortar. You must allow a minimum slope for drainage off a path: 1 inch per 10 feet of run or ¼ inch per foot from side to side.

Mixing mortar

Mortar recipes vary according to their intended use, but the ingredients are usually the same: cement, sand, possibly lime (or fireclay), and water. Either make your own or buy ready-to-mix mortar, which is more expensive but will save you time. To build a wall, you will need a mix consisting of 1 part portland cement, ½ part hydrated lime or fireclay, and 6 parts sand. This mixture is much like Type N, commonly sold for general use. In contrast, a typical mortar for paving and most other below-grade installations contains only 1 part portland cement and 3 parts sand.

Small amounts of mortar can easily be mixed by hand, but mortar can be caustic, so be sure to wear gloves when you work with it. Carefully measure the sand, cement, and lime into a wheelbarrow or similar container. Use a hoe to thoroughly mix the dry ingredients and form them into a pile. Make a depression in the center of the dry mix and pour some water into it. Mix, then repeat the process. When ready for use, mortar should have a smooth, uniform, granular consistency; it should also spread well and adhere to vertical surfaces (important when building a wall) but not "smear" the face of your work, which can happen when the mortar is too watery. Add water gradually until these conditions are met. Make only enough mortar to last a few hours; any more is likely to be wasted.

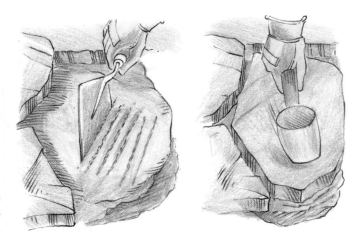

1. Dry-fit all stones, trimming if necessary. Then prepare a mortar mix just stiff enough to support the stones. Spread the mortar at least 1 inch deep, covering enough space to lay one or two stones at a time. Furrow the mortar with a trowel (above left). Set each stone in place, bedding it with a rubber mallet (above right), and checking for level. If a stone isn't level, lift it up and scoop out or add mortar as needed. Clean stones with a wet cloth as you work.

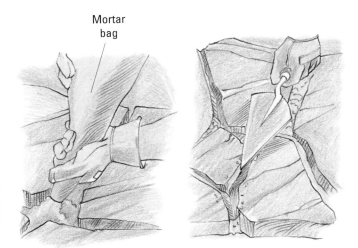

Mortar bag

2. Let the mortar set for 24 hours, then grout joints with the same mortar mix (plus an optional ½ to 1 part fireclay for workability, but no lime). If stone is a nonstaining type, work grout across stones and into joints with a wet sponge. Otherwise, squeeze grout into joints, then smooth with a mason's trowel as shown.

Trimming stone

Because most flagstones are irregular, you'll probably need to trim some pieces before setting them. You can keep this chore to a minimum, however, by carefully dry-fitting a design.

Wear gloves and safety glasses for even small trimming jobs. Chip off pieces with a mason's hammer or a brick set and hand sledge. To make a major cut, use the adjacent stone as a guide and proceed with a brick set and sledge, as shown below. It is often difficult to keep a stone from splitting or shattering beyond the cut line, so have some extra stone on hand.

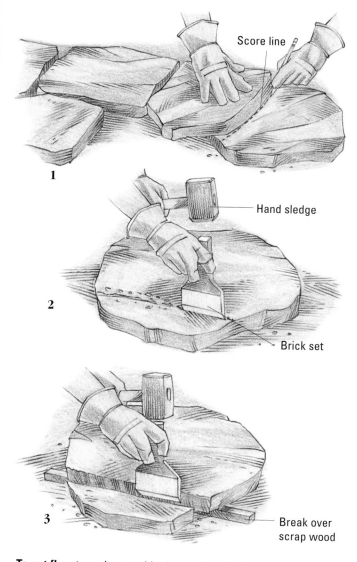

To cut flagstone, lay one block over its neighbor and trace its outline (1). Then score a groove in the stone to be cut (2). Finally, prop up the stone and split it with a sharp blow (3).

Mosaics in Mortar

Large flagstones and tiles aren't the only masonry units that can be laid in mortar. Small pebbles or pieces of broken tile can be arranged mosaic-style in geometric or fanciful patterns. The circle of stones above—the focal point of a short stone walk—is laid in mortar and soil. To be sure of your pattern, lay out the complete design first before mixing any mortar. You can also set river rock, fieldstone, and pebbles in a mortar bed, or mix them with larger stones for a formal look.

To set mosaics in mortar, spread a 1:3 cement-sand mortar mixture over a concrete slab, to a depth of ½ inch. The pieces must be placed in the mortar bed within 2 hours, so spread only as much as you can fill within that time; cut away any dry edges of mortar before spreading the next section. Keep the stones or tile in a pail of clean water, and set them in the mortar while they're still wet, pushing them deep enough so that the mortar gets a good hold on their edges—generally, just past the middle—then press down on them with a board to keep them level. Let the mortar set for 2 to 3 hours, then spread another thin layer over the surface and into the voids. Wash off any excess mortar before it sets.

INSTALLING A GRAVEL PATH

Gravel—either smooth river rock or the more stable crushed rock—makes a low-cost, fast-draining path that can complement a wide variety of informal and formal planting schemes. The first step in laying a gravel path is to excavate and install edging to hold the loose material in place. Then put down landscape fabric to discourage weeds. Gravel surfaces tend to shift when walked on, but the movement will be minimized if you use a compacted base of crushed rock or sand.

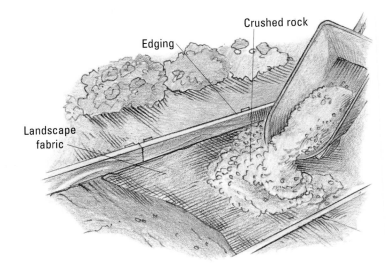

1. Install edgings first, then put down landscape fabric or plastic sheeting to protect against weeds. Pour decomposed granite or sand over the site, taking care not to dislodge the liner.

2. Rake the base material evenly over the path until it is of a uniform 1-inch thickness. As you rake, wet the material with a fine spray.

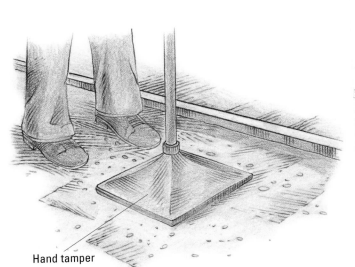

3. Using a vibrating power tamper or a hand tamper, pass over the wet base several times, packing it down firmly. This firm base aids drainage and helps keep the topcoat from shifting.

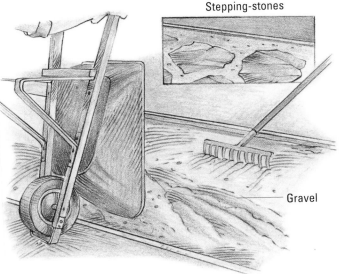

4. Spread the gravel at least 2 inches thick and rake it evenly over the base. If desired, place stepping-stones on the base so that their tops protrude slightly above the surrounding gravel.

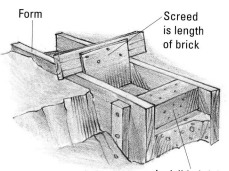

Form

Screed
is length
of brick

Invisible brick

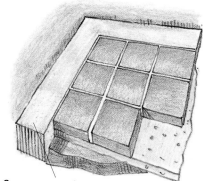

Fieldstones

Concrete mowing strip

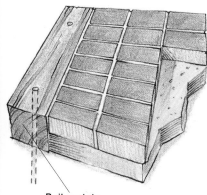

Railroad tie

A look at edgings

Whether you lay it, hammer it, set it, or pour it in place, a patio or walk almost always requires an edging. In addition to visually outlining the surface, an edging confines the pavement within the desired area—which is especially important when you are pouring concrete, working with loose materials such as gravel, or setting bricks or pavers in sand.

Several tried-and-true edging options are illustrated here. The most popular are made of 2-by-4 or 2-by-6 lumber, but for emphasis, you can use 4-by-4 or 6-by-6 material. Heavy timbers and railroad ties make strong edgings and interior dividers, especially when drilled and threaded with steel pipe. If your design calls for gentle curves, try pressure-treated 1 by 4s.

Another effective edging material is poured concrete. It is excellent for constructing invisible edgings underground, serving as a footing for mortared masonry units, or installing flush with a new walk. Bricks also establish a neat, precise edge. Set them directly in firm soil—horizontally, vertically, or even at an angle (but don't expect them to be very durable). And if you have random pieces of uncut stone, bear in mind that they make a perfect edging for a path in a rustic or naturalistic landscape.

Manufactured plastic or steel edgings are quite functional. These strips secure bricks or concrete pavers below finished paving height; they can be concealed with soil or sod. Flexible sections are convenient for tight curves.

For curbing paved areas, an edging is often installed after the base has been prepared and before the setting bed and paving are laid. String mason's lines around the perimeter, not only to mark the exact borders of the paving, but also to designate the outside top border of the edging. To achieve the correct edging height, you'll probably need to dig narrow trenches under the lines.

Wood posts

Finish board

Plastic edging

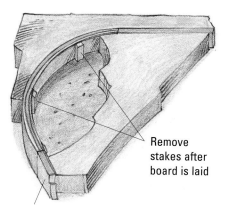

Remove
stakes after
board is laid

Pressure-treated 1 by 4

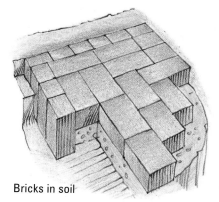

Bricks in soil

385

POURING A CONCRETE SLAB

Most of the work for a concrete path or patio lies in the preparation, which entails grading and formwork. Lay out stakes and mason's lines to mark the outline of the slab, allowing for at least a 1-inch drop for each 10 feet away from the house for drainage. If the exposed soil is soft, wet it and then tamp it firmly.

Wooden, steel, or copper dividers can be permanent partitions; they also serve as control joints to help prevent cracking and help break up the job into smaller, more manageable pours.

Be sure to add any required reinforcement to formwork before pouring. Check local building codes; usually, 6-inch-square welded wire mesh is the best choice for pavings.

See page 379 for instructions on mixing concrete. Pour large areas in sections, and be sure to have helpers on hand to assist with hauling and spreading the wet concrete. You'll need gloves to protect your hands from the concrete's caustic ingredients; wear rubber boots if you have to walk on the wet mix.

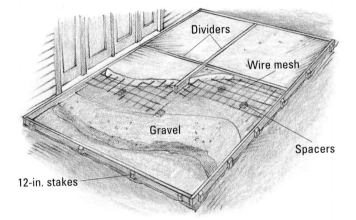

1. For rough grading, dig deep enough to allow for 4 inches of concrete plus 2 to 8 inches of gravel. Construct forms from 2 by 4s secured to 12-inch stakes, placing the form tops at finished slab height. Add welded wire mesh for reinforcement.

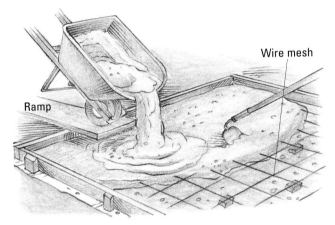

2. Begin pouring concrete at one end of form while a helper spreads it with a hoe or shovel. Work concrete up against form and tamp it into corners, but don't press it down too hard. A splashboard or ramp lets you pour it where you want it.

3. With a helper, move a 2-by-4 screed across the form to level concrete, using a rapid zigzag, sawing motion. A third person can shovel concrete into any hollows.

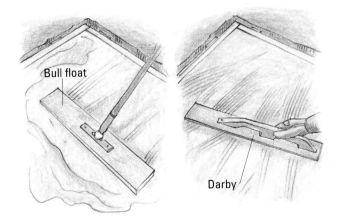

4. Initial floating smooths down high spots and fills small hollows left after screeding. As shown, use a darby for small jobs and a bull float with an extension handle for larger slabs.

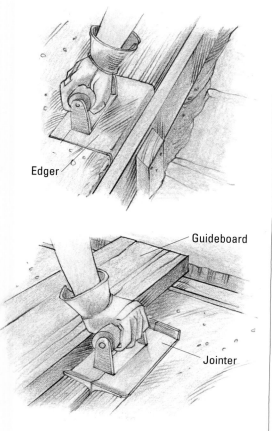

Edger

Guideboard

Jointer

5. Run the edge of a trowel between concrete and form. Then run an edger back and forth to create a smooth, curved edge (top). Make control joints every 10 feet with a jointer (above).

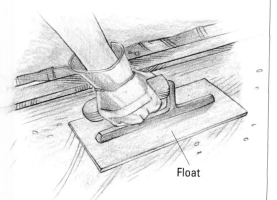

Float

6. Before the surface stiffens, give it a final floating with a wooden float. For a smoother surface, follow with a steel trowel. For a nonskid surface, drag a broom lightly across the concrete, without overlapping strokes.

Pouring a Footing

If you want to build a garden wall, you must give it a solid base or footing. Very low walls (no more than 12 inches) and dry-stone walls (see page 390) may only require a leveled trench or a rubble base; but mortared walls require a footing fashioned from concrete that is twice as wide and at least as deep as the wall's thickness. In cold-weather areas, extend the footing below the frost line. Add 6 inches to the trench depth for a bottom layer of gravel.

If you need to pour a post footing for a deck, fence, or overhead, see page 368. Use bags of ready-mixed concrete for these small jobs.

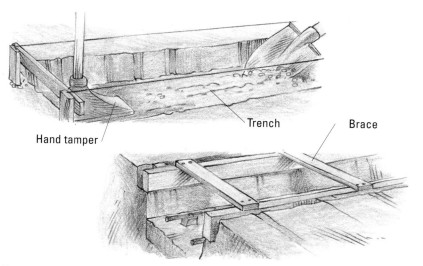

Hand tamper

Trench

Brace

1. Prepare a base for the footing by leveling and tamping the bottom of the trench and adding a 6-inch layer of gravel (top). Trenches in very firm soil may serve as forms; otherwise, build forms with 2-by lumber, stakes, and braces (above). Set any required reinforcing bars on a layer of broken bricks or other rubble.

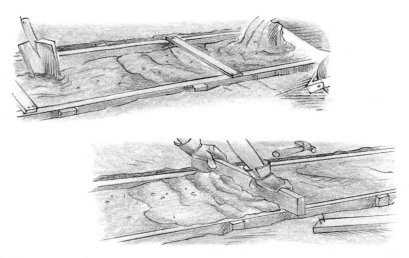

2. Pour concrete (above, top), and insert any vertical reinforcing bars required. Screed concrete level with tops of forms (bottom). Cover with a plastic sheet, leave to cure for 2 days, then remove the forms and begin to build the wall.

BUILDING A BLOCK WALL

For fast, inexpensive masonry wall construction, concrete blocks are the ideal material. They are heavy but fairly easy to work with, and these rugged units make strong, durable walls.

First, lay out a dry course, or row, of blocks, spacing them ³⁄₈ inch apart, and try to plan the wall so that no block cutting is necessary (you can also draw a plan on graph paper). If cutting is unavoidable, you can use the method described for bricks on page 381. Then you'll need to dig a trench for a strong, level concrete footing (for details, see page 387). Build the wall with a standard wall-building mortar (see page 382), but keep the mix slightly stiff. Otherwise, the heavy blocks may squeeze it out of the joints. A running bond pattern is the simplest to construct (see page 381).

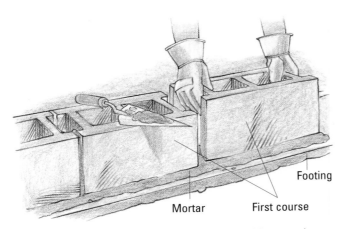

Mortar   First course   Footing

1. Spread a bed of mortar, 2 inches thick and wide enough for three blocks, over the footing. Then place the first-course corner block carefully, and press it down to form an accurate ³⁄₈-inch joint with the footing. Butter the ends of the next blocks with mortar, then set each one ³⁄₈ inch from the previous block.

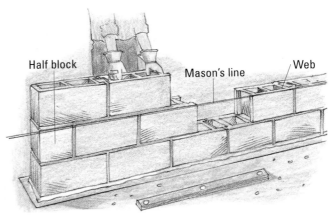

Half block   Mason's line   Web

2. Check level often as you build up leads (at least three courses high) at both ends. String a mason's line between corner blocks as a guide to keep blocks straight. Start each even-numbered course with a half block. Butter both webs and edges, making full bed joints.

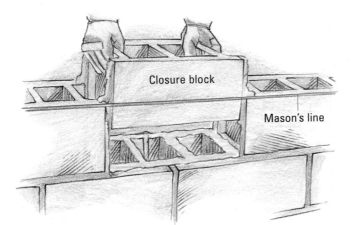

Closure block   Mason's line

3. Fill in blocks between the leads, keeping ³⁄₈-inch joint spacing. Be sure to check alignment, level, and plumb frequently. To fit the closure block, butter all edges of the opening and the ends of the block, then press it firmly into place.

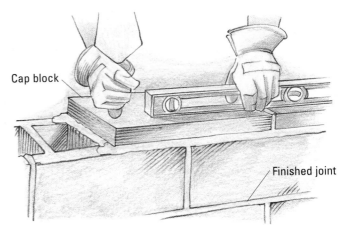

Cap block   Finished joint

4. As you work, finish joints with a jointer or a wooden dowel. Solid cap blocks, available in various thicknesses, provide the simplest way to top off the last course. Simply mortar them in place on full bed joints, as shown. Tap into place and level.

Applying veneer to a block wall

Many people find concrete block boring or feel that it doesn't blend well with their landscaping. If you are among them, consider building a block wall and dressing it up by applying a stucco or other veneer to its surface.

Professional landscapers often take advantage of concrete blocks' low cost and speed of assembly to build a wall, then they cover it with plastering stucco for attractive texture and shape. Though plastering is an acquired technique, an accomplished do-it-yourselfer might reasonably tackle a small garden wall.

Plastering a block wall is a two-part operation. The first layer—or "scratch coat"—should be about ³/₈ inch thick and must be applied after you have painted the wall with a concrete bonding agent or covered it with wire lath. Then rough up the scratch coat with a commercial tool or a batch of wires held together (hence the name *scratch*) to help the finish coat's "bite." Apply the finish coat to a thickness of ¼ inch; it may be precolored or painted later. When the sheen has dulled, give texture to the plaster's surface by floating on the finish coat with a steel trowel (with or without notches), a sponge, or a stiff brush.

For best results, buy plaster premixed. If the color is integral, consult with your supplier about coloring oxides, and plan to use a mix with white concrete and sand in it.

Another way to enhance a block wall is to apply a brick or stone veneer to it (see page 199). Although the resulting wall looks like solid masonry, it requires less labor and expense. You will need to place noncorrosive metal wall ties in the mortar joints in every other row of blocks, spacing them 2 to 3 feet apart. The ties must protrude beyond the blocks to help secure veneer units.

Lastly, mortar the veneer to the core. Bend the wall ties into the joints between the stones or bricks. As you build, completely fill the spaces between the wall and veneer with soupy mortar.

This tall privacy fence features 8 by 8, pure white stucco panels that sandwich sections made of closely spaced, dark green, vertical 2 by 4s.

Building a dry stone wall

The key to building a stone wall is careful fitting; the finished structure should appear to be a unit rather than a pile of rocks. A dry stone wall is constructed without mortar and depends upon the weight and friction of one stone on another for its stability. Not only is it simple to build, but it also has the attraction of allowing you to place soil and plants in the unmortared spaces as you lay the stones.

Use the largest stones for the foundation course, and reserve the longer ones for "bond" stones—long stones that run the width of the wall. Set aside broad, flat stones to cap the top of the wall.

Most dry stone walls slope inward on both surfaces; this tilting of the faces is called batter and helps secure the wall. To check your work, make a batter gauge by taping together a 2-by-4 board, a scrap block, and a carpenter's level, as shown below.

Batter gauge

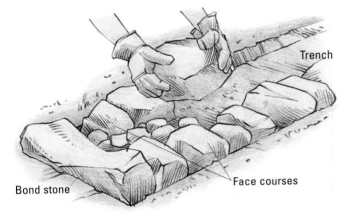

Trench

Face courses

Bond stone

1. Lay foundation stones in a trench about 6 inches deep. First, place a bond stone (one as deep as the wall) at one end; then position the two face courses at both edges of the trench. Choose whole, well-shaped stones for the face courses. Fill in the space between face courses with tightly packed rubble.

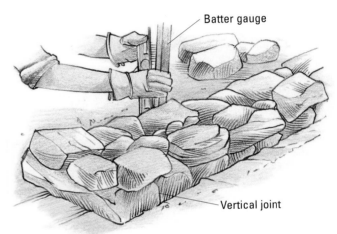

Batter gauge

Vertical joint

2. Lay stones atop the first course, staggering vertical joints. Select stones that fit together solidly, and tilt the stones of each face inward toward one another. Use a batter gauge on faces and ends of the wall to check the tilt. Place bond stones every 5 to 10 square feet to tie the wall together.

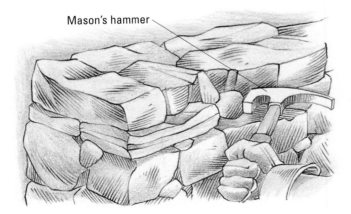

Mason's hammer

3. Continue to add courses, staggering vertical joints and maintaining the inward slope, so that gravity and the friction of the stones set one upon another will help hold the wall together. Gently tap small stones into any gaps with a mason's hammer.

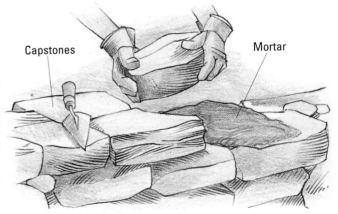

Capstones

Mortar

4. Finish the top with as many flat, broad stones as possible. For frost resistance, mortar the cap as shown. Don't rake (indent) these joints; level them flush with a piece of scrap wood to prevent water from collecting.

Retaining walls

If your home sits on a sloping lot or a hillside, a retaining wall may be needed to hold back the soil and prevent erosion. Homeowners have a choice of three basic wall-building materials—wood, stone, or concrete—and now a number of new modular masonry systems have been developed with the owner-builder in mind (see example below). These systems come with complete step-by-step instructions for installation.

Simple wood or masonry retaining walls, less than 3 feet high and on a gentle slope with stable soil, can be built by a do-it-yourselfer, but it's a good idea to consult your local building department for even a low retaining wall. Most communities require a building permit for any retaining wall and may require a soil analysis in any area suspected of being unstable.

In general, it's best to site your retaining wall so it results in the least possible disruption of the natural slope, but even so, extensive cutting and filling may be needed. The hill can be held back with a single wall or a series of low retaining walls that form terraces. Though terracing is less risky, both methods disturb the hill and should be designed by an engineer. If space permits, the safest approach is not to disturb the slope at all but to build the wall on the level ground near the foot of the slope and fill in behind it.

In any case, the retaining wall should rest on cut or undisturbed ground, never on fill. Planning for drainage is also essential. Usually, you'll need a gravel backfill to collect water that dams up behind the wall. Water in the gravel bed can be drained off through weep holes in the base of the wall or through a drainpipe that channels the water into a storm sewer or other disposal area.

RETAINING WALL OPTIONS

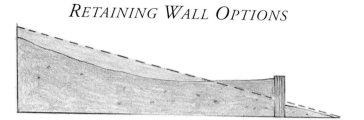

Slope is cut away and excess earth is moved downhill. Retaining wall now holds back long, level terrace.

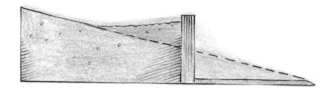

Earth is cut away and moved behind tall retaining wall. Result is level ground below, high, level slope behind.

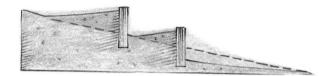

Total wall height is divided between two terraces, resulting in a series of level beds.

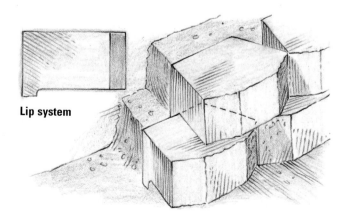

Lip system

Interlocking pin system

For low retaining walls or small raised planters, modular masonry systems are available in various styles and weights. Most use cast "lips" (above left) or interlocking pins (right)

to establish the setback and resist outward-pushing forces. Fiberglass or steel pins drop through holes in upper blocks and stop in grooves on units below, joining each to two beneath.

STEP-BUILDING BASICS

Laying out low, single, back-garden steps does not involve as much time and effort as planning runs of well-designed formal steps; the latter requires an understanding of proper proportions.

The flat part of a step is called the tread; the vertical part under the tread is the riser. Ideally, the depth of the tread plus twice the riser height should equal 25 to 27 inches. Based on an average length of adult stride, the ideal outdoor step should have a 6-inch-high riser and a 15-inch-deep tread, but riser and tread dimensions can vary. Risers should be no lower than 5 inches and no higher than 8 inches; tread depth should never be less than 11 inches. The overall riser-tread relationship should remain the same. All the risers in any one flight of steps, as well as all the treads, should be uniform in size.

To fit steps evenly, you must calculate the degree of slope. Using the drawing at top right as a guide, first calculate the distance from A to B; this is the rise, or change

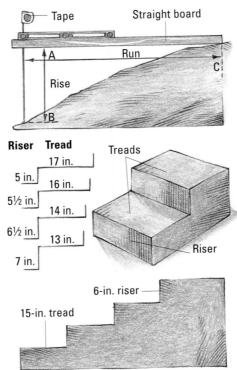

Ideal tread-riser relationship

in level, of the slope. The horizontal distance from A to C is called the run.

To determine the number of steps you will need, divide the desired riser height into the total rise of the slope (in inches). If the answer ends in a fraction (and it probably will), drop the fraction and divide that number into the total rise; this time, the resulting figure will give you the exact measurement for each of the risers. Then check the chart (left) to see if the corresponding minimum tread will fit the slope's total run.

Plan on a minimum width of 2 feet for utility steps and 4 feet for most other types of steps. If you want the steps to accommodate two people walking side by side, allow a width of 5 feet.

Rarely do steps fit exactly into a slope. More than likely, you will have to cut and fill the slope to accommodate the steps. If your slope is too steep for even 8-inch risers, remember that steps need not run straight up and down. Curves and switchbacks make the distance longer but the climb gentler.

Timbers or ties

Both 6-by-6 pressure-treated timbers and railroad ties make simple but rugged steps (risers). To begin, excavate the site and tamp the soil in the tread area firmly. Lay the ties or timbers on the soil, then drill a hole near both ends of each tie or timber. With a sledge, drive either ½-inch galvanized steel pipes or ¾-inch reinforcing bars through the holes into the ground.

Or, for extra support, pour small concrete footings (see page 387) and set anchor bolts in the slightly stiffened concrete. When the concrete has set (after about 2 days), secure the ties to the footings with the bolts.

Once the tie or timber risers are in place, fill the tread spaces behind them with concrete, brick-in-sand paving, gravel, grass, or another material.

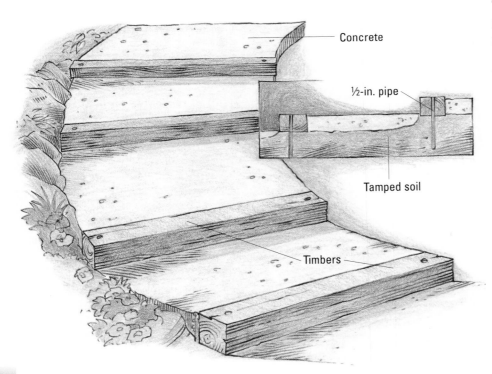

Wooden stairs

Formal wooden steps are best for a low-level deck or for easy access to a doorway. Make stringers, the wood framework that supports steps (see right), from 2 by 10s or 2 by 12s. If the steps are more than 4 feet wide, a third stringer will be needed in the middle.

Use galvanized bolts or metal joist hangers to secure stringers to a deck beam or joist; if you're running stringers off stucco siding or another masonry surface, hang them on a ledger, as shown. Note that when bolts are used, the first tread is below the surface of the interior floor or deck; when joist hangers are the fasteners, however, the first tread must be level with the floor.

Attach the stringers at the bottom to wooden nailing blocks anchored in a concrete footing. Build risers and treads from 2-by material cut to width; treads should overlap the risers below and may hang over slightly.

Riser

Ledger

Tread

Stringers

Anchor bolts

2-by-4 nailing block

Footing

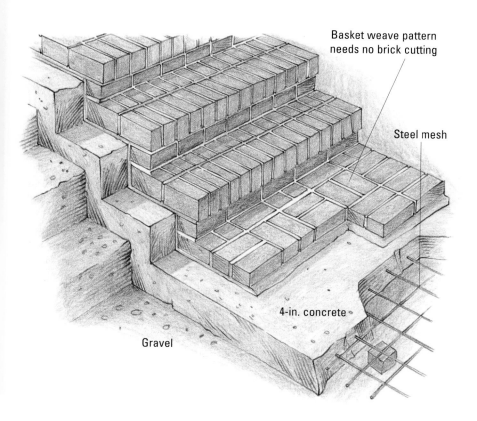

Basket weave pattern needs no brick cutting

Steel mesh

4-in. concrete

Gravel

Masonry steps

Steps can be built entirely of concrete, or, for a finished look, the concrete can be used as a base for mortared masonry units.

First, form rough steps in the earth. Allow space for at least a 6-inch gravel setting bed and a 4-inch thickness of concrete on both treads and risers. (In cold climates you will need 6 to 8 inches of concrete, plus a footing that is sunk below the frost line.) Include the thickness of any masonry units to tread-and-riser dimensions. Tamp filled areas thoroughly.

With 2-inch-thick lumber, build forms like those shown on pages 386–387. Lay the gravel bed, keeping it 4 inches back from the front of the steps; you will pour the concrete thicker at that potentially weak point. Reinforce with 6-inch-square welded wire mesh.

Pour and screed the concrete as for a poured concrete footing. To make treads more weather-safe, broom the wet concrete to roughen its surface, then cure as for a concrete footing (see page 387).

INSTALLING A GARDEN POND

With either a flexible plastic or rubber pond liner and a bit of elbow grease, even a beginner can fashion an average-size garden pond in a single weekend. (See page 185 for a discussion of easy-to-install rigid pond liners.)

Even a pond with an unusual shape should not present a problem. A liner can take almost any shape, accommodating curves and undulations. It's also possible to weld two pieces of liner together with solvent cement, or have the supplier do it for you.

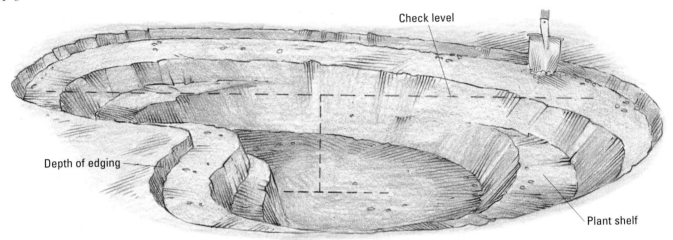

Check level

Depth of edging

Plant shelf

1. Mark the pond's outline with a hose or a length of rope. Dig all around the outline with a sharp spade; remove any sod, and keep it in a shady spot for later patching. Excavate the hole to the desired depth and width, plus 2 inches all around for a layer of sand. Dig down to the thickness of any edging material. Check level carefully, using a straight board to bridge the rim.

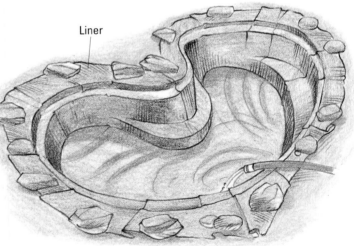

Liner

3. Open up the liner and let it soften in the sun. Then spread it over the hole, evening up the overlap all around. Place heavy stones or bricks around the perimeter to weigh it down, then slowly begin to fill the pond with water.

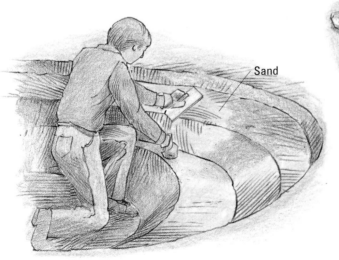

Sand

2. Next, remove all protruding roots and rocks and fill any holes with soil. Pack a 2-inch layer of clean, damp sand into the excavation. Smooth the sand with a board or a concrete float.

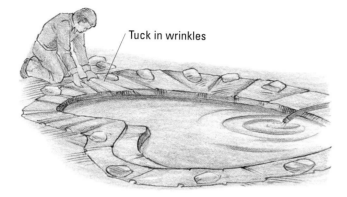

Tuck in wrinkles

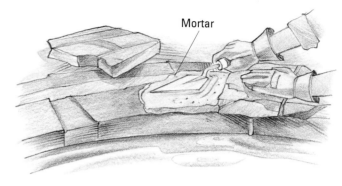

Mortar

4. Continue filling, tucking in wrinkles all around; as required, make pleats at hard corners (they won't be visible when the pool is filled). You can wade into the pool to tuck in the lining, but the water's weight will make it fit the contours of the hole.

5. When the pond is full, add overhanging edging: lay flagstones or brick in a thin bed of mortar. Next, bring the liner up behind the edging, then trim the liner. Drain the pool, clean it out, and refill it with fresh water.

Fountains and Falls

Water in motion, whether gently spilling, gurgling, or energetically tumbling, is always enchanting. Both fountains and waterfalls help bring the sparkle and the musical sounds of falling water into the garden.

Surprisingly, fountains can be simple to create. A wooden planter box, a metal basin, or a large pot, for example, can easily be converted into a small fountain. Just coat the inside of a wooden container or an unglazed pot with asphalt emulsion or epoxy paint, or use a flexible liner. Then drop in a submersible pump with a riser pipe and add water (in shallow water, a few rocks can conceal the pump).

For larger holding pools, many designers prefer precast rigid fiberglass or reinforced concrete. A wall fountain's raised holding pool is often of concrete or concrete block, covered with plaster or faced with brick, tile, or stone above the waterline. A submersible pump and water pipes can be combined to add a fountain to an existing wall. An electric switch, perhaps

located indoors, controls the pump-driven flow; a ball or three-way valve allows you to alter the flow to suit your taste. To automatically replace water lost through evaporation, hook up a float valve to the water supply line. A drain is also handy.

Waterfalls pose some unique design considerations. The major technical concern is waterproofing. Before plunging into construction, determine which pump, pipes, and other plumbing hardware you'll need to provide the desired flow. For a waterproof channel, use either a flexible liner, free-form concrete, a fiberglass shell or series of splash pans, or a combination of the above.

If you opt for a liner, position waterfall rocks carefully, making sure not to damage or displace the liner. Once the basic structure is complete, secure secondary stones and add loose rocks or pebbles to provide visual accents or to form a ripple pattern. Only creative experimentation will reveal the most pleasing sights and sounds.

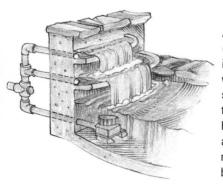

A formal wall fountain combines a raised holding pool, a masonry wall, and decorative spill shelves. Water tumbles from pipe outlets to spill shelves to a holding pool; a submersible pump sends it back around again.

Waterfall design calls for a watertight channel, natural-looking stones, and adequate camouflage for plumbing parts. A flexible liner is the simplest channel option; stone placement conceals the liner.

INSTALLING IRRIGATION SYSTEMS

The benefits of a permanent irrigation system are well known—water and time savings, healthier plants, and reduced maintenance. The information given on pages 332–333 can help you choose the best system for your garden. Shown here are installation procedures for the two main types of irrigation systems—sprinkler and drip.

Most systems can be attached to an existing water supply pipe (1-inch diameter or larger is best). Because drip systems require only low water volume and pressure, you may be able to connect a drip system to a convenient outdoor faucet; the manufacturer's literature will help you determine whether this is best for your situation. You will want to pick out some possible locations to place your valves. Consider how they might be concealed (they can be unsightly) and, if your system will be automated, where you'll put the timer and how far it is from an electrical connection.

No matter how you connect your system to the water supply, you will need proper filter, pressure regulator, and backflow devices. Filters ensure that emitters don't clog. Pressure regulators prevent too much water pressure from building up in the system and possibly forcing the emitter heads off the supply lines. Backflow devices, which are usually required by law, prevent irrigation water from backing up into the home water supply.

Whether or not your irrigation system is automated, check it frequently for broken or clogged sprinklers or drip emitters.

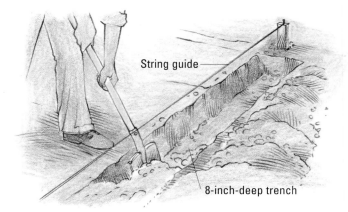

1. A sprinkler system must be laid underground. First, dig 8-inch-deep trenches for pipes. To keep trench lines straight, run string between two stakes.

2. Connect pipes to the water supply pipe, then attach control valve (with built-in antisiphon control valve) at least 6 inches above ground. Use thick-walled, ¾-inch PVC pipe.

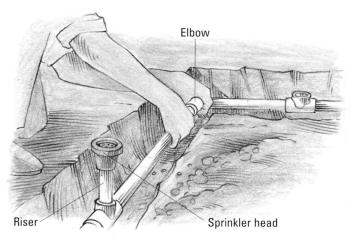

3. Assemble pipes from the control valve outward, fitting risers and sprinkler heads to elbows, tees, and side outlets. Joints may screw together or require PVC solvent cement.

4. Flush out pipes with heads removed. Then fill in trenches, mounding loose soil along center of trench. Tamp the soil firmly with a hand tamper. Avoid striking the sprinkler heads.

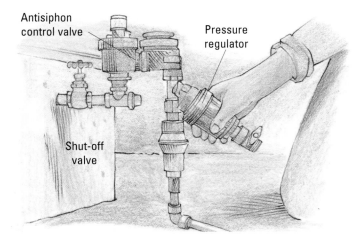

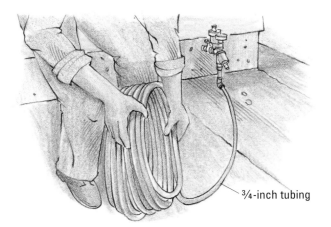

1. Drip irrigation system assembly starts with connecting the antisiphon control valve, filter, and pressure regulator to the water supply line (for hose-end system, use a hose bibb).

2. Connect ¾-inch flexible polyvinyl tubing and lay out main lines on the surface of the soil or in shallow trenches. For a sturdier system, use buried PVC pipe for main lines.

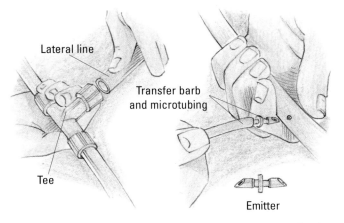

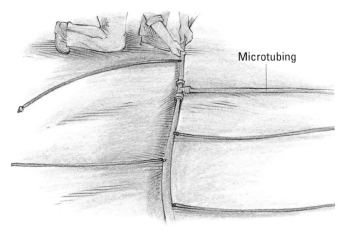

3. Lay out and attach lateral lines using tee connectors (left). Many kinds hold tubing without cement. Attach end caps, then insert emitters or transfer barbs for microtubing (right).

4. Flush system to ensure that all emitters work properly. Cover the lines with a thin layer of mulch, if desired, but leave the emitters and microtubing above ground.

Switching to Drip

If you have an existing sprinkler system with an underground distribution line of PVC pipe, you can simplify the installation of a drip system by retrofitting it. But if you have a galvanized pipe system, retrofitting it is less practical than replacing it, because over time pieces of flaking metal can clog the drip emitters.

Commercial products make switching to drip easy. At right are two retrofit kits for sprinkler systems. The system you choose depends on the layout of your garden and the number of sprinklers you plan to change.

Multioutlet bubbler heads

Generally, it's better to change the entire line on one valve to drip than to mix sprinklers and drip along it (if you have lawns and borders on the same line, for example). Because of different output from sprinklers and drip fittings, trying to adjust watering times on a mixed system is difficult. But in some cases you will have no choice.

The system shown at top delivers water through ¼-inch tubing and multioutlet bubbler heads. The simple retrofit shown at left uses only one riser; the other riser is capped, as shown.

BUILDING A RAISED BED

Raising your garden above the ground can solve some of the most frustrating problems gardeners face. These easy-to-build beds make it possible for plants to thrive where soil is poor, wildlife is hungry, or the growing season is short. And if you need easy access to your plants—to accommodate a disability or simply to eliminate back-bending labor—you can sit on the edge of the bed and garden in comfort.

Line the bottom of the bed with wire screening to keep out burrowing pests, or fit it with a PVC framework for bird netting. Fill the bed with the best soil you can. Good soil means that plants can be placed closer together, making a small area more productive.

A raised bed can be any size, but if it is more than 4 feet wide it will be difficult to reach the middle from either side. If the sides will double as benches, build the frame 18 to 24 inches high.

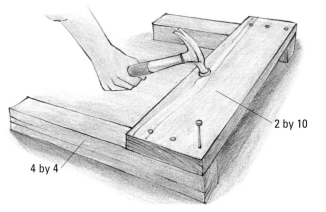

1. Orient a rectangular bed from north to south. For a 4-by-10-foot bed, first nail short sides of 2 by 10s to 3-foot-high 4-by-4 corner posts. Use rot-resistant lumber and galvanized nails.

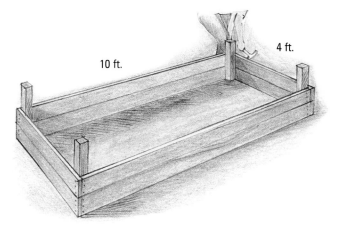

2. Flip over structure and nail 10-foot lengths to corner posts. For added strength, install wooden bracing or metal L-straps. Work on level ground so that bed is as square as possible.

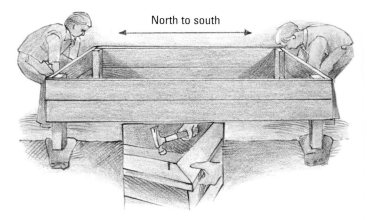

3. Set bed right side up and insert corner posts into predug foot-deep holes. Level if necessary. Cap the top with surfaced redwood 2 by 6s, with ends cut at a 45-degree angle (inset).

4. Mix 3 to 4 inches of new soil into the ground at the bottom of the bed to aid drainage. Line with wire screening, then add more soil. This 20-inch-deep bed holds about 2½ cubic yards of soil.

RAISED-BED STYLES

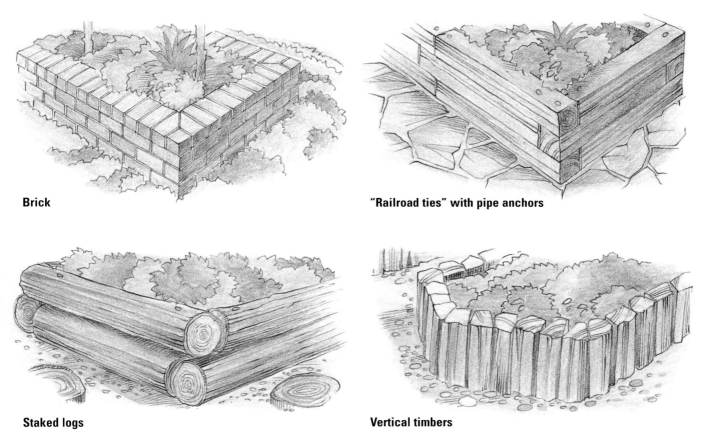

Brick

"Railroad ties" with pipe anchors

Staked logs

Vertical timbers

Easy-Access Gardening

It isn't easy to garden from a wheelchair, but it's not impossible. It takes thoughtful planning to give maximum access to planting areas. Here are some features that make a garden accessible.

Raised beds *can accommodate both flowers and edible plants. To put gardening chores within easy reach of a wheelchair, the beds should be about 16 inches tall and no more than 4 feet wide; they can be long or U-shaped, with the opening in the U just wide enough for a chair.*

Paved paths *about 4 feet wide can allow a chair to turn, maneuver, and glide easily. Ideally, the paths should be extensions of a paved patio at the rear of the house or of a porch or terrace at the front. If the house is at a higher level than the garden, a wide, gently sloping ramp can angle off a back deck.*

Hinged trellises *can be lowered to tend or gather crops such as peas and tomatoes.*

An automatic irrigation system *eliminates the need for routine watering. See pages 332–333 for options.*

Railings *for walks and ramps should be sunk in concrete footings for extra support.*

Special tools *are available with extra-long handles to reach into beds from a chair.*

Mulch *of fabric or loose materials reduces the need for frequent weeding, which can be a chore.*

Select low-maintenance plants. *Choose trees that don't drop a lot of litter, opt for a small lawn — or no lawn at all — and choose plants that don't require frequent maintenance or pest and disease control.*

WORKING SAFELY

Although the garden is not generally a hazardous place, any time you pick up a tool, climb a ladder, or start moving heavy materials, you can injure yourself—or someone else. If you are planning to carry out any of the landscape projects shown in the previous pages, follow the guidelines given here.

Safety accessories and clothing

Many masonry projects call for safety precautions. To protect yourself from flying particles of dust or rock when cutting stone or brick, wear safety goggles or a full face mask. Look for comfortably fitting, fog-free types made of scratch-resistant, shatterproof plastic. Dry portland cement is irritating to the eyes, nose, and mouth; wear a dust mask when mixing concrete.

Wet concrete and mortar are caustic to the skin, so wear heavy rubber gloves and tuck your sleeves into them. Also wear rubber boots if you must walk in the concrete to finish it off. Wash your skin thoroughly with water if wet mortar or concrete contacts it.

When using lumber products, protect your hands from wood splinters with all-leather or leather-reinforced cotton work gloves. If you are sanding wood, wear a disposable painter's mask. For work with solvents, finishes, or adhesives, wear disposable rubber or plastic gloves.

Working safely with power tools

Portable power tools can cause injuries in an instant. Handle these tools with respect, and follow some basic safety precautions.

Read the owner's manual before using any tool.

When you operate a power tool, try to do so without interruption or distraction. If possible, block off the work area to keep all visitors away—especially children and pets.

Never wear loose-fitting clothing or jewelry that could catch in a tool's mechanism. If you have long hair, tie it back.

Never use a power tool if you are tired or under the influence of alcohol or drugs.

Before you plug in a tool, check that safety devices such as guards are in good working order. Also, tighten any clamping mechanisms on the tool, ensure that the blade or bit is securely installed, and set up any necessary supports or clamps for securing the work.

Ensure that your hands and body—and the power cord— are well away from a tool's blade or bit.

Never stand on a wet surface when using a power tool that is plugged into an electrical outlet, unless the outlet is GFCI protected (see opposite page).

Never cut wet wood, and if you can't avoid cutting warped boards or must cut through a knot, be on your guard for kickback—when the tool lurches back out of the wood.

Make sure there are no fasteners in any lumber that you are sawing or drilling.

If a blade or bit jams in a piece of wood, turn off and unplug the tool before trying to extricate it. To keep your balance, don't reach too far with the tool; move closer to it and keep a stable footing.

Always allow the bit or blade to stop on its own before setting down the tool.

Unplug a tool before servicing or adjusting it and after you have finished using it.

Follow the manufacturer's specifications to lubricate and clean power tools, and make sure all blades and bits are sharp and undamaged.

If you are using a rented concrete mixer, read the instructions carefully. Never reach into the rotating drum with your hands or tools. Keep well away from the moving parts, and do not look into the mixer while it is running.

Working safely with electricity

Tools powered by electricity are essential for most outdoor construction projects. But unless a drill, circular saw, or other power tool is double-insulated, it must be properly grounded or it can give a serious shock. Double-insulated tools should be clearly marked (the plug will have only two prongs). When you are working in a damp area or outdoors, a ground fault circuit interrupter (GFCI) is essential.

When working outside, you will probably need to use an extension cord for your tools. Use the shortest extension cord possible (long cords can overheat, causing a fire hazard), and make sure it's rated for outdoor use. The longer the cord, the less amperage it will deliver, which means less power for the tool's motor. Look at the tool's nameplate to determine its amperage requirement. Avoid crimping the cord; don't run it through a door that will be continually opened and closed.

A main disconnect allows you to shut down your entire electrical system whenever you need to change a fuse or in case of an emergency. If you need to work on an outdoor switch, circuit, or outlet, you'll need to shut off power to a branch circuit. *Never* work on a live electrical circuit. Two typical disconnects are shown at right. Familiarize yourself with them before you start to work.

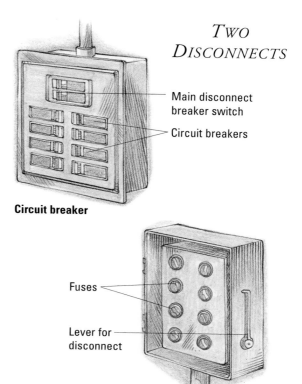

TWO DISCONNECTS

Main disconnect breaker switch

Circuit breakers

Circuit breaker

Fuses

Lever for disconnect

Fuse box

To lift heavy objects, spread your feet a comfortable width apart. Then bend your knees and, keeping your back straight, pick up the object—never bend at the waist or you could injure your back. If an object is very heavy, get help.

When working on a ladder, wear sturdy shoes with good traction. Overlap the sections of an extension ladder by three or four rungs, and tie the top of the ladder to a stable object. Haul up your equipment using a rope and bucket, as shown.

SUBJECT INDEX

Italic page numbers refer to pages on which there are relevant photographs or illustrations. **Boldface** page numbers indicate charts, lists, or plans.

PLANT INDEX

Italic page numbers refer to pages on which there are relevant photographs. **Boldface** page numbers indicate charts, lists, or plans.

PHOTOGRAPHY CREDITS

Credits from left to right are separated by semi-colons; credits from top to bottom are separated by dashes.

Back cover: Ian Adams; Jessie Walker; David Cavagnaro; Bert Klassen-Greg Ryan & Sally Beyer; Ken Druse, **1:** Gay Bumgarner, **2:** Kevin Sink, **3:** Scott Atkinson, **4–5:** Ian Adams, **6:** Mary Liz Austin (2)-Steve Mulligan; Greg Ryan & Sally Beyer, **9:** Gay Bumgarner, **10–11:** Janet Davis, **12–15:** Greg Ryan & Sally Beyer, **16–17:** Karen Bussolini courtesy Heliotrope Garden Design, **18–19:** Lynn Steiner, **20–21:** Greg Ryan & Sally Beyer, **22–23:** Jessie Walker, **24–25:** Janet Davis, **26–27:** Mike Grandmaison/GardenImage, **28–29:** Terry Donnelly, **30–31:** Ian Adams, **32–33:** Judith Bromley, **34–37:** Ian Adams, **38–47:** Jessie Walker, **48–49:** Judith Bromley, **50–51:** Ken Druse, **52–55:** Judith Bromley, **56–57:** Jerry Pavia, **58–61:** Bert Klassen, **62–65:** Andreas Trauttmannsdorff, **66–67:** Greg Ryan & Sally Beyer, **68–75:** David Cavagnaro, **76–79:** Ian Adams, **80–81:** David Cavagnaro, **82–83:** Ken Druse, **84–87:** Ian Adams, **88–89:** Steve Mulligan, **90–91:** Peter Wilson, **92–93:** Tom Stromme, **94–95:** Peter McEnroe, **96–99:** Cheryl Richter, **100–103:** Karen Bussolini, **104–105:** Gay Bumgarner, **106–109:** Kevin Sink/Midwestock **110–111:** Gay Bumgarner, **112–113:** Ian Adams, **114–115:** Gay Bumgarner, **116–117:** Karen Bussolini, **118–119:** Gay Bumgarner, **122:** Walter Chandoha-Bert Klassen, **123:** Kevin Sink/Midwestock-Leonard Philips-Judith Bromley, **128:** Phil Harvey, **130:** David Cavagnaro; Gay Bumgarner-Ian Adams, **131:** Gay Bumgarner-Jessie Walker, **132:** Ian Adams-Gay Bumgarner-Ian Adams, **133:** Gay Bumgarner-Bert Klassen, **134:** Phil Harvey, **136:** Jessie Walker; Jerry Harpur, Inc.-Charles Mann, **137:** Roger Foley-Derek Fell-Karen Bussolini, **138:** *Southern Living Magazine*-Roger Foley, **139:** *Southern Living Magazine* (2)-Gay Bumgarner, **140:** Derek Fell-Carole Ottesen, **141:** Roger Foley-Gay Bumgarner-Dency Kane, **142:** Dency Kane-Greg Ryan & Sally Beyer, **143:** Gay Bumgarner (2)-R. Todd Davis, **148:** Karen Bussolini/Jackson Scofield-Phil Harvey **149–151:** Phil Harvey, **152–153:** David Cavagnaro, **154:** Derek Fell, **155:** Derek Fell-Saxon Holt; e-presidio.com, **156:** Janet Davis-Gay Bumgarner, **157:** Peter Whiteley-Catriona Tudor-Erler, **158–159:** Derek Fell; **159:** Ernest Braun-Janet Davis, **161:** Karen Bussolini-Janet Davis, **162:** Gay Bumgarner-Walter Chandoha (2), **163:** Charles Mann, **164:** Jerry Pavia; Karen Bussolini, **165:** Gay Bumgarner; Dency Kane; Charles Mann-Ken Druse-Walter Chandoha-Michael Thompson, **166:** Karen Bussolini, **167:** Karen Bussolini; Dency Kane-Lynn Karlin, **168:** Walter Chandoha-Dency Kane, **169:** Tony Gianmarino/GardenImage; Gay Bumgarner-David Cavagnaro, **170:** Roger Foley, **171:** Derek Fell-Michael Thompson; Vixen Hill, **172–173:** David Cavagnaro, **173:** Gay Bumgarner-Judith Bromley-Gay Bumgarner, **174:** Karen Bussolini, **175:** Walter Chandoha-Gay Bumgarner-Ian Adams/GardenImage, **176:** R. Todd Davis-David Cavagnaro, **177:** Janet Davis-Karen Bussolini, **178–179:** Teena Albert, **180:** Jerry Pavia-Teena Albert, **181:** Dency Kane; Crandall & Crandall (2); Derek Fell, **182:** Walter Chandoha; Jerry Pavia-Gay Bumgarner; Karen Bussolini, **184:** Walter Chandoha; Gay Bumgarner, **185:** James Carrier (3), **186, 187:** Judith Bromley, **187:** Ken Druse-Greg Ryan & Sally Beyer, **188–189:** Alan & Linda Detrick/GardenImage, **189:** R. Todd Davis-Greg Ryan & Sally Beyer, **191:** Karen Bussolini, **192:** Derek Fell, **193:** Leonard Phillips, **194:** Gay Bumgarner; David Cavagnaro-Karen Bussolini; Greg Ryan & Sally Beyer, **195:** Karen Bussolini, **196:** Walter Chandoha, **197:** Liz Ball-R.Todd Davis, **198:** Derek Fell-Walter Chandoha, **200–201:** Gay Bumgarner, **202:** Jerry Pavia, **204:** David Cavagnaro, **205:** Jerry Pavia, **208:** Janet Davis-Gay Bumgarner-David Cavagnaro, **210:** David Cavagnaro; Gay Bumgarner-David Cavagnaro. **211:** *Southern Living Magazine* (3), **212:** Ivan Massar/Postive Images; Roger Foley-Derek Fell, **213:** R. Todd Davis; Judith Bromley-Karen Bussolini, **214:** Jerry Pavia, **215:** Jim Knopf/Johnson Books; Derek Fell, **216:** Jerry Pavia-R. Todd Davis-Saxon Holt, **218:** Saxon Holt, **219:** David McDonald; Norm Plate-Jerry Pavia, **220:** Arnaud Descat/MAP; Norm Plate, **221:** Derek Fell-Susan A. Roth; Lynne Harrison; R. Todd Davis, **222:** Derek Fell, **223:** Bill Johnson-R. Todd Davis-David Cavagnaro; Susan A. Roth, **224:** Jerry Pavia, **225:** Jerry Pavia-Gay Bumgarner-*Southern Living Magazine*, **226:** Tom Wyatt, **227:** Tom Wyatt; Phil Harvey-Norm Plate, **228:** David Cavagnaro; Derek Fell, **230:** *Southern Living Magazine;* Susanne Loosmoore, **231:** Jerry Pavia-Karen Bussolini; Cheryl Richter; Jerry Pavia-Judith Bromley-Karen Bussolini-Dency Kane, **232:** Gay Bumgarner-David Cavagnaro, **233:** Susanne Loosmoore-Jerry Pavia; David Cavagnaro, **234:** Cheryl Richter, **235:** Jerry Pavia, **236:** Richard Day/Daybreak-Jerry Pavia (2) **238:** David Cavagnaro-Derek Fell-David Cavagnaro, **240:** Jerry Pavia; Richard Hamilton-David Cavagnaro; Jerry Pavia (2); Alan & Linda Detrick, **241:** Tom Woodward-Jerry Pavia (2); Janet Davis; Saxon Holt, **242:** Jerry Pavia; Darrow Watt, **243:** Charles Mann; David Cavagnaro; Claire Curran; Jerry Pavia, **244:** Jerry Pavia-*Southern Living Magazine,* **246:** Saxon Holt-David Cavagnaro-Bill Johnson, **248:** Charles Mann-Gay Bumgarner-David Cavagnaro, **249:** Cynthia Woodyard; Claire Curran; Cynthia Woodyard; Michael Thompson, **250:** Cynthia Woodyard-Saxon Holt; Janet Davis, **251:** Janet Davis-Norm Plate-Karen Bussolini, **254:** David Cavagnaro (2)-Walter Chandoha, **256:** Greg Ryan & Sally Beyer, **257:** Jerry Pavia; David Cavagnaro; Jerry Pavia; R.Todd Davis, **258:** David Cavagnaro-Charles Mann-David Cavagnaro, **260:** Allan Mandell, **260:** Jerry Pavia (2); Allan Mandell; Pam Spaulding/Positive Images, **261:** Allan Mandell, **262:** Derek Fell-Richard Shiell-David Cavagnaro, **264:** Walter Chandoha-Allan Mandell; Jerry Pavia, **265:** David Cavagnaro, **266:** David Cavagnaro; Gay Bumgarner, **267:** Karen Bussolini-Carolyn Chatterton-Gay Bumgarner, **268–269:** Gay Bumgarner, **270:** Gay Bumgarner-Phil Harvey, **271:** Kathleen Brenzel-Peter Whiteley; Phil Harvey; David Belda-Kathleen Brenzel; Karen Bussolini, **272:** Norm Plate; Nancy Rotenberg-Phil Harvey, **273:** Norm Plate-Norm Plate-Sean Sullivan (2); Norm Plate, **274:** Jerry Pavia-Phil Harvey, **275:** Jerry Pavia; R. Todd Davis, **276:** Gay Bumgarner-Pam Spaulding/Positive Images, **277:** Gay Bumgarner (4), **278:** Karl Petze/S&H; Jonelle Weaver/Gardener's Eden; Cheryl Fenton/S&H-Phil Harvey-Karl Petze/S&H, **279:** Cheryl Fenton/S&H (3)-Richard Rethmeyer (2); Norm Plate, **280:** Gay Bumgarner, **281:** Greg Ryan & Sally Beyer (2); David Cavagnaro (2), **282:** Greg Ryan & Sally Beyer; Cheryl Richter (2), **283:** Gay Bumgarner; Andrew Lawson-Saxon Holt, **284:** John Tyson/GardenImage-Cheryl Richter, **285:** Mary Liz Austin-Hotshot/GardenImage, **286–287:** Judith Bromley, courtesy Craig Bergmann Landscape Design, **288:** Phil Harvey/Solutions; Deborah Jones/Gardener's Eden; Jim Sadlon/S&H, **289:** Norm Plate; Peter Whiteley-Phil Harvey, **290:** Gay Bumgarner-Suzanne Woodard, **291:** Richard Shiell; Hadco Lighting; Suzanne Woodard-Campbell, Harrington & Brear, Inc.; Hadco Lighting (2), **293:** Nightscaping (2)-Hadco Lighting (4), **294:** Terry Donnelly-Sean Sullivan, **295:** David Belda (2); Phil Harvey/S&H-Jim Sadlon/S&H; Karl Petze/ Gardener's Eden; Jonelle Weaver/Gardener's Eden-Jim Sadlon, S&H; Greg Ryan & Sally Beyer; Phil Harvey, **296:** Walter Chandoha, **297:** David Cavagnaro-Peter Whiteley; David Belda; Mick Hales-Deborah Jones/S&H, **298:** Talis Bergmanis-R. Todd Davis; Kay Shaw, **299:** John Tyson/GardenImage; Norm Plate, **300:** Mark Bolton/GardenImage-R. Todd Davis-Julie Sprott/GardenImage, **301:** Catriona Tudor-Erler-Jonelle Weaver-Richard Day/Daybreak; Ed Carey, **302:** R. Todd Davis, **303:** Karen Bussolini; Greg Ryan & Sally Beyer-Derek Fell-Cheryl Richter, **304–305:** Jim Reed, **306:** Terry Donnelly, **307:** David Cavagnaro, **308:** A. B. Sheldon, **309:** Jardin Botanique du Montreal, **310:** Hugh Palmer; Judith Bromley (2), **312:** Janet Davis, **313:** Jerry Pavia; Bill Beatty-Bill Johnson, **314:** Lynn Karlin-Karen Bussolini; Rob & Ann Simpson; Richard Day/Daybreak, **316:** Walter Chandoha-Derek Fell, **317:** Walter Chandoha, **318:** Carolyn Chatterton, **321:** Ken Druse-Karen Bussolini, **322:** Karen Bussolini, **323:** Charles Mann, **324:** Dwight Kuhn-Michael Thompson; Norm Plate, **325:** Marion Brenner-Tom Woodward; David Cavagnaro, **326:** Tony Stone, **327:** Jeff Greenberg/Folio, **328:** The Image Bank-Gay Bumgarner, **329:** Michael Thompson, **330:** Hank De Lespinasse; Judith Bromley, **331:** Jerry Pavia-David Cavagnaro, **332:** Darrow Watt; Norm Plate; Darrow Watt-Tom Wyatt (3), **333:** Norm Plate, **334:** Strybing Arboretum, **335:** Ned Therrien, **336–337:** Karen Bussolini, **360–361:** Roger Foley, **362:** Roger Foley, **363:** Smart Deck ®No-hassle Deck and Railing Systems by USPL , **364:** Phil Harvey, **365:** The Thompson Co., **369:** Phil Harvey, **372:** Phil Harvey-Peter Christiansen, **373:** Peter Whiteley, **374:** Derek Fell-Darrow Watt, **375:** Gay Bumgarner; Tom Wyatt, **376:** Tom Wyatt, **377:** Martien Vinkesteijn/GardenImage-R. Todd Davis, **378:** Jack McDowell (4)-Jerry Pavia, **379:** Phil Harvey, **382:** Tom Wyatt, **383:** Roger Foley, **389:** Gay Bumgarner, **397:** Norm Plate, **400:** Phil Harvey

ACKNOWLEDGMENTS

Special thanks to Kris S. Jarantoski, Chicago Botanic Garden; Neil Diboll, Prairie Nursery; Richard and Sue Eyre, Rich's Foxwillow Pines Nursery; Lyle Bergmann; Mary Louise and Leon Fidrych; Beth Stolley Drucker; Sharon W. Waltman, U.S.D.A. Natural Resources Conservation Service, National Soil Survey Center, Lincoln, NE; and all the homeowners who graciously allowed us to photograph their gardens.